Purchasing Power Parities of Currencies

Purchasing Power Parities of Currencies

Recent Advances in Methods and Applications

Edited by

D.S. Prasada Rao

School of Economics
The University of Queensland
Brisbane, Australia

Edward Elgar
Cheltenham, UK • Northampton, MA, USA

Published by
Edward Elgar Publishing Limited
The Lypiatts
15 Lansdown Road
Cheltenham
Glos GL50 2JA
UK

Edward Elgar Publishing, Inc.
William Pratt House
9 Dewey Court
Northampton
Massachusetts 01060
USA

A catalogue record for this book
is available from the British Library

Library of Congress Control Number: 2009928593

ISBN 978 1 84542 237 0

Printed and bound by MPG Books Group, UK

Contents

Figures

Tables

Contributors

Bart van Ark
Chief Economist, The Conference Board, New York, USA and Professor of Economics, University of Groningen, Groningen, Netherlands

Bettina Aten
Economist, Bureau of Economic Analysis, Washington DC, USA

Bert Balk
Professor of Economics, Erasmus University, Rotterdam, Netherlands and Statistics Netherlands, Netherlands

James Cuthbert
Retired Chief Statistician, Scottish Bureau of Statistics, Edinburgh, Scotland

Erwin Diewert
Professor of Economics, University of British Columbia, Vancouver, Canada

Steve Dowrick
Professor of Economics, The Australian National University, Canberra, ACT, Australia

Larry Dwyer
Professor of Tourism Studies, University of New South Wales, Sydney, Australia

Peter Forsyth
Professor of Economics, Monash University, Melbourne, Australia

Alan Heston
Professor of Development of Economics (retired), University of Pennsylvania, Philadelphia, USA

Robert Hill
Professor, Department of Economics, University of Graz, Austria and School of Economics, University of New South Wales, Australia

Yoshimasa Kurabayashi
Emeritus Professor of Economics, Hitotsubashi University, Tokyo, Japan

xi

D.S. Prasada Rao
Professor of Economics, The University of Queensland, Brisbane, Australia

David Roberts
International Comparisons Unit, OECD, Paris, France

Itsuo Sakuma
Professor of Economics, Senshu University, Tokyo, Japan

Sergey Sergeev
Senior Economist, Statistics Austria, Vienna, Austria

Marcel Timmer
Professor, Groningen Growth and Development Centre, University of Groningen, Groningen, Netherlands

Michael Ward (Late)
Senior Economist (retired), Development Economics Data Group (DECDG), World Bank, Washington DC, USA

Foreword

To measure the size and structure of the world economy and see how it has changed over time, we need (a) to measure growth in volume of Gross Domestic Product (GDP) in the component countries, eliminating inter-temporal change in prices and (b) in order to make cross–country comparisons, and aggregate measures of regional and world economic performance, we need to convert national currencies into a common purchasing power unit, eliminating inter–country difference in price level. We need PPPs for this as exchange rates are mainly a reflection of purchasing power of tradeable items and may move erratically because of capital movements. With these two measures one can then merge the growth and cross–section evidence to study the structure, size and movement of the world economy, and compare levels of national performance in space and time. This book makes a major contribution to the literature on purchasing power parities (PPPs). It is the latest in a flow of important studies which started in 1940. The eminent contributors are mainly concerned with presenting new methods of estimation, rather than new estimates of world performance. It is worth considering it in a historical perspective of the literature.

Colin Clark's *Conditions of Economic Progress* (Macmillan, 1940) was a first rough effort to supply PPPs, but he had to rely on limited price data of the Ford Motor company, his own comparisons for luxury goods and ILO material on rents. He had national income estimates for only 16 countries in his first edition. Most of these were derived from national statistical offices which had no common guidelines for constructing their GDP estimates.

The OEEC (Organisation for European Economic Cooperation) was created as an organ of the Marshall Plan in 1949 to promote European recovery, and estimate needs for American aid. The first OEEC publication on PPPs, *An International Comparison of National Products and the Purchasing Power of Currencies*, by Milton Gilbert and Irving Kravis (both pupils of Simon Kuznets at the University of Pennsylvania), appeared in 1954, with binary bilateral comparisons of expenditure for four European countries and the USA. In 1958, a companion study appeared, comparing eight European countries with the USA. At the same time Richard Stone was organising the standardisation of GDP estimates in member countries. There was another publication in 1959 by Deborah Paige and Gottfried Bombach, which compared output levels, rather than expenditure: *A Comparison of National Output and Productivity of the United Kingdom and the United States*. The quality of these three OEEC publications, and their degree of detail was much superior to the 1940 effort of Colin Clark. By 1961, OEEC had PPP estimates (some of them rough) for all of its 16 member countries, but this measurement activity stopped when OEEC was replaced by OECD in that year.

In 1965, the OECD Development Centre organised a meeting with Irving Kravis, Richard Ruggles and others to examine the possibility of resurrecting the PPP work to cover a wider range of countries. As a result, the Ford Foundation gave Kravis a $300 000 grant to start his International Comparison Project (ICP) in 1968. His main colleagues at the University of Pennsylvania were Alan Heston and Robert Summers. The ICP published three studies in 1975, 1978, and 1982. The third volume, *World Product and Income: International Comparisons of Real Gross Product* was a masterpiece. It covered 34 countries (3 Africa, 10 Asia, 6 Americas, 15 Europe) for the benchmark year 1975. It was more sophisticated than the OEEC as it was multilateral instead of binary. It involved collection of carefully specified price information by statistical offices for more than 2 000 representative items of consumption, investment and government services. It was meticulously transparent, describing exactly what had been done with clear and completely detailed presentation of the estimates. It used a new method of multilateralisation of the results known as Geary–Khamis (after the work of R. S. Geary and S. H. Khamis). This method provided transitivity and other desirable properties. It was used as a method for aggregating results at the basic heading level. It was used in conjunction with the commodity product dummy method invented by Robert Summers for filling holes in the basic data set. It did not include China, whose authorities would not have been willing to participate, but Kravis, who had been in the US army in China during the war, went on a US delegation to China in October 1979, and made a reduced information study of prices of 75 items in five cities, and rural areas adjacent to them (see 'An Approximation of the Relative Real per Capita GDP of the Peoples Republic of China', *Journal of Comparative Economics*, pp. 60–78, (5) 1981. Kravis' study exaggerated the level of Chinese per capita GDP performance and was superceded by Ren Rouen, *China's Economic Performance in International Perspective*, OECD, 1997.

The ICP (now International Comparison Programme) was taken over by the United Nations Statistical Division. It made two reports *World Comparisons of Real Gross Domestic Product and Purchasing Power* for 1980 and 1985, published in 1987 and 1994. The first covered 60 countries and the latter 64. The method was the same as that of Kravis, Heston and

Summers, but the methodological text was much shorter. Alan Heston and Robert Summers continued the work they had started with Kravis by regular publication of the Penn World Tables. These are necessarily rougher than the full ICP, as much more limited price information is used. However, they are very useful and filled many holes in the dataset; PWT 6.1 contained estimates for 169 countries. The United Nations dropped its ICP estimates which were taken over by the World Bank, which published its first estimates for 2005 in 2008. These are described as ICP estimates, but in fact deviate from the Kravis, Heston Summers methodology.

OECD reactivated its estimation of GDP and purchasing power parities in 1982. It did this in cooperation with Eurostat. The approach was similar to that of the ICP (see Michael Ward, *Purchasing Power Parities and Real Expenditure in the OECD*, 1985). OECD used the Geary–Khamis approach, which gives a weight to countries corresponding to the size of their GDP, so that a large economy like the USA has a strong influence on the results whereas Eurostat prefers a multilateral method in which all its member countries have an equal weight. This technique, EKS, is named for its inventors Eltötö, Koves and Szulc. Both OECD and Eurostat made studies of non–member countries, Eurostat on African countries and OECD on former communist countries.

Between 1989 and 2003, I made four studies of the world economy, published by OECD, with a much longer time horizon than other OECD studies. The 2003 book, *The World Economy: Historical Statistics* dealt with the period from 1 to AD 2001. I used the growing country coverage of studies for OECD countries, for Eastern Europe, Latin America, the Middle East, Asia and Africa to increase the GDP coverage for my benchmark year 1990. I had ICP type estimates for 70 countries which were 93.7 per cent of the world economy, Penn World Tables estimates for 84 countries which represented nearly 5.6 per cent of world GDP and proxy estimates for 48 non–covered countries which were about 0.7 per cent of world GDP (see p. 230 of the volume cited). In Maddison (2007) *Contours of the World Economy, 1–2030*, Oxford University Press, I updated these estimates to 2003 and made projections to 2030 (see pp.376–386).

In 2008, the World Bank published *Global Purchasing Power Parities and Real Expenditures, 2005 International Comparison Program*, It presents estimates of GDP and GDP per capita for 146 countries. The Bank used the results of five regional studies and linked them, using the EKS method of aggregation. The ranking of countries within each region could not be modified in the linking process, because the regions insisted on 'fixity'. The Bank refers to the total as 'world' estimates, but makes no proxy estimates for non–included countries. A major shortcoming is its disparaging attitude to the five previous ICP global studies (three by Kravis, Heston and Summers

and two for 1980 and 1985 by the UN Statistical office). These are dismissed
(p. 10) as being 'based on very old and very limited data', implying that any
discrepancy with these earlier findings cannot cast doubt on the new and
implausible results for China, India and some other countries. Kravis et al.
(1982) contained a detailed and sophisticated analysis explaining the
sensitivity of PPP results to different measurement techniqes which is
completely lacking in the World Bank book. An obvious shortcoming is the
scrapping of the Geary–Khamis measure of PPP in favour of the EKS method
favoured by bureaucrats. It gives all countries the same weight, whatever
their size, putting Luxemburg on a par with the USA. This method
systematically exaggerates the per capita income differential between rich
and poor countries. Geary–Khamis gives a weight to countries corresponding
to the size of their GDP and shows smaller differentials, The new estimates
of Chinese per capita income are much lower than my estimates and those
those previously issued by the World Bank in its World Development
Indicators. They are now 9.8 per cent of the US level in 2005, compared with
18.3 per cent using the Maddison approach. The per cent difference is bigger
than one might expect between an EKS and a Geary–Khamis measure. There
is therefore reason to ask whether the statisticians in charge of estimating
Chinese price levels did not exaggerate them. Michael Ward has suggested to
me that, in aiming at comparability with advanced countries, the Chinese
statisticians probably made 'a disproportionate selection of items at the
higher end of the product range'. Thus they failed to get a representative
consumption profile of the average Chinese household. This may also have
been the case for other Asian countries.

The contribution by David Roberts in this book provides a detailed
description of methods used in OECD whose estimates now cover 46
countries, including the Russian Federation and Israel, as shown in Table 2.4.
It now uses the EKS formula for aggregation in its published results. The
chapter by Bart van Ark and Marcel Timmer in this volume is concerned
with productivity measurement with PPPs derived by the industry of origin
approach pioneered by Paige and Bombach (1959). Their Groningen ICOP
(International Comparisons of Output and Productivity) group was founded
in 1983 and has made estimates for about 30 countries over the past two
decades. This approach is easier to implement for advanced countries which
have censuses of production which provide information on inputs as well as
outputs. The results are very useful for growth accounting, and determining
the locus of technical progress. Its database for 1997 provides comparisons of
output, inputs and productivity at a detailed industry level. They distinguish
between E-PPPs from expenditure studies and O-PPP results from the value
added approach. They contrast the value of the two approaches. Both have

advantages and disadvantages. They conclude that they should be regarded as complements rather than substitutes.

The present volume, Purchasing Power Parities of Currencies, edited by Prasada Rao, contains 13 essays. Most are concerned with complicated problems now at the cutting edge of PPP analysis, with innovative suggestions for sophisticated improvements of present techniques for estimating PPPs. When the new World Bank PPP estimates for 2011 emerge, readers of this book will be well equipped to scrutinise its methodological approach with a critical eye.

Angus Maddison
Visiting Professor
United Nations University (MERIT)
Maastricht, Netherlands

Professor Emeritus
University of Groningen
Groningen, Netherlands

Acknowledgements

I am grateful to all the contributors to this volume for the time and effort they have put into the preparation and subsequent revisions of their chapters. I also thank them for their patience with me during the delays in getting this edited volume to print. Particular thanks are due to Erwin Diewert and Bert Balk for their constant encouragement and gentle pressure to get the work on the volume completed. I also wish to thank the Edward Elgar Publishing Company for their patience and willingness to extend the deadline for the submission of the manuscript. I could not have devoted sufficient time to get the volume completed if it was not for the generous support from the School of Economics, The University of Queensland, Brisbane, Australia in the form of sabbatical leave under its Special Studies Program. The final stages of the preparation of the manuscript were undertaken while I was visiting the Groningen Growth and Development Centre at the University of Gronginen in the Netherlands and the Indira Gandhi Institute for Development Research in Mumbai, India. I thank these two institutions for the excellent facilities and generous support extended to me during my visits. Finally, I thank my wife, Visala, who has helped me with the painstaking job of formatting and proof–reading various chapters.

D.S. Prasada Rao
Editor

PART I

Introduction

1. Introduction

D.S. Prasada Rao

1.1 BACKGROUND

In a globalised world, researchers, analysts, governments, national and international organisations are constantly seeking to benchmark the performance of nations in terms of their growth and productivity levels and trends and examine evidence on catch–up and convergence across countries. Consequently, there has been a steady increase in the demand for internationally comparable aggregates such as gross domestic product (GDP), real per capita income, and their components including private consumption, general government consumption and investment. In addition to international comparisons at the economy level, considerable research has focused on the performance of different sectors, including agriculture, manufacturing and services sectors, across countries based on labour and total factor productivity measures as well as growth accounting studies.

International comparisons of economic aggregates require conversion of aggregates expressed in respective national currency units into a common currency unit and adjusting for differences in the purchasing power of currencies. *Purchasing Power Parities* of currencies (PPPs) are used for this purpose. Since the seminal work of Gilbert and Kravis, the need for reliable estimates of PPPs has been well recognised and the task is currently undertaken under the auspices of the International Comparison Program (ICP) supported by various international organisations including the United Nations, World Bank, OECD, Eurostat and the Asian and African Development Banks. The most recent phase of the ICP for the benchmark year 2005 has covered 146 countries covering all the regions of the world. Results from the 2005 ICP are now available on line on the ICP website (www.worldbank.org/data/icp). The use of PPPs in the construction of the Human Development Index (HDI) and in the estimation of global and regional poverty based on $1/day and $2/day international poverty lines has brought the ICP and PPPs into prominence.

Compilation of PPPs is a complex exercise as it involves collection and processing of price data from a large and diverse set of countries. Since the

3

beginning of the International Comparison Program at the University of Pennsylvania forty years ago, there have been significant methodological developments in the areas of price collection; index number methods for spatial price comparisons and PPPs; and in the application of the PPPs at the national and international level. However, due to the specialised nature of the field of international comparisons most of these developments have not found their way into the mainstream literature and remained obscure for practitioners as well as researchers. Though the last decade has seen an improvement in this situation as research in this area is getting published in refereed international journals there is a wealth of information that still remains in the form of reports and working papers that are difficult to access.

The main objective of this edited volume is to bring together a selected set of contributions from leading researchers covering important recent developments in the area of international comparisons. As the international statistical community is gearing towards an anticipated next round of the ICP for the 2011 benchmark year, the methodological developments presented in this volume are likely to play a significant role. The publication of this volume is timely as it contributes to a better understanding of the recently published results from the 2005 ICP and prepares the reader for the future rounds of the ICP.

1.2   AN OVERVIEW

The book is divided into four parts. Part I provides an introduction to the ICP and international comparisons in general. Contributions in Part II relate to the methods currently employed in international comparisons and chapters in this part describe recent methodological developments designed to improve the PPP estimates. As these methods are used in the derivation of multilateral price comparisons in the form of purchasing power parities and national accounts for the participating countries expressed in a common currency unit, these methods are known as system methods for PPP computation. Part III covers a new and fertile area for research on spatial linking for international comparisons based on similarity of price and quantity structures. The research focus here is on improvements to international comparisons that could result if cross–country comparisons are based on progressive linking of countries which are similar in their consumption patterns, price structures and level of development. The contents of the chapters are likely to have a significant influence on how international comparisons of prices and real incomes are undertaken in the future. The edited volume is concluded with three chapters in Part IV that provide a brief overview of the important uses and applications of PPPs for policy purpose at the national and international levels.

Following this brief introduction to this volume, Chapter 2, by Roberts, is designed to provide the reader with a basic understanding of the concept of PPPs and the methodology used in the compilation of PPPs as it is currently practised at the OECD and Eurostat. This is a lengthy chapter but it is designed to serve as a useful reference on the basic concepts and methods used.

The first chapter in Part II by Balk provides an overview of the aggregation methods for international comparisons and an evaluation of the methods available. The chapter has an excellent treatment of the axiomatic and economic theoretic approaches to international comparisons. Chapter 4 by Rao shows how the two aggregation methods, the EKS and the CPD methods currently used in international comparisons, can be generalised and improved through the use of a stochastic approach. The remaining chapters in this part deal with methods designed to provide additively consistent international comparisons. Dowrick examines, in Chapter 5, the substitution bias induced in international comparisons based on additive methods like the Geary–Khamis method and provides a method of correcting the bias and generating true international real income comparisons. Chapter 6 by Sakuma, Rao and Kurabayashi provides a formal discussion of the properties of matrix and additive consistency of aggregation methods and offers a new additively consistent method for international comparisons. The last chapter by Cuthbert highlights the importance of studying data structures and shows how a better understanding of the price and quantity structures contributes to the study of the performance of different additive methods. Cuthbert uses principal components analysis to identify data structures and examines how each principal component contributes to our understanding of the properties of different additive methods.

Part III is devoted to a discussion of recent developments associated with the use of spatial linking in international comparisons. A major problem associated with international comparisons is the absence of a natural ordering of the countries participating in international comparisons similar to what is available in temporal comparisons based on a chronological order. Chapter 8 by Diewert sets up a formal structure to measure similarity in price and quantity levels and structures across countries. A number of similarity indexes are proposed by Diewert which could be used in identifying an optimal spatial linking strategy for cross–country comparisons of prices. His chapter is followed by the chapter by Hill who pioneered the use of minimum spanning trees. Chapter 9 provides valuable insights into the use of spanning trees and discusses their robustness over time and illustrates the potential of this approach by demonstrating how prior restrictions could be imposed within this approach. Chapter 10 by Aten and Heston is an ideal follow up to Hill's chapter where the authors examine various practical issues encountered in the application of the spatial chaining methods for international comparisons of prices and real incomes. The last two chapters in this part deal with the exploration of data structures in developing suitable aggregation methods for international comparisons. In Chapter 11, Sergeev outlines a new method of identifying an international price structure that optimally represents the price structures observed in participating countries and uses the derived structure of international prices to compile PPPs and to compare real incomes.

Part IV consists of three chapters each devoted to a different type of application of PPPs from the ICP. Chapter 12 by Ward provides a comprehensive overview of the applications of PPPs for economic analysis and policy formulation at the national and international levels. Ward's chapter fills an important gap as it focuses in a large part on the uses of international comparisons at the national level. This chapter reflects the enormous experience of Ward who spent a large part of his life as an international civil servant as a producer and user of results from the ICP. Chapter 13 by van Ark and Timmer focuses on PPPs for international comparisons of sectoral output and productivity. Their chapter describes how ICP PPPs from the expenditure side of national accounts can be used in building sectoral comparisons. The last chapter by Dwyer, Forsyth and Rao presents an interesting application as to how PPPs from the ICP at the detailed level can be used in constructing indices of price competitiveness for destination countries as viewed by different types of tourists from various origin countries. Their chapter demonstrates how a wealth of data generated by the ICP can be used for meeting the needs of a specific sector like the tourism sector.

1.3   LAST WORD

This volume covers recent significant developments and equips the reader with the state–of–the–art techniques in the field of international comparisons of prices and real incomes. I have immensely enjoyed and learnt a great deal from reading these contributions through the editorial process and I sincerely hope that the readers also derive as much benefit from the contributions in this volume. Each chapter has a fairly exhaustive list of references related to the topics covered and the reader would find it useful to delve deeper through the studies cited in the chapters.

2. The Compilation of Purchasing Power Parities: the Eurostat–OECD Purchasing Power Parity Programme

David Roberts

2.1 INTRODUCTION

The Eurostat–OECD Purchasing Power Parity Programme was started in the early 1980s to compare the price and volume levels of GDP of the member states of the European Union (EU) and the member countries of the OECD.[1] This remains the Programme's purpose, although its coverage has been broadened to include countries that are neither EU member states nor OECD member countries.[2]

Before the price and volume levels of the GDPs of different countries can be compared, it is first necessary to express their GDPs, which are in national currencies and valued at national price levels, in a common currency at a uniform price level. Eurostat and the OECD use purchasing power parities (PPPs) to do this. PPPs are calculated with data collected specifically for the purpose. To illustrate how this is done, the chapter explains how Eurostat–OECD comparisons are carried out by describing the methods, organisation and procedures that were in place for the 2005 comparison. It also presents summary results of the 2005 comparison. The chapter draws heavily on the Eurostat–OECD methodological manual and the Eurostat–OECD report on the 2005 comparison (Eurostat and OECD; 2006; 2007).

Although Eurostat and the OECD apply the same methodology, there are differences in application. These differences arise because Eurostat makes comparisons of EU member states every year, while the OECD only makes comparisons of OECD member countries every three years. They also arise

---

[1] Eurostat is the statistical office of the European Communities.

[2] These are either countries that have applied to join the European Union or the OECD or countries of the former Soviet Union and the former Yugoslavia with which Eurostat and the OECD have programmes of technical cooperation in statistics.

because Eurostat co–ordinates a significantly larger number of participating countries than the OECD – over two-thirds of the countries participating in the joint comparisons are co-ordinated by Eurostat. It is for this reason that, when application differs, the chapter describes the approach of Eurostat rather than that of the OECD.[3]

2.2   BACKGROUND

2.2.1   Eurostat–OECD Approach

GDP can be estimated from the production side, the expenditure side and the income side. All three approaches will yield the same result in theory. Price and volume comparisons of GDP are based on the identity: value = price × volume. The values of income aggregates, unlike the values of production and expenditure aggregates, cannot be split into meaningful price and volume components. Price and volume comparisons of GDP can only be made from the production side or the expenditure side.

Eurostat–OECD comparisons are made from the expenditure side which identifies the components of final demand: consumption, investment and net exports. The reasons for this are: one, the inherent usefulness of making comparisons from the demand side; two, the difficulties of organising comparisons from the supply side which require data for both intermediate consumption and gross output; and three, the generally better comparability among countries of their detailed breakdowns of final expenditure on GDP.[4]

Comparing the values of final expenditure that countries make on GDP will not provide a comparison of the volumes of goods and services purchased in the countries unless the differences in their price levels have been removed. This can be done either by observing the volumes directly or by deriving them indirectly using a measure of relative prices to place the expenditures of the countries on the same price level. Prices are easier to observe than volumes and direct measures of relative prices usually have a smaller variability than direct measures of relative volumes. Eurostat–OECD comparisons estimate volumes indirectly.

---

[3] See 'Annex VI: Differences between Eurostat and OECD Comparisons' (Eurostat and OECD, 2006).

[4] The disadvantage of the expenditure approach is that, although it enables levels and structures of consumption and investment to be compared, productivity comparisons can only be made at the level of the whole economy. Individual industries are not identified on the expenditure side. In order to compare productivity at the industry level, international comparisons of GDP must be undertaken from the production side (see, for example, Paige and Bombach, 1959; Maddison and van Ark, 1989).

International volume comparisons of GDP depend on four conditions being met. These are: one, the definition of GDP is the same; two, the measurement of GDP is the same; three, the currency unit in which GDP is expressed is the same; and four, the price level at which GDP is valued is the same. GDP estimates of countries participating in Eurostat–OECD comparisons generally meet the first condition as they are compiled in line with one of the two complementary international systems of national accounts: the SNA 93 (United Nations, 1993) and the ESA 95 (Eurostat, 1996). But the measurement of GDP is not always equally exhaustive across all participating countries to satisfy the second condition. In particular, the GDP of countries with a large informal or underground sector may be underestimated, depending on how well the national accounts statisticians have been able to include these 'non–observed' activities in the GDP estimates. The third condition is not met except by countries in the Euro Area.[5] The GDP estimates of the majority of participating countries are expressed in different national currencies. Nor is the fourth condition met as the GDP estimates of participating countries are valued at national price levels.

To meet the last two conditions it is necessary to have conversion rates that both convert to a common currency and equalise the purchasing power of different currencies in the process of conversion – that is, conversion rates that are both currency converters and spatial price deflators. PPPs are such conversion rates.[6] When the GDPs of countries are converted to a common

---

[5] The Euro Area consists of Austria, Belgium, Finland, France, Germany, Greece, Ireland, Italy, Luxembourg, Netherlands, Portugal, Slovenia and Spain. Even though their GDPs are expressed in the same currency, that is in euros, their GDPs are not comparable because they are valued at national price levels.

[6] In their simplest form PPPs are nothing more than price relatives. For example, if the price of a hamburger in France is 2.84 euros and in the United States it is 2.20 dollars, the PPP for hamburgers between France and the United States is 2.84 euros to 2.20 dollars or 1.29 euros to the dollar. This means that for every dollar spent on hamburgers in the United States, 1.29 euros would have to be spent in France to obtain the same quantity and quality – in other words, the same volume – of hamburgers. Therefore, to compare the volumes of hamburgers purchased in the two countries, either the expenditure on hamburgers in France can be converted to dollars by dividing it by 1.29 or the expenditure on hamburgers in the United States can be converted to euros by multiplying it by 1.29. PPPs, however, are not only calculated for individual products, they are also calculated for product groups and for each of the various levels of aggregation up to and including GDP. In moving up the hierarchy of aggregation, PPPs remain price relatives, but price relatives that refer to increasingly complex assortments of goods and services. Hence, if the PPP for GDP between France and the United States is 0.97 euros to the dollar, it can be inferred that for every dollar spent on the GDP in the United States, 0.97 euros would have to be spent in France to purchase the same volume of goods and

currency using PPPs, they are also revalued at a uniform price level. They reflect only differences in the volumes of goods and services produced in the countries. As such, they are *real* measures or measures of volume.[7]

2.2.2   Data Requirements

The calculation of PPPs from the expenditure side requires each country participating in the comparison to provide a set of national annual purchasers' prices and a detailed breakdown of final expenditure on GDP. The prices should refer to a selection of products chosen from a common list of precisely–defined goods and services. The final expenditures should be broken down by product groups – called 'basic headings' – according to a common classification. Both prices and expenditures should refer to the year of the comparison – or 'reference year'. And both should cover the whole range of final goods and services included under GDP. Participating countries have also to provide annual average exchange rates and mid–year resident population for the reference year.

The prices reported by participating countries are used to calculate PPPs first at the product level, then at the basic heading level and finally at the various levels of aggregation above the basic heading level. The PPPs at the aggregation levels are calculated with the final expenditures that participating countries have supplied on the constituent basic headings as weights. The PPPs are used to convert national final expenditures on GDP into real final expenditures on GDP. The exchange rates are used to derive comparative

---

services. Purchasing the 'same volume of goods and services' does not mean that identical baskets of goods and services will be purchased in both countries. The composition of the basket will vary between countries and reflect differences in tastes and cultural backgrounds, but both baskets will, in principle, provide equivalent satisfaction or utility.

[7] Before PPPs became available, exchange rates had to be used to make international comparisons of GDP. While this provides GDP estimates that satisfy the third condition – they are all expressed in a common currency – it does not satisfy the fourth condition of equalising price levels. To do this, exchange rates would have to reflect the relative purchasing power of currencies in their national markets. And this they do not do. First, because exchange rates are determined by the supply and demand for different currencies and the supply and demand for currencies are influenced by factors such as capital flows between countries and currency speculation rather than the needs of international trade. And secondly, because many goods and services, such as buildings, all government services and most market services, are not traded internationally. GDPs of countries converted to a common currency using exchange rates continue to be valued at national price levels. They reflect both differences in the volumes produced in the countries and differences in their price levels. As such, they are *nominal* measures or measures of value.

price levels. They are also used as proxy PPPs for exports and imports when calculating the PPPs for GDP. The population data are used to compute real final expenditures per head.

2.2.3 Consistency

PPPs are primarily price deflators. The prices supplied by participating countries should be *consistent* with the methods of valuation used to estimate their final expenditures on GDP. Failure to observe this will result in biased volume measures. As expenditure = price × volume, volumes are obtained by dividing expenditures by prices. If the volumes are to be estimated correctly, the prices collected should be those used to derive the expenditures. Deflating with prices that are not consistent with those underlying the expenditure values will result in volumes being underestimated if the prices are too high or overestimated if the prices are too low.

In principle, the final expenditures on GDP that participating countries report for the reference year are estimated using national annual purchasers' prices of actual market transactions. Consistency requires participating countries to collect *national* prices – that is, prices that have been averaged over all localities of the country so as to take account of regional variations in prices. The national prices have to be *annual* prices – that is, prices that have been averaged over the days, weeks, months or quarters of the reference year so as to allow for seasonal variations in prices as well as general inflation and changes in price structures.

The national annual prices have to be *purchasers'* prices – where a purchaser's price is defined as the amount paid by the purchaser in order to take delivery of a unit of a good or service at the time and place required by the purchaser. It includes supplier's retail and wholesale margins, transport and insurance charges, non–deductible tax on products and sometimes, as in the case of certain items of machinery and equipment, installation costs. Finally, the national annual purchasers' prices have to be *market* or *transaction* prices – that is, the actual price for a transaction agreed on by the transactors. As such, it is the net price inclusive of all discounts, surcharges, rebates and, in the case of certain services, invoiced service charges and voluntary gratuities.

2.2.4 Comparability and Representativity

Besides being consistent with the final expenditures on GDP, the prices participating countries report must be for items that are *representative* of their final expenditure on GDP and which are *comparable* between them.

Comparability and representativity are not necessarily complementary requirements. Consumption patterns can vary from country to country for a variety of reasons including differences in tastes, cultures, climates, price structures, product availability and income levels. Products representative of the final expenditure of one country are not necessarily representative of the final expenditures of other countries, while products that are strictly comparable across countries are unlikely to be equally representative of them all. Failure to observe either of these two requirements will result in either an overestimation or underestimation of price levels and a corresponding underestimation or overestimation of volumes. Eurostat–OECD comparisons employ methods for selecting products and for calculating PPPs that are designed to respect both requirements. Inevitably compromises have to be made and, when they are, comparability is favoured over representativity.

Comparability
Products are said to be comparable if they have identical or equivalent physical and economic characteristics. Equivalence between products is defined as meeting the same needs with equal efficiency so that purchasers are indifferent between them and are not prepared to pay more for one than for the other. The pricing of comparable products ensures that differences in prices between countries for a product reflect 'actual' price differences and are not influenced by differences in quality. Pricing goods and services of constant quality avoids quality differences being mistaken for 'apparent' price differences and the consequent underestimation or overestimation of price levels.

Comparability is obtained in Eurostat–OECD comparisons by participating countries pricing product specifications that fully define the products in terms of the principal characteristics that influence their market prices. The approach is called 'specification pricing' and requires the characteristics of both the product and the transaction to be specified. Product specifications can be brand and model specific – that is, a specification in which a particular brand and model, or a cluster of comparable brands, is stipulated. Or they can be generic – that is, a specification where only the relevant technical parameters and other price determining characteristics are given and no brand or cluster of brands is designated. Generic specifications and, to a lesser extent, specifications with brand clusters are two of the ways of enabling countries to price items that are both comparable and representative. Another way is to permit countries to treat brand and model specifications as generic – that is, countries price products that match the characteristics specified other than those of brand and model which are considered to be indicative only. (This last option is only used in Eurostat–OECD comparisons when pricing equipment goods.)

Ideally, all product specifications would be brand and model specific so that countries would price products of identical quality. In practice, this is not possible for reasons of availability and representativity. Generic specifications have also to be employed and inevitably some variability in quality between the products priced by countries will occur. Quality differences can arise as the result of countries pricing items that do not match exactly the product specifications. They can also arise because, although the items priced appear to match the product specifications exactly, the product specifications are not precise enough to ensure that countries price items of the same quality. In most cases, these differences are identified when the price data are edited. Prices are not adjusted to compensate for differences in quality in Eurostat–OECD comparisons. Mismatches in quality are dealt with either by re–matching the prices reported or by discarding them.

Representativity
Representativity is a concept that relates to individual products within a basic heading. It has had to be introduced because there are no expenditure weights below the basic heading level with which to determine the relative importance of the various products priced for a basic heading. To ensure that there are enough prices to be compared between countries, participating countries are required to price both representative products (their products) and unrepresentative products (the products of others) within each basic heading. Representative products generally have a lower price level than unrepresentative products and, if this is not taken into account when calculating the PPPs for a basic heading, the PPPs will be biased. To avoid this, countries participating in Eurostat–OECD comparisons are required to do two things. The first is to ensure that there are representative products they can price in each basic heading when the product list is being finalised prior to price collection. The second is to identify which of the products they have priced within a basic heading are representative when reporting their prices.

Representativity is defined in terms of an individual country within a basic heading. A product is either representative or unrepresentative of the price level in country A for a given basic heading. It is representative, if in country A, its price level is close to the average for all products within the basic heading. Usually, though not necessarily, the purchases of the product will account for a significant proportion of the total purchases of all products covered by the basic heading. If not, the product will at least be sold in sufficient quantities for its price level to be typical for the basic heading.

In practice, basic headings can cover a heterogeneous mixture of products with significant disparities in their price levels. In these circumstances, representativity is defined in two stages. First in terms of the product types included in the basic heading – representative product types are those that account for the bulk of the expenditure on the basic heading. And then in terms of products within the representative product types – representative products are those whose price level is close to the average for all products of its type.

2.2.5   Equi–representativity

Because of the differences in price levels between representative products and unrepresentative products, a comparison based on products that are not equally representative of all participating countries will result in biased price relatives. Price levels for countries pricing a smaller number of representative products will be overestimated, while price levels for countries pricing a larger number of representative products will be underestimated. When putting together the product list for a comparison, it is important to ensure that it is 'balanced' or 'equi–representative' of all participating countries for each basic heading identified in the common expenditure classification. This does not mean that each country should price the same number of representative products for each basic heading because the method used by Eurostat–OECD comparisons to calculate PPPs for a basic heading ensures that any imbalance between countries in the number of representative products priced does not produce biased PPPs. The method requires each country to price a minimum of one representative product per basic heading. While this produces unbiased PPPs, it does not necessarily produce reliable PPPs. For that, each country needs to price that number of representative products which is commensurate with the heterogeneity of the products and price levels covered by the basic heading and its expenditure on the basic heading.

2.2.6   Classification of Final Expenditure on GDP

The Eurostat–OECD classification of final expenditure on GDP provides the structure around which the comparisons are organised. It is based on the expenditure–by–purpose classifications and the product classifications of the SNA 93 and the ESA 95. The classification consists of the seven main aggregates listed below. These are broken down into expenditure categories, expenditure groups, expenditure classes and basic headings. The most important of these aggregation levels is the lowest level, the basic heading level. Basic headings are the building blocks of a comparison. It is at the level of the basic heading that expenditures are defined, products selected, prices collected and edited, and PPPs first calculated and averaged.

In theory, a basic heading covers a group of similar well–defined goods or services. In practice, coverage is determined by the lowest level of final expenditure for which explicit expenditure weights can be estimated. This means that an actual basic heading can include a broader range of goods or services than is theoretically desirable. It also means that quasi–expenditure weights have to be assigned to indicate the relative importance – or representativity – of the products covered.

The seven main aggregates of the classification are currently broken down into 224 basic headings. This is the same breakdown as that used for the 2005 comparison. The principal features of the breakdown are as follows:

- *Individual consumption expenditure by (resident) households* is broken down by purpose into 147 basic headings (United Nations, 2000a). Expenditure at the basic heading level is defined according to the domestic concept – that is, irrespective of whether the household making the purchase in the domestic market is resident or not. To obtain expenditure by resident households, the expenditure in the country by non–residents is treated as a single amount and subtracted from the expenditure abroad by resident households (also treated as a single amount) to provide a global adjustment called 'net purchases abroad'. Global adjustment is necessary because most participating countries are unable to distinguish between the expenditures of resident and non–resident households at the basic heading level. For subsequent analysis, the 147 basic headings are also classified by type of product – that is, whether they consist predominately of non–durable goods, semi–durable goods, durable goods or services.[8]

- *Individual consumption expenditure by non–profit institutions serving households (NPISHs)* is broken down by purpose into six basic headings: housing, health, recreation and culture, education, social protection, and other services (such as religion, political parties, labour and professional organisations and environment protection) (United Nations, 2000b). By convention all final consumption expenditures of NPISHs are treated as being for the benefit of individual households. The breakdown is not optimal. Health and education should be broken down further in line with that applied for households and government. But the data available on NPISHs are not uniform across participating countries.

- Government final consumption expenditure is broken down by purpose and by type of service into *individual consumption expenditure by government* and *collective consumption expenditure by government*

---

[8] The distinction between non–durable goods and durable goods is based on whether the goods can be used only once or whether they can be used repeatedly or continuously over a period considerably more than a year. Durables also have a relatively high purchasers' price. Semi–durable goods differ from durable goods in that their expected lifetime of use, though more than one year, is significantly shorter and that their purchasers' price is substantially less.

(United Nations, 2000c). Individual consumption expenditure by government covers government expenditure on individual services – that is, services which households consume individually (housing, health, recreation and culture, education and social protection). Collective consumption expenditure by government is government expenditure on collective services – that is, services which benefit households collectively (general public services, defence, public order and safety, economic affairs, environment protection and housing and community services).

- *Individual consumption expenditure by government* is broken down into 29 basic headings. First, by purpose – housing, health, recreation and culture, education, social protection – and then, in the case of health and education, by whether the expenditure is the purchase of health or education services from market producers or for the production of health and education services by government itself.
- This distinction is important. The health and education services that government purchases from market producers are 'market services'. The health and education services that government produces itself are mainly 'non–market services'. The difference between market services and non–market services is that the former are sold at prices that are economically significant, while the latter are not. They are either provided free or sold at prices that do not cover their production costs. Expenditures on market services can be obtained by multiplying the quantities sold by the economically–significant prices they are sold at. The same prices can also be used to calculate the PPPs for market services. The absence of economically–significant prices for non–market services precludes their expenditures and their PPPs being derived in the same way as they are for market services. Instead, the convention adopted by national accountants, whereby expenditures on non–market services are estimated by summing up their costs of production, is respected. Consistency with the prices underlying the expenditure estimates is maintained by using the prices of inputs to calculate the PPPs for non–market services. This is referred to as the 'input–price approach'. To implement the input–price approach, the expenditures on non–market services need to be broken down by cost components.
- The expenditures on government–produced health and education services are broken down into five basic cost components as follows: compensation of employees, intermediate consumption, gross operating surplus (which in effect will be consumption of fixed capital as net operating surplus will be negligible), net taxes on production and receipts from sales (which is a negative cost component).
- *Collective consumption expenditure by government* is also broken down by basic cost components (collective services being non–market services by definition) into seven basic headings. There are seven rather than five basic headings because compensation of employees and intermediate

consumption are classified by type of service – that is, by whether they relate to defence or to collective services other than defence. Different prices are used to deflate these two components of defence expenditure.

- *Gross fixed capital formation* is broken down by type of product into 32 basic headings: one for products of agriculture, forestry, fisheries and aquaculture, twenty for machinery and equipment, nine for construction, one for computer software and one for other products n.e.c. (land improvement, mineral exploration and other intangible fixed assets) (Eurostat, 1998).
- *Change in inventories and acquisitions less disposals of valuables* are treated as two basic headings and not broken down further.
- *Balance of exports and imports* is treated as a single basic heading with no further breakdown.

2.2.7   Actual Individual Consumption

One feature of the classification not mentioned above concerns the derivation of actual individual consumption by households. The classification is an expenditure classification. Individual consumption expenditure is clearly structured by 'who pays' – households, NPISHs or government. Yet one of the principal aims of Eurostat–OECD comparisons is to compare what households in different countries actually consume at the various levels of aggregation. Results of comparisons are presented by 'who consumes' – households or government. Actual individual consumption by households is defined as the sum of the individual consumption expenditures of households, NPISHs and government.[9]

2.3   ORGANISATION OF COMPARISONS

2.3.1   Coverage and Frequency

During the 1980s, the Programme covered only OECD countries because at that time all EU member states were also OECD member countries. Eurostat was responsible for co–ordinating those OECD countries that were EU

---

[9] The transfer of the individual consumption expenditures of NPISHs and government to households is necessary because of the different ways individual services, particularly health and education services, are financed in participating countries. If it is not made, households in countries where NPISHs and/or government are the main providers of individual services will appear to consume a smaller volume of goods and services than households in countries where households themselves pay directly for the bulk of these services.

member states and the OECD was responsible for co–ordinating those OECD countries that were not. The OECD was also responsible for combining the two groups of countries in a single comparison. The 1990 Eurostat–OECD comparison covered 24 countries, of which 14 were co–ordinated by Eurostat and ten by the OECD. Since then, with the expansion of the European Union, the establishment of the European Economic Area, the identification of countries as candidates for EU membership and the inclusion of countries that are not members (or candidates for membership) of either the European Union or the OECD, the number of countries covered by Eurostat–OECD comparisons has risen to 46. For the 2005 comparison, 31 countries were co–ordinated by Eurostat and 15 by the OECD as shown in Table 2.1. As before, all countries were combined in a single comparison by the OECD.

Table 2.1   Countries participating in 2005 comparison

31 countries co–ordinated by Eurostat	27 member states of the European Union and the European Economic Area	*Austria, Belgium,* Bulgaria, Cyprus, *Czech Republic, Denmark,* Estonia, *Finland, France, Germany, Greece, Hungary, Ireland, Italy,* Latvia, Lithuania, *Luxembourg,* Malta, *Netherlands, Poland, Portugal,* Romania, Slovenia, *Slovak Republic, Spain, Sweden, United Kingdom*
	3 non–EU member countries of the European Economic Area	*Iceland, Norway, Switzerland*
	1 EU candidate country	*Turkey*
15 countries co–ordinated by the OECD	7 non–European members countries of the OECD	*Australia, Canada, Japan, Korea, Mexico, New Zealand, United States*
	6 Western Balkan countries	Albania, Bosnia–Herzegovina, Croatia, Macedonia, Montenegro, Serbia
	2 other countries	Israel, Russian Federation

Note: OECD member countries are shown in *italics*.

Until 1990, benchmark comparisons were made every five years – 1980, 1985 and 1990 – and all data were collected over an 18–month period centred on the reference year. In 1990, Eurostat and the OECD adopted the 'rolling benchmark' approach. With this approach, data collection is carried out in continuous cycles.[10] Each cycle takes three years and comprises ten price surveys. The advantages of the approach are that it reduces response burden on participating countries, it enables them to include the price surveys in their regular programme of data collection and it fosters continuity of expertise in their national statistical agencies. Also, by 'rolling' data collected in one year over to the next year, it is possible to make 'benchmark' comparisons annually. Since 1990, Eurostat has made comparisons yearly for EU member states, while the OECD, to reduce the financial burden on countries, has made comparisons every three years for OECD member countries – 1993, 1996, 1999, 2002 and 2005.[11]

Eurostat–OECD comparisons are therefore made every three years, with the 2005 comparison being the most recent completed. The cycle of price surveys for the 2005 comparison started in 2003 and finished in 2005. But data collection was not completed until the third quarter of 2007 when countries reported their final detailed estimates of final expenditure on GDP for 2005. Preliminary results of the comparison were released at the end of 2006. Final results were published at the end of 2007. Reports have been published on all joint comparisons (the reader can refer to various OECD publications such as OECD, 1987; 1992; 1993; 1995; 1996; 1999; Eurostat and OECD, 2004; 2007; Ward, 1985).

---

[10] The starting point of the rolling benchmark approach is the matrix of basic heading PPPs for the latest benchmark year. In each subsequent year, some of the basic heading PPPs are replaced by new PPPs calculated using prices collected during the year, while the basic heading PPPs that have not been replaced are extrapolated using price indices specific to these basic headings. The matrix is then aggregated to obtain PPPs for each level of aggregation up to the level of GDP for the year in question. The cycle of replacement, extrapolation and aggregation continues with about a third of all basic heading PPPs being recalculated each year. After three years, all the original basic heading PPPs in the matrix have been replaced and a new round of price surveys begins.

[11] The rolling benchmark approach requires regular reporting of price indices at the level of basic headings in order to extrapolate the prices of products not priced during the year. While participating countries generally have price indices of sufficient detail and reliability with which to extrapolate PPPs for consumer goods and services, most of them do not have price indices with which to extrapolate PPPs for capital goods. This means that capital items on the product lists must be priced every year if the rolling benchmark approach is to be applied. However, pricing capital items annually is expensive. Countries co–ordinated by Eurostat used to price annually, but they now price capital goods once every two years. PPPs for interim years are derived by a combination of extrapolation and interpolation. Countries co–ordinated by OECD have always priced capital goods once every three years. No estimates are made for interim years.

2.3.2   Actual Data Requirements

The range of final goods and services included in GDP covers consumer goods and services, government services, capital goods and services, inventories, valuables, exports and imports. Countries participating in Eurostat–OECD comparisons are expected to price only consumer products, capital goods and government services.

- *Consumer goods and services:* Participating countries are required to report purchasers' prices for consumer products with the possible exception of rents. The prices are to be collected from a variety of outlet types located in the capital city. This is the practice followed by the majority of countries. But some countries do not limit their price collections to capital cities and collect prices in other cities and towns as well. When averaged, these prices are considered to be national prices.

  To reduce the response burden that national statistical offices would have to shoulder if they were required to price the full set of consumer products in a single year, prices are collected over three years. The product list is divided into six parts. Two parts are surveyed each year: one part in the first half of the year, the other in the second half of the year. For the reference year t, one third of the prices that countries report for consumer products will refer to the year $t-2$, one third to the year $t-1$ and one third to the reference year t.

  In most cases, these prices are not national because they refer to the capital city. In all cases, they are not annual because they refer to a single point in time. Those countries that collect capital city prices are required to provide spatial adjustment factors with which to convert their capital city prices to national prices. All countries are required to provide temporal adjustment factors with which to centre the prices collected in the years $t-2$, $t-1$ and t on the reference year t. Spatial adjustment factors and temporal adjustment factors are to be supplied for each basic heading. Temporal adjustment factors are also to be supplied at the product level when the products are seasonal.

  For rents, countries have to provide national annual purchasers' prices. But, if their rent market is small or unrepresentative, they provide instead data on the quality and quantity of their housing stock so that volume measures can be estimated directly.
- *Capital goods and services:* Participating countries are required to report national purchasers' prices for capital goods. There are two price surveys: one for equipment goods, the other for construction. April prices are collected because it is too costly to monitor prices over the whole year. Prices for equipment goods are to be obtained from producers, importers, distributors or actual purchasers. The prices collected can be either for actual market transactions or for hypothetical market transactions. Prices

for construction are to be compiled using a set of standard construction projects covering different types of buildings and civil engineering works. Prices for the projects are to be at the level of prevailing tender prices.

• *Government services:* Participating countries are required to report the prices of the inputs used in the production of government services. Not all inputs are priced; only the most important – labour – is priced. Participating countries are required to provide the annual compensation of employees that government pays to a cross–selection of occupations in collective services, public health services and public education services.

Participating countries also have to provide expenditure weights, annual average exchange rates and mid–year resident population for the reference year. Countries supply details of their final expenditure on GDP for the reference year, *t*, twice. Provisional estimates are returned in September of year *t*+1. These are used to calculate the preliminary PPPs for *t* that are released in December of *t*+1. Final, or near final, estimates are returned in September of *t*+2. These are used to calculate the final PPPs for *t* that are released in December of *t*+2. Countries report expenditures weights directly to Eurostat and the OECD. Data on exchange rates and population are extracted by Eurostat and the OECD from in–house databases.

2.3.3 Price Surveys and Country Groups

The ten price surveys comprising a cycle are: the six surveys that cover consumer goods and services and take place once every three years; the two surveys that cover capital goods and take place once every two years (or every three years for countries co–ordinated by the OECD); and the two surveys, one covering actual and imputed rentals, the other covering compensation of employees paid to producers of government services, that take place every year (or every three years for OECD countries). The schedule and coverage of the price surveys for the 2005 comparison are given in Table 2.2.

Before each price survey for consumer products and each price survey for capital goods, there are meetings at which the participating countries, together with Eurostat and the OECD, select the products to be priced during the survey. An essential input into the selection process is the pre–survey that participating countries are required to conduct before the meeting to familiarise themselves with the situation in their domestic markets regarding the products about to be surveyed. The meetings have a direct bearing on the quality of the price collections carried out by countries.

Table 2.2   Schedule and coverage of the price surveys for 2005 comparison

Consumer Price Surveys (2003 to 2005)	
2003–1	Food; Non-alcoholic beverages; Alcoholic beverages; Tobacco.
2003–2	Clothing; Footwear; Goods and services for personal care; Personal effects.
2004–1	Materials for the maintenance and repair of the dwelling; Household appliances; Glassware, tableware and household utensils; Tools and equipment for house and garden; Goods for routine household maintenance; Audio-visual, photographic and information-processing equipment; Games, toys, hobbies, gardens, plants, flowers and pets; Newspapers, books and stationery.
2004–2	Personal transport equipment; Spare parts and accessories, fuels and lubricants for the operation of personal transport equipment; Equipment for sport, camping and open-air recreation; Catering services; Accommodation services.
2005–1	Cleaning, repair and hiring of clothing and footwear; Maintenance and repair services for the dwelling; Water supply and miscellaneous services relating to the dwelling; Electricity, gas and other fuels; Domestic and household services; Maintenance and repair services for personal transport equipment; Transport services; Postal services; Telephone and telefax services; Maintenance and repair services for major durables; Veterinary and other services for pets; Recreational and cultural services; Education services; Financial and other services not elsewhere specified.

Table 2.2   *Schedule and coverage of the price surveys for 2005 comparison*
   – continued

Consumer Price Surveys (2003 to 2005)	
2005–2	Furniture and furnishings; Carpets and floor coverings; Household textiles; Medical products, appliances and equipment; Outpatient services.

Other Price Surveys (2005)	
Equipment Goods	Fabricated metal products; General purpose machinery; Special purpose machinery; Electrical and optical equipment; Transport equipment.
Construction Projects	Residential buildings; Non–residential buildings; Civil engineering works.
Housing Services	Actual rentals for housing; Imputed rentals for housing.
Compensation of Employees	Collective services; Public health service; Public education services.

Experience shows that the effectiveness of these meetings depends on the number of products to be considered, the number of countries at the meeting and the thoroughness of the pre–survey carried out by countries prior to the meeting. The three variables interact. As the number of countries increases, the number of products increases. As the number of products increases, the quality of pre–survey work decreases. Experience also shows that this interaction can be a serious problem for meetings held to select consumer products where there are a large number of products to be considered. It is much less of a problem for meetings held to select capital goods where the number of products to be discussed is considerably smaller.

When the number of countries Eurostat co–ordinated rose from 21 to 31 in 1999, it was clear that meetings to select consumer products involving 31 countries discussing some four to five hundred products per survey would be unmanageable and detrimental to the quality of the comparison. For the purposes of organising the surveys of consumer prices, Eurostat divided the 31 countries into three groups with one of the countries in the group acting as group leader. The composition and leaders of the country groups established for the 2005 comparison are listed in Table 2.3.

Group leaders are only responsible for the six price surveys dealing with consumer goods and services. The other four price surveys remain the responsibility Eurostat and the OECD and are organised centrally by them.

Table 2.3   Country groups for the 2005 comparison

Country Group	Countries
Eurostat Countries	
Northern Group (led by Finland)	Denmark, Estonia, Finland, Iceland, Ireland, Latvia, Lithuania, Norway, Sweden, United Kingdom
Central Group (led by Austria)	Austria, Belgium, Czech Republic, Germany, Hungary, Luxembourg, Netherlands, Poland, Slovak Republic, Slovenia, Switzerland
Southern Group (led by Portugal)	Bulgaria, Cyprus, France, Greece, Italy, Malta, Portugal, Romania, Spain, Turkey
OECD Countries	
Western Balkan Group (led by Slovenia and the OECD)	Albania, Bosnia–Herzegovina, Croatia, Macedonia, Montenegro, Serbia, Slovenia
OECD Group (led by the OECD)	Australia, Canada, Israel, Japan, Korea, Mexico, New Zealand, Russian Federation, United States

2.3.4   Linking Country Groups

The country groups are organised by the group leaders to conduct their own surveys of consumer prices. Although prices are collected according to a common set of guidelines and following a common timetable, the products selected for pricing are not common to all groups. Each group is, in effect, a separate comparison. The Group data sets need to be combined before a comparison covering all participating countries can be made. The groups are linked using 'overlap products' – that is, products that are priced by two or more country groups.

To this end, Eurostat co–ordinates the surveys of consumer prices among its three country groups and the OECD co–ordinates the surveys between the OECD group and the Eurostat groups. This co–ordination is essential. Without it, price and volume comparisons of household final consumption expenditure could not be made between the three Eurostat groups or between European countries and non–European countries. Similar co–ordination is needed for the price surveys organised centrally by Eurostat and the OECD. It is the OECD's responsibility to ensure that the product lists for OECD countries for these surveys overlap sufficiently with those for Eurostat countries.

2.4   COLLECTION AND EDITING OF DATA

2.4.1   Consumer Goods and Services

Individual consumption expenditure by households covers the actual and imputed final consumption expenditure incurred by households on the goods and services they require to satisfy their individual needs. It accounts on average for over 60 per cent of GDP in participating countries. This makes it the most important of the seven main aggregates comprising final expenditure on GDP. As such, it is central to Eurostat–OECD comparisons.

One feature of Eurostat–OECD comparisons mentioned already is that prices for consumer goods and services are collected over a period of three years. The basket of products comprising household final consumption expenditure is divided into six parts with prices for two parts being surveyed each year. This requires the organisation of six separate price surveys. Each survey takes between 18 to 20 months to complete. Hence, within any calendar year, work is underway on five surveys: the two surveys of the previous year are being finalised; the two surveys of the current year are being carried out; and the first survey of the following year is being prepared.

Another feature of Eurostat–OECD comparisons, also mentioned already, is that there are too many participating countries for the six price surveys covering consumer goods and services to be managed centrally by either Eurostat or the OECD. Organisation is decentralised. Participating countries are divided into groups with one of the countries in the group acting as group leader (as shown in Table 2.3).

Product selection

Households purchase a large and diverse assortment of individual goods and services, but only a selection of these are priced for the purpose of calculating PPPs. The selection is made at the level of the basic heading. The object is to select a sample of products that reflects the principal expenditures on the basic heading – that is, to select from the products covered by the basic heading those that households are commonly buying.

Choosing a sample of products for a basic heading that can be priced over a number of countries is much more difficult than it is to select the products to be priced at the elementary level of a consumer price index (CPI) within a single country. Selection for a CPI can be left to the price collector whose choice may differ from outlet to outlet providing it does not change over time. This initiative cannot be allowed to price collectors collecting prices for spatial comparisons such as Eurostat–OECD comparisons. The products priced must be comparable across all participating countries pricing them and at all outlets at which the products are priced. If they are not, quality differences will be disguised as price differences leading to biased price relatives.

The products selected also have to be representative of each country's expenditure on the basic heading. But consumption patterns vary among countries. Products that are comparable across countries may be representative for some countries but not for others. For a comparison to be based on products that are both comparable and representative, participating countries have to price their own representative products and, as available, the representative products of others. Representative products usually have lower price levels than unrepresentative products and this will led to biased price relatives if the representativity of the products selected for the basic heading is unevenly distributed among participating countries. To avoid this, the selection of representative products for a basic heading should be equi–representative.

Product selection is made separately for each price survey. The object is to compile a product list for the survey that comprises an equi–representative selection of comparable products for each basic heading that is to be surveyed. To this end, countries participating in Eurostat–OECD comparisons are required to carry out a pre–survey beforehand. During the pre–survey, countries determine the availability and representativity of products proposed for the product list. They also verify whether the products have been specified in a form that ensures that countries pricing them will be pricing comparable products.

Group product lists
The selection of products for a price survey is organised by the group leaders in consultation with the other members of their group. The process commences with the group leaders attending the 'planning meeting' convened by Eurostat and the OECD. The purpose of the meeting is to agree on a common approach to the pre–survey and the survey itself. The exchange

and pooling of information between group leaders that begins at the planning meeting continues until the group product lists are finalised at the 'overlap meeting'.

Consultation with group members starts with the group leader sending them the 'pre-survey questionnaire'. The questionnaire is based on the product list used the last time the country group carried out the price survey and on market research carried out in the meantime by the group leader. The result is an amended and updated version of the previous product list. Some products will have been deleted, some will have been proposed for deletion, others will have had their specifications redefined, and new products, complete with their specifications, will have been added. The pre–survey questionnaire is an annotated first draft of the group product list for forthcoming price survey.

On receipt of the questionnaire, the group members carry out the 'pre–survey'. This involves visiting outlets to ascertain the availability, the comparability and the representativity of the products specified in the questionnaire. Countries use the findings of the pre–survey to reply to the questionnaire. They have a number of options: to accept or reject (possibly with modifications) the deletions proposed; to accept, reject or modify the redefined specifications and the specifications of the proposed new products; and to propose precisely–defined new products themselves. Countries are expected to support their modifications and proposals with technical documentation and pictures.

On the basis of the replies received from group members, the group leader revises the product list contained in the pre–survey questionnaire to produce the 'draft group product list'. On completion, the draft product list is circulated to group members for them to review prior to the 'group meeting'. The group meeting is convened by the group leader. It is attended by the group members, the other group leaders, Eurostat and the OECD. Its principal object is to complete the process started with the pre-survey – namely, the establishment of the 'final group product list' for the ensuing price survey.

The pre–survey and the group meeting provide the means whereby group members can ensure that the final group product list reflects the availability of comparable products in their domestic markets and is equally representative for all of them. Even so, the group product list agreed at the group meeting is not the final list.

Overlap products

Group product lists can be expected to differ from one country group to the other. Some of the products specified will be common to more than one group, but comparisons across the country groups cannot be left to chance.

Before the group product lists are finalised and countries begin price collection, Eurostat and the OECD convene a meeting with the group leaders. This is the 'overlap meeting' at which the group product lists are combined to make sure that, at each basic heading covered by the survey, there are enough overlap products to allow each country group to be compared with each of the other country groups.

When there are not enough overlap products for a basic heading, new ones have to be added. Overlap products can often be 'created' by combining the specifications of two products with similar characteristics by widening the range of one or more parameters. The process of creating overlaps begins during the group meetings which are held one after another and are attended by all group leaders. Because group leaders know what products are specified in their own draft group product list, they are able to propose modified or new product specifications to another group as appropriate. At the same time, they learn what products are available in the countries of the other groups and, if necessary, can modify their own group product list accordingly.

When participating countries receive the final product list for their group prior to price collection, they will find that it has been amended to provide the necessary overlaps between the groups. New products will have been introduced, some products on the original list will have had their specifications modified, while other products agreed to at the group meeting will have been omitted in order to accommodate the overlap products added and to avoid imbalances among the different types of products specified. Each overlap product has a code number that identifies which of the other groups it provides an overlap.

Product specifications
The product specifications used for Eurostat–OECD comparisons are either 'brand and model specific' or 'generic'. A brand and model specification designates the particular brand and model to be priced. A generic specification lists only the relevant technical parameters of the product to be priced. It does not identify any brand. A brand and model specification has a tight definition. Countries pricing a specification stipulating a specific brand and model are, in principle, pricing identical products. A generic specification has a looser definition. Countries pricing a generic specification are, in principle, pricing comparable products.

Particular importance is given to brand for two reasons. First, brands provide tight specifications that make possible the identification and pricing of goods that are exactly the same in the countries pricing them. Second, the brand itself may have a value. Consumers often perceive products with certain brand names as preferable to similar products sold under other brand names and are prepared to pay more for them. In such cases, the brand name is a price determining characteristic and should be included in the product specification.

Product specifications that are brand and model specific have two possible disadvantages. The brand and model stipulated may not be available or, if available, the brand and model may not be representative. Using clusters of comparable brands and models partly addresses these issues, particularly that of availability.

Generic specifications, especially those with too loose or too open–ended definitions, are susceptible to variations in quality. As neither Eurostat nor the OECD adjust prices to accommodate quality differences, it is important that the generic specifications are sufficiently detailed – or tight – to ensure that participating countries price products of similar quality.

Product specifications should be supported by pictures of the products they specified. Price collectors do not always envisage the same product from a written description. The pictures will show them what it is they have to price. Pictures are not necessary for all product specifications. They are less essential for brand and model specifications and more useful for generic specifications where they can help to reduce quality differences arising from misinterpretation. Countries participating in Eurostat–OECD comparisons are provided with pictures for a selection of product specifications.

Price collection

Price collection is the responsibility of the participating countries. Before they can begin price collection, they have a number of tasks to complete. These involve: selecting and contacting the outlets to be visited by price collectors; preparing the pricing materials and supplementary documentation for price collectors (including the translation of product specifications and survey guidelines into the national language if necessary); identifying which specifications on the final group product list are to be priced and, in the case of generic specifications, which brands are to be priced; and holding a meeting with price collectors to clarify issues such as how many items to be priced per basic heading, how many price observations per item, etc.

Selection of outlets

The selection of outlets is of particular importance because of the effect it will have on the average prices of the products to be surveyed. Different products have different distribution profiles. Some products are sold mostly in supermarkets, other products are sold mainly in specialist shops. Prices for the same product can change from outlet type to outlet type because the conditions under which it is sold vary.

'Conditions of sale' – such as the availability of advice from shop assistants, the provision of after-sales service and the ability to return defective goods – constitute a service element. If the service element changes from one outlet type to another, the product being purchased is not the same at both outlets even if it is physically identical. The difference in the service element is a quality difference and contributes to the price difference. If, when averaging the prices collected for the product, no account is taken of the different service elements of the outlets at which they were observed, the average price is likely to be too high or too low.

To avoid this, countries participating in Eurostat–OECD comparisons are required to select outlets so that the selection mirrors consumer purchasing patterns at various outlet types for the products being priced. If consumers buy 50 per cent of their clothing from departmental stores, 30 per cent from supermarkets and 20 per cent from specialist shops, then a sample of ten outlets would comprise five departmental stores, three supermarkets and two specialist shops. As the products being surveyed differ from price survey to price survey, the selection of outlets will also differ between surveys. By selecting outlets in this way, implicit weights are introduced to accommodate the varying service elements of outlets and their impact on price. Unbiased average prices are the result.

Location is another consideration that participating countries need to take into account when selecting outlets. The number of outlets selected in each location should be proportional to the area distribution of the volume of sales of the products in question. The location of selected outlets can be expected to differ from survey to survey.

A common starting point for the selection of outlets is the sample of outlets used for the CPI, but it is only a starting point. The product lists for Eurostat–OECD price surveys are larger than CPI lists, specifying products not included in the CPI. The CPI sample may not be ideal to collect reliable prices for these products because the selection of outlets by type is not in proportion to the volume of their sales of the products. In this case, it is necessary to augment the CPI sample with additional outlets. At the same time, because resources available for the price surveys are limited, the CPI sample may be too large and has to be reduced.

Number of products priced per basic heading
The number of products to be priced per basic heading will vary from basic heading to basic heading. It will depend on the heterogeneity of products covered by the basic heading and on the importance of the basic heading. The minimum that countries participating in Eurostat–OECD comparisons have to price is one representative product per basic heading as this provides for the calculation of unbiased PPPs. But as the object is to calculate PPPs that are also reliable, countries are expected to price more than one representative product per basic heading. In principle, they should price that number of

representative products that are commensurate with the price variation within the basic heading and their expenditure on the basic heading.

Participating countries are also required to price the representative products of other participants, otherwise it may not be possible to make a comparison. Which unrepresentative products a country should price depends on availability. Price collectors should not be asked to waste resources tracking down products that are not easily found. Also, it is desirable that the prices collected for unrepresentative products provide relatively reliable average prices. In this respect, countries are advised to prune the list of products they cannot price or cannot price without difficulty. Price collectors would then attempt to price all products remaining on the list.

Number of price observations per product

The number of prices to be collected for a product will differ from one basic heading to another. It will also differ from product to product within a basic heading. In general, the number of prices collected for a product determines the reliability of its average price. The larger the number of price observations, the more accurate the average price. The actual number depends on the degree to which the prices of the product vary and the degree of accuracy required. It also depends on the product specification, the tighter the specification the smaller the price variation.

On the assumptions that price variation is usually between 5 and 15 per cent and that the desired level of precision is 10 per cent, participating countries are advised that between 5 and 10 observations are required for brand specific specifications and between 15 to 20 observations are required for generic specifications.[12] These numbers refer to a single pricing location such as the capital city. They are indicative only. Each participating country has to decide on the number of price observations to be collected per product according to the type of specification being priced and the conditions prevailing in its market.

Prices collected

The object of the price surveys is to collect the prices that purchasers actually pay to sellers to acquire the goods and services specified on the final group product list at the time of the survey. As it is not practical to collect prices from purchasers, the prices are collected from sellers. Most sellers display the prices at which they are prepared to sell their products. But the prices at which products are offered for sale are not necessarily the prices at which

---

[12] Sample size is determined by $[t^2 CV^2/SE^2]$ where t is Student's t and which is assumed to equal 2 at 0.95 probability, CV, or coefficient of variation, is the product's price variation, and SE, or standard error, is the desired degree of accuracy.

they are actually sold. Price collectors observe offer prices but, before recording them as actual purchasers' prices, they have to establish whether the offer price includes all the relevant price components – such as delivery costs, VAT, discounts, service charges and gratuities – and, if not, adjust it accordingly.

Medical goods and services

Sales of most consumer goods and services involve a transaction between a seller and a single buyer. This is not always the situation with medical goods and services which can involve a transaction between a seller and two independent buyers. Such a situation arises when the medical products are paid for in part by a household and in part by the government. The purchasers' price that participating countries are required to report is the total price or the sum of the price paid by the household and the price paid by government. If composite prices are not used to calculate PPPs when they should be, the volume of medical products purchased will be twice what it should be.[13] Usually there are regulations that determine what the household should pay and what the government will pay and this information can be obtained from the government office responsible.

Seasonal products

Seasonal products are defined as those products for which both prices and the quantities sold vary substantially throughout the year. Usually, the patterns of variation are repeated from one year to the next. By this definition, certain fruits, vegetables, fish and flowers are obviously seasonal products. Various types of clothing are also seasonal products. So too are those goods that are sold in substantial amounts at prices well below 'normal' prices during seasonal sales. For the purposes of Eurostat–OECD comparisons, only seasonal food products warrant special treatment.

Annual prices for seasonal products, other than seasonal food products, are obtained as they are for non–seasonal products. Their survey prices are adjusted to annual averages using monthly temporal adjustment factors that participating countries extract from their CPI databases. The temporal

---

[13] Suppose that the quantity of a pharmaceutical product purchased is 1000 units and that the price per unit is €10 of which households pay €2 and government €8. In the national accounts, €2000 will be recorded as household expenditure and €8000 will be recorded as government expenditure. If the amounts actually paid – that is, €2 by households and €8 by government – are used to deflate these expenditures, it will seem that both households and government have each purchased 1000 units or 2000 units in total. But if the total amount paid – that is €10 – is used, households will appear to have purchased 200 units and government 800 units – a total of 1000 units.

adjustment factors are unweighted – that is, they are not weighted by the quantity sold in the corresponding month.

Annual prices for seasonal food products are obtained by adjusting survey prices with weighted temporal adjustment factors. This requires participating countries to provide monthly or quarterly weights in addition to an appropriate CPI sub–index for each seasonal food product they priced. The weights should be quantity weights reflecting the quantities of the item purchased throughout the survey year. If quantity weights are not available, expenditure weights based on expenditure on the item during the survey year should be provided instead.

Assigning representativity indicators

So that representative products can be distinguished from unrepresentative products when PPPs are calculated for a basic heading, countries participating in Eurostat–OECD comparisons are required to indicate which of the products they have priced are representative when reporting their prices. Representative products are designated by a 'representativity indicator'. Currently an asterisk (*) is employed and representative products are commonly referred to as 'asterisk products'.

Participating countries have problems identifying representative products. The problem is not with products that they themselves have proposed for the product lists because they are supposed to be representative. The problem lies with the products that other countries have proposed. The openness of domestic markets, particularly in the European Union, has progressively increased the availability of many of these products. And, without reliable expenditure data by product within basic headings, it is difficult to determine whether they are being sold in sufficiently large numbers to be representative.

Hence, the decision as to whether or not these products are representative has to be based on other data sources. Such sources include motor vehicle registration statistics, internet sites giving country–specific information on a range of 'best selling' products, and sales personnel at the outlets visited during the pre–survey and the price survey. The number of prices collected during the price survey can also be used as a measure of representativity. Finally, in the absence of any relevant data or informed opinion, the decision has to be subjective.

Housing services and the rent survey

Although housing services are part of individual consumption expenditure by households, they are not included in the survey cycle. They are covered by a special rent survey for which participating countries are not expected to collect data specifically but to extract them from existent statistical sources. The survey is held every year and is organised by Eurostat and the OECD and not by the group leaders. Data are collected on the rents paid by tenants, and on the rents imputed to owners–occupiers, for a selection of precisely–defined dwellings. Quantitative and qualitative data on the housing stock are also collected.[14]

The data on rents are used to calculate PPPs with which the final expenditures on actual and imputed rents are deflated to derive volume measures on housing services indirectly. The quantitative and qualitative data on housing stock are used to compute volume measures on housing services directly. These direct volume measures serve two purposes. They provide a check on the volume measures obtained indirectly. And, more importantly, they can be used in place of the indirect measures for those participating countries that do not have a sufficiently developed and representative rent market and so are not able to supply the data required on actual and imputed rents.

Reporting and validation of prices
Once price collection is finished, participating countries are required to enter their price observations on the electronic reporting form provided for each survey in the survey cycle. Countries send the completed reporting form to their group leader for validation.

Validation is an iterative process with reporting forms going backwards and forwards with questions and answers between group leaders and their group members. It has two distinct phases. The first phase is the intra–country editing. During this phase, the price observations of each group member are checked separately without reference to the price data of other group members. The second phase is the inter–country editing within country groups. During this phase, the average survey prices of each group member are checked against the average survey prices of other group members. As soon as both phases have been concluded to the satisfaction of all members of the group, the group leader returns the validated reporting forms to Eurostat.

On receipt of the reporting forms, Eurostat starts the third and final phase of validation: the inter–country editing across country groups. Again it is an iterative process, but this time between countries and Eurostat. As with second phase, it consists of checking the average survey prices of each country against the average survey prices of other countries, but this time all countries are involved and not just other group members. Validation finishes when both Eurostat and the countries agree on the average prices and the

---

[14] Number of rooms and usable area; with or without running water, inside toilet, electricity and central heating (or air conditioning).

underlying price observations. Once approved, the average survey prices are considered final.

The reporting, validation and approval of a survey's prices takes place in the ten months that follow price collection.

The three phases of validation have the same objective: to identify and eliminate non–sampling errors from the survey price data. Editing involves identifying prices that are outliers – that is, prices that are determined to be either too high or too low according to given criteria. Prices that are outliers are not necessarily wrong. But the fact that they are outliers suggests that they could be wrong and that they need to be verified. Intra–country editing looks for outliers among the individual prices that a country has collected for each product it has chosen to survey. Inter–country editing searches for outliers among the average survey prices that countries have reported for the same products within a basic heading.

Countries and group leaders are assisted in the identification of outliers by two software packages. The first package involves data entry on price input sheets and the generation of price output sheets flagging outliers. Price input and output sheets are designed specifically for intra–country editing of individual price observations. They are also the means by which price data are transmitted between countries, group leaders and Eurostat during the three phases of validation. The second package concerns the Quaranta editing procedure and the generation of Quaranta tables flagging outliers (Eurostat and University of Florence, 1996). Quaranta tables are used in both phases of inter–country editing of average survey prices.

Price input and output sheets are used solely to edit the prices of consumer goods and services collected by the six surveys constituting the survey cycle. These surveys are the only surveys for which countries report individual price observations. The Quaranta editing procedure has a broader application than editing the prices collected for consumer products. Quaranta tables are also used to edit the average survey prices for rents, compensation of employees, equipment goods and construction projects.

From average survey prices to national annual prices
The majority of participating countries conduct their price surveys only in the capital city, so the average survey prices are capital city prices. Two months after data collection is completed, countries reporting capital city prices are required to provide Eurostat spatial adjustment factors with which their capital city prices can be converted to national prices. A spatial adjustment factor is to be supplied for each basic heading surveyed. Eurostat adjusts the capital city prices to national prices, basic heading by basic heading, once the average prices for a survey have been validated. Participating countries

obtain the spatial adjustment factors from the surveys of regional price differences that they are required to conduct every six years.

The national survey prices, irrespective of whether they are adjusted capital city prices or national prices supplied directly by countries, refer to the point in time when the survey was conducted. They need to be adjusted to annual prices. At the end of each year, participating countries are required to provide Eurostat and the OECD monthly temporal adjustment factors for each basic heading under individual consumption expenditure by households. Those that refer to the basic headings that were surveyed during the year are used to adjust the national survey prices for these basic headings to national annual prices. Participating countries extract the temporal adjustment factors from their CPI data base.

2.4.2   Government Services

Government services are the services provided to households by government. They comprise individual services and collective services. Individual services are the services that government provide to specific identifiable households – that is, services, such as health and education, which benefit individual households. Collective services are those that government provide simultaneously to all members of the community – that is, services, such as defence and public order and safety, which benefit households collectively.

Market and non–market services
Collective services are produced by government. Individual services can be both produced by government and purchased by government from market producers. The individual services that government purchases from market producers are called 'market services' because they are sold at economically–significant prices that determine the amounts producers supply and purchasers buy. Being economically significant, the prices are used to value the outputs of market producers by multiplying the quantities produced by the prices at which they are sold. Thus, they are also the prices with which to calculate PPPs for market services.

The collective and individual services that government produces itself are referred to as 'non–market services' because they are not sold at economically significant prices. Instead, they are either provided free or sold at prices that do not cover their costs of production. Without economically–significant prices, it is not possible to value the outputs of non–market producers in the same way as the outputs of market producers are valued. National accountants value the outputs of non–market producers by summing the costs to produce them. To maintain consistency with the prices underlying these expenditures, it is necessary to use the purchasers' prices of inputs to calculate the PPPs for non–market services.

Treatment of market services

Collecting the economically–significant prices paid for market services is not as straightforward as it is for most consumer services. Purchases of individual services from market producers by government are financed differently from country to country. The government may buy the services, in full or in part, direct from the producers or it may reimburse households, in full or in part, after the households themselves have made the purchase. When both government and households pay the market producer, there are two purchasers and two prices.

The prices to be collected are 'total prices'. In countries where either government or households pay the whole purchasers' price direct to the market producer, the total price is the price that either government or households pay (irrespective of any subsequent reimbursement in the case of households). In countries where households pay only a portion of the purchasers' price to the market producer and the reminder is paid to the market producer by government, the total price is the composite price – that is, the sum of the non–reimbursable part paid by households and the part paid by government.

Although it is possible to collect total prices for individual services purchased by government from market producers in principle, it is difficult to collect internationally comparable total prices for health and education services in practice. For Eurostat–OECD comparisons, total prices are only collected for medical goods and services delivered to out–patients. Output prices are not collected for hospital services or education services. Reference PPPs are used instead.

Treatment of non–market services

Using purchasers' prices of inputs to calculate PPPs for non–market services is called the 'input–price approach'. It requires a breakdown of expenditure on non–market services by cost components. The five basic cost components identified in the Eurostat–OECD expenditure classification are the following: compensation of employees, intermediate consumption, gross operating surplus (which is essentially consumption of fixed capital as net operating surplus is likely to be negligible), net taxes on production and, a negative cost component, receipts from sales.

Eurostat–OECD comparisons only use the input–price approach for the three most important services produced by government: health, education and collective services. Reference PPPs are used for the remaining services: housing, recreation and culture, and social protection.

Survey of compensation of employees

Not all inputs are priced for Eurostat–OECD comparisons. Only the labour input is priced. Participating countries are required to provide the annual compensation of employees that government pays to employees in a cross-section of occupations in collective services, public health services and public education services during the reference year.[15] The compensation of employees collected for an occupation is a purchaser's price for a hypothetical market transaction – that is, what government would pay an employee of a specified seniority working in the occupation. In principle, the price is to be computed using government salary scales. In practice, it is often extracted from payroll statistics.

Countries are also required to report for each selected occupation: the standard number of hours worked per week, the number of working days with paid leave, the number of public holidays falling on working days during the reference year, and the percentage share of the occupation within the basic heading for which it has been selected. The standard number of hours worked per week and the number of working days taken as holidays are used to normalise the compensation of employees across countries. The norm applied is 1710 hours worked per year.[16] The compensation of employees of selected occupations working less or more than the norm are increased or decreased proportionally.

The percentage shares of the selected occupations within their basic headings should refer to the wider groups of employees that the selected occupations represent and not just to the employees in the selected occupations. The selected occupations are a sample. Each selected occupation represents a stratum of employees that have comparable occupations and similar levels of compensation of employees. The percentage shares are to relate to these occupational strata. They are used in conjunction with the standardised compensation of employees to obtain expenditure weights for each selected occupation that can be used when calculating PPPs for the basic heading to which it is assigned.

---

[15] Cleaner, caretaker, labourer, messenger, maintenance electrician, switchboard operator, secretary, draughtsman, book–keeping clerk, computer operator, policeman, social worker, civil engineer, sanitary engineer, public health nurse, public health physician, executive official I (without university degree), executive official II (with university degree); kindergarten teacher, primary school teacher, secondary school teacher, head teacher; hospital cook, typist, hospital administrator, laboratory assistant, physiotherapist, nursing auxiliary, nurse I, nurse II (operating theatre), nurse III (head of department), doctor I, doctor II (assistant head of department), doctor III (head of hospital department).

[16] 52 working weeks, each 38 hours duration, less 7 working weeks (or 35 working days) of paid leave and public holidays.

Validation of prices

Two edits should be carried out by participating countries before reporting the compensation of employees and related data to Eurostat and the OECD. The first edit is to look at the internal coherency of the data set. For example, it is usually the case that: doctors earn more than nurses; head teachers earn more than other teachers; officers in the army earn more than privates and so on. Income differentials between occupations that are contrary to expectations should be verified and the errors identified should be corrected.

The second edit is to check the consistency between the compensation of employees that are to be reported for the latest reference year and the compensation of employees that were reported for the previous reference year. Differences can be expected between the two data sets because the salary scales will have changed between the two periods. Discrepancies that cannot be explained in this way should be verified and the errors discovered should be corrected.

Eurostat and the OECD repeat these two edits. They also apply the Quaranta editing procedure to compare the price levels of the compensation of employees reported for the selected occupations across countries. The outliers identified through this procedure are returned to the countries reporting them for verification. Countries are required to either correct the compensation of employees originally reported or to confirm that they are correct.

Productivity adjustments

The input-price approach as applied in Eurostat–OECD comparisons does not take into account differences in productivity between the producers of non–market services in different countries. Non–market producers are assumed to be equally efficient so that the same level of input yields the same volume of output regardless of the country in which the non–market producer is operating. Given the extent to which income levels vary among participating countries, this assumption is difficult to defend. Differences in productivity are being disguised as price differences with output volumes being overestimated for countries whose cost of inputs are relatively low and underestimated for countries whose cost of inputs are relatively high.

The failure to take account of productivity differences between the producers of non–market services in different countries affects not only the PPPs and volume indices of health services, education services and collective services, but also the PPPs and volume indices of the main aggregates of which these expenditure categories are a part: actual individual consumption by households, actual collective consumption by government and GDP. It is the effect on the volume indices of these aggregates – particularly the volume indices of GDP – that is the primary concern.

The problem is not specific to international spatial comparisons, it is a problem for national temporal comparisons as well. But it is a much more serious problem for international comparisons as differences in the productivity of producers of non–market services are significantly larger between countries than are the year–to–year changes in productivity of non–market producers of individual countries. Even so, the majority of EU member states and OECD member countries have not been in favour of adjustments for productivity differences being employed in Eurostat–OECD comparisons. They argue that productivity adjustments are inevitably based on assumptions that cannot be verified without a genuine measurement of output. And, if output could be measured, then input methods would not be necessary.

2.4.3   Capital Goods and Services

Gross fixed capital formation (GFCF) in the Eurostat–OECD expenditure classification is broken down into three expenditure categories – equipment goods, construction projects and other products.[17] Eurostat–OECD comparisons are concerned with collecting prices and calculating PPPs for equipment goods and construction projects. With the exception of software, prices are not collected for other products and, as PPPs cannot be calculated for these items, reference PPPs are used instead.

GFCF is one of the more difficult and costly aggregates for which to collect internationally comparable and representative prices. One reason for this is the complexity and variability of the products being priced. It is because of this that Eurostat–OECD product specifications for equipment goods and construction projects are drawn up by engineers and quantity surveyors and not by statisticians. Another reason is that the expertise required to draw up the product specifications is also required to match and price them and this expertise is not usually available in most national statistical agencies. Typically the pricing of capital goods – particularly the pricing of construction projects – has to be contracted out to consultancy firms that specialise in engineering or in construction.

---

[17] Other products consist of: plantation, orchard and vineyard development; change in stocks of breeding stock, draught animals, dairy cattle, animals raised for wool clippings, etc.; computer software that a producer expects to use in production for more than one year; land improvement including dams and dikes which are part of flood control and irrigation projects; mineral exploration; acquisition of entertainment, literary or artistic originals; other intangible fixed assets.

2.4.4 Equipment Goods

The complexity of equipment goods, the variation in purchasing patterns among countries, the number of countries being compared and resource constraints requires the survey of equipment prices to focus on the pricing of comparable products. The approach adopted for the survey is the standard one of specification pricing. It involves the selection of a basket of precisely–defined products so that countries price to a constant quality and any price differences observed are 'pure' price differences. The selection is made in consultation with the countries participating in the comparison. The products are defined in terms of characteristics that influence their purchasers' price.

Product specifications
The characteristics specified cover both the product (performance, operation and quality) and the transaction (order size, discounts, delivery and installation). The products priced by countries should be identical, but, if they are not, they should at least be equivalent. The products priced do not necessarily have to be the same make and model and deviation from the technical parameters is tolerated. Transaction characteristics have to be respected because countries are required to report actual transaction prices and not list or catalogue prices.

All the products specified for the survey are new. Second–hand equipment goods bought by resident producers are only recorded as GFCF if they are purchased from non–residents and imports of second–hand equipment goods are not typical for the majority of countries participating in Eurostat–OECD comparisons. In addition, the quality of second–hand equipment goods varies considerably making it difficult to price comparable items without adjusting for quality differences. Quality adjustments are not a feature of Eurostat–OECD methodology. Countries are required to price only new items even when imported second–hand items are more representative.

Representativity
Representativity is introduced into the survey by including in the product list a number of alternative specifications for the same product. This allows the different factors that can influence a country's purchasing patterns, such as domestic producers, traditional trade links or average size of farms and factories, to be accommodated. Representativity is also introduced by allowing countries some flexibility in the interpretation of product specifications. Countries are expected to price representative products when it does not compromise comparability.

Flexibility in interpretation

To price products that are equivalent, countries have to match the technical parameters of the makes and models that are available in their market with the technical parameters of the make and model specified.[18] This requires flexibility in the interpretation of product specifications, but flexibility exercised with caution. Too liberal an interpretation will result in the loss of comparability, too strict an interpretation can mean that items cannot be priced. To avoid either of these extremes and to minimise quality differences, countries are provided with pricing guidelines. These usually allow a substitution when the parameter affected by the deviation contributes only a small share to the total price.

Sources of prices

Countries can obtain prices directly from producers, importers or distributors or from their catalogues. They may even obtain them from actual purchasers, if practical. The prices can be collected by whichever method, or combination of methods, countries find the most convenient – personal visit, telephone, letter, internet and so on. But whatever the source, whatever the method, strict conformity to the concept of purchasers' price is essential in all cases.

Some countries obtain prices through their producer price index (PPI). Either they are able to match the equipment good specifications directly with those used for the PPI or they request the PPI respondents who are producers of the types of equipment goods being surveyed to price the equipment good specifications. As PPIs generally collect basic prices, these need to be adjusted to purchasers' prices.

Validation of prices

Countries report average national purchasers' prices for the reference month of the survey year. Eurostat and the OECD use the Quaranta editing procedure to validate these average prices. But, because of the complexity of the items priced, the prices of equipment goods cannot be verified on the basis of price alone. The fact that prices for an item appear consistent across countries does not mean that the items priced are comparable across countries. Before applying the Quaranta editing procedure, Eurostat and the OECD compare the technical parameters of the products priced first. Products are sorted into groups on the basis of the comparability of their

---

[18] When matching products and deciding whether or not the one observed is a close substitute to the one specified, it is not just the number of parameters not matching that needs to be taken into account, but also the degree to which they differ. Products observed with 'near misses' on most, if not all, parameters could still be an acceptable substitute for the product specified.

technical parameters with those of their product specifications or with those of products priced by other countries.

Matched products have parameters that are either identical to those of their product specification or equivalent to those of their product specification or identical to those of a product priced by another country. (Unmatched products are discarded.) Grouping products in this way makes it easier to interpret the Quaranta editing procedure. If the prices reported for a product specification are shown to be consistent across countries, it is reasonable to assume that they refer to comparable items. Whereas when outliers are identified, the mistake, if any, is more likely to be an incorrect price than an incorrect match. Outliers are referred back to the reporting country. It is asked to confirm or to correct the price.

2.4.5   Construction Projects

The approach used for Eurostat–OECD construction price comparisons emphasises comparability. Participating countries are required to price a number of standard construction projects covering different types of residential buildings, non–residential buildings and civil engineering works. Countries are currently expected to price a total of nine projects – three residential buildings, three non–residential buildings and three civil engineering works.[19]

Bills of quantities

The standard construction projects are not actual constructions, but they designed to be representative of actual constructions to be found in participating countries. Each standard project is defined by a 'bill of quantities' and a set of technical drawings. The bill of quantities breaks down the project into a number of major components (earthworks, masonry, joinery and so on.) each of which comprises a number of elementary components (mechanical excavation of foundation trenches, supply, transport, dumping and compacting of crushed aggregate for foundation trenches and so on.).

Each elementary component is specified by a quantity. The total price for the elementary component is computed by multiplying the quantity specified by a unit price. By summing the total prices of its elementary components, a total price can be obtained for each major component. And, by summing the

---

[19] Countries select projects from the following: seven residential buildings – European house, Portuguese house, Nordic house, North American house, Japanese house, Australian–New Zealand house, apartment in an apartment block; five non–residential buildings – agricultural shed, European factory, Japanese factory, office block, primary school; and four civil engineering works – asphalt road, concrete road, bridge, and concrete sewer main.

total prices of the major components, an overall price for work done can be obtained. The overall price for work done is not the final price of the project. It needs to be augmented by architects' and engineers' fees and by non–deductible taxes on products in order to arrive at the desired purchasers' price.

Flexibility in interpretation

All countries pricing a particular standard project price the same bill of quantities so that, in principle, all of them are pricing a comparable product. In practice, this may not be so. Materials and methods of construction can vary between countries. National standards and regulations also vary between countries. Some flexibility of interpretation has to be allowed if countries are to provide representative prices.

Countries are provided with pricing guidelines to ensure that flexible interpretation does not become too liberal and result in marked differences in quality or in a different construction being priced. Usually, substitutions are acceptable when the components affected represent only a small share of the total price and the basic features of the construction remain unchanged. When substitutions are made, they should be clearly identified and explained in the bill of quantities.

Unit prices

The unit prices used in the bills of quantities must cover not only the contractor's direct cost for each of the specified elementary components (such as materials, labour, hire of equipment, sub–contractors' fees), but also the profits (or losses) of the contractor, general expenses (including share of main office overheads), and all preliminary expenses (including the cost of site preparation) connected with the construction.

The unit prices do not include architects' and engineers' fees and non–deductible VAT. As already mentioned, these are added after the overall price of work has been established. Nor do the unit prices include the expenditure incurred for the purchase of the land. But in this case no addition is made to the overall price of work either for the cost of the land itself or for the costs associated with the transfer of ownership.

Source of unit prices

The unit prices with which to value the elementary components of the bills of quantities can be obtained either from actual bills of quantities that have been valued for tenders submitted by construction companies or from one of the computerised systems of unit costs that major consultancy firms and research institutes maintain for the construction industry. If the first source is adopted, only unit prices from tenders that have been successful – or from tenders that can be considered realistic because they would permit the carrying out of work in good condition – should be used to value the standard construction projects.

If the second source is employed, the standard construction projects will be valued at resource cost and not at purchasers' prices. It is necessary to adjust the underlying unit costs to unit prices using the total prices of successful tenders to establish the level to which the unit costs have to be raised.

Validation of prices
Countries report the average national purchasers' price for the reference month of the survey year for each standard construction project they price. Before doing so, they are required to compare the bills of quantities of the projects priced in the current survey with the bills of quantities for the same projects from the previous survey. This is possible because the standard construction projects and their bills of quantities do not change – or change only marginally – from one survey to the next. The object is to see whether the contribution to the total price of each major component is approximately the same in both surveys and, if it is not, to check the unit prices of its elementary components across the two surveys. Errors identified in this way are to be corrected.

Eurostat and the OECD apply the Quaranta editing procedure to detect outliers by comparing the total prices for the standard construction projects across countries. Editing bills of quantities by total price alone is not sufficient. Outliers do not necessarily mean that the projects priced are not comparable, while, conversely, the absence of outliers does not necessarily mean that the projects priced are comparable. Additional validation at lower levels of aggregation is required.

The validation is carried out at the level of major components initially. An edit similar to the inter–temporal edit described above is employed instead. It involves matching the bills of quantities for the projects priced by countries and comparing them to establish whether the contribution of each major component to total price is approximately the same in each country. If it is not, the shares of the elementary components to the total price of the major component under review are then compared to see whether there are any questionable unit prices. Suspect unit prices are referred back to the countries reporting them for correction or confirmation that they are correct.

2.5   CALCULATION AND AGGREGATION OF PPPs

2.5.1   The Eltetö–Köves–Szulc (EKS) Method

The computation of PPPs for GDP is made in two stages. First, there is the calculation of unweighted PPPs at the basic heading level; then, there is the weighted aggregation of the basic heading PPPs up to the level of GDP. Eurostat and the OECD use the Eltetö–Köves–Szulc or EKS method both to calculate basic heading PPPs and to aggregate them.

Participating countries price both products that are representative of their national market and products that are representative of the national markets of others. As representative products generally have a lower price level than unrepresentative products, this has to be taken into account when calculating the PPPs for a basic heading otherwise the PPPs will be biased. Because there are no expenditure weights below the basic heading with which to determine the relative importance of the products priced for a basic heading, participating countries are required to indicate whether or not the products they priced are representative of their national markets when reporting their prices.

The information on representativeness, together with the prices to which it refers, is used to obtain unweighted PPPs at the basic heading level as follows:

- For each pair of countries, two PPPs are calculated. The first is the geometric mean of the price relatives for products representative of the first country; the second is the geometric mean of the price relatives for products representative of the second country. The geometric mean of these two PPPs is then taken to derive a single PPP between the two countries.
- By following this procedure each basic heading is provided with a matrix of binary PPPs. In some cases, the matrix is incomplete because it is not always possible to calculate a PPP directly between each pair of countries. In addition, the PPPs in the matrix are intransitive.[20]
- The matrix is made complete by taking the geometric mean of all the available indirect PPPs bridging the pairs of countries for which direct PPPs are missing.[21] This procedure does not always work, in which case it

---

[20] This means that in the case of three countries A, B and C, the ratio of the PPP between A and C and the PPP between B and C is not equal to the PPP between A and B: $PPP_{AC} / PPP_{BC} \neq PPP_{AB}$.

[21] An indirect PPP between two countries is one obtained by calculating it indirectly through a third country. Hence, in the case of three countries A, B and C, the indirect PPP for A on B via C is given as $_cPPP_{AB} = PPP_{AC} / PPP_{BC}$, where $_cPPP_{AB}$ is the indirect PPP and PPP_{AC} and PPP_{BC} are the direct PPPs for A and B on C.

is necessary to take PPPs from elsewhere in the comparison to act as proxies for the missing PPPs.

- The matrix is made transitive by applying the EKS procedure. Transitivity is achieved by replacing the PPP between each pair of countries by the geometric mean of itself squared and all the corresponding indirect PPPs between the pair obtained using the other countries as a bridge. The resulting EKS PPPs differ as little as possible from the original binary PPPs.[22]

The aggregation of basic heading EKS PPPs is undertaken at each level of expenditure up to the level of GDP as follows:

- For each pair of countries, the basic heading EKS PPPs are weighted, summed and averaged using first the expenditures on the basic headings of the first country as weights and then the corresponding expenditures of the second country as weights. This results in two weighted PPPs – a 'Laspeyres type' PPP and a 'Paasche type' PPP – the geometric mean of which gives a single 'Fisher type' or Fisher PPP between the two countries.[23]
- By following this procedure each level of aggregation is provided with a matrix of intransitive Fisher PPPs. Application of the EKS procedure makes the matrix transitive. This involves replacing each Fisher PPP by the geometric mean of itself squared and all the corresponding indirect Fisher PPPs obtained using each of the other countries as a bridge.
- The EKS PPPs are then used to convert the national expenditures in national currencies to real expenditures in a common currency.

The EKS method provides PPPs for each pair of countries in the comparison that are close to the PPPs that would be obtained if each pair of countries had been compared separately. This is because the EKS procedure in making the Fisher PPPs transitive minimises the differences between them

---

[22] In other words, the EKS method satisfies characteristicity. This is the property that requires the transitive multilateral comparisons between members of a group of countries to retain the essential features of the intransitive binary comparisons that existed between them before transitivity. A transitive multilateral comparison between a pair of countries is influenced by the price and quantity data of all other participating countries. Characteristicity requires that the impact of these influences should be kept to a minimum when they are introduced into the intransitive binary comparison. The extent to which the EKS PPP and the original binary PPP for a pair of countries differ depends on the degree of homogeneity among the price structures of the group of countries being compared.

[23] The qualifier 'type' is used because the terms 'Laspeyres', 'Paasche' and 'Fisher' are traditionally used in the context of temporal comparisons. Yet, like traditional Laspeyres and Paasche indexes, the Laspeyres and the Paasche type PPPs are, respectively, weighted arithmetic means and weighted harmonic means.

and the resulting EKS PPPs. It also provides real final expenditures that are neither additive nor subject to the Gerschenkron effect.[24, 25]

2.5.2   Missing PPPs and Reference PPPs

Sometimes there are a number of basic headings for which PPPs cannot be calculated for a country. Either the country has not priced a representative product or, if it has, other countries have not priced its representative product or, if they have, it has not priced their representative products. Consequently, no direct binary PPP can be calculated between it and any other country. In such cases, the PPPs for the countries and basic headings are taken either from a comparable basic heading – such as beef for veal – or from the next level of aggregation – such as meat for pork.

For a number of basic headings no prices are collected because, for various reasons, it is difficult to specify and to price products that are comparable across countries for them. PPPs based on price data that have been collected for other basic headings are used for these basic headings. Such PPPs are called 'reference PPPs'. They serve as proxies for the PPPs that would have been calculated had prices been collected for the basic headings for which no prices were collected. Reference PPPs are either PPPs for highly aggregated expenditure components, such as household final consumption expenditure, or PPPs for goods and services that are similar to the goods and services for which no prices were collected.

2.5.3   PPPs for European Union and the OECD

The EKS calculation as described above generates PPPs and real final expenditures for individual countries. It does not provide PPPs and real final expenditures for groups of countries such as the two groups used to present

---

[24] In other words, the real final expenditures for basic headings do not sum to the real final expenditures of the aggregates of which they are components. Similarly, the real final expenditures for the aggregates do not sum to real final expenditure on GDP.

[25] The Gerschenkron effect applies to aggregation methods that use either a reference price structure or a reference volume structure to compare countries. For methods employing a reference price structure, a country's share of total GDP (that is the total for the group of countries being compared) will rise as the reference price structure becomes less characteristic of its own price structure. For methods employing a reference volume structure, a country's share of total GDP will fall as the reference volume structure becomes less characteristic of its own volume structure. The EKS method does not use either a reference price structure or a reference volume structure when estimating real expenditures.

comparison results: the 27 EU member states (EU 27) and the 30 OECD member countries (OECD 30).

The PPPs and the real and nominal final expenditures for groups of countries are derived using the PPPs and the national expenditures in national currencies of their constituent countries. Before doing this, it is necessary to nominate a currency for each group. The euro is normally selected for EU 27 and the US dollar for OECD 30. It is also necessary to designate a reference country. Traditionally, Germany is chosen for this purpose. It should be noted that neither the choice of currencies nor the choice of reference country affects the final results because they are base country invariant.

Having selected the currencies for the groups and the reference country, the PPPs and the real and nominal final expenditures are calculated for the two groups as follows:

- First, the national expenditures in national currencies of the countries are converted to real final expenditures in 'German euros' using PPPs where Germany, or the euro in Germany, equals 1.00. Real final expenditures for the two groups are obtained by summing the real final expenditures of their constituent countries.
- Next, the national expenditures in national currencies of the countries comprising EU 27 are converted to nominal final expenditures in euros using exchange rates. These nominal final expenditures are then summed to obtain nominal final expenditures for EU 27. Nominal final expenditures in US dollars are similarly generated for OECD 30.
- Finally, the nominal final expenditures for the two groups are divided by their real final expenditures to provide PPPs for each group where Germany, or the euro in Germany, equals 1.00 – that is, euro per 'German euro' for EU 27 and US dollar per 'German euro' for OECD 30.

The PPPs and the real final expenditures for the country groups are, like the PPPs and real expenditures for the individual countries, based on the 'German euro' and Germany. For presentational purposes, the PPPs and the real final expenditures for both individual countries and country groups are rebased on the euro and EU 27 and the US dollar and OECD 30.

2.5.4   Fixity

The relative position of countries can change as the composition of the group of countries being compared changes. The results for the European Union are used for administrative purposes as well as for economic analysis. Consequently, Eurostat requires that only one set of results be recognised as the official results for the European Union. Eurostat and the OECD have therefore agreed that the official results for EU member states will remain unchanged when these countries are included in comparisons with a wider group of countries such as the OECD. This is referred to as the 'fixity convention'. The convention has been observed since the 1980 comparison. It now covers all countries that participate in both Eurostat comparisons and OECD comparisons irrespective of whether or not they are EU member states.

Fixity involves two groups of countries, one smaller than the other, with the smaller group being a sub–group of the larger group. For example, all countries covered in a Eurostat comparison are included in the larger Eurostat–OECD comparison. There are two sets of PPPs for the smaller group: the first set is that calculated for the group on its own, the second set is that calculated for the group as a sub–group of the larger group. Fixity requires that the first set replaces the second set in the larger comparison. This is achieved by taking the ratio of the geometric means of the two sets of PPPs and multiplying the first set of PPPs by the ratio so as to put them at the same overall level as the second set of PPPs. The procedure preserves the relationships between the countries in the sub–group and the relationships between the other countries in the larger group. It also preserves the relationship between the other countries and the sub–group as a whole.

2.6   SUMMARY RESULTS OF THE 2005 COMPARISON

Summary results of the 2005 Eurostat–OECD comparison are presented in Table 2.4. These are the PPPs for GDP and three sets of indices derived using the PPPs. The indices, all of which are based on the OECD, that is OECD = 100, cover GDP price levels, real GDP and real GDP per head. The PPPs and the indices comply with the fixity requirement.

Comparative price levels are the ratios of PPPs to exchange rates. They provide a measure of the differences in price levels between countries by indicating for a given aggregate the number of units of the common currency needed to buy the same volume of the aggregate in each country.[26] In Table 2.4, the aggregate is GDP and the common currency 'US dollars at average

---

[26] From the PPPs in Table 2.4, it can be seen that if a given volume of GDP costs 82 euros in the European Union, it costs 97 dollars in the United States and 12,600 yen in Japan. To compare these prices it is first necessary to express them in a common currency by converting them to 'OECD dollars' using exchange rates. The comparative price levels so derived show that if a given volume of GDP costs 102 OECD dollars in the European Union, it costs 97 OECD dollars in the United States and 114 OECD dollars in Japan. In other words, the general price level of the United States is only slightly lower than that of the European Union, but much lower than that of Japan.

OECD price levels' or 'OECD dollars'. At the level of GDP, comparative price level indices provide a measure of the differences in the general price levels of countries. Table 2.4 shows that the Nordic countries [Iceland (150), Denmark (138), Norway (133), Sweden (120), Finland (119)] and Switzerland (136) have the highest general price levels and that the Balkan countries [Bulgaria (37), Macedonia (38) Serbia (40), Montenegro (44), Bosnia–Herzegovina (45) Albania (47), Romania (47)] and the Russian Federation (44) have the lowest. A more complete presentation of these indices can be found in Table 2.5.

Table 2.4   Summary results of the 2005 comparison

Countries	PPPs for GDP	GDP Price Levels	Real GDP	Real GDP per Head
	National currency per USD[1]	*per cent of OECD Average*	*per cent of OECD Total*	*per cent of OECD Average*
Albania	47.2	47	0.05	18
Australia	1.35	103	1.98	113
Austria	0.850	106	0.83	117
Belgium	0.874	109	0.99	110
Bosnia–Herzegovina	0.707	45	0.07	22
Bulgaria	0.576	37	0.21	32
Canada	1.18	97	3.33	121
Croatia	3.83	64	0.17	46
Cyprus	0.412	89	0.05	84
Czech Republic	14.0	58	0.61	70
Denmark	8.28	138	0.54	116
Estonia	7.60	60	0.07	57
Finland	0.956	119	0.47	105
France	0.897	112	5.48	102
Germany	0.868	108	7.40	105
Greece	0.683	85	0.83	88
Hungary	125.0	63	0.51	59
Iceland	94.4	150	0.03	123
Ireland	0.995	124	0.46	131
Israel	3.61	81	0.46	78
Italy	0.851	106	4.79	96
Japan	126.0	114	11.39	104
Korea	767.0	75	3.02	74
Latvia	0.290	52	0.09	46

Continued

Table 2.4   Summary results of the 2005 comparison – continued

Countries	PPPs for GDP	GDP Price Levels	Real GDP	Real GDP per Head
	National currency per USD[1]	*per cent of OECD Average*	*per cent of OECD Total*	*per cent of OECD Average*
Lithuania	1.44	52	0.14	49
Luxembourg	0.897	112	0.10	241
Macedonia	18.5	38	0.04	25
Malta	0.241	70	0.02	70
Mexico	6.93	64	3.46	39
Montenegro	0.356	44	0.01	27
Netherlands	0.873	109	1.67	120
New Zealand	1.49	105	0.30	85
Norway	8.60	133	0.65	164
Poland	1.85	57	1.52	47
Portugal	0.688	86	0.62	69
Romania	1.38	47	0.60	32
Russian Federation	12.4	44	5.00	41
Serbia	26.5	40	0.19	30
Slovak Republic	16.7	54	0.25	55
Slovenia	0.597	74	0.14	79
Spain	0.746	93	3.48	94
Sweden	8.99	120	0.85	110
Switzerland	1.69	136	0.78	122
Turkey	0.844	63	1.65	27
United Kingdom	0.631	115	5.60	109
United States	0.972	97	36.42	144
European Union	0.823	102	38.31	91
OECD	1.00	100	100.0	100

[1] US dollars at average OECD price levels – that is, US dollars that have the same purchasing power in all 30 OECD countries and reflect the average price level over the OECD as a whole. Often referred as 'OECD dollars'.

The indices for real GDP and the indices for real GDP per head are measures of volume. The former are used to compare the economic size of countries, while the latter are used to compare the economic welfare of their populations.

From Table 2.4, it can be seen that the two largest economies are those of the European Union (38 per cent) and the United States (36 per cent), after which there comes Japan (11 per cent), the United Kingdom and Germany (5.6 and 7.4 per cent), France, Italy and the Russian Federation (at 5 per cent), Canada, Korea, Mexico and Spain (at 3 per cent), and then Australia, the Netherlands, Poland and Turkey (at 2 per cent). All the other countries have economies that are less than 1 per cent of the OECD total.

In terms of real GDP head, it can be seen from the Table that Luxembourg, with an index of 241, is well ahead of the other participating countries. But this figure has to be treated with some caution. One of the reasons for Luxembourg's high index is the large share of frontier workers in total employment (close to one quarter). These persons contribute to GDP and employment but are not included in the total population figure. Another reason is that GDP per head makes no allowances for international transfer payments such as profits received from abroad or remittances sent abroad. Gross national income (GNI) takes such flows into account. For some countries moving from GDP to GNI can markedly change the picture and put the figure for GDP per head into perspective. In the case of Luxembourg, when the switch to GNI is made, its index relative to the OECD average falls from 246 to around 200 indicating significant net transfers out of the country.

After Luxembourg come Norway (164), the United States (144), Ireland (131) and then Iceland, Switzerland, Canada and the Netherlands (all between 120 and 123). Interestingly, if GNI instead of GDP is used, Ireland falls from 131 to around 110 (because of net transfers out of the country) and Switzerland moves from 122 to over 130 (because of net transfers into the country).[27] A more comprehensive overview of the GDP per head indices can be found in Table 2.5.

2.6.1 Ranking or Grouping

Although real GDP and real GDP per head are often used to rank countries by economic size and economic welfare, neither the indices of real GDP nor the indices of real GDP per head should be used to establish a strict order of ranking. Instead, they are best used to assign countries to groups with similar GDP per head, as they are in Table 2.5, even though this can involve a degree of arbitrariness. Likewise, comparative price levels indices can be used to rank countries by their general price levels, but here too countries with similar price levels should be grouped together, as they are in Table 2.5, rather than ranked strictly. This is because PPPs are statistical constructs

---

[27] For most of the other countries for which GNI data are available, GDP and GNI rankings are similar.

rather than precise measures. While they provide the best available estimate
of the size of a country's economy, of the economic well–being of its
residents and of its general price level in relation to the other countries in the
comparison, they are, like all statistics, point estimates lying within a range
of estimates – the 'error margin' – that includes the true value.

Table 2.5   GDP per head and comparative price level, 2005 comparison

Countries with Indices of Real GDP per Head with a value:	
Greater than 125	Ireland, Luxembourg, Norway, United States
Between 100 and 124	Australia, Austria, Belgium, Canada, Denmark, Finland, France, Germany, Iceland, Japan, Netherlands, Sweden, Switzerland, United Kingdom
Between 75 and 99	Cyprus, Greece, Israel, Italy, New Zealand, Slovenia, Spain
Between 50 and 74	Czech Republic, Estonia, Hungary, Korea, Malta, Portugal, Slovak Republic
Between 25 and 49	Bulgaria, Croatia, Latvia, Lithuania, Macedonia, Mexico, Montenegro, Poland, Romania, Russian Federation, Serbia, Turkey
Less than 25	Albania, Bosnia–Herzegovina
Countries with Comparative Price Level Indices with a value:	
Greater than 125	Denmark, Iceland, Norway, Switzerland
Between 100 and 124	Australia, Austria, Belgium, Finland, France, Germany, Ireland, Italy, Japan, Luxembourg, Netherlands, New Zealand, Sweden, United Kingdom
Between 75 and 99	Canada, Cyprus, Greece, Israel, Korea, Portugal, Spain, United States
Between 50 and 74	Croatia, Czech Republic, Estonia, Hungary, Latvia, Lithuania, Malta, Mexico, Poland, Slovak Republic, Slovenia, Turkey
Less than 50	Albania, Bosnia–Herzegovina, Bulgaria, Macedonia, Montenegro, Romania, Russian Federation, Serbia

The error margins surrounding PPPs depend on the reliability of the expenditure weights and the price data as well as to the extent to which the particular goods and services selected for pricing by participating countries actually represent the price levels in each country. As with national accounts data generally, it is not possible to calculate precise error margins for PPPs or for the real GDP levels and comparative price levels derived from them.

2.7   CONCLUDING REMARKS

The next Eurostat–OECD comparison will be the 2008 comparison. Price collections are already underway. Preliminary results will become available at the end of 2009 and final results will be published at the end of 2010. The methods, organisation and procedures that are being used for the 2008 comparison are broadly similar to those described in the chapter for the 2005 comparison, but there are differences. For example, the selection of occupations for the survey of compensation of employees paid by government has been thoroughly revised; an output approach has been developed for education; and the compositions of the country groups have changed to accommodate the absorption of the Western Balkan Group by the Central and Southern Groups.

Both Eurostat and the OECD are aware that they are still on the learning curve as far as international comparisons of GDP are concerned. This motivates their search for improvement. Currently the focus is on advancing the quality and timeliness of the consumer price surveys. Special software has been developed to facilitate and encourage greater interaction between group leaders and countries. Among the outcomes expected are more equi–representative product lists, better defined product specifications and a reduction in the start–to–finish time for consumer price surveys from 18 to 12 months. Other efforts involve developing an output approach for health services, particularly hospital services, and revising the bill of quantities approach to pricing construction projects. It is anticipated that most, if not all, of these developments will be in place for the 2011 comparison.

REFERENCES

Eurostat (1996), *European System of Accounts 1995*, Luxembourg.
Eurostat (1998), Statistical Classification of Products by Activity in the European *Economic Community* (CPA 1996), Luxembourg.
Eurostat and OECD (2004), *Purchasing Power Parities and Real Expenditures, 2002 Results*, Paris.

Eurostat and OECD (2006) *Methodological Manual on Purchasing Power Parities*, Luxembourg and Paris.

Eurostat and OECD (2007) *Purchasing Power Parities and Real Expenditures, 2005 Results*, Paris.

Maddison A. and B. van Ark (1989), 'International Comparisons of Purchasing Power, Real Output and Labour Productivity: a Case Study of Brazilian, Mexican, and U.S. Manufacturing, 1975', *Review of Income and Wealth*, **35** (1), 31–55.

OECD (1987), *Purchasing Power Parities and Real Expenditures, 1985*, Paris.

OECD (1992), *Purchasing Power Parities and Real Expenditures, 1990, Volume 1, EKS Results*, Paris.

OECD (1993), *Purchasing Power Parities and Real Expenditures, 1990, Volume 2, GK Results*, Paris.

OECD (1995), *Purchasing Power Parities and Real Expenditures, 1993, Volume 1, EKS Results*, Paris.

OECD (1996), *Purchasing Power Parities and Real Expenditures, 1993, Volume 2, GK Results, Paris*.

OECD (1999), Purchasing Power Parities and Real Expenditures, 1996 Results, Paris.

Paige D. and G. Bombach (1959), *A Comparison of National Output and Productivity of the United Kingdom and the United States*, Paris: OEEC.

Quaranta V. (1996), 'A Data Quality Control Approach in Price Surveys for PPP Estimates', in *Improving the Quality of Price Indices: CPI and PPP*, Eurostat and University of Florence, Luxembourg, 305–321.

United Nations (1993), *System of National Accounts 1993*, New York.

United Nations (2000a), 'Classification of Individual Consumption According to Purpose (COICOP)', *Classification of Expenditure According to Purpose*, New York.

United Nations (2000b), 'Classification of the Purposes of Non–Profit Institutions Serving Households (COPNI)', *Classification of Expenditure According to Purpose,* New York.

United Nations (2000c), 'Classification of the Functions of Government (COFOG)', *Classification of Expenditure According to Purpose*, New York.

Ward. M., (1985), *Purchasing Power Parities and Real Expenditures in the OECD, 1980*, Paris: OECD.

PART II

System Methods for PPP Computation

3. Aggregation Methods in International Comparisons: an Evaluation

Bert Balk[*]

3.1 INTRODUCTION

International price and volume comparisons are carried out for a variety of purposes, at different levels of aggregation, and using different methods. The remainder of this book provides a clear illustration of this situation.

Apart from operational issues, comparing two countries at a time – a so–called bilateral comparison – is relatively simple, because one can borrow methods familiar from the field of intertemporal comparisons.[1] However, multilateral comparisons, that is, comparisons in which more than two countries at a time are involved, constitute a subject *sui generis*.

Multilateral international comparisons are not a simple translation of multilateral intertemporal comparisons. There are a number of differences, the most important of which is that, unlike time periods, countries do not exhibit a natural ordering.

By way of example I would like to draw attention to a recent comparison of health care costs across a number of countries, as reported by Schreyögg et al. (2008). For 8 European countries the costs of 5 hospital care episodes were compared, using 5 standardized cost categories. The next step was to decompose bilateral total cost ratios into price and volume components, using Fisher indices. This led to 8 different orderings, depending on the country chosen as reference. To obtain a single ordering, the authors had to use some transitivization method. They chose the EKS–method, but without arguing why. Anyway, the episode–specific purchasing power parities (PPPs) that were obtained differed considerably from other, more general, measures like exchange rates and PPPs at the level of GDP or medical care.

---

[*] The views expressed in this article are those of the author and do not necessarily reflect any policy of Statistics Netherlands. All rights with respect to Sections 3.2–7 remain with Cambridge University Press.

[1] Eichhorn and Voeller (1983), for example, provided a parallel treatment of intertemporal and interspatial comparisons within the axiomatic approach.

The intention of this chapter is to review some progress that has been made over the past decades in understanding the nature of the various methods proposed and/or used. As in the theory of intertemporal comparisons there are three main approaches: the axiomatic or test approach, the stochastic approach, and the economic approach. The first two approaches, and the history of methodological developments, were extensively discussed by Balk (2008). Therefore the present chapter concentrates on the economic approach, and results from other approaches will only be discussed insofar as relevant for the remainder of this book.

The architecture of this chapter is as follows. Section 3.2 deals with the necessary notation and definitions. Section 3.3 introduces bilateral comparisons. Section 3.4 discusses a number of methods, related by the fact that they are solutions to some minimization problem. Section 3.5 is devoted to the class of additive methods. Section 3.6 summarizes some results from the test approach. Section 3.7 briefly introduces methods based on spanning trees. Section 3.8 considers the economic approach with the assumption of country–specific preferences. The characteristic feature of this approach is that aggregate values are conceived as outcomes of optimization problems. Section 3.9 continues with the assumption of international preferences. Section 3.10, finally, concludes.[2]

3.2 NOTATION AND DEFINITIONS

It is assumed that we must compare countries[3] $1,...,I$ $(I \geq 3)$ with respect to some well–defined economic aggregate involving commodities which are arbitrarily labelled as $1,...,N$ $(N \geq 2)$. The price vector for country i, expressed in its own currency, will be denoted by $p^i \equiv (p_1^i,...,p_N^i) \in \Re_{++}^N$, and the corresponding quantity vector will be denoted by $x^i \equiv (x_1^i,...,x_N^i) \in \Re^N$ $(i = 1,...,I)$. Both vectors are assumed to pertain to the same period of time.[4] Some of the quantities could be negative, for instance in the case of imports. However, it is assumed that[5] $p^i \cdot x^j > 0$ for all $i,j = 1,...,I$. For all $i = 1,...,I$, $p^i \cdot x^i$ represents the value of country i's aggregate in its own currency.

---

[2] Sections 3.2–7 quote with permission from Balk (2008), to which the reader is referred for more, and more detailed results.

[3] The word 'country' is used as a shorthand for any kind of geographical entity.

[4] An additional layer of complexity emerges when one takes the time dimension explicitly into account. This leads to the problem of combined interspatial–intertemporal comparisons, as considered by Krijnse Locker and Faerber (1984) and, more recently, by Hill (2004).

[5] The dot denotes inner product: $\left[p^i \cdot x^j \equiv \Sigma_{n=1}^N p_n^i x_n^j \right]$.

The price index of country j relative to country i will be denoted by the ratio P^j/P^i, and the quantity index will be denoted by the ratio Q^j/Q^i $(i,j = 1,...,I)$.[6] This notation expresses the requirement that price and quantity indices be transitive.[7] A second, equally important requirement is that price index and quantity index satisfy the Product Test; that is, their product exhausts the value ratio:

$$\frac{P^j}{P^i}\frac{Q^j}{Q^i} = \frac{p^j \cdot x^j}{p^i \cdot x^i}(i,j = 1,...,I). \tag{3.1}$$

The ultimate purpose of most international comparisons is to compare 'real' aggregates of countries. The following definitions serve to make this notion precise. The volume of country i is defined as $p^i \cdot x^i / P^i$ $(i = 1,...,I)$,[8] and the volume share of country i in the aggregate volume of all I countries is defined as

$$Q^i \equiv \frac{p^i \cdot x^i / P^i}{\Sigma_{k=1}^{I} p^k \cdot x^k / P^k}$$

$$= \left(\sum_{k=1}^{I} (p^k \cdot x^k / p^i \cdot x^i)(P^k / P^i)^{-1} \right)^{-1} \tag{3.2}$$

$$= \left(\sum_{k=1}^{I} (Q^i / Q^k)^{-1} \right)^{-1} (i = 1,...,I).$$

The volume shares add up to 1. The second and third lines are added to show how volume shares can be calculated from a set of price index numbers or a set of quantity index numbers respectively.

The additive nature of the country–specific volume shares makes it possible to define volume shares for aggregates of countries as well. For example, the volume share of the union of countries i and j is simply given by $Q^i + Q^j$.

---

[6] The ratio P^j/P^i is usually called the purchasing power parity (PPP) of country j (or country j's currency) relative to country i (or country i's currency). Countries may have the same currency.

[7] On the consequence of requiring transitivity, see Balk (2008).

[8] In practice this is calculated as $p^i \cdot x^i /(P^i / P^k)$ for some choice of the numeraire country k.

3.3   BILATERAL COMPARISONS

To start with, consider a bilateral price comparison between two countries i and j. The price level of country j relative to country i can be measured by the Laspeyres price index

$$P^L(p^j, x^j, p^i, x^i) \equiv p^j \cdot x^i / p^i \cdot x^i, \qquad (3.3)$$

or by the Paasche price index

$$P^P(p^j, x^j, p^i, x^i) \equiv p^j \cdot x^j / p^i \cdot x^j. \qquad (3.4)$$

The interpretation of these indices depends of course on the aggregate under study. For instance, when we are studying household consumption, the Laspeyres price index compares the value of country i's household consumption at country j's prices to the value of this consumption at its own prices. Similarly, the Paasche price index compares the value of country j's household consumption at its own prices to the value at country i's prices.

A symmetric measure is provided by the Fisher price index, defined as the geometric average of the Laspeyres and the Paasche price index:

$$P^F(p^j, x^j, p^i, x^i) \equiv [P^L(p^j, x^j, p^i, x^i) P^P(p^j, x^j, p^i, x^i)]^{1/2}. \qquad (3.5)$$

The symmetry of the Fisher index with respect to the two countries involved implies that

$$P^F(p^i, x^i, p^j, x^j) = 1/P^F(p^j, x^j, p^i, x^i); \qquad (3.6)$$

that is, the Fisher index satisfies the Country Reversal Test.

Of course, many other indices could be used for making bilateral comparisons. Though such pairwise comparisons can be very insightful, the main drawback is that a complete comparison exercise delivers a square matrix of size I. Using symmetric indices does reduce the number of distinct comparisons to $I(I-1)/2$, but does not provide a single, transitive ordering of the countries.

3.4   METHODS BASED ON MINIMIZATION PROBLEMS

Gini–Elteto–Köves–Szulc (GEKS) Indices

We now turn to a truly multilateral comparison, that is, a comparison of all the I countries simultaneously. It is assumed that there is a set of positive country weights g_i $(i = 1,...,I)$. Such weights can be regarded as initial measures of country importance. Normalized weights, adding up to 1, are defined by $f_i = g_i / \Sigma_{i=1}^I g_i$ $(i = 1,...,I)$.

Consider the following minimization problem

$$\min_{p^1,...,p^I} \sum_{i=1}^I \sum_{j=1}^I g_i g_j [\ln P^F(p^j, x^j, p^i, x^i) - \ln(P^j / P^i)]^2 , \qquad (3.7)$$

that seeks to determine transitive, multilateral price indices which approximate as good as possible the intransitive, bilateral Fisher price indices. The weights $g_i g_j$ are used to discriminate between all the pairwise comparisons.[9] The solution of this problem is

$$\left(\frac{P^j}{P^i}\right)_{GEKS} = \prod_{k=1}^I [P^F(p^j, x^j, p^k, x^k) P^F(p^k, x^k, p^i, x^i)]^{f_k} \ (i, j = 1,...,I). \quad (3.8)$$

If all the weights are the same, which implies that $f_k = 1/I$ $(k = 1,...,I)$, then expression (3.8) reduces to the EKS–formula proposed independently by Elteto and Köves (1964) and Szulc (1964). The last formula was, however, already proposed by Gini (1924).

An interesting way of interpreting the GEKS price index[10] (3.8) is to notice that each of the factors $P^F(p^j, x^j, p^k, x^k) P^F(p^k, x^k, p^i, x^i)$ provides a 'price index' for country j relative to country i, calculated via a 'bridge' country k. Since there are I choices for k, it is rather natural to take an average of all of those factors as the final index.

It is important to notice that, according to expression (3.8), the price indices $(P^j / P^i)_{GEKS}$ depend not only on the prices and quantities of the

---

[9]   Rao (this volume) considers a generalization of this procedure, whereby the weights $g_i g_j$ are replaced by weights g_{ij}. See also Rao and Timmer (2003), where the weights g_{ij} are indicators of the reliability of the bilateral comparisons.

[10]   A more appropriate name would be 'GEKS–Fisher' index, to distinguish this index from the 'GEKS–Törnqvist' index to be introduced in Section 3.8.

countries i and j, but also on the prices and quantities of all the other countries involved. Thus if we extend the set of countries, all price index numbers must be recalculated. This is one of the features distinguishing multilateral price indices from bilateral price indices.

The GEKS quantity indices can be obtained from expression (3.8) by using expression (3.1), the fact that the weights f_k add up to 1, and the Factor Reversal property of the Fisher price and quantity indices. The indices read

$$\left(\frac{Q^j}{Q^i}\right)_{GEKS} = \prod_{k=1}^{I} [Q^F(p^j,x^j,p^k,x^k)Q^F(p^k,x^k,p^i,x^i)]^{f_k} \quad (i,j=1,...,I). \quad (3.9)$$

where the Fisher quantity index for country j relative to country I is defined by

$$Q^F(p^j,x^j,p^i,x^i) = [(p^i \cdot x^j / p^i \cdot x^i)(p^j \cdot x^j / p^j \cdot x^i)]^{1/2}. \quad (3.10)$$

Notice that the GEKS quantity indices (3.10) can also be obtained by interchanging prices and quantities in the GEKS price indices (3.8). Thus the GEKS indices satisfy the Factor Reversal Test.

Van IJzeren–type Indices

The minimization problem (3.7) can be rewritten as

$$\min_{p^1,...,p^I} \sum_{i=1}^{I} \sum_{j=1}^{I} g_i g_j [\ln(P^F(p^j,x^j,p^i,x^i)P^i / P^j)]^2. \quad (3.11)$$

Van IJzeren (1987) showed that in this problem the Fisher index can be replaced by the Laspeyres or Paasche index without effect on the solution. Consider now the following, a slightly different minimization problem

$$\min_{p^1,...,p^I} \sum_{i=1}^{I} \sum_{j=1}^{I} g_i g_j P^L(p^j,x^j,p^i,x^i)P^i / P^j. \quad (3.12)$$

One can prove that this problem has a unique, positive solution $P_Y^1,...,P_Y^I$, which is determined up to a scalar factor. Thus, although not expressible in explicit form, the price indices P_Y^j / P_Y^i $(i,j=1,...,I)$ are completely determined, as are the quantity indices via relation (3.1). They depend on the prices and quantities of all the I countries. The method defined by expression (3.12) is known as the third, balanced method of van IJzeren

From the first–order conditions of minimization problem (3.12) it is simple to show that the van IJzeren price and quantity indices satisfy the Factor Reversal Test.

Alternatively one could consider the minimization problem

$$\min_{p^1,...,p^I} \sum_{i=1}^{I} \sum_{j=1}^{I} g_i g_j P^P(p^j, x^j, p^i, x^i) P^i / P^j, \tag{3.13}$$

which differs from the foregoing problem (3.12) in that the Paasche index is used instead of the Laspeyres. One can also prove that this problem has a unique, positive solution, determined up to a scalar factor.

This (relatively unknown) method has been proposed by Gerardi (1974), as a variation of van IJzeren's method. The price and quantity indices from the Gerardi–van IJzeren system likewise satisfy the Factor Reversal Test.

Other Indices

Closely related to the GEKS indices are indices according to generalizations of Fisher's (1922) 'blended system' and Diewert's (1986) 'own share system'. Still other methods were developed by Kurabayashi and Sakuma (1982, 1990), called YKS and Q–YKS. Both are related to the van IJzeren method which was defined by expression (3.12).

A Closing Remark

All the methods discussed in this section effectively provide a mapping from a vector of initial country weights $(f_1,...,f_I)$ to a vector of volume shares $(Q^1,...,Q^I)$. This is a continuous mapping from the I–dimensional unit simplex into itself. According to Brouwer's Fixed Point Theorem (see Green and Heller 1981) such a mapping has a fixed point. Thus in all the formulas one can replace f_k (or g_k) by Q^k $(k = 1,...,I)$. The solution vector must of course then be obtained by a suitable numerical iteration method.

3.5 ADDITIVE METHODS

A multilateral comparison method is called *additive* when

$$Q^i \propto \pi \cdot x^i \ (i = 1,...,I), \tag{3.14}$$

where $\pi \equiv (\pi_1,...,\pi_N)$ is some price vector. Expression (3.14) says that the volume share of country i is proportional to the aggregate value of this country's quantities at prices π. Since $\Sigma_{i=1}^I Q^i = 1$, expression (3.14) implies that

$$Q^i = \frac{\pi \cdot x^i}{\Sigma_{i=1}^I \pi \cdot x^i} (i = 1,...,I).$$ (3.15)

Using the product relation (3.1), this in turn implies that

$$P^i \propto \frac{p^i \cdot x^i}{\pi \cdot x^i} (i = 1,...,I).$$ (3.16)

Thus each purchasing power parity P^i is proportional to a Paasche–type price index, comparing country i's price vector p^i to the price vector π. When the proportionality factor in the last expression equals 1, the method is called *strongly additive*.

The virtue of an additive method is its simple interpretation, as evidenced by the foregoing expressions. The use of a common price vector enables us to compare the quantity structures of an aggregate across countries in a very straightforward way. The intertemporal analogue is to express the value of an aggregate through time in 'constant prices'.

The basic problem, of course, is how to pick the price vector π. The symmetric treatment of countries suggests that π must be some average of the country–specific price vectors p^i. Accordingly, π is called a vector of 'international prices'.

The Geary–Khamis (GK) Method

By far the best known member of the class of strongly additive methods was proposed by Geary (1958) and popularized, via Khamis (1972), by its use in the International Comparison Project (Kravis et al., 1975). This method consists of the following set of definitions,

$$\pi_n = \frac{\sum_{i=1}^I p_n^i x_n^i / P^i}{\sum_{i=1}^I x_n^i} \quad (n = 1,...,N)$$

$$P^i = p^i \cdot x^i / \pi \cdot x^i \quad (i = 1,...,I),$$ (3.17)

which actually is a system of equations that must be solved. Each international price π_n can be regarded as the unit value of commodity n, after having converted the country–specific values $p_n^i x_n^i$ to a common currency. One could also say that each country–specific price p_n^i is deflated by the purchasing power parity P^i, and that a weighted average of the p_n^i / P^i is taken, the weights being quantity shares $x_n^i / \sum_{j=1}^{I} x_n^j$. Put otherwise, π is not a vector of average prices, but a vector expressing some average price *structure*.

One can show that this system has a unique solution for volume shares, price indices, and international prices.

The particular definition of the international prices, as given in the first equation of (3.17), is the point of much criticism levelled against the GK method. By virtue of its definition the vector π tends to resemble the price structure of the largest country involved in the comparison exercise,[11] say ℓ. But then, as one verifies easily,

$$\frac{Q_{GK}^i}{Q_{GK}^\ell} = \frac{\pi \cdot x^i}{\pi \cdot x^\ell} \approx \frac{p^\ell \cdot x^i}{p^\ell \cdot x^\ell}, \tag{3.18}$$

which is the Laspeyres quantity index of country i relative to country ℓ. Depending on the market orientation of the aggregate (producer or consumer), this index is generally felt to be an under– or over–estimate of the 'true' quantity index. This alleged bias is called the Gerschenkron effect, after its discovery by Gerschenkron (1951). In intertemporal comparisons it finds its parallel in the substitution bias.

An obvious remedy is to look for alternative definitions of the international prices. Doing so, Cuthbert (1999) developed the Generalized Geary–Khamis method, of which not only the GK method but also the Iklé (1972) method appear to be particular cases. Hill (2000a) developed the 'equally weighted GK method'.

Other Additive Methods

Also differing from the GK method by the definition of international prices, is the KS–S method proposed by Kurabayashi and Sakuma (1981, 1990). Recently, Sakuma et al. (2000) developed an interesting variant of the KS–S method. The defining system of equations of the new (SRK) method is

---

[11] Khamis (1998) denies this: 'No country is large enough (with respect to all commodities) to produce such an effect.'

$$\pi_n = \alpha \sum_{i=1}^{I} (p_n^i / P^i)(p^i \cdot x^i / p^i \cdot \sum_{j=1}^{I} x^j) \quad (n=1,...,N)$$

$$P^i = p^i \cdot x^i / \pi \cdot x^i \qquad (i=1,...,I).$$

(3.19)

It is interesting to compare this system of equations to the GK system (3.17). In the GK system the country–specific deflated prices p_n^i / P^i are weighted with commodity–specific quantity shares $x_n^i / \sum_{j=1}^{I} x_n^j$. Using prices p_n^i, these quantity shares can be expressed as value shares $p_n^i x_n^i / p_n^i \sum_{j=1}^{I} x_n^j$. Now in the SRK system the country–specific deflated prices are weighted with aggregate value shares $p^i \cdot x^i / p^i \cdot \sum_{j=1}^{I} x^j$. These weights are the same for every commodity. Each of these weights can be interpreted as the volume share of country i based on its own price vector, or as the Paasche–type quantity index for country i relative to the aggregate of all countries.

It is easily seen that the first equation of (3.19) is an instance of the more general definition,

$$\pi_n = \sum_{i=1}^{I} g_i (p_n^i / P^i)(n=1,...,N),$$

(3.20)

where the scalars g_i $(i=1,...,I)$ are positive country weights. Choosing now

$$g_i = P^i / p^i \cdot \sum_{j=1}^{I} x^j \ (i=1,...,I)$$

(3.21)

leads to the (Standardized Structure) method as proposed by Sergeev (this volume).[12] It is straightforward to infer that this method leads to volume shares of the form

$$Q_S^i = \frac{\sum_{k=1}^{I} p^k \cdot x^i / p^k \cdot \overline{x}}{\sum_{i=1}^{I} \sum_{k=1}^{I} p^k \cdot x^i / p^k \cdot \overline{x}} (i=1,...,I)$$

(3.22)

where $\overline{x} \equiv \sum_{j=1}^{I} x^j$. Since the unknown P^i's in the numerator of (3.21) and the denominator of (3.20) cancel, there is no need to solve a system of equations, and the concept of international prices becomes superfluous. The corresponding quantity indices can be expressed as

---

[12] According to the interpretation of Cuthbert in a letter to Sergeev dated 4 October 2000.

$$\frac{Q_S^i}{Q_S^j} = \frac{\Sigma_{k=1}^{I} Q^L(p^i, x^i, p^k, \overline{x})}{\Sigma_{k=1}^{I} Q^L(p^j, x^j, p^k, \overline{x})} (i, j = 1, ..., I). \tag{3.23}$$

The right–hand side of this expression is a ratio of average Laspeyres quantity index numbers, each relating countries i and j to the aggregate of all countries, using prices of a third country k.

3.6 SOME RESULTS FROM THE TEST APPROACH

How do we discriminate between the methods discussed in the previous two sections? The classical approach – the landmark in the area of intertemporal comparisons being Fisher (1922) – is to set up a system of tests or desirable properties and find out which method fails which tests. This is the approach followed by Kravis et al. (1975) in their pathbreaking work on international comparisons. The properties they thought most important were (formulated in our jargon) that price and quantity indices be transitive, that these indices satisfy the Product Test, that all countries be treated symmetrically, and that the method of comparison exhibits additive consistency.

The first two properties are maintained here from the outset (see Section 3.2). Furthermore, a quick perusal of the methods discussed in Sections 3.3 and 3.4 leads to the conclusion that in all these methods the countries are indeed treated symmetrically. The fourth property, however, is open for debate. On the one hand it seems to favour only additive methods but on the other hand it is not able to discriminate between the various additive methods.

Diewert (1986, 1987, 1999) more rigidly formulated a set of tests for multilateral comparisons (abbreviated as MTs). Balk (1989) modified these tests by incorporating country weights. All these tests emphasize the fact that the primary purpose of any international comparison is to make volume comparisons. Price indices play only an intermediary role. Consequently, the tests are framed in terms of volume shares, which are here understood to be functions of all the prices, quantities, and country weights (if any). Thus, formally, $Q^i = Q^i(p^1, ..., p^I, x^1, ..., x^I, g_1, ..., g_I)$ for $i = 1, ..., I$.

This set of tests can informally be summarized as follows:[13]

• MT1 requires that volume shares must be positive, must add up to 1, and must exhibit continuous behaviour in all variables.

---

[13] For formal definitions and alternatives the reader is referred to Balk (2008).

- MT2p requires that if all the countries have the same price structure, then the volume shares reduce to a simple additive form.
- MT2x requires that if all the quantity vectors are proportional to each other, then the volume shares are equal to the factors of proportionality.
- MT3 requires that if the prices remain unchanged but a certain country expands with a certain factor, then the volume shares behave accordingly.
- MT4 requires that differing inflation rates but equal quantity growth rates leave the volume shares invariant.
- MT5–MT7 formulate obvious invariance requirements: invariance to choice of the units of measurement, symmetric treatment of countries, and symmetric treatment of commodities, respectively.
- MT8 considers the situation where one or more countries are disaggregated, and requires consistency of the volume shares.
- MT9 stipulates that 'small' countries shall not influence the volume shares of 'large' countries unduly.

All the methods introduced in Sections 3.3 and 3.4, and many more, have been subjected to these ten tests.[14] It appears that there is no method that satisfies all the tests. The GEKS method violates only tests MT3 and MT8. The methods of van IJzeren, Gerardi–van IJzeren, GK, and SRK violate only one test, namely MT3. Sergeev's method violates MT3, MT8 and MT9.

A novel, quite natural test proposed by Diewert (1999) concerns monotonicity: each volume share Q^i must be increasing in the components of the vector x^i $(i = 1,...,I)$. He was able to show that van IJzeren's method satisfies this test.[15] By analogy, the Gerardi–van IJzeren method also satisfies this test. Diewert also showed that when $I = 2$, the GK method does not satisfy the monotonicity test. However, it remains to be seen what happens when $I \geq 3$. Finally, whether the SRK method satisfies this test is still an open question. Thus, the evidence here is, for the time being, inconclusive.

3.7   METHODS BASED ON SPANNING TREES

Transitive price and quantity indices can also be constructed by the procedure of chaining. However, as noticed in Section 3.1, countries do not exhibit a natural ordering. Given I countries, there appear to be $I(I-1)/2$ bilateral

---

[14] See Balk (1996) and (2008) for proofs and additional results.
[15] He actually proved it for the unweighted case, that is, where $g^i = 1/I$ $(i=1,...,I)$, but there is no reason to suppose that this proof does not hold in the general case.

index numbers (provided that the Country Reversal Test holds) and I^{I-2} possible ways to link the countries together without creating any cycles. Put otherwise, there exist I^{I-2} spanning trees. How could we choose some 'optimal' spanning tree?

The natural approach is to use some measure of proximity and to order the countries according to this measure. In the time series context this measure is simply given by the length of the time span separating any two periods. Due to the unidirectional flow of time, this leads to a unique ordering, independent of the data. In the spatial context the ideal of data–independency of the ordering must be given up.

Hill (1999a, 1999b) developed two methods that allow the data to determine the 'optimal' spanning tree. Multilateral indices are then obtained by linking together bilateral indices as specified by the spanning tree. To give an example, suppose that we must compare country j to country i. If, according to the spanning tree, the countries appear to be adjacent, then the price index of j relative to i is defined as $P(p^j, x^j, p^i, x^i)$ for some bilateral index satisfying the Country Reversal Test. But if the countries j and i are connected via, say, countries k and l respectively, then the price index of j relative to i is defined as the chained index $P(p^j, x^j, p^k, x^k)P(p^k, x^k, p^l, x^l)P(p^l, x^l, p^i, x^i)$. The device used in both methods for obtaining an 'optimal' spanning tree is the so–called Paasche–Laspeyres spread.[16]

A practical motive for finding and using 'optimal' spanning trees is the prospect of economizing on data. Recall that a multilateral method such as GEKS requires knowledge of all $I(I-1)/2$ bilateral index numbers. Suppose now that, based on a full data set for a certain period, we have obtained an 'optimal' spanning tree. Under the assumption that this structure remains stable over a certain time span, for later periods it is sufficient to compute only the $I-1$ bilateral index numbers which are required by the spanning tree. This could save on the amount of data as well as lead to an appreciable gain in accuracy of the bilateral comparisons, since the data can be chosen such as to make the bilateral comparisons as accurate as possible without the need of imposing excessive data requirements on 'far off' countries.

Examples and robustness results can be found in Hill (1999a, 1999b and this volume). It appears that, although the minimum–spanning trees are not stable over time, they generate similar clusters of countries. It also appears that the multilateral index numbers are less sensitive to the choice of the underlying spanning tree than one might suspect. Similar conclusions were reached by Heston et al. (2001).

---

[16] Alternative (dis–)similarity measures are considered by Diewert (this volume).

3.8 THE ECONOMIC APPROACH: COUNTRY–SPECIFIC PREFERENCES

In this section I review the economic approach to the comparison of economic aggregates. The characteristic feature of the economic approach is that the value of any such aggregate is conceived as being the outcome of an optimization problem, and that the objects of interest for the comparison are not the resulting quantity vectors as such, but the indifference curves or production possibility frontiers to which these vectors belong.[17] Put otherwise, the objects for the comparison are sets of quantity vectors between which substitution is allowed, either from the consumer or the producer point of view.

Let the aggregate under consideration be household consumption and suppose that each country is inhabited by a representative household whose preference structure is represented by a utility function $U^i(x)$ $(i = 1,...,I)$. The dual cost (or expenditure) functions are defined by $C^i(p,u) \equiv \min_x \{p \cdot x \mid U^i(x) \geq u\}$, where $u \in \text{Range}\, U^i(x)$ indicates a standard of living. Notice that $C^i(p,u) = p \cdot x^i(p,u)$, where $x^i(p,u) \equiv \arg\min_x \{p \cdot x \mid U^i(x) \geq u\}$ denotes the vector of cost minimizing quantities. If each cost function is continuously differentiable, then $x^i(p,u) = \nabla_p C^i(p,u)$.[18] The usual regularity conditions are supposed to hold.

The basic assumption of the economic approach is that for each actual country i, quantity vector x^i is optimal at the country i price vector p^i; that is, for some value u^i the following equations hold:

$$x^i = x^i(p^i, u^i)(i = 1,...,I),\qquad(3.24)$$

and thus

$$p^i \cdot x^i = C^i(p^i, u^i)(i = 1,...,I).\qquad(3.25)$$

If each cost function is continuously differentiable, then the foregoing equations imply that

---

[17] Van Veelen and Van der Weide (2008) (unnecessarily) restrict the economic approach to the case of (common) international preferences as treated in the next section.

[18] Notation: $\nabla_x f(x)$ denotes the vector of first–order derivatives of $f(x)$ with respect to x.

$$w^i = \nabla_{\ln p} \ln C^i(p^i, u^i)(i = 1, ..., I), \tag{3.26}$$

where w^i is the actual country i vector of commodity value shares $(i = 1, ..., I)$.

There are now two rather natural ways of measuring the price level of country j relative to country i. The first is by the Laspeyres–perspective cost of living index

$$C^i(p^j, u^i) / C^i(p^i, u^i), \tag{3.27}$$

which measures the relative cost of achieving country i 's standard of living at the prices of country j and i respectively. The second is by the Paasche–perspective cost of living index

$$C^j(p^j, u^j) / C^j(p^i, u^j), \tag{3.28}$$

which measures the relative cost of achieving country j 's standard of living at the prices of country j and i respectively. Both measures are equally plausible but will in general deliver different outcomes. We can look for some intermediate index; that is, an index P^j / P^i satisfying

$$C^i(p^j, u^i) / C^i(p^i, u^i) = (P^j / P^i)t$$
$$tC^j(p^j, u^j) / C^j(p^i, u^j) = P^j / P^i \quad (t > 0). \tag{3.29}$$

Generalizing this to all the I countries means that we must solve the following equation

$$\prod_{i=1}^{I} \left(\frac{C^i(p^j, u^i)}{C^i(p^i, u^i)} \frac{P^i}{P^j} \right)^{f_i} = \prod_{i=1}^{I} \left(\frac{C^j(p^i, u^j)}{C^j(p^j, u^j)} \frac{P^j}{P^i} \right)^{f_i} \quad (j = 1, ..., I), \tag{3.30}$$

where $f_i \ (i = 1, ..., I)$ are normalized country weights. The solution appears to be

$$\frac{P^j}{P^i} = \prod_{k=1}^{I} \left[\left(\frac{C^k(p^j, u^k)}{C^k(p^k, u^k)} \frac{C^j(p^j, u^j)}{C^j(p^k, u^j)} \right)^{1/2} \left(\frac{C^k(p^k, u^k)}{C^k(p^i, u^k)} \frac{C^i(p^k, u^i)}{C^i(p^i, u^i)} \right)^{1/2} \right]^{f_k} \tag{3.31}$$

$$(i, j = 1, ..., I).$$

Each term of this product consists of a Fisher–perspective cost of living index of country j relative to country k times the Fisher–perspective cost of living index of country k relative to country i. Thus the structure of expression (3.31) is similar to the structure of expression (3.8), and we could call (3.31) the economic GEKS price index.[19]

In order to make this expression operational it is assumed that each country–specific cost function has the translog functional form with second–order coefficients which are the same across countries; that is, it is assumed that

$$\ln C^i(p,u) = \alpha_0^i + \sum_{n=1}^{N} \alpha_n^i \ln p_n + \beta_1^i \ln u + \frac{1}{2} \sum_{n=1}^{N} \sum_{n'=1}^{N} \alpha_{nn'} \ln p_n \ln p_{n'} +$$

$$\frac{1}{2} \beta_{11} (\ln u)^2 + \sum_{n=1}^{N} \gamma_n \ln p_n \ln u \quad (u > 0)(i = 1,...,I) \quad (3.32)$$

with the usual restrictions to ensure linear homogeneity of the cost function in prices. Applying the Translog Identity, due to Caves et al. (1982b), one then obtains the following identity:

$$\frac{1}{2}\left[\ln \frac{C^k(p^j,u^k)}{C^k(p^k,u^k)} + \ln \frac{C^j(p^j,u^j)}{C^j(p^k,u^j)}\right] = \quad (3.33)$$

$$\frac{1}{2}\left[\nabla_{\ln p} \ln C^k(p^k,u^k) + \nabla_{\ln p} \ln C^j(p^j,u^j)\right] \cdot \left[\ln p^j - \ln p^k\right] (j,k = 1,...,I)$$

where $\ln p$ denotes the vector $(\ln p_1,...,\ln p_N)$. Using expression (3.26), this equation reduces to

$$\frac{1}{2}\left[\ln \frac{C^k(p^j,u^k)}{C^k(p^k,u^k)} + \ln \frac{C^j(p^j,u^j)}{C^j(p^k,u^j)}\right] = \frac{1}{2}\sum_{n=1}^{N}(w_n^k + w_n^j)\ln(p_n^j / p_n^k) \quad (3.34)$$

$$= \ln P^T(p^j,x^j,p^k,x^k)(j,k = 1,...,I)$$

---

[19] Instead of (3.31), Armstrong (2001a) considered mean–of–order–λ indexes $P^j / P^i = (\sum_{k=1}^{I} f_k (C^k(p^j,u^k)/C^k(p^i,u^k))^\lambda)^{1/\lambda}$ $(i,j = 1,...,I)$ with f_k $(k = 1,...,I)$ such that transitivity is ensured. Armstrong (2002) proceeded by assuming that each country–specific cost function $C^i(p,u)$ has a CES functional form. The parameters were estimated on OECD data for 24 countries, 115 commodities, and years 1990, 1993 and 1996. Index numbers for two members of the class of mean–of–order–λ indexes were compared to GEKS and GK results.

But this in turn means that expression (3.31) reduces to

$$\frac{P^j}{P^i} = \prod_{k=1}^{I} \left(P^T(p^j,x^j,p^k,x^k)P^T(p^k,x^k,p^i,x^i) \right)^{\frac{1}{k}} \quad (i,j=1,...,I). \quad (3.35)$$

This expression is the same as expression (3.8), except that Fisher indices are replaced by Törnqvist indices.[20] The corresponding economic quantity index Q^j/Q^i is obtained by applying the product relation (3.1).

The foregoing derivation basically generalizes the result of Caves et al. (1982a). This result was obtained in the context of the input side of production, departing from a transformation function and assuming constant returns to scale. Notice that such an assumption was not needed here.

A different approach was followed by Rao and Salazar-Carrillo (1988). Conditional on a certain price vector π, the economic purchasing power parity of country i was defined by

$$P^i \equiv \frac{C^i(p^i,u^i)}{C^i(\pi,u^i)} \quad (i=1,...,I), \quad (3.36)$$

which has the form of a Paasche–perspective cost of living index. The vector π was determined by requiring that for each commodity the sum of the quantities which are optimal at π equals the sum of the actual quantities; that is,

$$\sum_{i=1}^{I} x_n^i(\pi,u^i) = \sum_{i=1}^{I} x_n^i \quad (n=1,...,N). \quad (3.37)$$

The next step is to notice that every country–specific pair (p^i,x^i) can be rationalized by a country–specific Cobb-Douglas cost function

$$C^i(p,u) \equiv F(u) \prod_{n=1}^{N} p_n^{w_n^i} \quad (i=1,...,I), \quad (3.38)$$

where w_n^i are the actual commodity n value shares of country i $(n=1,...,N; \ i=1,...,I)$ and $F(u)$ is monotonicly increasing in u. Under this assumption expression (3.36) reduces to

---

[20] The indices defined by expression (3.35) are therefore called 'GEKS–Törnqvist' indices.

$$P^i = \prod_{n=1}^{N} (p_n^i / \pi_n)^{w_n^i} \ (i = 1,...,I).$$ (3.39)

Now the Cobb–Douglas cost function implies that the cost minimizing quantities are given by $x_n^i(p,u) = (w_n^i / p_n) C^i(p,u)$ $(n = 1,...,N)$. Substituting this into equation (3.37), rearranging terms, and making use of definition (3.36) together with the rationality assumption (3.25), one finally obtains that

$$\pi_n = \frac{\sum_{i=1}^{I} w_n^i C^i(\pi, u^i)}{\sum_{i=1}^{I} x_n^i} = \frac{\sum_{i=1}^{I} p_n^i x_n^i / P^i}{\sum_{i=1}^{I} x_n^i} (n = 1,...,N).$$ (3.40)

These are the same international prices as in the GK method (3.17). The purchasing power parities, however, are different. The system (3.39) – (3.40) must be solved numerically.

3.9 THE ECONOMIC APPROACH: INTERNATIONAL PREFERENCES

The next approach simplifies things by assuming that in all countries the same (international) preference structure prevails; that is,

$$C^i(p,u) = C(p,u)(i = 1,...,I).$$ (3.41)

Under this assumption, expression (3.36) reduces to

$$P^i = \frac{C(p^i, u^i)}{C(\pi, u^i)} = \frac{p^i \cdot x^i}{C(\pi, u^i)} (i = 1,...,I),$$ (3.42)

where the second equality is based on the basic assumption (3.25). Then, using the product relation (3.1), we find that

$$\frac{Q^j}{Q^i} = \frac{C(\pi, u^j)}{C(\pi, u^i)} (i, j = 1,...,I);$$ (3.43)

that is, the economic quantity index of country j relative to country i is given by the minimum cost to achieve the standard of living u^j relative to the minimum cost to achieve the standard of living u^i, conditional on a certain price vector π. The right–hand side of this equation is known as being a money metric (or Allen) standard of living index. For a fixed π the index is indeed transitive. The basic issue, of course, is how to pick the price vector π.[21]

Suppose for a start that the preference structure exhibits homotheticity. This is equivalent to the supposition that the cost function can be factored as

$$C(p,u) = F(u)C(p,1), \tag{3.44}$$

where $F(u)$ is monotonicly increasing in u. Under homotheticity the economic quantity index (3.43) reduces to

$$\frac{Q^j}{Q^i} = \frac{F(u^j)}{F(u^i)}(i,j=1,...,I), \tag{3.45}$$

which is independent of prices. An important implication is that the following inequalities hold:

$$\frac{Q^j}{Q^i} = \frac{C(p^i,u^j)}{C(p^i,u^i)} \leq Q^L(p^j,x^j,p^i,x^i) \tag{3.46}$$

$$\frac{Q^j}{Q^i} = \frac{C(p^j,u^j)}{C(p^j,u^i)} \geq Q^P(p^j,x^j,p^i,x^i). \tag{3.47}$$

These inequalities are due to the fact that the optimality assumption (3.24) implies that x^j attains the standard of living u^j and therefore, by the definition of the cost function, $C(p^i,u^j) \leq p^i \cdot x^j$. Similarly, $C(p^j,u^i) \leq p^j \cdot x^i$. In addition, relation (3.25) was used.

Based on these two inequalities, a reasonable approximation to Q^j/Q^i appears to be the geometric average of $Q^L(p^j,x^j,p^i,x^i)$ and $Q^P(p^j,x^j,p^i,x^i)$, which is $Q^F(p^j,x^j,p^i,x^i)$.

But also, for any set of country weights f_k $(k=1,...,I)$, adding up to 1, one obtains that

---

[21] For the details of this approach, see Hill (2000b) and Kakwani and Hill (2002). The basic assumption of a common preference structure can be tested by revealed–preference analysis; see Dowrick and Quiggin (1994).

$$
\begin{aligned}
\frac{Q^j}{Q^i} &= \prod_{k=1}^{I}\left(\frac{F(u^j)}{F(u^k)}\frac{F(u^k)}{F(u^i)}\right)^{f_k} \\
&= \prod_{k=1}^{I}\left(\frac{F(u^j)C(p^k,1)}{F(u^k)C(p^k,1)}\frac{F(u^k)C(p^i,1)}{F(u^i)C(p^i,1)}\right)^{f_k} \\
&= \prod_{k=1}^{I}\left(\frac{C(p^k,u^j)}{C(p^k,u^k)}\frac{C(p^i,u^k)}{C(p^i,u^i)}\right)^{f_k} \quad (i,j=1,...,I),
\end{aligned}
\tag{3.48}
$$

where the last line was obtained by using the homotheticity assumption (3.44). Again, our optimality assumption implies that x^j attains the standard of living u^j and therefore, by the definition of the cost function, $C(p^k,u^j) \le p^k \cdot x^j$. Similarly, $C(p^i,u^k) \le p^i \cdot x^k$. Applying these inequalities to the numerators in expression (3.48) and using (3.25) for the denominators, we obtain the following inequality for the economic quantity index:

$$
\begin{aligned}
\frac{Q^j}{Q^i} &\le \prod_{k=1}^{I}\left(\frac{p^k \cdot x^j}{p^k \cdot x^k}\frac{p^i \cdot x^k}{p^i \cdot x^i}\right)^{f_k} \\
&= \prod_{k=1}^{I}\left(Q^L(p^j,x^j,p^k,x^k)Q^L(p^k,x^k,p^i,x^i)\right)^{f_k} \quad (i,j=1,...,I).
\end{aligned}
\tag{3.49}
$$

By a similar reasoning we find that

$$
\frac{Q^j}{Q^i} \ge \prod_{k=1}^{I}\left(Q^P(p^j,x^j,p^k,x^k)Q^P(p^k,x^k,p^i,x^i)\right)^{f_k} \quad (i,j=1,...,I). \tag{3.50}
$$

We have thus obtained a second set of upper and lower bounds for the economic quantity index Q^j/Q^i. A reasonable approximation to this quantity index, retaining transitivity, is then provided by the unweighted geometric average of the right–hand sides of (3.49) and (3.50); that is, we set

$$
\frac{Q^j}{Q^i} \sim \prod_{k=1}^{I}\left(Q^F(p^j,x^j,p^k,x^k)Q^F(p^k,x^k,p^i,x^i)\right)^{f_k} \quad (i,j=1,...,I). \tag{3.51}
$$

But this is the GEKS–Fisher index (3.9). We have thus obtained the result that under identical homothetic preferences the GEKS–Fisher quantity index provides a reasonable approximation to the economic quantity index which was defined by expression (3.43).

A subtle modification of the foregoing reasoning leads to a result that sheds light on the method of chaining as discussed in Section 3.6.

Suppose that all the countries are connected by a spanning tree, and that countries i and j are connected to each other via countries $k_1, ..., k_L$. We can then write, instead of expression (3.48),

$$
\begin{aligned}
\frac{Q^j}{Q^i} &= \frac{F(u^{k_1})}{F(u^i)} \frac{F(u^{k_2})}{F(u^{k_1})} \cdots \frac{F(u^j)}{F(u^{k_L})} \\
&= \frac{C(p^i, u^{k_1})}{C(p^i, u^i)} \frac{C(p^{k_1}, u^{k_2})}{C(p^{k_1}, u^{k_1})} \cdots \frac{C(p^{k_L}, u^j)}{C(p^{k_L}, u^{k_L})} (i, j = 1, ..., I),
\end{aligned}
\tag{3.52}
$$

where the last line was again obtained by using the homotheticity assumption. As in the foregoing this leads to the following upper bound for the economic quantity index:

$$
\frac{Q^j}{Q^i} \le Q^L(p^{k_1}, x^{k_1}, p^i, x^i) Q^L(p^{k_2}, x^{k_2}, p^{k_1}, x^{k_1}) \cdots Q^L(p^j, x^j, p^{k_L}, x^{k_L}) \tag{3.53}
$$

$$
(i, j = 1, ..., I).
$$

But we can also write, by virtue of the homotheticity assumption,

$$
\begin{aligned}
\frac{Q^j}{Q^i} &= \frac{F(u^{k_1})}{F(u^i)} \frac{F(u^{k_2})}{F(u^{k_1})} \cdots \frac{F(u^j)}{F(u^{k_L})} \\
&= \frac{C(p^{k_1}, u^{k_1})}{C(p^{k_1}, u^i)} \frac{C(p^{k_2}, u^{k_2})}{C(p^{k_2}, u^{k_1})} \cdots \frac{C(p^j, u^j)}{C(p^j, u^{k_L})} (i, j = 1, ..., I),
\end{aligned}
\tag{3.54}
$$

which leads to the lower bound

$$
\frac{Q^j}{Q^i} \ge Q^P(p^{k_1}, x^{k_1}, p^i, x^i) Q^P(p^{k_2}, x^{k_2}, p^{k_1}, x^{k_1}) \cdots Q^P(p^j, x^j, p^{k_L}, x^{k_L}) \tag{3.55}
$$

$$
(i, j = 1, ..., I).
$$

A reasonable approximation to the economic quantity index Q^j / Q^i is then provided by the geometric mean of the two bounds,

$$\frac{Q^j}{Q^i} \approx Q^F(p^{k_1},x^{k_1},p^i,x^i)Q^F(p^{k_2},x^{k_2},p^{k_1},x^{k_1})\cdots Q^F(p^j,x^j,p^{k_L},x^{k_L}) \quad (3.56)$$

$$(i,j=1,...,I).$$

Hence, under the assumption of identical homothetic preferences the chained Fisher quantity index provides also a reasonable approximation to the economic quantity index which was defined by expression (3.43).[22]

Homotheticity is a great but very restrictive assumption. In a recent paper Quiggin and Van Veelen (2007, p. 376) remarked that

> The great attraction of the representative consumer assumption and the even stronger assumption that the representative utility function is homothetic is that it permits a sensible economic interpretation to be given to statements that are commonly made using index numbers.

The assumption means that, given a vector of country–specific prices, increasing the standard of living would lead to an equi–proportionate increase of all the quantities consumed. This is patently unrealistic. Afriat (1972, p. 28) already observed that

> ... it is an overwhelmingly significant fact of experience that the rich, whether individuals or countries, have things that the poor do not have at all, let alone in corresponding proportions. Deliberately to overlook this in a system of calculation that seeks to make general comparisons leaves the significance of such calculation quite obscure, even as to the locus of injustice.

It is clear that under nonhomotheticity the choice of the vector π becomes a matter of importance. Using the definition of the cost function, expression (3.42) can be rewritten as

$$\sum_{n=1}^{N}\pi_n x_n(\pi,u^i) = \sum_{n=1}^{N}(p_n^i/P^i)x_n^i \,(i=1,...,I). \quad (3.57)$$

In Neary and Gleeson's (1997) approach the vector π is determined by adjoining this system of equalities across countries by a similar system of equalities across commodities:

---

[22] An extension of this technique, by taking the minimum and maximum respectively over all spanning trees, leads to the tight upper and lower bounds as derived by Dowrick and Quiggin (1997). Notice that $Q^F(p',x',p,x) = 1/Q^L(p,x,p',x')$.

$$\sum_{i=1}^{I} \pi_n x_n(\pi, u^i) = \sum_{i=1}^{I} (p_n^i / P^i) x_n^i \ (n = 1,...,N). \tag{3.58}$$

Rearranging terms, the complete system of equations appears to be

$$\pi_n = \frac{\sum_{i=1}^{I} p_n^i x_n^i / P^i}{\sum_{i=1}^{I} x_n(\pi, u^i)} \qquad (n = 1,...,N) \tag{3.59}$$

$$P^i = C(p^i, u^i) / C(\pi, u^i) \ \ (i = 1,...,I).$$

Neary and Gleeson (1997) called this the Geary–Konüs system.[23] In a later publication, Neary (2004) called the system of equations (3.59) the Geary–Allen International Accounts (GAIA). Given a functional form for the cost function, this system of equations must be solved numerically to obtain the purchasing power parities.

The problem, of course, is how to obtain an appropriate functional form for the cost function. A flexible functional form requires at least $1 + (N+1) + (N+1)(N+2)/2$ parameters to be estimated, whereas the number of data points is $I \times N$. Since in any realistic comparison exercise the number of commodities N will exceed by far the number of countries I, the estimation of a flexible form is a mission impossible unless we are given more data points per country.

Neary and Gleeson (1997) therefore assumed that the international preference structure could be represented by the Stone–Geary utility function (Linear Expenditure System), which leaves only a modest number of $2N - 1$ parameters to be estimated. Using price and expenditure data for 11 commodities and 16 countries coming from the ICP 1970 survey, they calculated price and quantity index numbers and compared these to the corresponding GK and GEKS results. This exercise was repeated by Hill (2000b) on 1990 data for 24 OECD countries and 11 commodities.

Neary (2004) assumed that the international preferences were represented by the (Quadratic) Almost Ideal Demand System. The QAIDS system appears to have $N(N+5)/2 - 2$ free parameters. The demand system was estimated on data for 11 commodities and 60 countries coming from the ICP 1980 survey. There appeared to be little to choose between the index numbers

---

[23] It is straightforward to verify that if the international preference structure is of the Leontief fixed coefficients type, which means that $C(p,u) = F(u)p \cdot a$ for some quantity vector a, then the system (3.59) reduces to the Geary–Khamis system (3.17).

generated by the AIDS or the QAIDS system. Neary's overall conclusion was that the index numbers generated by the QAIDS system were closer to the GEKS index numbers than to those of Geary–Khamis, but markedly different from both.

3.10 CONCLUSION

Looking back one could say that though we have learned quite a lot, the lessons are not all pointing in the same direction. Put otherwise, there appears to be no unique, award–winning method. However, some methods have better credentials than others. A brief recapitulation here may be sufficient.[24]

The centre stage among the methods discussed in Section 3.3 was occupied by the GEKS–Fisher price and quantity indices (expressions (3.8) and (3.9)). From the economic viewpoint this pair of indices can be rationalized by assuming identical homothetic preferences across all the countries (see expression (3.51)). Assuming non–homothetic country–specific preferences which are not 'too' different – in mathematical form this is expressed by (3.32) – leads us to the GEKS–Törnqvist price index (3.35). From the empirical viewpoint it can be expected that the GEKS–Fisher and the GEKS–Törnqvist indices closely approximate each other. The GEKS–Fisher volume shares appear to violate only the tests MT3 and MT8. However, as documented in Section 3.3, the GEKS–Fisher indices are bracketed by the van IJzeren and the Gerardi indices, both of which do satisfy the test MT8. Thus, there is reason to expect that the GEKS–Fisher's failure of satisfying MT8 is not 'too' bad. Moreover, as demonstrated by van IJzeren (1987) on a numerical example, the weights are not particularly influential, so that it is virtually harmless to set all the (normalized) weights equal to $1/I$.

Using a data–driven spanning tree as basis for the construction of a system of chained indices seems to be an area for further research. As indicated in the previous section, chained Fisher quantity indices can be defended from the economic angle, provided that one is willing to assume identical homothetic preferences.

A comparison of the structural features of an economic aggregate is best served by employing an additive method. Economically seen, such a method does not allow substitution behaviour. Judged from the viewpoint of tests, the choice seems to be between the GK and SRK methods. The issue here is to find a method that suffers least from the Gerschenkron effect. There is reason

---

[24] Armstrong (2001b) compared a large number of aggregation methods on 1990 data for 24 OECD countries and 158 commodities. This interesting exercise made clear once more that the choice of method really matters.

to expect that in this respect the GK method must be preferred to the SRK method.

REFERENCES

Afriat, S.N. (1972), 'The Theory of International Comparisons of Real Income and Prices', in D.J. Daley (ed.), *International Comparison of Prices and Output, Studies in Income and Wealth*, **37**, New York: National Bureau of Economic Research.

Armstrong, K.G. (2001a), 'Microeconomic Foundations for the Theory of International Comparisons', *Journal of Economic Theory*, **101**, 585–601.

Armstrong, K.G. (2001b), 'What Impact does the Choice of Formula have on International Comparisons?', *Canadian Journal of Economics*, **34**, 697–718.

Armstrong, K.G. (2002), 'Empirically Estimated 'True' PPP Indexes', mimeograph, Department of Economics, Carleton University, Ottawa.

Balk, B.M. (1989), 'On van IJzeren's Approach to International Comparisons and its Properties', *Statistical Papers/Statistische Hefte*, **30**, 295–315.

Balk, B.M. (1996), 'A Comparison of Ten Methods for Multilateral International Price and Volume Comparison', *Journal of Official Statistics*, **12**, 199–222.

Balk, B.M. (2008), *Price and Quantity Index Numbers: Models for Measuring Aggregate Change and Difference*, New York: Cambridge University Press.

Caves, D.W., L.R. Christensen and W.E. Diewert (1982a), 'Multilateral Comparisons of Output, Input, and Productivity using Superlative Index Numbers', *Economic Journal*, **92**, 73–86.

Caves, D.W., L.R. Christensen and W.E. Diewert (1982b), 'The Economic Theory of Index Numbers and the Measurement of Input, Output, and Productivity', *Econometrica*, **50**, 1393–1414.

Cuthbert, J.R. (1999), 'Categorisation of Additive Purchasing Power Parities', *The Review of Income and Wealth*, **45**, 235–249.

Diewert, W.E. (1986), 'Microeconomic Approaches to the Theory of International Comparisons', Technical Working Paper No. 53, Cambridge MA: National Bureau of Economic Research. Abridged version, entitled 'Test Approaches to International Comparisons', in W.E. Diewert and A.O. Nakamura (eds) (1993), *Essays in Index Number Theory, Volume 1*, Amsterdam: North–Holland.

Diewert, W.E. (1987), 'Index Numbers', in *The New Palgrave: a Dictionary of Economics: Volume 2*, in J. Eatwell (ed.), London: Macmillan. Reprinted in W.E. Diewert and A.O. Nakamura (eds), (1993), *Essays in Index Number Theory, Volume 1*, Amsterdam: North–Holland.

Diewert, W.E. (1999), 'Axiomatic and Economic Approaches to International Comparisons', in *International and Interarea Comparisons of Income, Output and Prices*, in A. Heston and R.E. Lipsey (eds), Studies in Income and Wealth, **61**, Chicago and London: University of Chicago Press.

Diewert, W.E. (this volume), 'Similarity Indexes and Criteria for Spatial Linking'.

Dowrick, S. and J. Quiggin (1994), 'International Comparisons of Living Standards and Tastes', *American Economic Review*, **84**, 332–341.

Dowrick, S. and J. Quiggin (1997), 'True Measures of GDP and Convergence', *American Economic Review*, **87**, 41–64.

Eichhorn, W. and J. Voeller (1983), 'Axiomatic Foundation of Price Indexes and Purchasing Power Parities', in W.E. Diewert and C. Montmarquette (eds), *Price Level Measurement*, Ottawa: Statistics Canada; also reprinted in W.E. Diewert (ed.) (1990), *Price Level Measurement*, Amsterdam: North–Holland.

Eltetö, Ö. and P. Köves (1964), 'On an Index Computation Problem in International Comparisons', (in Hungarian), *Statiztikai Szemle*, **42**, 507–518.

Fisher, I. (1922), *The Making of Index Numbers*, Boston, MA: Houghton Mifflin.

Geary, R.C. (1958), 'A Note on the Comparison of Exchange Rates and Purchasing Power between Countries', *Journal of the Royal Statistical Society: A*, **121**, 97–99.

Gerardi, D. (1974), *Sul Problema della Comparazione dei Poteri d'Aquisto della Valute, Istituto di Statistica, Universita degli Studi di Padova*. Series Papers.

Gerschenkron, A. (1951), *A Dollar Index of Soviet Machinery Output, 1927–28 to 1937*, Santa Monica, CA: Rand Corporation.

Gini, C. (1924), 'Quelques Considérations au Sujet de la Construction des Nombres Indices des Prix et des Questions Analogues', *Metron*, **4**, 3–162.

Green, J. and W.P. Heller (1981), 'Mathematical Analysis and Convexity with Applications to Economics', in K.J. Arrow and M.D. Intriligator (eds) *Handbook of Mathematical Economics, Volume 1*, Amsterdam: North–Holland.

Heston, A., R. Summers and B. Aten (2001), 'Price Structures, the Quality Factor, and Chaining', *Statistical Journal of the United Nations ECE*, **18**, 77–101.

Hill, R.J. (1999a), 'Comparing Price Levels Across Countries Using Minimum-Spanning Trees', *The Review of Economics and Statistics*, **81**, 135–142.

Hill, R.J. (1999b), 'International Comparisons Using Spanning Trees', in A. Heston and R.E. Lipsey (eds), *International and Interarea Comparison of Income Output and Prices*, Studies in Income and Wealth, **61**, Chicago and London: University of Chicago Press.

Hill, R.J. (2000a), 'Measuring Substitution Bias in International Comparisons Based on Additive Purchasing Power Parity Methods', *European Economic Review*, **44**, 145–162.

Hill, R.J. (2000b), 'Constructing Bounds on Per Capita Income Differentials Across Countries', *Scandinavian Journal of Economics*, **102**, 285–302.

Hill, R.J. (2004), 'Constructing Price Indexes Across Space and Time: the Case of the European Union', *American Economic Review*, **94**, 1379–1410.

Hill, R.J. (this volume), 'Comparing Per Capita Income Levels Across Countries Using Spanning Trees: Robustness, Prior Restrictions, Hybrids and Hierarchies'.

IJzeren, J. van (1955), 'Over Verschillende Methoden ter Berekening van Pariteiten ten behoeve van Internationale Koopkrachtvergelijking', *Statistische en Econometriche Onderzoekingen (C.B.S.)*, **10**, 101–132.

IJzeren, J. van (1956), *Three Methods of Comparing the Purchasing Power of Currencies*, Netherlands Central Bureau of Statistics, Statistical Studies, **7**, Zeist: De Haan.

IJzeren, J. van (1987), *Bias in International Index Numbers: a Mathematical Elucidation*, Dissertation, Hungarian Academy of Sciences (private edition).

Iklé, D.M. (1972), 'A New Approach to the Index Number Problem', *Quarterly Journal of Economics*, **86**, 188–211.

Kakwani, N. and R.J. Hill (2002), 'Economic Theory of Spatial Cost of Living Indices with Application to Thailand', *Journal of Public Economics*, **86**, 71–97.

Khamis, S.H. (1972), 'A New System of Index Numbers for National and International Purposes', *Journal of the Royal Statistical Society: A*, **135**, 96–121.

Khamis, S.H. (1998), 'Measurement of Real Product: Some Index Number Aspects', Paper presented at the 25th General Conference of the IARIW, Cambridge, UK.

Kravis, I.B., Z. Kenessey, A. Heston and R. Summers (1975), *A System of International Comparisons of Gross Product and Purchasing Power*, Baltimore and London: Johns Hopkins University Press.

Krijnse Locker, H. and H.D. Faerber (1984), 'Space and Time Comparisons of Purchasing Power Parities and Real Values', *Review of Income and Wealth*, **30**, 53–83.

Kurabayashi, Y. and I. Sakuma (1981), 'An Alternative Method of Multilateral Comparisons of Real Product Constrained with Matrix Consistency', paper presented at the 17th General Conference of the IARIW, Gouvieux, France.

Kurabayashi, Y. and I. Sakuma (1982), 'Transitivity, Factor Reversal Test and Matrix Consistency in the International Comparisons of Real Product', Discussion Paper 54, Institute of Economic Research, Hitotsubashi University, Tokyo.

Kurabayashi, Y. and I. Sakuma (1990), *Studies of International Comparisons of Real Product and Prices*, Tokyo: Kinokuniya Company and Oxford: Oxford University Press.

Neary, J.P. (2004), 'Rationalizing the Penn World Table: True Multilateral Indices for International Comparisons of Real Income', *American Economic Review*, **94**, 1411–1428.

Neary, J.P. and B. Gleeson (1997), 'Comparing the Wealth of Nations: Reference Prices and Multilateral Real Income Indexes', *Economic and Social Review*, **28**, 401–421.

Quiggin, J. and M. van Veelen (2007), 'Multilateral Indices: Conflicting Approaches?', *Review of Income and Wealth*, **53**, 372–378.

Rao, D.S.P. (this volume), 'Generalised Eltetö–Köves–Szulc and Country–Product–Dummy Methods for International Comparisons'.

Rao, D.S.P. and J. Salazar–Carrillo (1988), 'A General Equilibrium Approach to the Construction of Multilateral Index Numbers', in J. Salazar–Carrillo and D.S.P. Rao (eds), *World Comparison of Incomes, Prices and Product*, Amsterdam: North–Holland.

Rao, D.S.P. and M.P. Timmer (2003), 'Purchasing Power Parities for Industry Comparisons Using Weighted Eltetö–Köves–Szulc (EKS) Methods', *Review of Income and Wealth*, **49**, 491–511.

Sakuma, I., D.S.P. Rao and Y. Kurabayashi (2000), 'Additivity, Matrix Consistency and a New Method for International Comparisons of Real Income and Purchasing Power Parities', paper presented at the 26th General Conference of the IARIW, Cracow, Poland. Revised version in this volume.

Schreyögg, J., O. Tiemann, T. Stargardt and R. Busse (2008), 'Cross–country Comparisons of Costs: the Use of Episode–Specific Transitive Purchasing Power Parities with Standardized Cost Categories', *Health Economics*, **17**, S95–S103.

Sergeev, S. (this volume), 'Aggregation Methods Based on Structural International Prices'.

Szulc, B. (1964), 'Index Numbers of Multilateral Regional Comparisons', (in Polish), *Przeglad Statistyczny*, **11**, 239–254.

Veelen, M. van, and R. van der Weide (2008), 'A Note on Different Approaches to Index Number Theory', *The American Economic Review*, **98**, 1722–1730.

4. Generalised Elteto–Köves–Szulc and Country–Product–Dummy Methods for International Comparisons

D. S. Prasada Rao[1]

4.1 INTRODUCTION

The International Comparison Program is the principal source of data on purchasing power parities of currencies and internationally comparable economic aggregates such as the real gross domestic product, private consumption, investment and government expenditure. The recently completed phase of the International Comparison Program (ICP) for the year 2005 had a global coverage with 146 participating countries from all the regions of the world. A general survey of the concepts and methods used as well as extensive tables containing results from the 2005 ICP round are available from World Bank (2008), ADB (2007). Roberts (this volume) provides an excellent overview of the organisation and implementation of ICP for the OECD and Eurostat countries. A major step in any international comparison exercise is the aggregation of commodity level price and quantity data. Aggregation of price–quantity data is undertaken at two different levels. First stage aggregation is at the detailed item level, and second stage is at a more aggregated level usually referred to as the *basic heading level*.[2] In view of the multilateral nature of the comparisons it is widely accepted that index number methods employed in such an aggregation exercise should satisfy a

---

[1] This is an extensively revised version of a paper by the author presented at the international seminar on purchasing power parities held at the World Bank, Washington, DC in February, 2001. The author wishes to thank Bettina Aten, Bert Balk, Erwin Diewert, Golamreza Hajarghasht, Alan Heston, Christopher O'Donnell and Marcel Timmer for their comments on various aspects covered in this chapter.

[2] See Roberts (this volume) for a detailed description of basic headings and various issues relating to price and expenditure data used in the process of aggregation.

number of properties, including *transitivity, country symmetry, additivity* and are also usually expected to preserve a degree of *characteristicity.*[3]

Two aggregation methods, viz., the Eltetö–Köves–Szulc (EKS) and the country–product–dummy (CPD) methods for aggregation, played a major role in the 2005 ICP. The Technical Advisory Group (TAG)[4] recommended the use of the CPD method[5] for aggregation below the basic heading level and the EKS method was recommended for purposes of aggregation above the basic heading level. The Group also recommended the use of the Geary–Khamis method in compiling international comparisons that are additively consistent and publishing them in a set of supplementary tables for those who are interested in the analysis of size and structure of GDP. The main objective of the chapter is to examine in the EKS and CPD methods in detail and propose generalisations of these methods. Given the newly acquired status of the EKS method as the preferred method of aggregation for international comparisons, it is necessary to examine the EKS method and see if further improvements could be made. In contrast, the CPD method has long been considered to be a statistical technique that can be used in filling gaps of missing price data. In the early phases of ICP work, the CPD method was used as a method of aggregation below the basic heading level. The CPD method, due its econometric nature, could be extended and generalised to provide a comprehensive framework for international comparisons. A major objective of the present chapter is to demonstrate the versatility of the CPD method and show how the CPD model can be used in generating various methods of aggregation currently in use in international comparisons.

The outline of the chapter is as follows. Section 4.2 describes the notation used in the chapter and establishes a few concepts that are central to index number methods for international comparisons. Section 4.3 examines the EKS method briefly and proposes a generalised EKS system which allows for differential weights for each binary comparison reflecting the general reliability of the binary comparison. Numerical results based on alternative specification of weights are also presented. Section 4.4 is devoted to the CPD method and its generalisations. The section will examine various aspects of the CPD method to illustrate its role in the future rounds of the ICP.

---

[3] See Balk (1996 and this volume) for a discussion of several axiomatic properties expected of index numbers methods used in international comparisons. More details of these properties are available in Kravis et al. (1982) and Diewert (1999).

[4] See the ICP World Bank website (www.worldbank.org/data/icp) for more details about the constitution and the role of the technical advisory group for the 2005 ICP.

[5] A variant of the CPD method, the country-product-representativeness-dummy (CPRD) method, was recommended as a method for aggregating price data below the basic heading level when information on *representativity* is available.

4.2　NOTATION

The following notation is used throughout the chapter. Let p_{ij} and q_{ij} represent, respectively, the price and quantity of i-th commodity in j-th country. We consider a multilateral comparison with M countries and N commodities. If the commodities represent items below the basic heading level, quantity data or information on weights are usually not available. Prices are expressed in national currency units for a specific quantity unit of the commodity. If price data are not collected or not available for a given commodity in a given country, the corresponding price is considered to be missing. If the commodities represent aggregates, at or above the basic heading level, then price and quantity data are usually available. At the aggregate level, price data are usually in the form of purchasing power parities, expressed relative to a numeraire currency unit. Quantity data are derived indirectly using the value aggregates in national currencies and PPPs.

We also use PPP_j to denote the purchasing power parity of j-th country currency (relative to a numeraire currency) which measures the number of national currency units that have the same purchasing power as one unit of the numeraire currency unit. When we turn to the discussion of the country–product–dummy (CPD) method, we will make use of P_i which denotes the average international price of i-th commodity. The natural logarithms of PPP_j and P_i are, respectively, denoted by π_j and η_i.

4.3　THE ELTETÖ–KÖVES–SZULC METHOD

The EKS method, proposed by Eltetö and Köves (1964) and Szulc (1964),[6] is designed to construct transitive multilateral comparisons from a matrix of binary/pairwise comparisons derived using a formula which does not satisfy the transitivity property. The basic premise underlying the EKS method is that a direct comparison between two countries, j and k, is the best way to compare the price levels in the two countries. If the binary comparisons compiled using a particular index number formula are not transitive, then the aim should be to compile transitive comparisons which remain as close as possible to the binary comparisons. Thus the EKS method seeks to preserve characteristicity of a binary comparison in its attempt to provide a transitive multilateral method.

---

[6]　It is now well recognised that Gini (1924) proposed this method in 1924. We will continue to refer to this as the EKS method as it is commonly the case with most publications of international organisations.

The EKS method in its original form uses binary Fisher PPPs (F_{jk}: $j,k=1,..M$) as building blocks to construct a transitive multilateral system. However, the EKS technique can be applied to any other binary index number system that satisfies time–reversal or country–reversal test. Rao and Banerjee (1986) used the EKS technique on a range of binary index numbers including the Tornqvist index and the binary form of the Geary–Khamis index. The following discussion will focus on the original EKS formulation using the Fisher binary index but is equally applicable in other cases.

The computational form for the EKS index, for a pair of countries j and k is given by

$$EKS_{jk} = \prod_{l=1}^{M} \left[F_{jl} \cdot F_{lk} \right]^{1/M} \tag{4.1}$$

where F_{jk} denotes the Fisher price index number for country k with country j as the base.

Computation of F_{jk} differs depending upon the level of aggregation at which the formula is applied. For purposes of aggregation at levels above the basic heading, Fisher formula used in PPP computations is essentially the same is standard Fisher index formula which is the geometric mean of the Laspeyres and Paasche indices. However, the Fisher index used for aggregation below the basic heading level (where quantity or expenditure data are not available), the formula is a bit different.[7] These aspects are discussed in further detail when generalisations of EKS are considered at levels below the basic heading level.

The EKS method in (4.1) produces comparisons which are transitive. In addition, these indices also satisfy an important least squares property that indices in (4.1) deviate the least from the pairwise Fisher binary comparisons.[8] The least squares property is in line with the property of characteristicity espoused in Drechsler (1973). Since Fisher index is considered to be ideal and possesses a number of desirable properties,[9] the EKS method has a certain appeal since it preserves the Fisher indices to the extent possible, while constructing multilateral index numbers.

Equation (4.1) defines the EKS index as an unweighted geometric average of the linked (or chained) comparisons between countries j and k using each of the countries in the comparisons as a link. A major problem with the EKS formula is that it gives equal weights to all linked comparisons, $\left[F_{jl} \cdot F_{lk} \right]$, effectively assuming that they are all of equal reliability. Following Rao

---

[7] These indices may be termed 'Laspeyres-type', 'Paasche-type' and 'Fisher-type' indices in that they use the basic ideas of these indices.

[8] A formal proof of this is given in Rao and Banerjee (1986).

[9] See Diewert (1978) for a discussion of the properties of the Fisher index.

(1997) and Rao et al. (2002), it can be argued that in practice it is possible to show that some link comparisons are intrinsically more reliable than others. For example if we are interested in a comparison between the US and Germany we may consider linked comparisons through economies of similar size and development like Japan or the UK to be more reliable than linked comparisons through countries at a different level of development like India or the Philippines. Similarly, in many international comparison exercises we find that some pairwise Fisher indices are based on price data for many commodities while in other cases comparisons are based on prices for only one or two items. Obviously comparisons in the case of the former would be more reliable than those based on fewer items. The generalised EKS method is designed to take into account any additional information on the reliability of the binary measures when constructing the EKS multilateral indices.

4.3.1   Generalised EKS Method

In proposing a generalisation that makes it possible to derive weighted EKS index numbers, we first show that the EKS indices can be derived using a regression framework and that the indices in equation (4.1) are least squares estimates of the unknown parameters in a suitably specified regression model. The second step then is to use the stochastic properties of the disturbance terms to introduce a system of weights into the construction of the EKS index numbers.

We start with the basic framework for the EKS which seeks to derive a set of index numbers I_{jk} which are transitive and at the same time minimise the log–distance from the Fisher binary indices. This can be achieved by solving the following optimisation problem which minimises:

$$\sum_j \sum_k (\ln I_{jk} - \ln F_{jk})^2$$

subject to the transitivity restriction: $I_{jk} = I_{jl} I_{lk}$ $\forall j,k,l$ (4.2)

Although the optimisation problem appears complex it can be handled easily once the problem is reparametrised using the following commonly known property associated with transitivity.

Result: A multilateral system of index numbers, I_{jk} $(j,k=1,2,...,M)$, satisfies transitivity property if and only if there exist M numbers $\pi_1, \pi_2,..., \pi_M$ such that, for all j and k

$$ln\ I_{jk} = \pi_k - \pi_j$$

This result shows that transitivity reduces the number of unknowns in the matrix of transitive indices. Even though there are M^2 elements in the matrix of binary comparisons, once we impose transitivity we can construct each and every element of the matrix once the π's are known.

Using this result, the problem in (4.2) can be restated as one of finding π_1, $\pi_2,..., \pi_M$, which minimise

$$\sum_j \sum_k (\pi_k - \pi_j - \ln F_{jk})^2 \qquad (4.3)$$

Then the required index I_{jk} is defined as the ratio $\exp(\hat{\pi}_k)/\exp(\hat{\pi}_j)$ where (^) shows that these are solutions to the minimisation problem. After some simple algebraic manipulation it can be shown that the EKS index is related to the solution above as:

$$EKS_{jk} = \frac{\exp(\hat{\pi}_k)}{\exp(\hat{\pi}_j)} = \exp(\hat{\pi}_k - \hat{\pi}_j)$$

Considering equation (4.3) further, it is evident that $\hat{\pi}$'s are the ordinary least squares estimators of π's (which are the best linear unbiased estimators) in the following model specification

$$\ln F_{jk} = \pi_k - \pi_j + u_{jk}$$
$$with \quad E(u_{jk}) = 0 \quad and \quad v(u_{jk}) = \sigma^2 \qquad (4.4)$$

Given the model specification in (4.4), it is possible to discriminate between indices for different pairs of countries using some indicators of reliability. Suppose we know that the Fisher index between countries 1 and 2 is less reliable then the corresponding observation in the regression model, (4.4) will have a higher variance.

4.3.2   Modelling Reliability through Heteroskedastic Disturbances

It is possible to incorporate this additional information about reliability through heteroskedastic disturbances in the regression model. Thus we can use the following model:

$$\ln F_{jk} = \pi_k - \pi_j + u_{jk}$$

$$\text{with} \quad E(u_{jk}) = 0 \quad \text{and} \quad v(u_{jk}) = \frac{\sigma^2}{w_{jk}} \tag{4.5}$$

where w_{jk} is a measure of reliability. If w_{jk} is large we consider that particular Fisher index, F_{jk}, to be reliable. Modified EKS indices can be obtained by applying generalised least squares or ordinary least squares to the transformed model:

$$\sqrt{w_{jk}} \ln F_{jk} = \sqrt{w_{jk}} \pi_k - \sqrt{w_{jk}} \pi_j + u^*_{jk}$$

$$\text{with} \quad E(u^*_{jk}) = 0 \quad \text{and} \quad v(u^*_{jk}) = \sigma^2 \qquad \forall j,k = 1,..M, \ j \neq k$$

Applying least squares to the transformed equation gives the following normal equations to be solved for the unknown parameters:

$$\begin{bmatrix} \sum\limits_{j\neq 1}^{M} w_{1j} & -w_{12} & \cdot & \cdot & -w_{1M} \\ -w_{21} & \sum\limits_{j\neq 2}^{M} w_{2j} & & & -w_{2M} \\ \cdot & & & & \\ \cdot & & & & \\ -w_{M1} & -w_{M2} & \cdot & \cdot & \sum\limits_{j\neq M}^{M} w_{Mj} \end{bmatrix} \begin{bmatrix} \hat{\pi}_1 \\ \hat{\pi}_2 \\ \cdot \\ \cdot \\ \hat{\pi}_M \end{bmatrix} = \begin{bmatrix} -\sum\limits_{j\neq 1}^{M} w_{1j} \ln F_{1j} \\ -\sum\limits_{j\neq 2}^{M} w_{2j} \ln F_{2j} \\ \cdot \\ \cdot \\ -\sum\limits_{j\neq M}^{M} w_{Mj} \ln F_{Mj} \end{bmatrix} \tag{4.6}$$

We note here that the matrix on the left–hand side is singular and of rank $M–1$. This means that the solutions to (4.6) are unique up to a factor of proportionality. So we can only solve for $\hat{\pi}_1,...,\hat{\pi}_M$ after restricting one of the $\hat{\pi}$'s at a given level. If we set $\hat{\pi}_1 = 0$, this implies that $PPP_1 = \exp(\hat{\pi}_1) = 1$ and that currency of the first country is used as the numeraire or the reference currency. For example, it is a common practice to use the US dollar as the reference currency in comparisons within the ICP. Given the regression model in equation (4.4), it is possible to use statistical packages after defining the dependent and independent variables (in this case they are dummy variables). The new PPPs or modified PPPs based on weighted EKS method are given by

$$PPP_j = \exp(\hat{\pi}_j)$$
$$\text{with} \quad PPP_1 = \exp(\hat{\pi}_1) = 1 \tag{4.7}$$

Before we turn to the actual application of the generalised EKS method we make a few observations. First, the generalization proposed here differs from those discussed in Balk (this volume) and Dikhanov (1994). Their generalisations are based on country–specific weights reflecting the relative size of the countries under consideration. Second, the general notion of equal weights to all the linked comparisons is usually interpreted as a *democratic* approach to international comparisons where all the countries are treated equally and given equal weight[10] But the basic philosophy underlying the EKS method that a direct binary comparison is the best for a comparison between two given countries, say *j* and *k*. This principle is relaxed and replaced by the notion that the EKS should track a binary comparison only when the binary comparison is reliable and the comparison is made between two similar countries. This is an idea that received considerable attention through the *minimum spanning tree* approach proposed by Hill (1999) and this volume) and various attempts have been made to measure reliability through measures of similarity in the price and quantity vectors.[11] Finally, we note that the procedure can be applied when the binary Fisher index number in equations (4.1 and 4.4) is replaced by any other binary index such as the Tornqvist index. We now turn to the actual application of the generalised EKS system for comparisons within the ICP.

4.3.3 Weighting Schemes for the Generalised EKS System

Implementation of the generalised EKS method requires the specification of the weights matrix underlying the heteroskedastic disturbances in equation (4.4). The weights matrix then determines the weights for different linked comparisons involved in the EKS method. It is necessary to specify the matrix of weights to make the method operational.

In this section we examine alternative specifications of weights suitable for aggregation below the basic heading level and above the basic heading level. The aggregation strategies at these two levels are different reflecting the nature of the data available. Below the basic heading level we have only price data and no quantity or weights data are available. However, for

---

[10] See Dikhanov (1994) for a discussion of this aspect.

[11] See Diewert (this volume) for a comprehensive discussion of the construction of similarity measures and Hill (this volume) and Aten and Heston (this volume) for an application of some similarity measures in identifying the best possible chains of comparisons.

aggregation above the basic heading level we have expenditure share weights available which can be used in the compilation of the index numbers.[12]

4.3.4   Generalised EKS System for Aggregation below the Basic Heading Level

The idea of using a stochastic specification for EKS method for aggregation below the basic heading level is not new. Cuthbert and Cuthbert (1989) used a similar approach in their treatment of 'representative' or 'characteristic' items. We refer to their result in one of the alternative models considered below.

Before discussing the possible application of the generalised EKS system for aggregation at levels below the basic heading, it is necessary to quickly examine the current specification of the EKS system used for aggregation at this level within the ICP. Two possible scenarios concerning availability of data can be considered here. First scenario, which is not all that common, is the case where price observations are available for all the items that comprise a given basic heading in all the countries representing a complete price tableau. The second case is where prices are observed and recorded for only a subset of items in each country, items priced differ across different countries. In the exposition below, we follow Ferrari and Riani (1998) and Ferrari et al. (1996). This case of incomplete tableaux is more commonly encountered as not all products used within the ICP can be priced in all the countries.

We consider the cases of complete and incomplete tableaux separately and suggest, in each case, possible specification of the weights, w_{jk}, that can be used in computing generalised EKS indices.

(i) EKS procedure when a price tableau is complete
In this case, since quantity weights are not available, the EKS PPPs for a given basic heading are derived using an unweighted geometric mean of the price ratios of all the commodities for the two countries j and k.

$$EKS_{jk} = \prod_{i=1}^{N} \left[\frac{p_{ik}}{p_{ij}} \right]^{1/N} \tag{4.8}$$

where the commodities listed within the basic heading range from i=1 to N.[13]

---

[12] See the ICP Handbook available on the ICP website at the World Bank, www.worldbank.org/data/icp.

[13] Normally a different notation is needed to denote the range of commodities within a basic heading level. Where it is obvious just a general range (i=1,2, ...,N) is used

(ii) EKS procedure when a price tableau is incomplete

We consider the case where only N_j and N_k out of N commodities (within a given basic heading) are priced. If N^*_{jk} is the number of commodities priced in both countries, j and k, then the EKS indices are computed using the following Fisher–type binary indices.

$$F_{jk} = \prod_{i \in N^*_{jk}} \left[\frac{p_{ik}}{p_{jk}} \right]^{1/N^*_{jk}} \tag{4.9}$$

The binary index is defined as the geometric average of price relatives of commonly priced items. Since indices in (4.9) are not transitive, the EKS procedure, in (4.1), is used in generating transitive PPPs at the basic heading level.

An obvious point for consideration here is the link between the reliability of a binary comparison and the number of items that are commonly priced. Obviously the ideal situation is where all the items are priced. It can be postulated that reliability is directly proportional to the number of items that are commonly priced, with formula in (4.9) breaking down where there are no commonly priced items. Therefore, it can be argued that the normal EKS procedure can be replaced by a weighted EKS procedure.

In this case a natural specification for w_{jk} is the proportion of the number of goods in the basic headings that are priced in both countries. Thus, we suggest the use of

$$w_{jk} = \frac{N^*_{jk}}{N}$$

where N and N^*_{jk}, respectively, denote the number of commodities in the basic heading and the number of commodities that are priced in both countries j and k.

(iii) EKS procedure with an incomplete price tableau and representative goods

In instances where the price tableau is incomplete, some of the items that are priced in a country are likely to be representative or characteristic (and therefore important) of the consumption in the basic heading under consideration, and the others are not representative. The Eurostat and OECD follow the following version of the EKS procedure. The Fisher index between countries j and k, for the given basic heading, is computed as a

---

to denote the commodity list that is relevant for the computation of a particular PPP.

geometric average of the Laspeyres– and Paasche–type indices based on prices of representative items alone. If n_j represents the set of representative commodities in country j for which prices are also available in country k, then the Laspeyres–type index is computed as

$$L_{jk} = \prod_{i \in n_j} \left[\frac{p_{ik}}{p_{ij}} \right]^{1/n_j}$$

and the Paasche–type index, based on the number of representative commodities in k which are also priced in country j, is defined as

$$P_{jk} = \prod_{i \in n_k} \left[\frac{p_{ik}}{p_{ij}} \right]^{1/n_k}$$

and the Fisher index[14] is given by

$$F_{jk} = \sqrt{L_{jk} P_{jk}} = \sqrt{ \prod_{i \in n_j} \left[\frac{p_{ik}}{p_{ij}} \right]^{1/n_j} \cdot \prod_{i \in n_k} \left[\frac{p_{ik}}{p_{ij}} \right]^{1/n_k} } \qquad (4.10)$$

The resulting Fisher indices do not satisfy transitivity. The current practice at Eurostat and the OECD is to apply the EKS procedure as in equation (4.1) to the matrix of Fisher–binary indices in (4.10). This procedure is described in OECD (1999). Ferrari and Riani (1998) examine various properties of the EKS index based on Fisher binaries in (4.10).

The quality or reliability of these indices will necessarily depend upon the number of representative items of a country for which prices are available in both countries. If n_j and n_k are both low, then the Fisher index in (4.10) is less reliable. Cuthbert and Cuthbert (1989, p.43) use a parametric or stochastic approach to derive the following expression for variance of $\ln F_{jk}$:

$$\operatorname{var}(\ln F_{jk}) = \frac{\sigma^2}{4} \left[\frac{1}{n_j} + \frac{1}{n_k} + \frac{2n_{jk}}{n_j n_k} \right] \qquad (4.11)$$

where n_j and n_k are the number of commodities representative in countries j and k respectively, and n_{jk} denotes the number of goods which are characteristic in both j and k.

---

[14] This is essentially a Fisher-type index as it is the geometric mean of Laspeyres-type and Paasche-type index numbers.

In this case the generalised EKS indices can be generated by using the following specification for w_{jk}. We use

$$w_{jk} = 1 / \left(\frac{1}{4} \left[\frac{1}{n_j} + \frac{1}{n_k} + \frac{2n_{jk}}{n_j n_k} \right] \right). \tag{4.12}$$

The use of weights specified in (4.12) is designed to adjust for differences in the number of representative products priced in different countries.

Given the time frame for the preparation of this chapter and due to lack of published price data for goods priced in different countries, no attempt has been made here to empirically implement these generalisations of the EKS method.[15] However, Rao and Timmer (2003) present results based on an application of such weighting schemes for the derivation of consistent multilateral comparisons of manufacturing sector purchasing power parities. Recently, Hill and Timmer (2006) considered the specification of the weights, w_{jk}, when the bilateral index is constructed using the Tornqvist index number formula.[16]

4.3.5 Generalised EKS System for Aggregation Above the Basic Heading Level

In this section we focus on the EKS method as it is applied in international comparisons for aggregation above the basic heading level. Here commodities refer to basic headings and prices are essentially PPPs for different countries for the basic heading under consideration. Thus the formula currently used in computing purchasing power parity for currency of country k with currency of country j as the reference is given by:

$$EKS_{jk} = \prod_{i=1}^{N} \left[F_{ji} \, F_{ik} \right]^{1/M}.$$

where the Fisher index between two countries j and k is defined as:

---

[15] In the recently completed global comparisons for the 2005 ICP, data on representativity could not be reliably compiled (see Roberts, this volume, for a discussion of this issue).

[16] As the binary Tornqvist index can be shown to be equivalent to a least squares estimator of a parameter of a suitably specified regression model (see Selvanathan and Rao, 1992), it is possible to derive a measure of reliability based on the standard error associated with the estimated parameter. This aspect was utilised in Rao et al. (1995) and also Hill and Timmer (2006).

$$F_{jk} = \left[\frac{\sum\limits_{i=1}^{N} p_{ik}q_{ij}}{\sum\limits_{i=1}^{N} p_{ij}q_{ij}} \cdot \frac{\sum\limits_{i=1}^{N} p_{ik}q_{ik}}{\sum\limits_{i=1}^{N} p_{ij}q_{ik}} \right]^{1/2}$$

The Fisher index here is the standard geometric mean of the Laspeyres and Paasche price index numbers.

Now we turn to the specification of the weights matrix necessary for the generalised EKS index where weights reflect a measure of reliability associated with each of the Fisher binary indices that are used in the EKS index shown above. We look at several alternatives.

(i) Weights based on Hill's Distance Function

Here we consider a measure of reliability that is based on the spread between Laspeyres and Paasche index numbers. Beginning from the work of Bortkiewicz (1924), it is generally accepted that the Paasche–Laspeyres spread reflects variability in the price and quantity ratios as well as the strength of the correlation between the price and quantity ratios over time or across countries.[17] Hill (1999) provides a formal measure of reliability based on this spread and discusses various properties of this measure. The distance between two countries j and k (d_{jk}) is measured for all j and k by

$$d_{jk} = \left| \ln\left(\frac{L_{jk}}{P_{jk}} \right) \right| \qquad (4.13)$$

where L_{jk} and P_{jk} respectively refer to Laspeyres and Paasche index numbers. We note here that the distance measure in (4.13) is the same whether the price index numbers or quantity index numbers are used. Since a large value of d_{jk} represents a larger spread between the Laspeyres and Paasche indices, we postulate that the weights needed for our weighted EKS method are inversely proportional to the distance function. Thus, for all j and k $(j \neq k)$ the weights are defined as:

$$w_{jk} = \frac{1}{d_{jk}}$$

---

[17] See Dikhanov (1994) for a discussion of the Paasche-Laspeyres spread as a measure of reliability. Van Ark et al. (1999) provide a decomposition of the spread into the different components along these lines for many binary ICOP comparisons.

If only one item was matched, the weight is set at zero. The weights matrix can be compiled using the basic price and quantity/expenditure data available for the purpose of compiling PPPs.

(ii) Weights based on economic distance

Here we consider economic distance, as measured by the relative levels of real per capita income, as a measure of reliability of the direct comparison between a pair of countries.

$$d_{jk} = \left| \ln(Y_j) - \ln(Y_k) \right| \tag{4.14}$$

where Y represents the real per capita income of a given country.[18] In this case, the matrix of weights is defined with a typical element defined as:

$$w_{jk} = 1/d_{jk}$$

This specification implies that, if two countries are at a similar stage of development, price structures between such countries are likely to be similar, thus resulting in a more reliable comparison. Comparisons between countries at a comparable stage of development are assigned higher weights in the weighted EKS procedure described above. This distance function was used in Selvanathan and Rao (1992) in generating generalised Tornqvist index numbers.

(iii) Similarity in price structures

The preceding specifications of the weights and distances are largely driven by the fact that binary comparisons between countries which are dissimilar (in terms of price and/or quantity structures) are intrinsically less reliable, and, therefore, less emphasis needs to be placed on the preservation of such binary comparisons. If capturing similarity in price structure is the main purpose, it is possible to obtain measures of price similarity and use them directly in the computation of generalised EKS Indices.

---

[18] It is obvious that there is a degree of circularity in the use of real per capita income which requires the knowledge of PPPs, which are to be estimated using the generalised EKS method. It is possible to use a two-step or iterative procedure instead of a more involved maximum likelihood procedure which can simultaneously estimate all the parameters (including the distance function) involved.

We use two similarity indexes drawn from the past literature.[19] If s_{jk} is a measure of price similarity between two countries j and k, then we can assign w_{jk} that is proportional to the similarity index, which implies that higher the value of s_{jk} implies more the weight assigned to the particular comparison within the generalised EKS framework. The following similarity indices are used in the empirical illustration.

Similarity index 1:

$$s_{jk} = \frac{\sum_{i=1}^{n} W_i \, p_{ij} \, p_{ik}}{\sqrt{\sum_{i=1}^{N} W_i \, p_{ij}^2 \, \sum_{i=1}^{N} W_i \, p_{ik}^2}} \tag{4.15}$$

where p_{ij} and p_{ik} respectively denote prices of i–th commodity in countries j and k; and W_i is the weight attached to i–th commodity. This index is drawn from Kravis et al. (1982). Kravis et al. suggest the use of a global expenditure share of i–th commodity (such a definition might require a suitable measure of global expenditure and the share of the commodity under consideration).

Similarity index 2:

$$s_{jk}(k) = \frac{\sum_{i=1}^{N} (p_{ij}q_{ik})(p_{ik}q_{ik})}{\sqrt{\sum_{i=1}^{m} (p_{ij}q_{ik})^2 \, \sum_{i=1}^{m} (p_{ik}q_{ik})^2}} \quad \text{and} \quad s_{jk}(j) = \frac{\sum_{i=1}^{m} (p_{ij}q_{ij})(p_{ik}q_{ij})}{\sqrt{\sum_{i=1}^{m} (p_{ij}q_{ij})^2 \, \sum_{i=1}^{m} (p_{ik}q_{ij})^2}} \tag{4.16}$$

These similarity indices, proposed in van Ark et al. (1999), depend upon the quantities in countries j and k. In this study, we propose to use the geometric average of $s_{jk}(j)$ and $s_{jk}(k)$ in (4.16) to define the weights required in the generalised EKS method.

Given the nature of the generalisations involved, it is possible to arrive at a number of alternative specifications for the matrix of weights. Only a few options are canvassed in this chapter. Since the generalisations suggested here are based on a regression framework, it would be possible to undertake

---

[19] There are several similarity indices proposed by Diewert (this volume) but empirical implementation of the new indices will be considered in future research. However the actual implementation would be very similar to what is discussed and illustrated in this chapter.

specification testing to choose between alternative specifications for the weighting matrices.

4.3.6 Numerical Illustration

A number of these alternative specifications are applied to the 1993 OECD results at the basic heading level. The illustration is restricted to the goods and services under the private consumption expenditure aggregate. All the prices are in the form of PPPs for the basic headings expressed using the US dollar as the numeraire currency. National expenditures for different basic headings are used in deriving implicit quantities. PPPs for the private consumption expenditure, derived using Fisher, standard EKS, and generalised EKS indices based on Hill's distance function, economic distance, and the two similarity indices discussed in equations (4.15) and (4.16), are presented in Table 4.1.

Table 4.1 shows PPPs with the USA as the base country. The Fisher and EKS parities are shown in the last columns. Results reported in the first four columns here are based on several variants of the EKS. Differences between the EKS and the generalised EKS, relative to Fisher binaries, are not as pronounced as expected.[20] This may be due to the fact that the empirical application involves only OECD countries. Results in the table demonstrate the feasibility of generalising the EKS method accounting for differing levels of reliability of the binary comparisons.

4.4 GENERALISED COUNTRY–PRODUCT–DUMMY (CPD) METHOD

The CPD method represents a simple regression approach to explain levels of prices of commodities in different countries. The method was originally proposed by Summers (1973) as a simple econometric tool to fill gaps in price data collected in early phases of the ICP conducted by Kravis and his associates at the University of Pennsylvania. The method was considered suitable for the purpose of aggregation below the basic heading level and it was considered as a major alternative to the EKS method for aggregation of price data at the item level. In the recently completed 2005 ICP, the CPD

---

[20] Similar observations were made by Rao and Timmer (2003) and Hill and Timmer (2006) where the generalised EKS method was used with different measures of reliability in deriving PPPs for manufacturing sector comparisons. While there is no a priori reason why the generalised EKS indices should be so close to the unweighted EKS indices this is an aspect that requires further research.

method was recommended by the Technical Advisory Group[21] for the ICP as the best suited method for aggregation at this level. At the same time, in recent years the scope of the CPD method has been enhanced considerably due to recent work on a generalised CPD method where weights are used in conjunction with the basic CPD regression model. The weighted CPD has been shown to generate various multilateral systems including: the Rao (1990) system for multilateral comparisons (Rao, 2005); several formulae including Tornqvist and the Geary–Khamis method for the case of two countries (Diewert, 2005); and the Iklé and the multilateral Geary–Khamis

Table 4.1   Purchasing power parities, OECD, 1993 (US dollar = numeraire) – generalised EKS method with alternative weights

| Country | Hill (1999) | Real Income Selvanathan and Rao (1992) | Price Similarity | | | |
			Van Ark et al. (1999)	KHS (1982)	Fisher	EKS
GER	2.16	2.12	2.12	2.13	2.04	2.14
FRA	6.96	6.81	6.86	6.90	6.63	6.90
ITA	1576.31	1538.77	1554.91	1563.42	1593.43	1564.76
NLD	2.20	2.16	2.18	2.19	2.08	2.19
BEL	40.37	39.42	39.64	39.89	38.83	39.90
LUX	39.33	37.86	37.78	38.04	38.28	38.05
UK	0.68	0.66	0.67	0.67	0.70	0.67
IRE	0.70	0.69	0.69	0.69	0.70	0.69
DNK	9.67	9.39	9.55	9.61	9.72	9.61
GRC	201.95	196.61	198.79	199.96	203.45	200.07
SPA	126.45	123.34	124.58	125.38	130.90	125.41
PRT	131.99	128.06	130.24	131.04	133.82	131.10
AUT	14.60	14.26	14.35	14.43	14.90	14.44
SUI	2.26	2.20	2.24	2.25	2.18	2.25
SWE	10.68	10.40	10.53	10.59	10.87	10.60
FIN	6.98	6.78	6.88	6.92	7.06	6.9
ICE	93.76	91.33	92.51	93.02	95.09	93.12
NOR	9.94	9.71	9.76	9.83	9.68	9.83
TUR	6735.85	6579.64	6636.33	6672.74	6851.69	6680.63
AUS	1.42	1.38	1.39	1.41	1.41	1.40
NZL	1.61	1.57	1.58	1.60	1.62	1.59
JAP	202.65	196.62	200.14	201.14	185.18	201.49
CAN	1.30	1.29	1.29	1.30	1.28	1.30
USA	1.00	1.00	1.00	1.00	1.00	1.00

---

[21] For more details on the composition of the group and its recommendations, see the ICP website at the World Bank: www.worldbank.org/data/icp.

methods (Hajarghasht and Rao, 2008). Rao (2004) provides a comprehensive overview of the CPD methods and its applications. The main objective of this section is to provide an overview of some of the main features of the weighted CPD method.

4.4.1 CPD Method – the Basic Model

The method postulates that the observed price of a commodity, say i-th commodity in j-th country, p_{ij}, is the product of three components: the purchasing power parity or the general price level in a country relative to other countries (denoted by PPP_j); the price level of the i-th commodity relative to other commodities (denoted by P_i) and a random disturbance term v_{ij}. This basic premise is often referred to as the *law of one* price. The basic model underlying the CPD method can be stated as:

$$p_{ij} = PPP_j \, P_i \cdot v_{ij}$$

It can be expressed in a logarithmic form as:

$$\ln p_{ij} = \ln PPP_j + \ln P_i + \ln v_{ij}$$
$$= \pi_j + \eta_i + u_{ij} \tag{4.17}$$

The disturbance term u_{ij} is assumed to have zero mean and constant variance, σ^2.

In order to estimate π_j $(j=1,...M)$ and η_i $(i=1,...N)$ the model can be written in the form of a standard regression model.

$$\ln p_{ij} = \pi_1 D_1 + \pi_2 D_2 + ... + \pi_M D_M + \eta_1 D_1^* + \eta_2 D_2^* + ... + \eta_N D_N^* + u_{ij} \tag{4.18}$$

where D_j's and D_i^*'s are respectively country and commodity dummy variables with the property that

$D_j =$ 1   if price observation p_{ij} belongs to country j
      0   otherwise
and

$D_i^* =$ 1   if price observation p_{ij} refers to i-th commodity
      0   otherwise.

The model derives its title, CPD model, from equation (4.18) where all the independent variables are essentially dummy variables representing either countries or commodities.

It is possible to estimate the parameters of the model using ordinary least squares estimation (LS) procedure. Under the assumption of normality of the disturbances, u_{ij}, the resulting estimator is also the maximum likelihood (ML) estimator. We note here that the LS and ML methods accord equal weight to each of the price observations. Thus it may be possible to considered the application of weighted LS or ML procedures. This aspect is pursued later in this section.

From the model, (4.18), it is obvious that irrespective how big the data set we have, it is impossible to estimate all the parameters due to the presence of perfect multicollinearity. So it is customary to estimate the parameters of the model after imposing a linear restriction. The simplest approach is to set one of the parameters to zero. In our application of the CPD method we set $\pi_1 = 0$, or equivalently $PPP_1 = 1$. Since country 1 in our list is the United States, all the PPPs and commodity specific effects (η_i) are all estimated using US dollar as the numeraire currency.

4.4.2   CPD Method for Aggregation below the Basic Heading Level

The CPD method, since the time it was first proposed by Summers (1973), has long been considered as a systematic method of filling gaps in the price tableau prior to the computation of PPPs at the basic heading level. However, the CPD method can be used directly as a method of aggregation below the basic heading level.

In the first instance, if the price tableau is complete then PPPs from the CPD method are equal to the geometric average of price relatives (see Ferrari et al., 1996; Rao, 2004 for a proof of this results), which, incidentally, is the EKS index stated in equation (4.8). Thus the EKS and CPD methods for aggregation below the basic heading level provide the same PPPs, and, therefore, there is no real need for a choice between the two methods.

When the price tableau is incomplete, then the CPD method produces a transitive set of PPPs taking into account all the price information[22] in a single step. In this case, the EKS and CPD methods are likely to produce different results but the CPD method is then preferable as it makes use of all the available price information.

CPD model with information on representativeness
In the ICP work where countries set out to price a long list of items prepared by the ICP team, it is generally found that some items priced in a country

---

[22] An exception to this result is the case where price data for certain commodities are available in only one country (see Ferrari et al., 1996).

may not be representative.[23] Modified EKS method described in equation (4.10) and its variant are used currently in the OECD–Eurostat comparisons (Roberts, this volume). Cuthbert and Cuthbert (1989) made an initial attempt to extend the standard model to incorporate any bias induced by price information pertaining to commodities that are not characteristic or not representative in a given country. For this purpose an additional dummy variable, R, is introduced. This is defined as:

$R = 1$ if the price observation, p_{ij}, refers to an item that is *not representative*
  0 if the price observation refers to a *representative item.*

The CPD model is modified to include R as an additional explanatory variable. The resulting model, referred to as the CPRD model, is given by:

$$\ln p_{ij} = \sum_{j=1}^{M} \pi_j D_j + \sum_{i=1}^{N} \eta_i D_i^* + \delta R + u_{ij} \qquad (4.19)$$

This model can be estimated using ordinary least squares estimation procedure. The ICP Handbook (World Bank, 2006) provides a detailed discussion of the properties of the CPRD model and it shows that the CPRD model offers robust results compared to the simple EKS method and its variants in the presence of data on representativeness of items priced in different countries.

Given the nature of the specification of the regression model underlying the CPD method, until recently the model has not been fully investigated in the international comparison context. It is only since 1995 there has been considerable attention on this method and in the following discussion we summarise some of the recent developments which serve to demonstrate that the CPD method can be generalised to provide a framework for computing PPPs and international prices for aggregation above the basic heading level.

4.4.3 Generalised CPD method for Aggregation above the Basic Heading Level

Before we proceed, we note that the distinguishing feature of aggregation above the basic heading level is the availability of information on expenditures and expenditure weights for each of the items in different countries. As noted earlier, the prices at the basic heading are essentially PPPs derived after aggregating price data below the basic heading level and

---

[23] See Roberts (this volume) for a detailed discussion of *representativity* and *comparability* which are competing concerns when item lists are prepared.

quantities are indirectly defined using the observed expenditure for each basic heading which is expressed in respective national currency units.

Weighted CPD model

Rao (2005)[24] considered a generalisation of the CPD method by making use of the quantity and value data directly into the CPD method. The basic idea behind this generalisation comes from the fact that the standard CPD regression model attempts to track the (logarithm) of the observed prices using an unweighted residual sum of squares. However in the spirit of the standard index number approach, a more appropriate procedure would be to find estimates of the parameters that are likely to track the more important commodities more closely. This is achieved by minimising a weighted residual sum of squares, with each observation weighted according to the expenditure share of the commodity in a given country. Thus the generalised CPD method suggests minimisation of:

$$\sum_{j=1}^{M}\sum_{i=1}^{N} w_{ij}\left[\ln p_{ij} - \sum_{j=1}^{M}\pi_j D_j - \sum_{i=1}^{N}\eta_i D_i^*\right]^2 \qquad (4.20)$$

with respect to the unknown parameters π_j and η_i. The minimisation here is conducted after weighting each observation according to its value share. This is equivalent to the application of ordinary least squares after transforming the equation to yield

$$\sqrt{w_{ij}}\ln p_{ij} = \pi_1\sqrt{w_{ij}}D_1 + \pi_2\sqrt{w_{ij}}D_2 + ... + \pi_M\sqrt{w_{ij}}D_M + \eta_1\sqrt{w_{ij}}D_1^* + ... + \eta_N\sqrt{w_{ij}}D_N^* + v_{ij}$$

$$(4.21)$$

where $w_{ij} = \dfrac{p_{ij}q_{ij}}{\sum\limits_{i=1}^{N} p_{ij}q_{ij}}$ is the value share of i-th commodity in j-th country.[25]

The approach underlying equation (4.21) is similar to the M–estimator approach followed in standard econometrics where a weighted sum of squares of residuals is minimised irrespective of the covariance matrix of the disturbances.

---

[24] The generalisation discussed here was originally proposed by Rao (1996) and was eventually published in Rao (2005).

[25] The approach advocated here is in contrast the stochastic approach to index number described in Clemments and Izan (1981, 1987), Selvanathan (1989) and Selvanathan and Rao (1992) where variance of the disturbance term in (4.18) is considered to be inversely proportional to the expenditure share of the commodity.

Equivalence of Generalised CPD and Rao–System for International Comparisons

Though the CPD method provides estimates of PPPs and international prices, P_is, this method has never been really considered as a viable alternative to the Geary–Khamis system or as a system for aggregation above the basic heading level. This is partly due to the fact that the CPD method has always been considered in its unweighted formulation.

Rao (2005) has shown that the PPPs and international prices resulting from the application of least squares to the weighted model (4.21) are identical to those resulting from the Rao (1990) method for international comparisons. The Rao–system (1990) is a variant of the Geary–Khamis system based on the use of log–linear equations and weights based on expenditure shares. The Rao–system consistss of $(M+N)$ log–linear equations involving M purchasing power parities PPP_j $(j = 1,...,M)$ and N international prices P_i $(i = 1,...,N)$. These are:

$$PPP_j = \prod_{i=1}^{N}\left(\frac{p_{ij}}{P_i}\right)^{w_{ij}} \quad \text{and} \quad P_i = \prod_{j=1}^{M}\left(\frac{p_{ij}}{PPP_j}\right)^{\overset{*}{w_{ij}}} \tag{4.22}$$

where w_{ij} is the value share of i–th commodity and

$$\overset{*}{w_{ij}} = w_{ij}\Big/\sum_{j=1}^{M} w_{ij}$$

is the share of value share of j–th country with respect to i–th commodity. Rao (1990) provides a proof of the existence and uniqueness (up to a factor of proportionality) of the solution for the unknown parities and international prices.

Among other characteristics of the Rao–system, the weighting system employed in the Rao–system is invariant to the size of the country, unlike the Geary–Khamis system, since it uses essentially value shares as a basis for weighting. Therefore international comparisons resulting from this method are less likely to be subject to the Gerschenkron effect.[26]

Equivalence of the Rao–system (see Rao, 2005) and the generalised CPD method can be established using the equivalence of the normal equations from least squares method applied to (4.21) and equations in (4.22) that define the Rao–system. This equivalence supports possible use of the CPD method, and its generalisations, for purposes of aggregation both below and

---

[26] See Dikhanov (1994) for a discussion of the Gerschenkron effect and its magnitude for different index number systems including the GK and the Rao–system.

above the basic heading level. In contrast to the Geary–Khamis method, the generalised CPD and the Rao methods are closer to Tornqvist indices due to the use of geometric averaging and value–share information.[27] Once the additive consistency condition is relaxed, the case for using generalised CPD method becomes stronger. The generalised CPD method also makes it feasible to compute standard errors associated with the PPPs resulting from the Rao–system. Table 4.2 shows the PPPs from weighted and unweighted CPD methods and contrasts them with the Fisher and EKS PPPs. All the PPPs are computed using the 1993 OECD data at the basic heading level.

Table 4.2   Purchasing power parities for OECD countries, 1993 (US dollar = numeraire) – weighted CPD method

Country	Fisher	EKS	CPD Unweighted	Weighted
GER	2.05	2.14	2.14	2.03
FRA	6.63	6.90	7.25	6.55
ITA	1593.43	1564.76	1724.86	1504.04
NLD	2.08	2.19	2.17	2.06
BEL	38.83	39.90	40.94	37.89
LUX	38.28	38.05	40.78	35.82
UK	0.70	0.67	0.68	0.64
IRE	0.70	0.69	0.75	0.67
DNK	9.72	9.62	9.78	9.13
GRC	203.45	200.07	221.65	188.47
SPA	130.90	125.41	136.56	118.54
PRT	133.82	131.10	152.64	129.03
AUT	14.90	14.44	15.76	13.73
SUI	2.18	2.25	2.31	2.18
SWE	10.87	10.60	10.99	10.08
FIN	7.06	6.93	7.43	6.60
ICE	95.09	93.12	100.33	89.54
NOR	9.68	9.83	10.47	9.23
TUR	6851.69	6680.63	7578.89	6321.67
AUS	1.41	1.40	1.44	1.33
NZL	1.62	1.59	1.66	1.53
JAP	185.18	201.49	220.65	187.43
CAN	1.28	1.30	1.32	1.23
USA	1.00	1.00	1.00	1.00

---

[27] It is well known that the Tornqvist index is an exact and superlative index number (Diewert, 1978) for binary comparisons and the binary version of the Rao-system can be shown to be pseudo-superlative index number. Further numerical values of the Rao-binary system are usually close to the Tornqvist and Fisher binary indices.

Results in Table 4.2 show clear differences between PPPs from weighted and unweighted CPD methods. The weighted CPD methods are comparable to the EKS and Fisher PPPs. Results from the weighted CPD appear to be generally lower than the corresponding EKS and Fisher PPPs.

Since the CPD and its generalisations are rooted in standard regression framework, it is possible to extend the CPD model in a number of directions designed to handle various measurement issues. A few of these extensions are briefly discussed below.

4.4.4 Generalised CPD under Different Distributional Assumptions

In this section we briefly discuss the recent work by Hajarghasht and Rao (2008) where it is shown that a range of multilateral methods can be derived using the CPD model and the application of the weighted likelihood methods under different distributional assumptions.

We recall the basic CPD model in equation (4.17):

$$p_{ij} = PPP_j \cdot P_i \cdot v_{ij}$$

or,

$$\ln p_{ij} = \ln PPP_j + \ln P_i + \ln v_{ij} = \pi_j + \eta_i + u_{ij}$$

where v_{ij} *and* u_{ij} are random disturbance terms. Hajarghasht and Rao (2008) have established the following results under different distributional specifications for v_{ij} in the multiplicative form of the CPD model.

Lognormal distribution
If the disturbances, v_{ij}, are lognormally distributed or u_{ij} is normally distributed with mean equal to 0 and variance equal to σ^2, then the weighted maximum likelihood estimator, with expenditure share weights, of the unknown parameters of π_j and η_i are identical to those obtained using the Rao–system. This result easily follows from the fact that the weighted least squares estimator for the CPD model is the same as the weighted maximum likelihood estimator when the disturbances are lognormally distributed.

Inverse gamma distribution
If the disturbances in the CPD model follow a gamma distribution then we have, following Hajarghasht and Rao (2008),

$$\frac{1}{v_{ij}} = \frac{P_i PPP_j}{p_{ij}} \sim gamma(r, r)$$

The choice of the same parameter r for the two parameters of the gamma distribution ensures that the expected value of the disturbance term is equal to 1.[28]

The result established by Hajarghasht and Rao (2008) shows that under the assumption of inverse gamma distribution for the disturbances the weighted least squares estimator of π_j and η_i result in *PPPs* and P_is that are identical to those derived from the Iklé system, defined as:

$$\frac{1}{PPP_j} = \sum_{i=1}^{N}\left(\frac{p_i}{P_{ij}}w_{ij}\right) \text{ for } j=1,2,\ldots M \text{ and } \frac{1}{P_i} = \sum_{j=1}^{M}\left(\frac{PPP_j}{P_{ij}}w_{ij}^{*}\right) \text{ for } i=1,2,\ldots N$$

Dikhanov (1994) has a detailed exposition of the Iklé system and its properties. An important implication of this result is that it would be possible to derive the standard errors associated with PPPs from the Iklé system using the generalised CPD approach when the disturbances follow an inverse gamma distribution.[29]

If the disturbances of the CPD model follow a gamma distribution, then the weighted maximum likelihood estimators of the parameters π_j and η_i and the resulting *PPPs* and P_is would be identical to those derived using a multilateral system similar to the Rao–system defined using arithmetic averages in the place of geometric averages.

The CPD model and the Geary–Khamis method
Lastly, we refer to the result which establishes a link between the CPD model and the Geary–Khamis method discussed in Hajarghasht and Rao (2008). Their result establishes that the GK *PPPs* and *Ps* are the method of moments estimators of the parameters in the CPD model (4.18) for a particular selection of moment conditions.[30] This result establishes for the first time that a stochastic approach can be adopted for the GK system with the possibility of deriving standard errors for the GK system.

4.4.5   CPD and the Tornqvist Index Numbers

The CPD technique can be used in generating Tornqvist index numbers for binary comparisons, thus providing multilateral generalisations that are

---

[28] For further details on the lognormal, gamma and inverse-gamma distributions used here, the reader is referred to Johnson et al. (1994).

[29] Hajarghasht and Rao (2008) also provide an empirical illustration of the results discussed here.

[30] A full description of this result cannot be presented here without adding significantly to the length of the chapter. So the reader is referred to Hajarghasht and Rao (2008) for further details.

identical to those proposed in Caves et al. (1982). Suppose we start with the CPD specification in (4.17). Suppose we are interested in a binary comparison between two countries j and k. The CPD model in (4.17) then yields:

$$\ln p_{ij} = \pi_j + \eta_i + u_{ij}$$

$$\ln p_{ik} = \pi_k + \eta_i + u_{ik}$$

If we are only interested in price level comparisons involving π_j and π_k, then by taking the difference of these equations, we have

$$\ln p_{ik} - \ln p_{ij} = \pi_k - \pi_j + v_{ijk} \qquad (4.23)$$

Given price data, equation (4.23) can be used in estimating $(\pi_k - \pi_j)$. If a weighted least squares approach is used in estimating $(\pi_k - \pi_j)$, with weights that are averages of expenditure shares in k and j, the resulting estimator of $(\pi_k - \pi_j)$ equals the Tornqvist index. If equation (4.23) is applied to data involving all pairs of countries $(j,k = 1,2,...M)$ then the weighted least squares estimates coincide with the CCD indices proposed in Caves et al. (1982). Proof of this result can be found in Selvanathan and Rao (1992).

4.4.6 Quality Adjustments and the Generalised CPD Method

The CPD model is often referred to as a hedonic model where the price determining characters are restricted to just the country in which the commodity is priced and the commodity itself. Naturally, the CPD model can be extended to include other characteristics including the outlet from which the item is priced. If $Z_1, Z_2, ..., Z_Q$ represent a set of quality characteristics that are deemed to be relevant in a particular empirical problem,[31] and if these quality characteristics are noted for each item across all the countries, then the appropriate CPD model with quality adjustments would be:

$$\ln p_{ij} = \sum_{j=1}^{M} \pi_j D_j + \sum_{i=1}^{N} \eta_i D_i^* + \sum_{q=1}^{Q} \theta_q Z_{qij} + u_{ij} \qquad (4.24)$$

The model in (4.24) provides estimates of π_js (and, therefore, PPP_js) after making adjustments for differences in quality of the products that are priced.

---

[31] In the context of making adjustments for quality differences in the process of constructing price index numbers, it is more appropriate to use CPD method for aggregation below the basic heading level.

The use of a CPD model incorporating quality adjustments was suggested in Kokoski et al. (1999) in the context of inter–area price comparisons, and Carter-Hill et al. (1997) where a model similar to (4.24) was used in examining housing prices over time. Actual empirical application of model (4.24) has significant data requirements in the form of observations on quality characteristics. Models similar to (4.24) are also canvassed in Tripplet (2000).

4.4.7   Generalised CPD Method Accounting for Spatial Autocorrelation in Price Structures

The CPD model and its generalisations described in equations (4.18) and (4.19) assume that price observations from different countries are independently distributed. Therefore, in the basic CPD model, the disturbances are assumed to have a mean equal to zero and have the same variance and are not autocorrelated. Under these assumptions least squares estimates of the parameters are the best linear unbiased estimators. Generally it is possible to test and adjust for the presence of heteroscedastic disturbances. In the previous sub–sections we considered several distributional assumptions, lognormal, gamma and inverse gamma distributions, and derived a link between the CPD method and methods like the Iklé and the GK methods.

In the context of the CPD model, the effect of the possible presence of autocorrelation among disturbances across countries for a specific commodity, the presence of spatial autocorrelation, has not been investigated. Aten (1996) has demonstrated the existence of spatial autocorrelation and analysed the presence of patterns in relative price structures across geographical regions. Presence of spatially autocorrelated disturbances implies that the use of ordinary least squares no longer provides the most efficient estimates of the parameters involved.

In this section we briefly touch upon some of the main features of the generalised CPD model with spatially autocorrelated disturbances. Before embarking on the testing and specification issues, it is useful to find an interpretation of the disturbances in the CPD model.

From the basic CPD model in (4.17), we have:

$$u_{ij} = \ln p_{ij} - \pi_j - \eta_i = \ln\left(\frac{p_{ij}}{PPP_j} / P_i\right) \qquad (4.25)$$

From equation (4.25) it is evident that the disturbance term for i–th commodity in j–th country is the logarithm of domestic price of i–th commodity, p_{ij}, converted to a common currency unit using PPP_j, expressed relative to the international price of i–th commodity. Thus the disturbance term provides a measure of price levels relative to international average prices, for each commodity in each country.

We use a simple structure for the spatial autocorrelation. For a given weights matrix, $\mathbf{W}$, we postulate that disturbances for a given commodity, i, represented by the vector $\mathbf{u_i}$ follow a first order autoregressive scheme given by:

$$\mathbf{u_i} = \rho_i \mathbf{W} \mathbf{u_i} + \mathbf{v_i} \quad \text{with} \quad |\rho_i| \leq 1$$

where $\mathbf{v_i}$ is a vector of random disturbances which are independently and identically distributed. The parameter, ρ_i, is the autocorrelation coefficient.

Given the nature and scope of the present chapter, no attempt is made here to provide details of the testing procedures and econometric methods of estimation. However some selected empirical results are provided to stimulate further interest in this topic.

The empirical results presented make use of the 1985 global comparison results from the ICP for 56 countries with eight aggregated expenditure categories. The presence of spatial autocorrelation is likely to be more pronounced when countries from different continents and at different levels of development are included. Data for the study is drawn from United Nations (1994).

In order to model spatial autocorrelation, it is necessary to specify a matrix of spatial weights, $\mathbf{W}$, where a typical element w_{jk} is a measure of spatial proximity of countries j and k. Spatial proximity does not necessarily imply physical distance, it could represent economic distance as measured by the level of trade between the two countries. However, in the following empirical illustration we simply use the physical distance between countries, as measured by the distance between capital cities, is used.[32]

Once the $\mathbf{W}$ matrix is specified, then ordinary least squares residuals are used in calculating a statistic, Moran's I–statistic, to test the presence of spatial autocorrelation. The test is conducted for different commodity groups.

Results in Table 4.3 indicate the presence of significant spatial autocorrelation for all the commodity groups, with the exception of transport.

---

[32] The author is grateful to Bettina Aten for providing data on $\mathbf{W}$ matrices. Moran's I-statistic is asymptotically normally distributed with a non-zero mean.

Table 4.3   Moran's I–statistic test for the presence of spatial autocorrelation

Commodity	I–statistic	Z–statistic (for significance testing)
1. Food	0.50009	3.57*
2. Clothing	0.47059	3.39*
3. Rent	0.32952	2.40*
4. Furniture	0.53808	3.88*
5. Medical	0.39672	2.93*
6. Transport	0.07829	0.67
7. Education	0.57515	4.09*
8. Others	0.55644	3.99*

Note: * indicates significance at 5% level.

The next step in the process of obtaining efficient estimates of the PPPs is the estimation of spatial autocorrelation coefficients for each of the commodity groups. These are presented in Table 4.4. The estimated correlation coefficients are all positive and the coefficient is very low for transport, which is consistent with results in Table 4.3.

Table 4.4   Spatial autocorrelation coefficients (ρ_i) for aggregated commodity groups

Commodity	Estimated value of ρ
1. Food	0.6607
2. Clothing	0.5199
3. Rent	0.7423
4. Furniture	0.5324
5. Medical	0.4069
6. Transport	0.1998
7. Education	0.5206
8. Others	0.4814

In Table 4.5, we present the purchasing power parities computed using the weighted CPD method (second column) and the maximum likelihood estimates (column 3) where spatial autocorrelation is explicitly accounted for.

*Table 4.5   Purchasing power parities using weighted CPD method
(base country: United States)*

Country	Weighted CPD Method	
	No autocorrelation	**With spatial auto correlation**
Germany	2.523	2.4973
France	7.179	6.8801
Italy	1254.807	1153.5172
Netherlands	2.470	2.2877
Belgium	44.512	36.5288
Luxembourg	42.619	39.4496
UK	0.559	0.4912
Ireland	0.692	0.5846
Denmark	10.055	9.1397
Greece	71.638	61.7066
Spain	88.771	77.1777
Portugal	69.140	55.6519
Austria	16.774	14.5587
Finland	6.185	5.3332
Norway	8.981	9.0290
Sweden	8.241	9.3838
Australia	1.211	1.0848
New Zealand	1.260	1.1068
Japan	211.178	185.8307
Canada	1.214	1.2818
USA	1.000	1.0000
Turkey	159.097	157.6794
Hong Kong	4.301	4.2127
Korea	430.709	420.7753
Thailand	7.238	6.6428
India	4.077	3.2916
Iran	62.831	61.2501
Sri Lanka	6.236	5.0552
Pakistan	3.866	3.6958
Philippines	5.878	5.7402
Botswana	2.142	0.4946
Egypt	0.234	0.2130
Ethiopia	0.687	0.7281
Kenya	4.037	3.8456
Malawi	0.376	0.3042
Mauritius	2.410	1.9289
Nigeria	0.766	0.6978
Sierra Leone	1.885	1.8109
Swaziland	0.516	0.4905
Tanzania	13.878	12.9100

Continued

Table 4.5   Purchasing power parities using weighted CPD method
(base country: United States) – continued

Country	Weighted CPD Method	
	No autocorrelation	With spatial auto correlation
Zambia	2.278	0.8820
Zimbabwe	0.439	0.4237
Benin	85.718	66.7808
Cameroon	127.908	111.0988
Congo	160.106	144.7286
Ivory Coast	133.409	126.4336
Madagascar	221.650	239.0097
Mali	155.009	161.1177
Morocco	2.015	1.9055
Rwanda	33.283	30.8601
Senegal	121.524	116.0764
Tunisia	28.135	0.2043
Poland	71.234	66.5788
Hungary	15.768	13.4411
Yugoslavia	93.237	93.7417
Bangladesh	6.038	5.9270

Results in Table 4.5 clearly demonstrate the feasibility of using weighted CPD method for international comparisons. The last column shows PPPs when the presence of spatial autocorrelation is accounted for. PPPs in the last column differ significantly from the standard weighted CPD results which is generally an indication that spatial autocorrelation in the disturbances is accounting for misspecification in the CPD model. There was a significant reduction in the standard errors (not reported here) associated with these estimates.

On the basis of these results it appears that significant differences in PPPs can result when the disturbances are spatially autocorrelated. It would be useful to examine further and check if the differences represent the effects of misspecification bias due to omission of some price determining characteristics like the outlet effect and systematic quality differences.

4.5 CONCLUSIONS

The chapter examined in detail the EKS and CPD methods for aggregation in the context of international comparisons, and discussed a number of generalisations of these methods that could enhance their applicability. A salient feature of the results presented here is that there is scope to use a stochastic approach to the compilation of PPPs and improve upon the standard EKS and CPD based PPPs. The chapter presented a general econometric approach to the construction of EKS indices and then used this approach to extend the EKS method to assign different weights to different binary comparisons reflecting their reliability. The procedure outlined can be applied for levels below and above the basic heading level. The chapter also examined the CPD method in considerable detail. Historically, the CPD method has always been considered as an aggregation method for the compilation of PPPs below the basic heading level. Based on recent results relating to the CPD method, the present chapter argues that the generalised version of the CPD method can be used to generate a range of commonly used multilateral methods including the Geary–Khamis, Iklé and the Rao methods. We have also shown that the CPD method is versatile in handling a range of data related issues. The fact that the CPD method uses a stochastic specification makes it possible to extend the model to incorporate quality factors and additional information based on the presence of correlation between relative price levels across countries. From the results presented in the chapter, it is clear that the CPD method and its variants are likely to play an important role in international comparisons of prices and real incomes in the future.

REFERENCES

ADB (2007), *Purchasing Power Parities and Real Expenditures*, Asian Development Bank, Manila.

Ark, van B., E.J. Monnikhof and M.P. Timmer (1999), 'Prices, Quantities and Productivity in Industry: a Study of Transition Economies in a Comparative Perspective', in *International and Interarea Comparisons of Income, Output and Prices*, in A. Heston and R.E. Lipsey (eds), *Studies in Income and Wealth*, **61**, Chicago and London: University of Chicago Press.

Aten, B (1996), 'A Mapping of International Prices', *Review of Income and Wealth*.

Aten, B and A.H. Heston (this volume), 'Chaining Methods for International Real Product and Purchasing Power Comparisons: Issues and Alternatives'.

Balk, B.M. (1996), 'A Comparison of Ten Methods for Multilateral International Price and Volume Comparison', *Journal of Official Statistics*, **12**, 199–222.

Balk, B.M. (this volume), 'Aggregation Methods in International Comparisons: an Evaluation'.

Bortkiewicz, L. von (1924), 'Zweck und Struktur einer Preisindexzahl', *Nordisk Statistik Tidskrift*, **3**.

Carter-Hill, R., J.R. Knight and C.F. Sirmans (1997), 'Estimating Capital Asset Price Indexes', *Review of Economics and Statistics*, **79**, 226–233.

Caves, D.W., L.R. Christensen and W.E. Diewert (1982), 'Multilateral Comparisons of Output, Input and Productivity Using Superlative Index Numbers', *Economic Journal*, **92**, 73–86.

Clements, K.W. and H.Y. Izan (1981), 'A Note on Estimating Divisia Index Numbers', *International Economic Review*, **22**, 745–47.

Clements, K.W. and H.Y. Izan (1987), 'The Measurement of Inflation: a Stochastic Approach', *Journal of Business and Economic Statistics*, **5**, 339–350.

Cuthbert, J.R. and M. Cuthbert (1989), *On Aggregation Methods for Purchasing Power Parities, Working Paper No. 56*, OECD Department of Economics and Statistics, Paris.

Diewert, W.E. (1978), 'Superlative Index Numbers and Consistency in Aggregation', *Econometrica* **46**, 883–900; reprinted as pp. 253–273 in W.E. Diewert and A.O. Nakamura (eds.) (1993) *Essays in Index Number Theory, Volume 1*, Amsterdam: North-Holland.

Diewert, W.E. (1999), 'Axiomatic and Economic Approaches to International Comparisons', in A. Heston and R.E. Lipsey (eds) *International and Interarea Comparisons of Income, Output and Prices, Studies in Income and Wealth*, **61**, Chicago and London: University of Chicago Press.

Diewert, W.E. (2004), 'On the Stochastic Approach to Linking Regions in the ICP', Paper prepared for the DECDG of the World Bank, Washington DC.

Diewert , W.E. (2005), 'Weighted Country Product Dummy Variable Regressions and Index Number Formulae', *Review of Income and Wealth*, **51**, 561–570

Diewert, W.E. (this volume), 'Similarity Indexes and Criteria for Spatial Linking'.

Dikhanov, Y. (1994), '*Sensitivity of PPP-based Income Estimates to Choice of Aggregation Procedures*', paper presented IARIW session on International Comparison; General Conference of the International Association for Research in Income and Wealth, St.Andrews, New Brunswick, Canada, 21–27, August 1994.

Drechsler, L. (1973), 'Weighting of Index Numbers in Multilateral Comparisons', *Review of Income and Wealth*, March.

Eltetö, O. and P. Köves (1964), 'On an Index Number Computation Problem in International Comparison' (in Hungarian), *Statisztikai Szemle* **42**, 507–518.

Ferrari, G. and M. Riani (1998), 'On Purchasing Power Parities Calculation at the Basic Heading Level', *Statistica*, **LVIII**, 91–108.

Ferrari, G., G. Gozzi and M. Riani (1996), 'Comparing GEKS and EPD Approaches for Calculating PPPs at the Basic Heading Level', in *Improving the Quality of Price Indices: CPI and PPP*, Eurostat.

Gini, C. (1924), 'Quelques Considérations au Sujet de la Construction des Nombres Indices des Prix et des Questions Analogues', *Metron*, **4**, 3–162.

Hajarghasht, G and D.S. Prasada Rao (2008), 'Stochastic Approach to Index Numbers for Multilateral Price Comparisons and their Standard Errors', CEPA Working Paper Series, WP 05/08, University of Queensland, Brisbane, Austalia.

Hill, R.J. (1999), 'Chained PPPs and Minimum Spanning Trees' in Lipsey and Heston (eds) *International and Interarea Comparisons of Income, Output and Prices*, in A.Heston and R.E. Lipsey (eds), *Studies in Income and Wealth*, **61**, Chicago and London: University of Chicago Press, pp. 109–120.

Hill, R.J. (this volume), 'Comparing Per Capita Income Levels Across Countries Using Spanning Trees: Robustness, Prior Restrictions, Hybrids and Hierarchies'.

Hill, R.J. and M.P. Timmer (2006), 'Standard Errors and Weights in Multilateral Price Indexes', *Journal of Business and Economic Statistics* **24** (3), 366–377.

Johnson, N.L., S. Kotz and N. Balakrishnan (1994), *Continuous Univariate Distributions*, **I** (2nd ed.), New York: John Wiley & Sons.

Kokoski, M.F., B.R. Moulton and K.D. Zieschang (1999), 'Interarea Price Comparisons for Heterogeneous Goods and Several Levels of Commodity Aggregation', in *International and Interarea Comparisons of Income, Output and Prices*, in A. Heston and R.E. Lipsey (eds), *Studies in Income and Wealth*, **61**, Chicago and London: University of Chicago Press, pp. 327–364

Kravis, I.B., A.W. Heston and R. Summers (1982), *World Product and Income: International Comparisons of Real Gross Domestic Product*, Baltimore, MD: Johns Hopkins University Press.

Maddison, A. and D.S. Prasada Rao (1996), 'A Generalized Approach to International Comparisons of Agricultural Output and Productivity' *Research Memorandum GD–27*, Groningen: Groningen Growth and Development Centre.

OECD (1987, 1996 and 1999), *Purchasing Power Parities and Real Expenditures,* Paris: Department of Economics and Statistics.

Rao, D.S. Prasada (1990), 'A System of Log–change Index Numbers for Multilateral Comparisons', in J. Salazar–Carrillo and D.S. Prasada Rao (eds) *Comparisons of Prices and Real Product in Latin America*, Amsterdam: North–Holland.

Rao, D.S. Prasada (1996), 'On the Equivalence of the Generalized Country–Product–Dummy (CPD) Method and the Rao–System for Multilateral Comparisons', Working Paper No. 5, Centre for International Comparisons, Philadelphia: University of Pennsylvania.

Rao, D.S. Prasada (1997), 'Aggregation Methods for International Comparison of Purchasing Power Parities and Real Income: Analytical Issues and Some Recent Developments', *Proceedings of the International Statistical Institute*, 51st Session, 197–200.

Rao, D.S. Prasada (2004), 'The Country–Product–Dummy Method: a Stochastic Approach to the Computation of Purchasing Power Parities in the ICP'. Paper presented at SSHRC Conference on Index Numbers and Productivity Measurement, 30 June–3 July, Vancouver.

Rao, D.S. Prasada (2005), 'On the Equivalence of Weighted Country–Product–Dummy (CPD) Method and The Rao–System for Multilateral Price Comparisons', *Review of Income and Wealth*, **51**, 571–580.

Rao, D.S. Prasada and K.S. Banerjee (1986), 'A Multilateral System of Index Numbers based on Factorial Approach', *Statistiche Hefte*, **27**, 297–312.

Rao, D.S. Prasada, A. Maddison and B. Lee (2002), 'International Comparison of Farm Sector Performance: Methodological Options and Empirical Findings for Asia-Pacific Economies, 1900–94', in Maddison et al. (eds) *The Asian Economies in the Twentieth Century*, Cheltenham, UK and Northampton, MA., USA: Edward Elgar, pp. 27–52.

Rao, D.S Prasada., E.A. Selvanathan and D. Pilat, (1995), 'Generalized Theil–Tornqvist Indices with Applications to International Comparisons of Prices and Real Output', *Review of Economics and Statistics*, **77**, 352–360.

Rao, D.S. Prasada, and M.P. Timmer (2003), 'Purchasing Power Parities for Manufacturing Sector Price Comparisons Using New Multilateral Index Number Methods', *Review of Income and Wealth*, **53**, 372–378.

Roberts, D. (this volume), 'The Compilation of Purchasing Power Parities: the Eurostat–OECD Purchasing Power Parity Programme'.

Selvanathan, E.A. (1989), 'A Note on the Stochastic Approach to Index Numbers', *Journal of Economics and Business Statistics*, **7**, 471–474.

Selvanathan, E.A. and D.S. Prasada Rao (1992), 'An Econometric Approach to the Construction of Generalised Theirl–Tornqvist Indices for Multilateral Comparisons', *Journal of Econometrics*, **54**, 335–346.

Summers, R. (1973), 'International Price Comparisons Based Upon Incomplete Data', *Review of Income and Wealth*, **19**, 1–16.

Szulc, B. (1964), 'Index Numbers of Multilateral Regional Comparisons' (in Polish), *Przeglad Statystyczny* **3**, 239–254.

Triplett, J. (2000), 'Hedonic Valuation of "Unpriced" Banking Services: Application to National Accounts and Consumer Price Indexes', Draft paper presented at the NBER, Summer Institute.

United Nations (1994), *World Comparisons of Real Gross Domestic Product and Purchasing Power*, New York.

World Bank (2006), *The ICP Handbook*, http://web.worldbank.org/WBSITE /EXTERNAL/DATASTATISTICS/ICPEXT/0,,contentMDK:20962711~menuPK: 2666036~pagePK:60002244~piPK:62002388~theSitePK:270065,00.html; Accessed on 15 November, 2008.

World Bank (2008), *Global Purchasing Power Parities and Real Expenditures: 2005 International Comparison Program*, Washington, DC.

5. True International Income Comparisons Correcting for Substitution Bias

Steve Dowrick

5.1   INTRODUCTION

This chapter explains and applies a new method for making international comparisons of economic aggregates such as per capita GDP. The principal advantage of the method is that the GDP numbers can be given a clear–cut interpretation in terms of standard welfare economic theory. They are True Index numbers – following the definition of Afriat (1984) – in that they represent the money–metric utility of a representative consumer who is maximising utility subject to the budget–constraint and prices of each country. We do not impose any parametric form for the utility function – other than the constraint that bilateral index ratios lie between the Paasche and Laspeyres ratios – nor do we rely on any particular price vector. Instead we make use of results in multilateral index number theory to give non–parametric bounds to the deviation of the index number for each country from the sample mean.

It is well known that the use of market exchange rates to translate international incomes into a common currency introduces a traded sector bias. Whilst exchange rates tend to equate purchasing power over traded goods and services, much of world production is for domestic consumption only. Wide variations across countries in the prices of non–traded goods and services are not reflected in the market for foreign exchange (FX). So FX–converted incomes do not reflect the relative purchasing power of consumers in their own countries. Indeed, the Balassa–Samuelson argument suggests that FX income comparisons tend to exaggerate international income differentials by ignoring the lower cost of living that is typically observed in poorer economies, due to cheaper labour–intensive services in the non–traded sector.

The International Comparison Program (ICP) has conducted detailed and standardised price surveys across many countries. The ICP has also established a method for valuing aggregates such as real GDP. Instead of using currency market rates of exchange, the ICP measures the value of *per capita* GDP bundles at constant international prices. The calculations of average international prices and real GDP are carried out using the Geary–Khamis (GK) method. The results of the ICP approach have been extended across countries and over time to produce the Penn World Tables. These tables, described in Summers and Heston (1991), are the principal source of data for international comparisons of real GDP that have been used in many hundreds, if not thousands, of studies.

The ICP approach typically results in substantial revisions to FX valuations of relative incomes. Comparing the USA with Mali, for example, the ratio of *per capita* 1980 GDP is 57 at market rates of exchange. The ICP data reveal, however, that non–traded goods and services are much cheaper, relative to traded goods, in Mali than they are in the USA. So the ICP's estimate of the real US/Mali GDP ratio is much lower, a ratio of 34.

It is not so well known, however, that the ICP approach to comparing real incomes can be just as problematic as the exchange rate approach. The problem is that fixed price indices are subject to substitution bias, as pointed out by Gerschenkron (1951) and Kravis and Lipsey (1991). ICP analysts have themselves described the bias, in Kravis et al. (1982, p.7), in these terms:

> The issue arises out of a familiar problem in price and quantity index number construction. ...Valuation at other than own prices tends to inflate the aggregate value of the bundle of goods because no allowance is made for the substitutions in quantities toward the goods that are relatively cheap. ... The practical importance of this issue ... may loom large in comparisons between countries that have widely divergent price and quantity structures.

Whilst recognising the problem of substitution bias, ICP researchers have not in the past been able to quantify the extent of the bias. Alternative methods of aggregation such as the EKS (Elteto–Köves–Szulc method) have been used by the OECD (1992), in part because of the intuition that they are likely to reduce substitution bias. But lacking any measure of the actual magnitude of the bias it has been difficult to evaluate the relative merits of the EKS and GK methods.

Hill (2000) has addressed the problem of measuring substitution bias, adopting two utility–based approaches to establishing bounds on income comparisons. He estimates the parameters of the linear expenditure system, which is derived from the Stone–Geary utility function, to derive utility numbers for each country. He notes the sensitivity of the income ratios to the choice of the reference price vector, illustrated by his finding that the

USA/Turkey ratio could be as high as 7 or as low as 3.5, bounds which encompass the GK ratio of 3.7. His second approach is to assume homothetic preferences, implying that income comparisons based on expenditure function ratios are invariant to the reference price vector. This enables him to tighten the bounds on the US/Turkey ratio to the interval (5.4, 4.0), establishing that the GK measure substantially overvalues the relative income of the poorer country.

This latter approach is similar to that used by Dowrick and Quiggin (1997), Whereas Hill examines only bilateral comparisons, Dowrick and Quiggin develop results on the multilateral properties of true index numbers, building on the pioneering work of Afriat (1981). In order to illustrate their method and to highlight the magnitudes of bias involved, it is worth explaining results with respect to a particular problem. Using the ICP data set for 1980 GDP *per capita* in 60 countries, what is the ratio of real GDP *per capita* in the richest country, the USA, relative to that in Mali, one of the very poorest? As discussed above, exchange rate comparisons give a measure of 57, whilst the GK method reduces the ratio to 34. These values for the US/Mali GDP *per capita* ratio are displayed in Figure 5.1, along with some alternative index numbers.

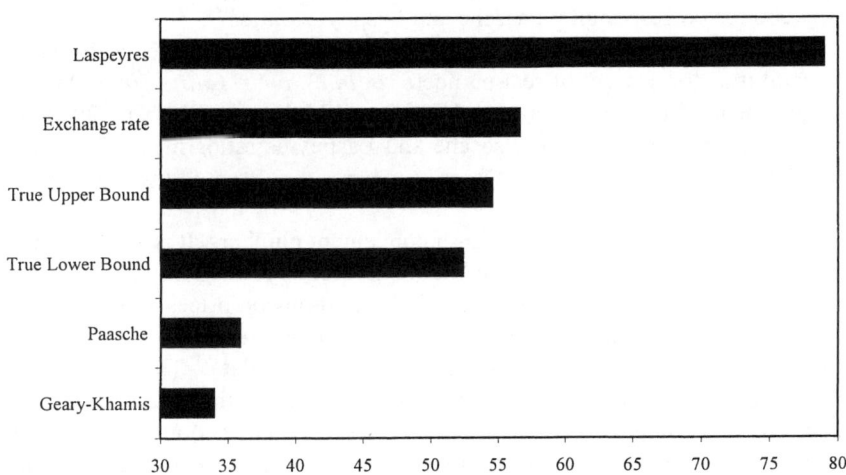

Source: Author's calculations from United Nations (1987)

Figure 5.1   Alternative measures of the 1980 per capita GDP ratio, USA/Mali

The Paasche and Laspeyres indices indicate the GDP ratios which are obtained by evaluating the GDP bundles at US prices or Mali prices respectively. These are intuitively informative indices since they measure the relative values which consumers in either country would put on the consumption bundle of the other. Substitution bias implies that the former will understate the true ratio, whilst the latter will overstate it. If we were concerned only with these two countries it might make sense to choose the geometric mean of the Paasche and Laspeyres ratios, the Fisher ideal index, as our best guess for the true income ratio. That yields an estimate of 53.

There is, however, a well–known problem with the Fisher index: it is intransitive in multi–country comparisons. For example, if we include Brazil in our comparisons, the Fisher index for USA/Mali does not equal the product of the indices for USA/Brazil and Brazil/Mali.

Afriat's solution to this problem can be viewed as a generalisation of the Fisher approach. The attractiveness of the Fisher index is that it is a compromise between the Paasche and Laspeyres indices. But it is the specificity of the Fisher compromise – choosing the geometric mid–point – which makes transitivity impossible. Afriat's solution comes from asking the more general question: 'is there any set of real income numbers for our 3 (or n) country problem such that the income ratio for each pair of countries lies between the corresponding Paasche and Laspeyres ratios?'.

If such a set of numbers does exist, the GDP ratios will necessarily satisfy transitivity: for any set of real numbers (a, b, c), $a/c = (a/b) . (b/c)$. Afriat's requirement that the US/Brazil and the Brazil/Mali ratios lie *between* rather than *at the mid–point* of the Paasche and Laspeyres ratios makes it feasible that there may exist such a set of numbers – a 'true index' in Afriat's terminology.

The Afriat index is not just a set of convenient numbers. It is a true welfare measure. Afriat (1981) has a remarkable theorem showing that the existence of such a true index, for a given set of observations on prices and quantities, is equivalent to the existence of a common homothetic preference relationship (or utility function) that rationalises the data.[1] That is to say, if there exists a set of Afriat index numbers, then there must also exist some common homothetic utility function such that any country's observed consumption bundle maximises the utility of a representative consumer facing the prices and budget constraint of that country. Moreover, the Afriat index numbers yield bilateral ratios that are the money–metric utility ratios.

In general, if a true index does exist it will not be unique – but we can establish upper and lower bounds to each of the bilateral ratios. These will be tighter than the Paasche–Laspeyres bounds. Using the Afriat method, as

---

[1] This equivalence is explained further by Varian (1982).

described later in this chapter, we find that the true utility–consistent US/Mali GDP ratio lies between 52 and 55.[2]

Using these true bounds as our benchmark, we can evaluate the degree of bias in different methods of aggregation. Referring to Figure 5.1 we see that the exchange rate measure lies above the true upper bound. The exchange rate undervalues Mali GDP by at least five percentage points. We can see that the GK method corrects for the bias inherent in exchange rate valuations of poor countries relative to rich countries; but the substitution bias of the fixed–price method means that the GK measure has over–valued Mali's true GDP by at least one third.

This example highlights one of our principal findings: neither exchange rate comparisons nor the ICP measures constitute a true index of welfare. Whilst the exchange rate comparison understates the relative value of incomes in poor countries, the GK method tends to overstate it.

The next section of this chapter develops a model which allows us to analyse the problems of exchange rate comparisons and various methods of correction for purchasing power parity before presenting the true index method. Then we present our True Index results and an evaluation of the GK and EKS indices.

5.2 A MODEL OF EXCHANGE RATE BIAS AND GEARY–KHAMIS BIAS

Until the 1980s, the data used for international comparisons of income levels were derived from national GDP data, converted to a common currency such as the US dollar using currency market exchange rates. This approach suffers from well known deficiencies. Countries differ greatly in the relative prices of traded and non–traded goods. This phenomenon has been analysed by Balassa (1964), Samuelson (1964) and Bhagwati (1984). Real wages are low in countries with low labour productivity, so non–traded labour–intensive services are cheap relative to capital–intensive traded goods. Market exchange rates are more likely to equate international prices in the traded sector than in the non–traded sector of the economy. Consequently, markets tend to undervalue the currencies of poor countries in relation to their domestic purchasing power. Hence the common experience of international

---

[2] We can interpret these numbers as saying that the representative consumer is at least as well off with the Mali GDP bundle as if they had been offered 1/55 of the USA's *per capita* GDP bundle, whereas the representative consumer is at least as well off with the USA bundle as if they had been offered 52 times the typical Mali bundle.

travellers that their money will go much further in India or Indonesia than it will in Western Europe.

A much improved approach was adopted in the United Nations' International Comparisons Project (now Program), The ICP's initial results were published in Kravis et al. (1982) and have been reviewed by Kravis and Lipsey (1991), This approach began with an attempt to produce internationally comparable estimates of prices of a highly disaggregated bundle of commodities. The ICP studies define purchasing power parity (PPP) for a particular commodity as the number of units of currency required to purchase the same amount of the good as a unit of the numeraire currency can purchase. These disaggregated PPPs are then used to evaluate nominal national accounts data to provide quantity comparisons such as real *per capita* consumption of a particular good. Whilst there are bound to be problems in comparing the quality of differentiated products and of non–marketed services, it is generally acknowledged that the disaggregated ICP estimates are the best available for consistent comparisons across many countries of real quantities of, say, cereals or furniture or medical services.

It is much less clear, however, that the ICP estimates of quantity aggregates such as GDP are the best available. Indeed, there are two different methods of aggregation in common use. The OECD (1992, 1993) have published separate volumes of real income comparisons using their currently preferred Eltetö–Köves–Szulc (EKS) method and the Geary–Khamis (GK) method of aggregation. It is this latter method that has been used as the basis for the Penn World Tables.

The GK method evaluates the per capita quantity bundles at 'international prices' to produce a quantity index of 'real' GDP. One of the attractive features of the method is additivity: the GK valuation of GDP can be broken down by category to produce measures of, say, real investment or real private consumption and these categories add up to total GDP. The major problem of this method is, however, the tendency towards substitution bias that is a feature of constant price indexes. If the international price vector used in the GK aggregation corresponds more closely to Italian than Japanese prices it will tend to mis–state the true value of the consumption bundle in Japan. In particular, we can imagine a situation where the representative consumer is equally well off in either country, in that she is indifferent between the *per capita* GDP bundles of the two countries. But Japanese consumers face lower prices for fish, so they purchase less pasta and more fish. The GK method, which values fish at the higher Italian prices, will suggest that GDP is higher in Japan than in Italy.[3]

---

[3] Neary (2004) has proposed a variant of the GK method whereby the actual expenditures in a country are replaced by the virtual expenditures that a reference

In order to analyse these two sources of bias in international comparisons, we make use of a simple model of two trading economies, as developed by Dowrick and Akmal (2005), Each produces a non–traded labour–intensive service. Only Country 1 is able to produce an intermediate good, A, which might be an agricultural product. Both countries manufacture a final tradeable good, M, using labour and the intermediate good. The production technologies exhibit constant returns to scale and are identical across countries, except that private knowledge (due to research and/or education) in the second country makes labour more productive in its manufacturing sector. Comparative advantage in manufacturing leads the high productivity country to export manufactures and import the intermediate good.

To keep the model simple we assume Cobb–Douglas production functions in manufacturing, we treat labour as the only factor of production, we disregard transport costs for trading the intermediate and manufactured goods and we assume competitive pricing behaviour in product and labour markets, including free trade. We assume that all goods and services must be produced, traded and consumed within the one time period. The production side of the economy in country *i* can be summarised as follows:

$$S^i = L^i_s$$
$$A^1 = L^1_a$$
$$M^i = (\lambda^i L^i_m)^\alpha . (A^i_m)^{1-\alpha} \quad ; \quad i=1,2 \quad (5.1)$$

where $Z = S, A, M$ represent the domestic output of services, intermediate goods and manufactured goods respectively; L^i_z represents the amount of labour employed in production sector Z; and λ^i is the productivity of labour in country i's manufacturing sector.

Given the assumptions of constant returns to scale and competitive pricing, we can solve for the price of the manufactured good in country i, P^{iM} in terms of the domestic currency input prices for labour and the intermediate good, w^i and P^{iA}:

$$P^{iM} = a (w^i/\lambda^i)^\alpha . (P^{iA})^{1-\alpha}$$
$$\text{where } a = 1 / [\alpha^\alpha . (1-\alpha)^{1-\alpha}]. \quad (5.2)$$

We normalise prices and productivity by setting the wage and productivity level in country 1 to unity. We can then use λ (>1) without a superscript to represent manufacturing labour productivity in the high productivity country 2. This allows us to derive the price vector for country 1 as:

---

consumer would make if they were to achieve their actual living standard at a notional set of world prices.

$$\mathbf{P^1} = (P^{IS}, P^{IA}, P^{IM}) = (1, 1, a) \tag{5.3}$$

The exchange rate is E units of currency 2 per unit of currency 1. Ignoring transport costs, the domestic price of the intermediate good in country 2 is E. This determines the price of the manufactured good, using (2) as: $P^{2M} = a(w^2/\lambda)^\alpha . E^{1-\alpha}$. But trade in the manufactured good requires $P^{2M} = E . P^{1M} = aE$. These conditions fully determines the wage in country 2 as $w^2 = \lambda E$, that is to say productivity–adjusted factor–prices are equalised across the traded sectors.

By assumption, there are no differences across countries in the productivity of labour in the production of non–traded services. The price of services is simply the wage. It follows that services are relatively expensive in the high–productivity, high–wage country. The price vector is:

$$\mathbf{P^2} = (\lambda E, E, aE) \tag{5.4}$$

We analyse demand and welfare by assuming common Cobb–Douglas preferences for consumers:

$$U^i(s^i, m^i) = (s^i)^\beta . (m^i)^{1-\beta} \tag{5.5}$$

where s and m refer to *per capita* consumption of services and manufactured goods. The budget share of services is β in each country. Given that *per capita* income in each country equals the wage, the *per capita* consumption bundles, $\mathbf{q}^i = [q^{iS}, q^{iM}]$ are:[4]

$$\begin{aligned} q^1 &= [\,\beta, (1-\beta)/a\,]\ ; \\ q^2 &= [\,\beta, \lambda(1-\beta)/a\,]. \end{aligned} \tag{5.6}$$

Substitution of the consumption bundles into the common utility function gives the true *per capita* income ratio between the two countries:

$$U^2 / U^1 = \lambda^{1-\beta} \tag{5.7}$$

These findings are summarised in the following propositions from Dowrick and Akmal (2001):

---

[4] We assume that the productivity differential and relative population size are such that it is feasible for country 1 to produce all of the intermediate good demanded in both countries.

Proposition 1 (Dowrick and Akmal): With free trade in intermediate and manufactured goods and competitive pricing, a country with higher productivity in manufacturing will exhibit the following features:
1. *per capita* real income is higher;
2. non–traded services are more expensive relative to manufactures.

In this model, *per capita* National Income and Gross Domestic Product are identical and, measured in local currencies, are simply equal to the wage. So the GDP or income ratio that is obtained by exchange rate comparison is simply w^2/Ew^1. Substituting in our expressions for wages, we get the FX income ratio:

$$FX^2 / FX^1 = \lambda \tag{5.8}$$

which leads to the second proposition.

Proposition 2 (Dowrick and Akmal): Traded sector bias in FX comparisons
International comparisons of *per capita* income which use market exchange rates overstate true income differentials.

Proof: From (5.7) and (5.8), where $U^2 > U^1$, $0<\beta<1$ and $\lambda > 1$,
$(FX^2 / FX^1) = \lambda^\beta (U^2 / U^1) > U^2 / U^1$.

This proposition is a restatement of the Balassa–Samuelson results. The overstatement of true income differentials is due to traded sector bias in exchange rate measures of real income. Whilst the free trade exchange rate, E, achieves purchasing power parity for traded goods, purchasing power parity for non–traded goods and services is higher, λE.

We turn now to the measurement of the international income ratio by the Geary–Khamis method. This method values each country's GDP at 'world prices'. The world price of manufactures, relative to services, is constructed as a weighted average of the relative prices of all the countries in the GK system. For the purposes of our model we have considered only two countries, but we can allow for other countries with a range of productivity levels in the GK system. We represent the GK price vector as:

$$P^{GK} = (P^{GK,S}, P^{GK,M}) = (1, a/g) \tag{5.9}$$

writing the relative price of manufactures in the international price vector as a/g to indicate that this corresponds to the price of manufactures in a hypothetical country with a productivity parameter of g. If the world economy is dominated by countries richer than country 2, g will be greater than λ. If, on the other hand, the rest of the world is poorer than country 1, g will be less than unity.

The Geary–Khamis measure of real GDP *per capita* for country i is the *per capita* consumption bundle evaluated at world prices: $\mathbf{q}^i \cdot \mathbf{P}^{GK}$. The GK income ratio is:

$$GK^{2,1}(g) = \frac{GK^2(g)}{GK^1(g)} = \frac{\beta + (1-\beta)\lambda/g}{\beta + (1-\beta)/g} \tag{5.10}$$

Whether this under or over–states the true income ratio depends on the value of g. We summarise the relationship in our third proposition.

Proposition 3 (Dowrick and Akmal): Substitution bias in Geary–Khamis comparisons
A bilateral international comparison of *per capita* income which values expenditure at constant prices will understate the true income differential if the constant price vector corresponds to that of the high productivity country, or the prices of an even richer country.

Proof: From (5.7) and (5.10), the ratio of the constant price (GK) income ratio to the true income ratio is $R(g)$:

$$R(g) = \frac{GK^{2,1}(g)}{U^2/U^1} = \frac{\beta g + (1-\beta)\lambda}{[\beta g + (1-\beta)]\lambda^{1-\beta}} \tag{5.11}$$

From (5.11), for $\lambda>1$, $R_g<0$. For $0<\beta<1$, $R(\lambda)<1$. It follows that R must be less than 1 and decreasing in g for all $g>\lambda$.

Proposition 3 formalises and extends the notion of substitution bias in fixed price comparisons. It is well known that the use of country 1's prices is likely to exaggerate country 2's welfare – since goods that are in high demand in 2, because of their relative cheapness, will be overvalued at 1's prices. (In other words, the Laspeyres quantity index is usually larger then the Paasche index – and this must be the case if the underlying preferences are common and homothetic.) It follows that valuing demand at country 1's prices will tend to overstate the true income ratio, if 1 is poorer than 2, and vice versa. This implication of substitution bias in the measurement of inequality is sometimes referred to as the *Gerschenkron Effect*, after Gerschenkron (1951). Nuxoll (1994) has shown that the Gerschenkron effect will also apply when the income ratio between country 1 and country 2 is measured at the prices of some third country, if relative prices and quantities are inversely correlated across all three countries. Our proposition formalises Nuxoll's result in the context of an explicit model where prices, quantities and the true income ratio are endogenously determined by tastes and technology.

The extent of these biases can be illustrated in a numerical example where non–traded services comprise half of total expenditure, i.e. $\beta=0.5$, and the productivity ratio between the two countries is ten, i.e. $\lambda=10$. From (5.7), the true income ratio is $10^{0.5} = 3.16$. The FX comparison, however, gives an income ratio of ten, overstating the true income ratio by a factor greater than three. In contrast, when 'international prices' correspond to the prices of a high productivity country ($g=50$), the GK income comparison in (5.10) yields an income ratio of only 1.2, understating the true income ratio by a factor of 2.7.

This example demonstrates the point that the extent of substitution bias in fixed price comparisons can be just as severe as the problem of exchange rate bias. It is particularly relevant in our analysis of bias in the ICP approach to aggregation, because the GK method of construction of the vector of 'international prices' is heavily weighted towards the price structures of the large OECD economies, particularly the USA. Nuxoll (1994) finds that the prices used in the Penn World Tables correspond most closely to those of a developed, rather than developing, economy.

5.3 THE CONSTRUCTION OF TRUE MULTILATERAL INDICES AND THEIR BOUNDS

We present an overview of the theoretical results derived by Dowrick and Quiggin (1997) which provide a basis for establishing the magnitude of bias in income comparisons. Our starting point is a set of n observations, indexed by i, of price and quantity vectors, $(\mathbf{p}^i, \mathbf{q}^i)$, where the prices are those faced by a representative consumer and the quantities are the consumption bundles chosen subject to their budget constraint. Afriat (1981) and Varian (1983) give conditions under which the data are consistent with a common homothetic utility function. Homotheticity implies that, for a given utility function $u(\mathbf{q})$, the expenditure ratio $E[u(\mathbf{q}^1), \mathbf{p}] / E[u(\mathbf{q}^2), \mathbf{p}]$ is unique – independent of the choice of p. This means that it is possible to represent preferences by a money–metric utility function that is independent of the choice of base prices. We follow Afriat (1984) in referring to a set of expenditure ratios so derived as a 'true' quantity index.

The key to the construction of true price and quantity indices is the minimum path matrix which is derived from the matrix of Laspeyres quantity ratios using an algorithm proposed by Varian (1982). The first step is to construct the Laspeyres matrix $\mathbf{L}$, where the element $L_{ij} = \log(p_i q_j / p_i q_i)$ is the log of the Laspeyres ratio. Each element L_{ij} is then replaced by its minimum path, M_{ij}, which is defined as:

$$M_{ij} \equiv min.(k,...,m) \, [L_{ij}, (L_{ik} + L_{kl} + ... + L_{mj})] \qquad (5.12)$$

from which we construct the minimum path matrix, $\mathbf{M} = \{M_{ij}\}$.

The intuition for the minimum path procedure is straightforward. The Laspeyres index is a lower bound to the true ratio. If the Laspeyres indices tell us that country A is at least 10 per cent richer than B, and B is at least 15 per cent richer than C, then we deduce that A must be at least 25 per cent richer than C. If it is the case that the Laspeyres index between A and C is 0.9, indicating only an 11 per cent gap, we can replace that entry in the matrix with the lower number 0.8 corresponding to the 25 per cent gap. The algorithm proposed by Varian (1982) implements this procedure for all possible sequences of chained bilateral comparisons.

Afriat has shown that if and only if the diagonals of $\mathbf{M}$ are zero, a true index representation is possible and the underlying common preferences are homothetic. Furthermore, tight bilateral bounds on the true logarithmic quantity index $(a_1, a_2, .. , a_n)$ are given by the elements of the minimum path matrix:

$$-M_{ji} \leq (a_j - a_i) \leq M_{ij} \qquad i,j = 1, ..., n \qquad (5.13)$$

where $(a_j - a_i)$ is the log of the true index ratio. Any true (Afriat) index, $a = (a_1, .. , a_n)$, must satisfy these bilateral inequalities for each i,j.

If a set of price and quantity data satisfies the Afriat–Varian test, implying that a finite minimum path matrix does exist, the non–parametric definition of the underlying utility function, which is required only to be homothetic, implies that there is no unique true index. Indeed, each row and each column of the minimum path matrix constitutes a true quantity index. A result from Dowrick and Quiggin (1997) does, however, allow us to establish bounds to the range of true indices.

Proposition 4 (Dowrick and Quiggin): Let $\mathbf{A+} \equiv (c1, .., cn)$ represent the vector of column means of the minimum path matrix, $\mathbf{M}$; let $\mathbf{A-} \equiv (-r1, ..,-rn)$ represent the vector of negative row means; and define the 'ideal Afriat index' as $\mathbf{A*} \equiv (\mathbf{A+} + \mathbf{A-}) / 2$

1. $\mathbf{A*}$, $\mathbf{A^+}$ and $\mathbf{A^-}$ are true indexes;
2. A_i^+, A_i^- and A_i^* are the bounds and mid–point of $(a_i - \Sigma_i a_i/n)$;
3. $\mathbf{A*}$ is equivalent to the Fisher ideal index when $n=2$.

This Proposition can be illustrated from the analysis of the 1980 ICP data. Calculation of row and column averages of the minimum path matrix reveals that the USA's true *per capita* GDP was at least 486 per cent and at most 526 per cent of the unweighted sample average. Table 5.1 shows the corresponding upper and lower bounds for Greece, Pakistan, and Mali. These bounds are taken from the column and row means (A^+ and A^-) of the minimum path matrix. The geometric averages of these bounds constitute the Afriat Ideal Index, A^*.

It is interesting to note that the construction of the Afriat ideal index matches closely the construction of the EKS index. The ideal Afriat index number for observation *i* is the difference between the *i*th row average and the *i*th column average of the minimum path matrix. Exactly the same procedure is used to calculate the EKS index numbers, except that it is the log Laspeyres matrix which is used.

Table 5.1   *Bounds on true indexes of per capita GDP 1980 for selected countries, relative to the sample mean for 53 ICP countries*

	Max (a+) per cent	Min (a–) per cent	Mean (a*) per cent
US	526	486	506
Greece	216	196	205
Pakistan	42	39	41
Mali	10	9	9

Source: Author's calculations using data from United Nations (1987)

In the next section we use the true multilateral methodology to evaluate the GK and EKS indices. The method of evaluation involves first of all establishing the extent to which the bilateral GDP ratios implied by each index satisfy the Afriat bilateral inequalities. We can also examine whether the GK and EKS indices satisfy the multilateral conditions given by Proposition Dowrick and Quiggin.

5.4   ANALYSING BIAS IN THE GK AND EKS INDICES

The 1980 ICP data set was analysed using 128 categories of expenditure for 53 countries satisfying the Afriat–Varian test of common homothetic preferences. Whilst the ICP data set for 1980 covers 60 countries, the data for seven economies (Norway, Spain, Hungary, Poland, Yugoslavia, Tanzania and Zimbabwe) failed to satisfy the test for common homothetic preferences at this level of disaggregation.

Our comparisons of the GK and EKS indices with the true bounds are summarised in Table 5.2 and listed in full in the Appendix (Table A.5.1). There are 53 × 52 = 2756 bilateral tests implied by the Afriat inequalities in (13) for our 53–country sample. More than one third of the GDP ratios from the Geary–Khamis index lie outside the true bounds; 22 per cent of the EKS ratios fail the test.

Turning to the measures of distance from the sample mean, we find that 39 out of the 53 GK measures lie outside the true bounds defined in part 2 of Proposition D&Q, whilst only 10 of the EKS measures violate these bounds. This does not tell us how close the two indexes are to the true index, so a further measure reported here is to take the log ratio of each index number to the Afriat ideal index and then calculate the standard deviation. We find that the GK numbers tend to lie further from the true index than are the EKS numbers, but they are considerably closer than the exchange–rate measure of GDP.

Table 5.2   Tests of 1980 GK and EKS quantity indices against true index bounds

	Exchange–rate	Geary–Khamis	EKS
Violations of bilateral bounds		1031 (37%)	619 (22%)
Violations of bounds relative to sample mean		39 (74%)	10 (19%)
Standard deviation of log of ratio to the Afriat ideal index	0.39	0.10	0.04

Source: Author's calculations using data from United Nations (1987).

These comparisons are probably best appreciated in diagrammatic form. Figure 5.2 shows the levels for each of the indexes of GDP *per capita*. Each index has been normalised to the geometric mean of the 53 country GK index, $2625. The exchange rate conversion, also in 1980 US dollars, is displayed as well. The data are listed in the Appendix (Table A.5.1). Countries are ordered, left to right, in descending values of the Afriat ideal index. The continuous lines represent the upper and lower true bounds. It is apparent that the exchange rate measures tend to overstate the true incomes of the rich countries and to understate the true incomes of the poor countries. There is some suggestion that the opposite is true of the GK index, but the scaling of the diagram makes it difficult to distinguish the measures at the lower end of the income distribution.

It is easier to distinguish the EKS and GK measures from the true bounds in Figure 5.3. Here we display distance (the log ratio) from the Afriat ideal index. We can read the information in Figure 5.3 as follows. Taking the richest country, the USA, we can read on the vertical axis that the GK measure of GDP is approximately –0.18 relative to the Afriat ideal index. That is to say, the GK method underestimates true US GDP by over 19 per cent – to be precise, by the ratio exp(0.175) = 1.191. We can also see that the EKS index for the US is close to the Ideal Afriat index, which is represented by the zero line, and that it lies within the true bounds.

We have already noted that 62 per cent of the GK measures, relative to the sample mean, lie outside the bounds. There is also a discernible tendency for the GK index to underestimate rich country GDP, relative to the sample mean, and to overestimate true GDP for the poorer countries.

On the basis of this data analysis, we can conclude that the GK index is much closer to a true index than is the exchange rate measure, but there is a tendency for the GK corrections to exchange rate bias to 'overshoot'. The extent of underestimation for the richest countries goes up to nearly 20 per cent, while the level of overestimation for the poorest 27 countries goes over 30 percent in some cases.

Visual inspection of Figure 5.3 confirms the statistical analysis summarised in Table 5.2. The EKS index lies within the multilateral bounds in the majority of cases and is substantially closer to the Afriat ideal index than the GK measure for almost every country.

5.5   CONCLUDING COMMENTS

The principal contribution of this chapter has been to apply Afriat's multilateral true index methodology in order to establish the range of substitution bias inherent in various measures of cross–country 'real' GDP. The results show that the two most commonly used methods of comparing real GDP across countries, the GK and EKS methods, are successful in reducing the bias in exchange rate comparisons which come from the failure of exchange rates to take account of non–traded prices. However, as predicted by our model, the fixed price basis of the GK measures does impart a substantial degree of substitution bias. It overstates the true income levels of poor countries relative to rich countries.

Where countries are diverse in their levels of development, substitution bias can be substantial. Our sample of 53 ICP countries in 1980 ranged from the very richest to the very poorest countries in the world with true income levels varying by ratios up to 50. In this context the typical level of substitution bias in the GK measure, relative to the mean, is around 10 per

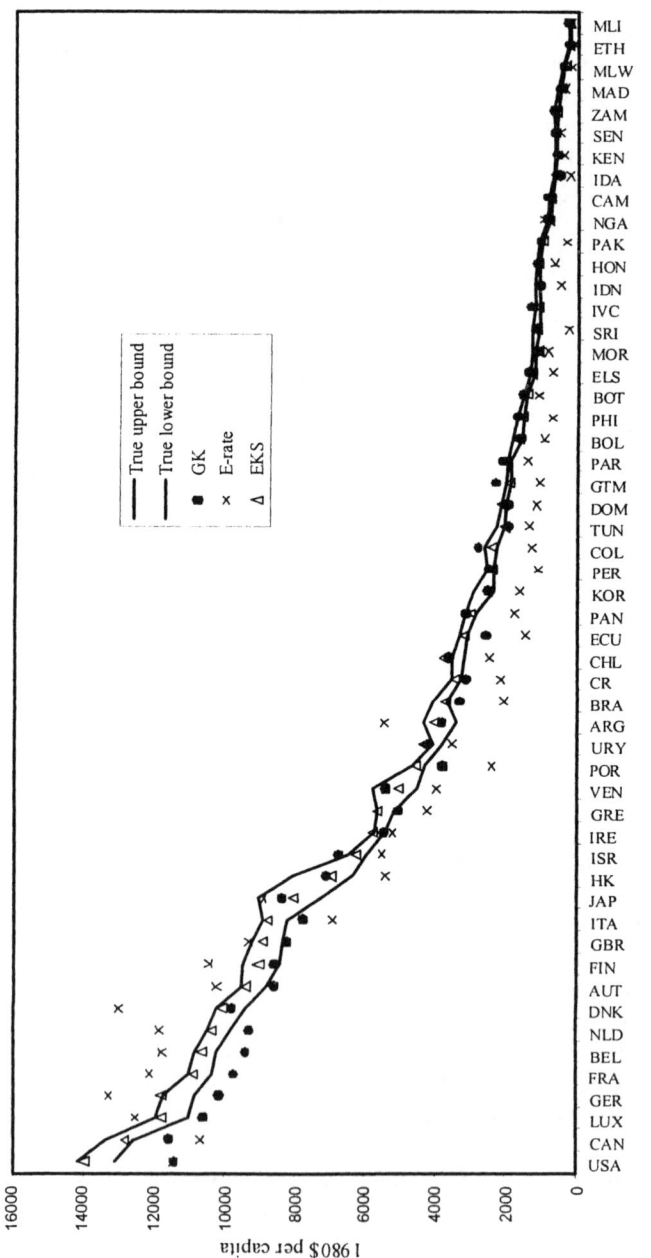

Source: Author's calculations using data from United Nations (1987).

Figure 5.2 Comparison of GK, EKS and FX with true bounds for 53 countries

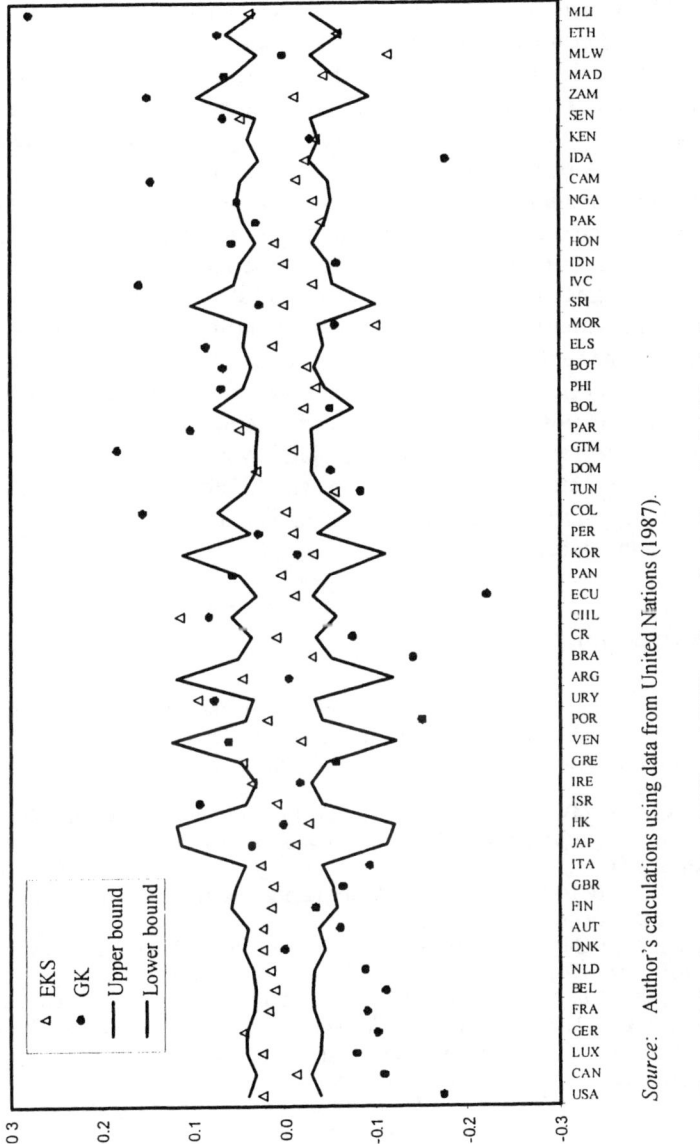

Source: Author's calculations using data from United Nations (1987).

Figure 5.3 Deviations of GK and EKS indexes from the ideal Afriat index

137

cent; in some cases the magnitude of the bias in bilateral comparisons approaches 50 per cent.

We observe that the degree of substitution bias in the EKS index was substantially less than in the GK. This reflects the similarity between the method by which the EKS index is constructed and the method that we have outlined for constructing the Ideal Afriat Index.

One conclusion could be that the EKS index, which is easier to construct because it does not require the minimum path algorithm, could be used as an approximation to the true index. Against this view, however, is the argument that the merits of the true index method are substantial enough to make it worthwhile pursuing despite the relative complexity of its computation. Most importantly, the true index method yields results which are utility–consistent. For those observations that pass the test for common homothetic utility, the index has a clear interpretation in terms of standard welfare economics. It gives money–metric measures of levels of utility which correspond to the notion that the representative consumer of country A is at least as well off as if they had been allocated some multiple of the consumption bundle of country B. Moreover, the non–parametric method of calculating the bounds of true indices emphasises that any single valued comparison of price or quantity aggregates is inherently imprecise. There is an irreducible degree of indeterminacy in any index number exercise. The true index method gives bounds to that indeterminacy.

REFERENCES

Afriat, S.N. (1981), 'On the Constructability of Consistent Price Indices Between Several Periods Simultaneously', in A. Deaton (ed.), *Essays in the Theory and Measurement of Consumer Behaviour*, Cambridge: Cambridge University Press, 133–161.

Afriat, S.N. (1984), 'The True Index', in A. Ingham and A.M. Ulph (eds), *Demand, Equilibrium, and Trade: Essays in Honor of Ivor F. Pearce*, New York: St. Martin's Press, 37–56.

Balassa, B. (1964), 'The Purchasing Power Parity Doctrine: a Reappraisal', *Journal of Political Economy*, **72 (6)**, 584–596

Bhagwati, J. (1984), 'Why are Services Cheaper in the Poor Countries', *Economic Journal*, **94** (374), 279–286.

Dowrick, S. and Md. Akmal (2005), 'Contradictory Trends in Global Income Inequality: a Tale of Two Biases', *Review of Income and Wealth*, **51**, 201–229.

Dowrick, S. and J. Quiggin (1997), 'True Measures of GDP and Convergence', *American Economic Review*, **87**, 41–64.

Gerschenkron, A. (1951), *A Dollar Index of Soviet Machinery Output, 1927–28 to 1937*. Santa Monica, CA: Rand Corporation.

Hill, R.J. (2000), 'Measuring Substitution Bias in International Comparisons Based on Additive Purchasing Power Parity Methods', *European Economic Review*, **44** (1), 145–162.

Kravis, I.B., A.H. Heston and R. Summers (1982), *World Product and Income: International Comparisons of Real Gross Product*, Baltimore: Johns Hopkins University Press.

Kravis, I.B. and R.E. Lipsey (1991), 'The International Comparison Program: Current Status and Problems', in Peter Hooper and J. David Richardson (eds), *International Economic Transactions, Issues in Measurement and Empirical Research*, Chicago: University of Chicago Press.

Neary, P.J. (2004), 'Rationalizing the Penn World Table: True Multilateral Indices for International Comparisons of Real Income', *American Economic Review* **94** (5), 1411–1428.

Nuxoll, D.A. (1994), 'Differences in Relative Prices and International Differences in Growth Rates', *American Economic Review*, **84** (5), 1423–1436.

OECD (1992), *1990 Purchasing Power Parities and Real Expenditures Volume 1*, Paris: OECD.

OECD (1993), *1990 Purchasing Power Parities and Real Expenditures: GK results Volume 2*, Paris: OECD.

Samuelson, P.A. (1964), 'Theoretical Notes on Trade Problems', *Review of Economics and Statistics*, **46** (2), 145–154.

Summers, R. and A.H. Heston (1991), 'The Penn World Table (Mark 5)', *Quarterly Journal of Economics*, **106** (2), 327–368.

United Nations & Commission of the European Communities (1986), '*World Comparisons of Purchasing Power and Real Product for 1980: Phase IV of the International Comparison Project: Part Two*', New York: United Nations.

United Nations and Commission of the European Communities (1987), Part II, *Detailed Results for 60 countries*, New York: United Nations.

Varian, H.R. (1982), 'The Non–parametric Approach to Demand Analysis', *Econometrica*, **50** (4), July, 945–973.

APPENDIX

Table A.5.1   Measures of real GDP per capita (1980$)

	TRUE AFRIAT INDICES			OTHER INDEXES		
	A*	A+	A−	GK	E–Rate	EKS
USA	13 629	14 171	13 095	11 447	11 447	13 961
Canada	12 965	13 373	12 582	11 615	10 686	12 801
Luxembourg	11 510	11 980	11 059	10 626	12 539	11 795
W.Germany	11 305	11 778	10 851	10 200	13 260	11 807
France	10 711	11 070	10 363	9 780	12 127	10 901
Belgium	10 551	10 872	10 229	9 436	11 795	10 659
Netherlands	10 178	10 530	9 838	9 316	11 831	10 343
Denmark	9 838	10 291	9 405	9 831	12 977	10 071
Austria	9 173	9 537	8 822	8 625	10 264	9 385
Finland	8 946	9 480	8 442	8 641	10 456	9 068
U.K.	8 804	9 283	8 350	8 253	9 326	8 909
Italy	8 553	8 919	8 209	7 788	6 931	8 773
Japan	8 119	9 081	7 259	8 414	8 919	8 028
Hong Kong	7 129	8 030	6 323	7 136	5 423	6 946
Israel	6 198	6 464	5 949	6 800	5 508	6 254
Ireland	5 575	5 750	5 410	5 480	5 206	5 779
Greece	5 394	5 659	5 146	5 097	4 231	5 650
Venezuela	5 110	5 779	4 523	5 432	3 965	5 019
Portugal	4 456	4 647	4 277	3 832	2 414	4 542
Uruguay	3 944	4 081	3 812	4 259	3 535	4 336
Argentina	3 862	4 346	3 429	3 843	5 457	4 044
Brazil	3 854	4 056	3 663	3 349	2 076	3 737
Costa Rica	3 419	3 540	3 301	3 173	2 158	3 451
Chile	3 361	3 562	3 175	3 650	2 482	3 768
Ecuador	3 226	3 328	3 127	2 586	1 474	3 188
Panama	3 011	3 162	2 864	3 185	1 784	3 024
Korea	2 620	2 928	2 345	2 583	1 627	2 540
Peru	2 438	2 530	2 350	2 508	1 129	2 414
Columbia	2 428	2 612	2 260	2 838	1 305	2 424
Tunisia	2 167	2 260	2 080	1 993	1 375	2 052
Dom. Rep.	2 084	2 147	2 024	1 980	1 168	2 150

Continued

Table A.5.1   Measures of real GDP per capita (1980$) – continued

	TRUE AFRIAT INDICES			OTHER INDEXES		
	A*	A+	A–	GK	E–Rate	EKS
Guatemala	1 941	2 000	1 882	2 333	1 097	1 921
Paraguay	1 924	1 980	1 867	2 131	1 428	2 022
Bolivia	1 716	1 852	1 591	1 632	963	1 680
Philippines	1 625	1 699	1 553	1 740	731	1 568
Botswana	1 489	1 542	1 439	1 592	1 130	1 453
El Salvador	1 301	1 360	1 245	1 417	737	1 316
Morocco	1 269	1 321	1 220	1 200	864	1 148
Sri Lanka	1 194	1 321	1 079	1 226	282	1 194
Ivory Coast	1 167	1 231	1 105	1 368	1 272	1 130
Indonesia	1 162	1 219	1 108	1 097	494	1 164
Honduras	1 145	1 180	1 110	1 212	679	1 156
Pakistan	1 064	1 113	1 017	1 097	351	1 022
Nigeria	850	893	808	894	992	824
Cameroon	788	826	751	911	829	777
India	680	699	661	570	245	664
Kenya	656	682	631	637	420	634
Senegal	643	662	625	687	508	674
Zambia	629	691	572	730	650	622
Madagascar	534	565	506	570	371	512
Malawi	414	427	402	415	203	370
Ethiopia	264	281	248	284	136	249
Mali	255	263	248	337	202	265

Source: Author's calculations using data from United Nations (1987).

Notes: 1. A*, A+ and A– are the Ideal Afriat index and the upper and lower true bounds. A* has been normalised to the geometric mean of the Geary–Khamis index, calculated from ICP data for 53 countries in 1980.

2. EKS is calculated from ICP data for the 53 country sample, normalised to the geometric mean of the Geary–Khamis index.

3. Geary–Khamis and Exchange rate measures are from UN (1986) where the GK measure is normalised so that the US value equals its nominal value.

6. Additivity, Matrix Consistency and a New Method for International Comparisons of Real Income and Purchasing Power Parities

Itsuo Sakuma, D.S. Prasada Rao and Yoshimasa Kurabayashi

6.1 INTRODUCTION

International comparisons of real incomes and compilation of purchasing power parities (PPPs) are activities undertaken under the auspices of international organisations such as the World Bank, OECD, EU, Asian and African Development Banks. The World Bank assumed the role of the global coordinator for the recently completed round of the International Comparison Program (ICP) and detailed results of these comparisons are available from World Bank (2008). Details of the 2005 ICP and its implementation using the OECD–Eurostat region as an illustrative example are presented in Roberts (this volume). Roberts (this volume) details various steps involved in the process of compiling PPPs and real incomes.

Two major components can be identified in any international comparisons exercise. The first component involves the painstaking process of identifying the product lists; gathering detailed price data from all the countries in the comparisons; and the second component requires proper aggregation of the price and quantity or value data compiled leading to meaningful estimates of purchasing powers of currencies and real incomes in different countries. The issue of aggregation formed the subject matter for research by several researchers over the last three decades. These concerted research efforts over time have led to a large range of aggregation or index number methods available for purposes of international comparisons. A review of various approaches used in identifying a suitable method of aggregation is presented in Balk (2008 and this volume).

The problem of choice of a suitable method for international comparisons from a variety of index number methods obviously points towards the need for criteria for selection of a suitable method. A number of properties, that can be used in assessing the suitability of a given aggregation method, have been discussed in the literature (see Kravis et al., 1982). These include among others: transitivity, base invariance, commensurability, additivity, matrix consistency and characteristicity. Balk (1996 and 2008) and Diewert (1986) provide a more formal list of such properties in the form of tests, similar to the Fisher's tests for index numbers, for comparisons over time, and assess several competing aggregation methods.

However, the main focus of the chapter is on the property of additivity.[1] Additivity is a property of the national accounts that underpin GDP and its components. Additivity is a property that ensures that real aggregates, at constant prices, also add up within the national accounts. Within the many aggregation procedures, the Geary–Khamis (GK) method is the best known aggregation procedure satisfying additivity. Over the years several international organisations have debated the relative merits of the Geary–Khamis method and the Elteto–Köves–Szulc (EKS) method, the latter does not satisfy additivity but is supposed to preserve characteristicity in the context of multilateral international comparisons. The OECD has decided to publish international comparison results based on the EKS method and then to provide supplementary results based on an additive method like the Geary–Khamis method.[2] A similar approach is followed in the more recently completed 2005 round of the ICP where the global and regional comparisons are based primarily on the EKS method and supplementary results based on the Geary–Khamis method are available for structural analysis.

A property closely associated with additivity is the property of matrix consistency, so close that the distinction between these two properties is often blurred. Even the exposition in Kravis et al. (1982) does not offer a discussion of the distinction between these two properties. A number of aggregation methods based on the matrix consistency property have been proposed in the literature, the most significant are the Kurabayashi–Sakuma (1981) and the van IJzeren (1956, 1987) class of methods.[3]

---

[1] See Balk (2008) for a discussion on the implications of transitivity under the economic approach. Cuthbert (this volume) also deals with the properties of a number of additively consistent methods for the compilation of PPPs.

[2] For results based on the EKS and the GK methods for the ICP 2005 for the Asia–Pacific region see *Purchasing Power Parities and Real Expenditures*, www.adb.org/ Documents/Reports/ICP–Purchasing–Power–expenditures / default. asp, Manila, Philippines.

[3] See Balk (2008 and this volume) for a more detailed description of these methods.

An important objective of the chapter is to offer formal definitions and descriptions of additivity and matrix consistency and discuss the link between these two concepts. In the literature, Geary–Khamis method has been the main aggregation procedure possessing the additivity.[4] The present chapter provides a new method for aggregation, which may be described as a variant of the Kurabayashi–Sakuma class of methods of aggregation, that satisfies the additivity and matrix consistency properties. Various properties of the method are investigated in the chapter.

A brief outline of the chapter is as follows. Section 6.2 establishes the notation used in the chapter. Section 6.3 deals with the additivity and matrix consistency properties used in international comparisons and it discusses the link between these two properties. In Section 6.4 a new aggregation method for international comparisons of prices and real income is outlined and a numerical illustration based on the 1990 OECD benchmark comparisons is provided. Results from the new method are presented and contrasted with the results derived using the Geary–Khamis method.

6.2   NOTATION

The following notation is used throughout the chapter. As the chapter deals with multilateral comparisons of price and quantities, it is assumed that price and quantity data are available for N countries and M commodities. Let

$\mathbf{P}$ be a $M \times N$ matrix of prices;

$\mathbf{Q}$ be a $M \times N$ matrix of quantities;

p_{ij} and q_{ij} represent, respectively, price and quantity of i–th commodity in j–th country;

$\bar{\mathbf{p}}$ be a column vector of order M consisting of elements $\bar{p}_i$ representing the international average price of i–th commodity;

PPP_j representing the purchasing power parity between the currency of country j and the currency of the base or numeraire country (number of units of currency of country j equivalent in purchasing power to one unit of numeraire currency);

$\mathbf{q}$ be a column vector of order N consisting of elements of q_j representing the aggregate quantity measure associated with country j;

$\mathbf{V}$ be the value matrix of order $M \times N$ with typical element $v_{ij} = p_{ij} \, q_{ij}$; and

---

[4] There are methods like Iklé (1972) that satisfy the property of matrix consistency. In recent literature, Cuthbert (1999) introduced a class of generalized Geary–Khamis indices that satisfy additivity. See Cuthbert (this volume) for a comparative assessment of different additive methods.

i be a column vector consisting of elements that are all equal to unity.

A few comments are in order. The prices for any given commodity are expressed in respective national currency units and, therefore, cannot be added across countries. Thus it is necessary to either normalise prices in each country or convert each country's prices into a common currency unit using a currency conversion factor such as purchasing power parity (PPP) associated with a given currency. The quantity measure, q_j, associated with country j, reflects the total volume of country j relative to a numeraire country or the world or simply expressed in a form that is directly comparable to the quantity measure of another country. Ratios of quantity measures can be interpreted as quantity index numbers.

6.3   ADDITIVITY AND MATRIX CONSISTENCY

As stated in the introduction, these two concepts, additivity and matrix consistency are intricately connected and the distinction between these two methods has not always been clear. For purposes of exposition, the concept of matrix consistency is dealt with first and then additivity concept is described.

Matrix Consistency

The idea of matrix consistency was explained in the Phase III ICP report by Kravis et al. (1982, p. 72) as

> Quantities expressed in value terms in matrix form, defined for n countries and m goods categories, should be stated in such a way that (1) the values for any category will be directly comparable between countries, and (2) the values of for any country will be directly comparable between categories.

The first requirement states that quantity measures derived at different levels of aggregation be such that the quantity measures can be compared across countries, including the level that includes the full set of commodities. The second requirement allows the possibility of defining quantity measures at any desired level of aggregation that can be used in the first requirement.

The requirement of matrix consistency requires the use of a set of international average prices, defined for each of the commodities in the complete list of commodities using observed national prices, such that the ratios of quantity measures q_k/q_j for two countries represent a quantity index number. The quantity measures q_j for each country j are determined up to a factor of proportionality as·

$$q_j = \lambda \sum_{i=1}^{M} \bar{p}_i q_{ij} \, , j = 1, 2, \ldots, N \qquad (6.1)$$

where $\bar{p}_i$ represents the international average price of i–th commodity such that the prices are all expressed in units that are comparable across countries and commodity groups. Matrix consistency requires that equation (6.1) holds for all sub–groups of commodities.

While matrix consistency requires that international average prices are defined, there is no explicit mention of the need to obtain measures for price comparison such as the purchasing power parities (PPPs) of currencies. However, PPPs can be defined indirectly as

$$PPP_j = \frac{\sum_{i=1}^{M} p_{ij} q_{ij}}{q_j} = \frac{1}{\lambda} \frac{\sum_{i=1}^{M} p_{ij} q_{ij}}{\sum_{i=1}^{M} \bar{p}_i q_{ij}} \qquad (6.2)$$

Equation (6.2) implies that purchasing power parities of currencies can also be defined as ratios of the value aggregates at national and international average prices. A further implication of matrix consistency that follows from equation (6.2) is that the national value aggregate for each country converted into a common currency unit using PPP_j is equal to the constant price value of the country–j quantity vector augmented by a constant. That is

$$\sum_{i=1}^{M} \bar{p}_i q_{ij} = \frac{1}{\lambda} \frac{\sum_{i=1}^{M} p_{ij} q_{ij}}{PPP_j} \qquad (6.3)$$

The LHS of equation (6.3) is the quantity measure required for purposes of matrix consistency.

Another point to be made about matrix consistency is that to make the concept operational, that is to be able to actually derive internationally comparable quantity measures, it is still necessary to define international average prices. This objective is achieved by different methods in different ways. The Geary–Khamis method defines international average prices directly using PPP_js in equation (6.2). The Kurabayashi–Sakuma (1981) approach defines average prices using normalised national price data. Similar approach is also used in the van IJzeren (1987) class of methods.

The concept of additivity and its relationship with matrix consistency are discussed below.

Additivity or Additive Consistency

Following several papers of Khamis (1984 and 1996, for example), additive consistency is defined as the requirement that for each country the national value aggregate expressed in national currency units converted into a common currency unit using purchasing power parities should be equal to the value aggregate derived by valuing the quantity vector of a country at international average prices, $\bar{p}_i$ for $i = 1, 2, ..., M$. In algebraic form,

$$\frac{\sum\limits_{i=1}^{M} p_{ij} q_{ij}}{PPP_j} = \sum\limits_{i=1}^{M} \bar{p}_i q_{ij} \tag{6.4}$$

Equation (6.4) ensures that national accounts presented at constant prices are consistent with value aggregates adjusted for price differentials using purchasing power parities. Note that the requirement in equation (6.4) is stipulated at the aggregate level only. That is what makes it different from the concept of *full additivity* discussed in Kravis et al. (1982).

Equation (6.4) is very similar to equation (6.3), derived from the matrix consistency concept, the only difference being that equation (6.3) requires the equality to hold with a factor of proportionality constant $1/\lambda$. The relationship between the additivity and matrix consistency concepts can be highlighted using the following result.

Result: Additivity implies matrix consistency but the converse is not true.

Additivity implies matrix consistency trivially with the proportionality constant $\lambda = 1$. The fact that the converse is not true can be established using the following example drawn from Rao (1997). For purposes of illustration, consider a simple van IJzeren system based on a simple additive specification for $\bar{p}_i$'s. The system is defined for $i=1,2,...,N$ and $j = 1,2,...,M$, as

$$\bar{p}_i = \frac{1}{N} \sum\limits_{j=1}^{N} p_{ij} / PPP_j \qquad \text{and} \qquad \frac{1}{PPP_j} = \frac{\sum\limits_{i} \bar{p}_i q_{ij}}{\sum\limits_{i} p_{ij} q_{ij}} \tag{6.5}$$

In proposing this method, it is argued that it has a unique solution when solved iteratively, at each iteration normalising e_j. It can be shown that such an iterative procedure converges to a unique positive solution, and therefore it can be considered as a viable additively consistent method.

However, a simple substitution of $\bar{p}_i$ into $1/PPP_j$ leads to a system for which no non–trivial solution exists. This observation is in contrast to the statement just above, which claims to provide a positive solution to the system.

An explanation for this paradox is as follows. Additivity constraint in equation (6.4) together with a linear function for $\bar{p}_i$'s will lead to a system of equations for $1/PPP_j$'s in the form

$$\mathbf{Ax} = \mathbf{x} \qquad \text{or} \quad (\mathbf{I-A})\mathbf{x} = 0 \tag{6.6}$$

Non–trivial solutions exist if ($\mathbf{I-A}$) is singular. This in turn implies that the matrix A has 'unity' as an eigenvalue.

However if additivity restriction is replaced by matrix consistency requirement in equation (6.3)

$$\sum_{i=1}^{M} \bar{p}_i q_{ij} = \frac{1}{\lambda} \frac{\sum_{i=1}^{M} p_{ij} q_{ij}}{PPP_j} \qquad \text{or} \qquad \frac{1}{PPP_j} = \lambda \frac{\sum \bar{p}_i q_{ij}}{\sum_i p_{ij} q_{ij}} \tag{6.7}$$

Then it leads to a system

$$\mathbf{Ax} = \lambda\mathbf{x}$$

($\lambda \neq 1$) which can be shown to have a positive solution. But for ($\lambda = 1$) only a trivial solution is feasible.

This example clearly demonstrates the crucial nature of the difference between the concept of matrix consistency and additivity in the context of discussing aggregation methods for international comparisons. This result has prompted Rao (1997, p.199) to postulate the following conjecture.

> In general most systems, like those due to Iklé, Gerardi and van IJzeren, additivity condition is imposed with a factor of proportionality built into it as shown in [3.7]. From the discussion, it appears that if additivity in the form specified in the original work of Geary and Khamis, and as described in [4], then the Geary–Khamis system may be conjectured to be the only additively consistent system. This discussion shows that it is nearly impossible to construct additively consistent systems similar to the GK system.

In the next section of the chapter, this answer to the conjecture is shown to be negative by providing an alternative to the Geary–Khamis system which has additive consistency property. Cuthbert (1999) has provided a class of generalised Geary–Khamis methods which also possess this property.

6.4   A NEW AGGREGATION METHOD

In this section, a new aggregation method which is derived as a variant of the Kurabayashi–Sakuma (1981) (KS) class of methods is outlined. The method uses the same basic framework as that used in the KS class of methods, but satisfies additional properties such as commensurability and additivity property discussed in Section 6.3.

Within the KS framework, a world price vector, $\bar{p}$, and a quantity measure vector, q, with elements q_j representing the relative size of the country j quantity are determined using a simultaneous equation system. In order to simplify the notation, the total value in each country is denoted by GDP_j, such that

$$GDP_j = \sum_{i=1}^{M} p_{ij}q_{ij}$$

A feature of the KS method is that the purchasing power parities are not defined directly from the method, but rather defined indirectly as

$$PPP_j = \frac{GDP_j}{q_j} \tag{6.8}$$

Once the quantity measures are derived, then PPP_j can be derived using equation (6.8). The world price and quantity vectors are defined using the following system of interdependent equations.

$$Q'\bar{p} = \lambda q$$
$$Pq = \mu\bar{p} \tag{6.9}$$

These two equations lead to the following equations, each of which imply a slightly different eigenvalue problem. The equations are:

$$PQ'\bar{p} = \lambda\mu\bar{p} = \alpha\bar{p} \tag{6.10}$$

$$Q'Pq = \lambda\mu q = \alpha q \tag{6.11}$$

In order to make the KS method operational, it is necessary to normalise the price matrix so that Pq in equation (6.9) is well defined. In actual empirical applications, the matrix is usually replaced by a normalised price matrix S, leading to

$$\mathbf{SQ'\overline{p}} = \lambda\mu\overline{\mathbf{p}} = \alpha\overline{\mathbf{p}}$$

$$\mathbf{Q'Sq} = \lambda\mu\mathbf{q} = \alpha\overline{\mathbf{p}}$$

Existence of unique (up to a factor of proportionality) positive solutions for $\mathbf{q}$ and $\overline{\mathbf{p}}$ is shown using the Frobenius–Perron Theorem and the eigenvalue α is the Frobenius–Perron root. Within the framework of the KS specification of equations (6.9), there is no guarantee that the resulting eigenvalue is equal to unity. In fact in most cases, the eigenvalue is not equal to 1.

Several specifications of the S matrix were considered in the past, including the numeraire and simplex methods of normalising the national prices leading to several variants of the KS method. However, both of these normalisations fail to satisfy the property of commensurability that is considered to be a standard requirement for index numbers. In this chapter, a new normalisation is proposed leading to a new method for international comparisons.

A New Method for International Comparisons

This method was originally proposed in 2000 (see Sakuma et al., 2000) as a way of deriving a commensurable Kurayabashi–Skuma (CKS) method. However, as the proposed method also provides an aggregation method which satisfies strict additivity as discussed in the paper, the method is increasingly being referred to as the Sakuma, Rao and Kurabayashi (SRK) method.[5]

Consider the following normalisation of the price data for different countries. The normalisation proposed here normalises the price of each commodity in a given country by the total value of the global quantities so that the normalsed global value is set to unity. The S matrix of normalised prices is given by

$$\mathbf{S} = \mathbf{P} \times \widehat{\mathbf{P'\overline{q}}^{-1}} \tag{6.12}$$

where $\overline{\mathbf{q}}$ is the vector of aggregate quantities such that

$$\overline{q}_i = \sum_{j=1}^{N} q_{ij} \;.$$

---

[5] See Balk (this volume) and Cuthbert (this volume) where the method is referred to as the SRK method. We follow the recent trend and refer to it as the SRK method.

The symbol $\wedge$ over a column vector denotes a diagonal matrix whose diagonal elements are formed using the elements of the column vector.

Given the new normalisation, the world price vector, $\bar{\mathbf{p}}$, and quantity measure vector, $\mathbf{q}$, are obtained as solutions from the following set of equations.

$$\mathbf{Q}'\mathbf{P} \times \widehat{\mathbf{P}'\bar{\mathbf{q}}}^{-1}\mathbf{q} = \alpha\mathbf{q} \tag{6.13}$$

and

$$\mathbf{P} \times \widehat{\mathbf{P}'\bar{\mathbf{q}}}^{-1}\mathbf{Q}'\bar{\mathbf{p}} = \alpha\bar{\mathbf{p}} \tag{6.14}$$

The following sequence of theorems establishes the most important properties of the new method.

Theorem 1: The systems of equations in (6.13) and (6.14) both have a unit eigenvalue.

Proof: Consider first, equation system (6.13). We have

$$\mathbf{Q}'\mathbf{P} \times \widehat{\mathbf{P}'\bar{\mathbf{q}}}^{-1}\mathbf{q} = \alpha\mathbf{q}$$

which can be re–written as

$$\mathbf{Q}'\hat{\bar{\mathbf{q}}}^{-1}\hat{\bar{\mathbf{q}}}\mathbf{P}\,\widehat{\mathbf{P}'\hat{\bar{\mathbf{q}}}\mathbf{i}}^{-1}\mathbf{q} = \alpha\mathbf{q}.$$

We note, firstly, that column sums of the matrix $\mathbf{Q}'\hat{\bar{\mathbf{q}}}^{-1}$ are all equal to 1. Secondly, it can also be seen that column sums of $\hat{\bar{\mathbf{q}}}\mathbf{P}\mathbf{P}'\hat{\bar{\mathbf{q}}}^{-1}$ are all equal to one. These two conclusions follow from the structure of the matrices.

Next, we note that if all the column sums (or row sums) of a square matrix A are equal to 1, then A has a unit eigenvalue. Proof of this follows from the fact that eigenvalues of A, denoted by $\lambda(\mathbf{A})$, satisfy the following inequalities.

$$\min r_i \leq \lambda(\mathbf{A}) \leq \max r_i$$
$$\min s_j \leq \lambda(\mathbf{A}) \leq \max s_j$$

where

$$r_i = \sum_{j=1}^{n} a_{ij} \quad \text{and} \quad s_j = \sum_{i=1}^{n} a_{ij}$$

denote respectively the row and column sums. See Nikaido (1968, p.108) for a proof of the statement.

Further we note that, if **B** is a matrix of size N x M and **C** is a matrix whose size is M x N, and if all column sums of **B** and all column sums of **C** are equal to 1, then all column sums of the (product) matrix **D** = **BC** are also equal to 1. The proof follows from the fact that the column sums can be written as:

$$\sum_{i=1}^{N} d_{ij} = \sum_{i=1}^{N}\sum_{k=1}^{M} b_{ik} \cdot c_{kj} = \sum_{k=1}^{M} c_{kj} \left[\sum_{i=1}^{N} b_{ik} \right] = 1,$$

Given all the observations above, it follows that the equation (6.13) can be written as

$$\mathbf{A}\mathbf{q} = \alpha\,\mathbf{q}$$

where matrix **A** has all column sums equal to 1, and with $\lambda(\mathbf{A})$ equal to 1. This concludes proof of Theorem 1. Similar proof can be constructed to show that eigenvalue in equation (6.14) is equal to unity.

Corollary: The new aggregation method derived using the matrix consistency property satisfies additivity since it satisfies the Rao–Khamis unit root constraint for additivity.

The Corollary to Theorem 1 shows that answer to the conjecture in Rao (1997) is in the negative since these results show that the new aggregation method satisfies additivity property as stipulated in Rao (1997) with a unit eigenvalue.

Theorem 2:   International comparisons from the solutions of (6.13) and (6.14) satisfy the commensurability property.

Proof: International comparisons are said to satisfy commensurability if the volume and price comparisons derived using the method, in the form of vectors **q** and $\bar{\mathbf{p}}$ are invariant to changes in the unit of measurement. Suppose units of measurement are changed so that the new price and quantity matrices are denoted by $\mathbf{P}^*$ and $\mathbf{Q}^*$. Then

$$\mathbf{P}^* = \hat{\omega}\,\mathbf{P} \quad and \quad \mathbf{Q}^* = \hat{\omega}^{-1}\,\mathbf{Q}$$

Then by direct substitution of $\mathbf{P}^*$ and $\mathbf{Q}^*$ into equations (6.13) and (6.14) it can be shown that the resulting quantity comparisons $\mathbf{q}^*$ are identical to **q** prior to the change in the units of measurement.

Theorem 3:   In the case of binary comparisons with $N=2$, the new method provides the following explicit solutions for the PPPs,

$$PPP_1 = 1 \ and \ PPP_2 = \frac{(F_{12})^2}{[EM_{12}]}$$

where F and EM respectively denote the Fisher and Edgeworth–Marshall index number formulae.

Proof: Consider equation (6.13). We have

$$Q'P \times \widehat{P'\bar{q}}^{-1} q = \alpha q.$$

It is easy to see that

$$Q'P = \begin{bmatrix} \sum\limits_{i=1}^{M} p_{i1}q_{i1} & \sum\limits_{i=1}^{M} p_{i2}q_{i1} & \cdots & \sum\limits_{i=1}^{M} p_{in}q_{i1} \\ \sum\limits_{i=1}^{M} p_{i1}q_{i2} & \sum\limits_{i=1}^{M} p_{i1}q_{i2} & \cdots & \sum\limits_{i=1}^{M} p_{i1}q_{i2} \\ \cdots & \cdots & \cdots & \cdots \\ \sum\limits_{i=1}^{M} p_{i1}q_{iM} & \sum\limits_{i=1}^{M} p_{i1}q_{iM} & & \sum\limits_{i=1}^{M} p_{i1}q_{iM} \end{bmatrix}$$

and

$$\widehat{P'\bar{q}}^{-1} = \begin{bmatrix} \dfrac{1}{\sum\limits_{i=1}^{M} p_{i1}\bar{q}_i} & 0 & \cdots & 0 \\ & \dfrac{1}{\sum\limits_{i=1}^{M} p_{i1}\bar{q}_i} & \cdots & 0 \\ \cdots & \cdots & \cdots & \cdots \\ 0 & 0 & \cdots & \dfrac{1}{\sum\limits_{i=1}^{M} p_{i1}\bar{q}_i} \end{bmatrix}$$

Using these two expressions, the system of equations in (6.13) can be written as:

$$L^{**} q = q \tag{6.15}$$

$$\text{where } \mathbf{L}^{**} = \left(\ell_{ij}^{**}\right) = \left(\frac{\sum\limits_{k=1}^{M} p_{kj} q_{ki}}{\sum\limits_{k=1}^{M} p_{kj} \bar{q}_{k}}\right).$$

Now consider the special case of the general system above with N=2 where the number of countries involved is equal to 2. Then the required vector of quantity ratios, **q**, can be solved from the following system of two linear homogeneous equations in as many unknowns.

$$\begin{bmatrix} 1 - \dfrac{\sum\limits_{i=1}^{M} p_{i1} q_{i1}}{\sum\limits_{i=1}^{M} p_{i1}(q_{i1} + q_{i2})} & -\dfrac{\sum\limits_{i=1}^{M} p_{i2} q_{i1}}{\sum\limits_{i=1}^{M} p_{i1}(q_{i1} + q_{i2})} \\[2em] -\dfrac{\sum\limits_{i=1}^{M} p_{i1} q_{i2}}{\sum\limits_{i=1}^{M} p_{i2}(q_{i1} + q_{i2})} & 1 - \dfrac{\sum\limits_{i=1}^{M} p_{i2} q_{i2}}{\sum\limits_{i=1}^{M} p_{i2}(q_{i1} + q_{i2})} \end{bmatrix} \begin{bmatrix} q_1 \\ q_2 \end{bmatrix} = \begin{bmatrix} 0 \\ 0 \end{bmatrix}$$

The matrix on the LHS is singular since each column sum is equal to zero, which shows that there is a non–trivial solution for the unknown (q_1, q_2). Suppose we let $q_2 = 1$ and then solve for the unknown q_1, we get

$$q_1 = \frac{\sum\limits_{i=1}^{M} p_{i2} q_{i1} / \sum\limits_{i=1}^{M} p_{i2}(q_{i1} + q_{i2})}{\sum\limits_{i=1}^{M} p_{i1} q_{i1} / \sum\limits_{i=1}^{M} p_{i1}(q_{i1} + q_{i2})} = \frac{1/(1+P_{12})}{1/(1+P_{21})}$$

where P_{12} and P_{21} are Paasche quantity index numbers for countries 2 and 1 respectively with the remaining country as the base. It can be shown similarly that if $q_1 = 1$, then solution for q_2 is given by

$$q_2 = \frac{1/(1+P_{21})}{1/(1+P_{12})} \tag{6.16}$$

Now we turn to the formulae for the purchasing power parities (PPPs) for the currencies of the two countries. The parities can be derived using the relationship between volume indicators q_j ($j=1$ and 2) and PPP_j ($j=1$ and 2) given by:

$$q_j = \frac{GDP_j}{PPP_j} \quad for \ j=1 \ and \ 2 \tag{6.17}$$

where GDP_j denotes the gross domestic product of country j, expressed in the currency units of country j. Given equation (6.17), we can derive expressions for PPP_j using equation (6.16). Using currency of country 1 as the numeraire, we have

$$PPP_2 = \frac{GDP_2 / q_2}{GDP_1 / q_1} = \frac{\sum\limits_{i=1}^{M} p_{i2}q_{i2} / q_2}{\sum\limits_{i=1}^{M} p_{i1}q_{i1} / q_1}$$

$$= \frac{\sum\limits_{i=1}^{M} p_{i2}q_{i2}}{\sum\limits_{i=1}^{M} p_{i1}q_{i1}} \cdot \frac{\sum\limits_{i=1}^{M} p_{i2}q_{i1} / \sum\limits_{i=1}^{M} p_{i2}(q_{i1} + q_{i2})}{\sum\limits_{i=1}^{M} p_{i1}q_{i2} / \sum\limits_{i=1}^{M} p_{i1}(q_{i1} + q_{i2})}$$

$$= \frac{P_{12}^{\,price} . L_{12}^{\,price}}{\sum\limits_{i=1}^{M} p_{i2}(q_{i1} + q_{i2}) / \sum\limits_{i=1}^{M} p_{i1}(q_{i1} + q_{i2})} = \frac{\left(F_{12}^{\,price}\right)^2}{EM_{12}^{\,price}}$$

where F denotes the Fisher index number and EM denotes the Edgeworth–Marshall price index numbers for country 2 with country 1 as the base.

The analytical expressions in Theorem 3 for the volume indices and the underlying PPPs serve as a guide to the results derived under the new method outlined in this chapter. The PPPs are linked to the Fisher index of prices as well as the well–known Edgeworth–Marshall price index which can also be expressed as a function of the Laspeyres and Paasche index numbers. Sergeev (this volume) expresses this result in an equivalent way where the Fisher index is shown to be a geometric mean of the SRK binary index (ratio of PPP_2 to PPP_1) and the Edgeworth–Marshall (EM) binary index.

6.5   EMPIRICAL ILLUSTRATION

In this section we provide an empirical illustration of the SRK (CKS) method described in Section 6.4. The illustration uses data drawn from the international comparisons exercise undertaken at the OECD for the benchmark year 1993. Since the results shown are for purposes of illustration only, the aggregation undertaken here considers data at a very aggregate level.

The data set covers 24 OECD member countries. The following is a listing of the commodity groups for purposes of aggregation. Only summary categories are selected for the purpose of this illustration. The categories are:

1. Food, Beverages and Tobacco
2. Clothing and Footwear
3. Gross Rent, Fuel and Power
4. House Furnishing and Operations
5. Medical Care
6. Transport and Communications
7. Recreation and Education
8. Other Expenditure
9. Construction
10. Producer durables
11. Net Exports
12. Government

Since these categories represent commodity groups, prices for these items are in the form of purchasing power parities derived at the category level within the international comparison exercise at the OECD. The quantities for each of these groups are then obtained by converting the nominal expenditures (in national currencies) into a common currency unit using the purchasing power parities of currencies for each of the groups. In this exercise, the item 'net exports' is dropped since the net exports can be either negative or positive unlike the rest of the items. Thus treatment of such an item necessarily depends upon the conventions used. So the results presented below are based on all the items with the exception of net exports. It is customary to use exchange rates for the conversion of Net Exports. The remaining 11 categories constitute what is usually referred to as *domestic absorption*.

Results from the SRK method and the Geary–Khamis method are presented in Table 6.1. Table 6.1 shows that the SRK method works very well. In fact the results obtained are quite close to those obtained using the Geary–Khamis method. Such a result is to be expected since the data used in the computations are already aggregated and presented for each of the commodity groups. For example, the international comparison work normally is based on 200 or more basic headings whereas the illustration here is based only on 11 categories (12 categories less one for exports).

Table 6.1   *Volume comparisons between OECD countries – SRK and GK methods*

Country	SRK Method			Geary–Khamis Method		
	Volume Ratio	Popula-tion	Per capita volume	Volume Ratio	Popula-tion	Per capita volume
Germany	0.204	63.232	0.813	0.205	63.232	0.814
France	0.183	56.420	0.815	0.183	56.420	0.816
Italy	0.172	57.663	0.749	0.172	57.663	0.749
Netherlands	0.042	14.947	0.705	0.042	14.947	0.707
Belgium	0.030	9.967	0.750	0.030	9.967	0.752
Luxembourg	0.001	0.381	0.896	0.001	0.381	0.897
UK	0.164	57.411	0.719	0.164	57.411	0.718
Ireland	0.006	3.503	0.439	0.006	3.503	0.438
Denmark	0.016	5.140	0.759	0.015	5.140	0.758
Greece	0.015	10.123	0.375	0.015	10.123	0.376
Spain	0.082	38.959	0.531	0.082	38.959	0.532
Portugal	0.015	9.377	0.402	0.015	9.377	0.402
Austria	0.024	7.718	0.786	0.024	7.718	0.786
Switzerland	0.025	6.796	0.943	0.026	6.796	0.944
Finland	0.015	4.986	0.764	0.015	4.986	0.765
Iceland	0.001	0.256	0.773	0.001	0.256	0.773
Norway	0.012	4.241	0.702	0.012	4.241	0.703
Sweden	0.027	8.559	0.797	0.027	8.559	0.796
Turkey	0.056	56.473	0.251	0.056	56.473	0.251
Australia	0.051	17.066	0.753	0.051	17.066	0.754
NZ	0.008	3.379	0.598	0.008	3.379	0.598
Japan	0.419	123.540	0.853	0.420	123.540	0.854
Canada	0.095	26.620	0.895	0.095	26.620	0.895
USA	1.000	251.394	1.000	1.000	251.394	1.000

Note: Population data in thousands; volume ratio and per capita volumes are expressed relative to USA (USA=1.00).

Results in Table 6.2 show that the international price structures derived under the two methods are essentially very similar. The government has prices above average but all the other commodity groups have international price levels below unity.

The main point to note about the results in Tables 6.1 and 6.2 is that they adequately demonstrate the feasibility of the SRK (CKS) method and that it is possible to construct variations of the Kurabayashi–Sakuma method that satisfy the property of commensurability.

Table 6.2   International prices from GK and SRK methods

Commodity Group	GK International Prices	SRK International Prices
Food, Beverages and Tobacco	0.86911	0.85944
Clothing and Footwear	0.86925	0.87807
Gross Rent, Fuel and Power	0.87399	0.89717
House Furnishing and Operations	0.89869	0.88692
Medical Care	0.87692	0.86520
Transport and Communications	0.87322	0.87067
Recreation and Education	0.87504	0.87419
Other Expenditure	0.87349	0.88261
Construction	0.90960	0.89725
Producer durables	0.82943	0.83213
Government	1.25124	1.25635

6.6   CONCLUSIONS

The main objective of the present chapter is to demonstrate that it is possible to specify variants of the Kurabayashi–Sakuma (1981) method for international comparisons which satisfy the property of commensurability and also satisfy the property of additivity. Previous versions of the KS method failed to satisfy this property, thus limiting its applications in the area international comparisons. The new method, termed the SRK method, is defined in Section 6.4. A number of important properties are established. It is shown that it is possible to provide analytical expressions for the volumes as well as purchasing power parities of currencies when the number of countries included is equal to 2. In addition, the chapter has also succeeded in providing an answer to the conjecture made by Prasada Rao (1997) that Geary–Khamis method is the only method that satisfies additive consistency in the framework of Rao–Khamis where the eigenvalues involved in equations that provide solutions for the parities and volumes must be equal to unity. In this chapter, a method which is different from the Geary–Khamis method is shown to satisfy the additive consistency property, thus providing a negative answer to the Rao conjecture. Thus, it appears that it may be feasible to construct other variants which satisfy the additive consistency property.

REFERENCES

Balk, B.M. (1996), 'A Comparison of Ten Methods for Multilateral International Price and Volume Comparison', *Journal of Official Statistics*, **12**, 199–222.

Balk, B.M. (2008), *Price and Quantity Index Numbers: Models for Measuring Aggregate Change and Difference*, New York: Cambridge University Press.

Balk, B.M. (this volume), 'Aggregation Methods in International Comparisons: an Evaluation'.

Cuthbert, J.R. (1999), 'Categorisation of Additive Purchasing Power Parities', *Review of Income and Wealth*, **45**, 235–249.

Cuthbert, J.R. (this volume), 'Implicit Data Structures and Properties of Selected Additive Indices'.

Diewert, W.E. (1986), 'Microeconomic Approaches to the Theory of International Comparisons', *NBER Technical Working Paper* No. 53.

Iklé, D.M. (1972) 'A New Approach to Index Number Theory.' *Quarterly Journal of Economics,* **86**, 188–211.

IJzeren, J. van (1956), *Three Methods of Comparing the Purchasing Power of Currencies*, Netherlands Central Bureau of Statistics, Statistical Studies, No. 7, Zeist: De Haan.

IJzeren, J. van (1987), *Bias in International Index Numbers: a Mathematical Elucidation*, Dissertation, Hungarian Academy of Sciences (private edition).

Khamis, S.H. (1984), 'On Aggregation Methods for International Comparisons', *Review of Income and Wealth*, **30**, 195–205.

Khamis, S.H. (1996), 'Consistency in Aggregation Principle for Multilateral Comparisons of Purchasing Power Parities and Real Product', in D.S. Prasada Rao and J. Salazar–Carrillo (eds), *International Comparisons of Prices, Output and Productivity*, Amsterdam: North Holland, 187–193.

Kravis, I.B., A.H. Heston and R. Summers (1982), *World Product and Income – International Comparisons of Real Gross Product*, Baltimore, MD and London: Johns Hopkins University Press.

Kurabayashi, Y. and I. Sakuma (1981), 'An Alternative Method of Multilateral Comparisons of Real Product Constrained with the Matrix Consistency', a paper presented at 17th General Conference of the International Association for Research in Income and Wealth, 17–22 August, Gouvieux, France.

Nikaido, H. (1968), Convex Structures and Economic Theory, New York and London: Academic Press.

Rao, D.S. Prasada (1997), 'Aggregation Methods for International Comparison of Purchasing Power Parities and Real Income: Analytical Issues and Some Recent Developments', *Bulletin of the international Statistical Institute*, **57–1**, 197–200.

Roberts, D. (this volume), 'The Compilation of Purchasing Power Parities: The Eurostat–OECD Purchasing Power Parity Programme'.

Sakuma, I., D.S.P. Rao and Y. Kurabayashi (2000), 'Additivity, Matrix Consistency and a New Method for International Comparisons of Real Income and Purchasing Power Parities', Paper presented at the 26th General Conference of the IARIW, 27 August – 2 September, Cracow, Poland.

Sergeev, S. (this volume), 'Aggregation Methods Based on Structural International Prices'.

World Bank (2008), *Global Purchasing Power Parities and Real Expenditures: 2005 International Comparison Program*, Washington, DC: World Bank.

7. Implicit Data Structures and Properties of Selected Additive Indices

James Cuthbert

7.1 INTRODUCTION

The purpose of this chapter is to consider the comparative properties of a number of different additive methods of constructing purchasing power parities (PPPs) when applied to a real world data set – and to relate the properties of the PPPs to the underlying structure of the data set. The research reported here is an extension of earlier work by Cuthbert (1999, 2000, 2001), and has been carried out following a suggestion made at the meeting at the World Bank in 2001, on 'PPPs for International Comparisons', that further consideration of additive methods would be useful. The data set used is 1985 data provided by the World Bank: while now fairly aged, this data set was chosen because it was regarded as being both extensive and of high quality. I am grateful to the World Bank for making this data set available. Responsibility for the opinions expressed here is entirely the author's. The structure of the chapter is as follows.

Section 7.2 defines what is meant by an additive PPP volume index, and then introduces the particular additive indices to be studied in this chapter. Two specific sub–classes are defined first: first of all, the sub–class of strongly additive indices (essentially equivalent to the class of Generalised Geary–Khamis (GGK) indices defined by Cuthbert (1999)) and secondly the sub–class of van Ijzeren indices. The specific indices studied in the chapter are as follows: the Geary–Khamis (GK) and Iklé indices, both belonging to the GGK sub–class: the equal weighted van Ijzeren (VY) index, the standardised structure (SS) index, and the Sakuma–Rao–Kurabayashi (SRK) index, which are all members of the van Ijzeren sub–class: and finally the Own–Weights (OW) index.

Section 7.3 considers the data set used in the study, that is, World Bank data relating to 1985. The structure of the data set is examined by using appropriate indicators of price and quantity structure. It is shown that the 57 countries in the data set fall into natural groupings based on the similarities of their price structures. It is also shown that the data set exhibits strong negative price quantity correlation. Both of these features will be shown to be very relevant to understand the comparative behaviour of the different indices being studied.

Section 7.4 is a brief digression, introducing an appropriate distance metric for use on price vectors, which will be required in the subsequent analysis.

Section 7.5 considers the results of applying the six additive index methods to the data set. It also develops an appropriate methodology for examining the structure of the resulting method–by–country matrix of volume estimates, in terms of a form of principal component analysis. It is shown that 98 per cent of the variability in the method–by–country matrix can be described in terms of two principal components. The next two sections examine the nature of these principal components and relate them to the underlying structure of the data.

Section 7.6 considers the first principal component, which accounts for 93 per cent of the variability in the data. Aggregation methods (like the GK and SRK), which compute international prices by weighting together country price vectors by weights which are proportional to country volumes, give relatively lower volume estimates for certain countries (typically advanced economies), than methods which adopt a more uniform weighting system. This arises because international prices for the former group of aggregation methods are closer to the individual price structures for the advanced group of countries: interacting with the negative price quantity correlations in the data structure, this gives rise to the observed effect under the first principal component. This is a typical Gerschenkron type effect.

Section 7.7 examines the second principal component: while only accounting for 5.4 per cent of the variability in the data, this component is nevertheless of considerable interest. It turns out that this component is essentially a contrast between GGK and van Ijzeren type indices: and it is related to the degree of negative price quantity correlation for particular commodities. Countries which have a high proportion of their expenditure on commodities for which there is a strong negative price quantity correlation have relatively smaller volumes under GGK as compared with van Ijzeren indices.

7.2 ADDITIVE INDICES

Let p_{ij} denote the price of item i in country j, ($i = 1, ...I$; $j = 1, ...J$), and let q_{ij} be the quantity: we assume that prices and quantities are strictly positive. Any aggregation method which computes international prices, π_i, and then defines the volume measure of country j as

$$v_j = \sum_i \pi \alpha_{ij}$$

is said to be an *additive* method.

In almost all the additive methods used in practice, the international price vector π is computed by weighting together the (deflated) price structures of individual countries. In this chapter, we shall restrict attention to additive methods where international prices can be computed as *arithmetic* averages of the deflated price structures of individual countries. More specifically, all of the aggregation methods to be considered are members of the following general class of aggregation methods:–

Let $A = A[P,Q]=[\alpha_{ij}]$ be a matrix of positive weights, satisfying the normalisation condition that

$$\sum_j \alpha_{ij} = 1 \text{ for all } i,$$

(where the individual elements α_{ij} may be functions of the prices and quantities P and Q). Then the weight matrix A defines an additive aggregation method in terms of the following equations in π_i, e_j and λ, namely,

$$\pi_i = \sum_j e_j p_{ij} \alpha_{ij} \qquad \text{for all } i \qquad (7.1)$$

$$e_j = \lambda \frac{\sum_i \pi_i q_{ij}}{\sum_i p_{ij} q_{ij}} \qquad \text{for all } j \qquad (7.2)$$

For any positive vectors π, e, and positive scalar λ, providing a solution to the simultaneous equations (7.1) and (7.2), then π defines international prices and e defines the corresponding vector of expenditure deflators, (the reciprocal of PPPs). Equation (7.1) means that international prices are constructed as a weighted average of deflated country prices: equation (7.2) says that the expenditure deflators are proportional to country real volumes divided by country expenditures.

It is relevant to make three comments about this general definition of additive aggregation methods:

(a) First of all, it is clear that the solutions to equations (7.1) and (7.2) are not unique, up to a multiplicative constant. Thus, if π, e and λ are a set of positive solutions, so is $k\pi$, ke and λ, for any positive constant k. This is a trivial complication. The way around is to specify one particular country, say country b, as base country, and to take the unique solution of equations (7.1) and (7.2) which also satisfies the condition

$$\sum_i \pi_i q_{ib} = \sum_i p_{ib} q_{ib}.$$

(b) The requirement for the term λ in equation (7.2) has nothing to do with the trivial scaling indeterminacy at (a), but relates to a much deeper difficulty. If π is eliminated from equations (7.1) and (7.2) by substituting (7.1) into (7.2), then it follows that the vector e must be the maximal left eigenvector of a particular positive matrix, and λ^{-1} is the corresponding maximal eigenvalue. In general, this eigenvalue will not equal 1, (except in an important special case – see below). So in general, unless the term λ is included in equation (7.2), no positive solutions to equations (7.1) and (7.2) will exist.

(c) The normalisation constraint, that the row sums of $\mathbf{A}$ are equal to one, is critical. Relaxing this condition has a commensurate scaling effect on the value of λ: so, in effect, λ is indeterminate unless an appropriate normalisation convention is adopted for $\mathbf{A}$. Failure to be clear about the normalisation of $\mathbf{A}$ can be the source of much confusion.

Generalised Geary–Khamis method

An important question about the system of equations (7.1) and (7.2) is – under what conditions is the value of λ equal to 1. This, for example, was effectively the condition imposed by Geary (1958), in his original paper defining the GK index: he regarded it as an 'essential' property. An almost complete answer to the question of when $\lambda = 1$ was given by Cuthbert, (1999). The two results proved by Cuthbert were as follows:–

(a) If α_{ij} is of the form

$$\alpha_{ij} = \frac{\beta_j q_{ij}}{\sum_j \beta_j q_{ij}} \quad ,$$

for some positive vector β, then $\lambda = 1$;

and the more difficult partial converse result

(b) if $\mathbf{A} = \mathbf{A}(\mathbf{Q})$ is a function of $\mathbf{Q}$ only, and if $\lambda = 1$ in equations (7.1) and (7.2), then

$$\alpha_{ij} = \frac{\beta_j q_{ij}}{\sum_j \beta_j q_{ij}} \quad \text{for some positive vector } \beta.$$

Cuthbert (1999) denoted the condition that $\lambda = 1$ as being *strong additivity*.

He also denoted an aggregation system defined by weights where

$$\alpha_{ij} = \frac{\beta_j q_{ij}}{\sum_j \beta_j q_{ij}} \tag{7.3}$$

as being a *Generalised Geary Khamis*, (GGK), aggregation system.

Cuthbert's results thus imply that all GGK aggregation systems are strongly additive: and that all strongly additive methods where the weights are functions only of **Q** are GGK.

In this chapter, two specific GGK methods are considered. These are defined as follows:

(a) Geary Khamis, (GK) index: $\beta_j = 1$ for all j in equation (7.3). (This index was originally defined by Geary (1958).)

(b) Iklé index: $\beta_j = v_j^{-1}$, where $v_j = \sum_i \pi_i q_{ij}$ for all j in equation (7.3). (This index was originally defined by Iklé (1972) using a different formulation. See Cuthbert (1999) for a proof that Iklé's original formulation is equivalent to the definition given here.)

In the GK index, therefore, countries with larger volumes have larger weights when the deflated prices of the individual countries are weighted together to form international prices: in contrast, under the Iklé index, countries with large volumes have no intrinsically greater weight in constructing international prices than countries with smaller volumes. As a shorthand, we shall say that indices where large countries have larger weights are 'non–democratic', while indices where country weights are independent of volume scale effects are 'democratic'. This shorthand notation of course is not meant to imply any value judgement.

Van Ijzeren Indices

The next sub–class of additive indices we shall consider are the so–called van Ijzeren indices: (Van Ijzeren (1987)). In equations (7.1) and (7.2) and, if, in equation (7.1),

$$\alpha_{ij} = \alpha_j \text{ for all } i, \text{ where } \alpha_j \geq 0 \text{ and } \sum_j \alpha_j = 1, \qquad (7.4)$$

then the aggregation method is said to be a *van IJzeren type* index. Clearly, an α_{ij} which satisfies equation (7.4) cannot satisfy equation (7.3): so the van Ijzeren indices are a distinct sub–class from the GGK indices, and have $\lambda \neq 1$.

The three specific van IJzeren indices considered for the purposes of the present study are:

(a) The equal weighted van IJzeren index, (referred to here as the VY index). This is defined by taking $\alpha_j = J^{-1}$ for all j in equation (4). The VY is thus a democratic index.

(b) The Standardised Structure (SS) index, introduced, (using a different formulation), by Sergeev (this volume): It can be shown that the SS index is equivalent to a van Ijzeren index, with

$$\alpha_j \propto \frac{1}{[\sum_k e_j p_{kj}(q_{k1} + \ldots + q_{kJ})]},$$

(where ' $\propto$ ' stands for 'is proportional to').

In words, this means that the SS index has weights which are inversely proportional to total world volumes evaluated at the deflated prices of country j. Usually, these weights are likely to be fairly uniform, so one would expect the SS index normally to be a fairly 'democratic' type index.

(c) The Sakuma–Rao–Kurabayashi (SRK) index, introduced, (using a different formulation), by Sakuma, Rao and Kurabayashi (this volume). It can be shown that the SRK index is equivalent to a van IJzeren index, with weights

$$\alpha_j \propto \frac{\sum_i p_{ij} q_{ij}}{[\sum_k p_{kj}(q_{k1} + \ldots + q_{kJ})]}$$

These weights will tend to apportion weights to individual countries almost in proportion to their individual volumes: so the

SRK will be a 'non–democratic' index.[1]

The final additive index we consider is not a member of either the GGK or van IJzeren sub–classes. This index is the Own Weights (OW) index: See, for example, Dikhanov, (1997). The OW index is defined as follows. Let

$$\theta_{ij} = \frac{p_{ij}q_{ij}}{\sum\limits_{i} p_{ij}q_{ij}},$$

that is, the expenditure share of item i in country j. The weights α_{ij} in equation (7.1) are then defined as

$$\alpha_{ij} = \frac{\theta_{ij}}{\sum\limits_{k} \theta_{ik}}.$$

The OW index is likely to be fairly 'democratic'.

7.3   THE STRUCTURE OF THE DATA SET

The data set used comprises data on expenditures, and prices relative to the USA, for 57 countries and 139 items, provided by the World Bank, and relating to 1985. For the purposes of the present study, three items (changes in stocks, net purchases abroad, and net exports of goods and services) were excluded from the calculation – since these are balancing items for which expenditures may be positive or negative. The indices were therefore computed on a data set comprising 136 items and 57 countries. The first step in the analysis was to convert the data to prices and quantities by dividing the expenditures by the relative prices: thus the 'prices' used in the study are actually relative prices to the USA, and the 'quantity units' for each item are the amounts of that item which can be bought for one US dollar in the USA. This particular choice of unit has no effect, of course, on the calculation of any of the indices.

The purpose of this section is to examine the structure of the basic set of price and quantity data so that, later on, the behaviour of the different indices

---

[1] Note that in their original paper, Sakuma et al. introduced their index as an example of an index with eigenvalue $\lambda = 1$: that is, as an index which, in terms of the notation used here, is strongly additive. However, the fact that the eigenvalue in the SRK paper is apparently equal to 1 is an artefact of lack of precision about normalisation of the weight matrix: see comment (c) above on page 163.

can be related to features of the data set structure. Examining the structure of a set of price and quantity data is a non–trivial problem, however, since what is required is an approach which is independent of:

(a) changes in the units in which the quantities of individual items are measured; and

(b) changes in the currency units in which prices are measured in different countries.

This was a problem considered by Cuthbert (2000): the approach developed in that paper was to define indicators of price structure and quantity structure which were independent of both (a) and (b) above – and which essentially measured the extent to which a given p_{ij} or q_{ij} deviated from a simple multiplicative model defined in terms of item and country effects.

An improved version of Cuthbert's (2000) approach is used in this chapter. More specifically, let π_i and e_j be the international prices and price deflators arising from the Iklé direct volume aggregation method. Then the price structure indicator, IP, is defined as

$$IP_{ij} = \frac{e_j p_{ij}}{\pi_i}. \tag{7.5}$$

The quantity structure indicator is defined symmetrically, as follows, in terms of the Iklé direct price aggregation method.

More specifically, consider the 'direct price' analogue of the Iklé method, which defines an international basket, χ_i, and volume deflator f_j, as positive solutions to the following sets of equations:

$$\chi_i = \sum_j f_j q_{ij} \frac{\beta_j p_{ij}}{\sum_k \beta_k p_{ik}} \quad \text{for all } i$$

$$f_j = \frac{\sum_i p_{ij} \chi_i}{\sum_i p_{ij} q_{ij}} \quad \text{for all } j$$

$$\beta_j = [\sum_i p_{ij} \chi_i]^{-1} \quad \text{for all } j.$$

Then the quantity indicator IQ is defined as

$$IQ_{ij} = \frac{f_j q_{ij}}{\chi_i} \tag{7.6}$$

There is thus a direct symmetry between the indicators of price and quantity structure defined in equations (7.5) and (7.6): this is a desirable property. Moreover, both sets of indicators are independent of the quantity units in which individual items are measured, of changes in currency units, and of choice of base country. The Iklé was chosen as the reference index for calculating these indicators because the Iklé direct price index is independent of changes in the currency units in individual countries – unlike many other direct price indices. However, as the work reported in Cuthbert (2000), makes clear, the types of indicator defined in equations (7.5) and (7.6) are robust in terms of choice of a different reference index for computation purposes.

As in Cuthbert (2000), the internal structure of the price data set was examined by calculating the correlations between countries for the values of *logIP*. One way of summarising the structure of the resulting correlation matrix is to draw a dendrogram.[2] The dendrogram indicates that there is indeed considerable structure in the matrix of price data, with similar and neighbouring countries tending to have highly positively correlated price structures. The figure indicates that there are three main groupings of countries, as classified on their price structures: these might loosely be categorised as advanced economies, Africa, and non–advanced Asia.

A similar process of constructing a nearest neighbour dendrogram was also carried out based on the logIQ correlations, and it is interesting that this quantity data gives rise to a broadly similar set of country groupings.

Finally, for each country, the correlations between the *logIP* and *logIQ* values were calculated. This calculation shows clear evidence of negative correlation between the price and quantity structures within each country, with the correlations lying between -0.14 and -0.45 for all countries. This confirms the accepted wisdom that goods which are relatively high volume in a given country tend to be relatively low priced, and vice versa. This is an expected feature of the data set which, as we will see, is of great significance as regards the comparative behaviour of the different aggregation methods.

7.4   A METRIC FOR MEASURING DISTANCES BETWEEN PRICE VECTORS

This section represents a short, but important, digression from the main flow of the chapter. One of the things we will want to do later is to have a suitable measure of the distance between different price vectors. Such a measure,

---

[2]   See Cuthbert (2000) for a description of the method used in building dendrograms from the *logIP* and *logIQ* matrices.

however, in addition to having the usual properties of a distance measure, should also have a number of special properties appropriate for dealing with price data. In particular, we would want the distance between two vectors of prices to be independent of:

(a) changes in the units in which the quantities of individual items are measured; and

(b) changes in the currency units in which prices are measured in different countries.

More formally, if **x** and **y** are positive vectors of prices, and D is a distance measure between **x** and **y**, then we want to find a measure D satisfying the following properties:–

(a) $D(\mathbf{x},\mathbf{y}) \geq 0 \quad \forall \mathbf{x},\mathbf{y}.$

(b) $D(\mathbf{x},\mathbf{y}) = D(\mathbf{y},\mathbf{x}) \quad \forall \mathbf{x},\mathbf{y}.$

(c) $D(\mathbf{x},\mathbf{y}) = 0 \iff \mathbf{x} = k\mathbf{y}$ for some scalar k.

(d) for vector $\alpha > 0$, define $\alpha\mathbf{x} = \{\alpha_i x_i\} \ \forall i$:
then $D(\alpha\mathbf{x},\alpha\mathbf{y}) = D(\mathbf{x},\mathbf{y}) \ \forall \alpha,\mathbf{x},\mathbf{y}.$ (This property means that the distance between price vectors is invariant to the choice of quantity unit for measuring the quantities of individual items.)

(e) For scalars $k_1, k_2, > 0$, $D(k_1\mathbf{x},k_2\mathbf{y}) = D(\mathbf{x},\mathbf{y}) \ \forall k_1, k_2.$ (This property means that the distance between price vectors is invariant to changes in the unit of currency in either country.)

(f) $D(\mathbf{x},\mathbf{y}) \leq D(\mathbf{x},\mathbf{z}) + D(\mathbf{z},\mathbf{y}) \ \forall$ positive vectors $\mathbf{x},\mathbf{y},\mathbf{z}.$ (This property is the standard triangle inequality which all good distance measures should satisfy.)

It is possible to define a distance measure satisfying all these properties. The author has devised the Mean Absolute Deviation (MAD) measure, defined as follows:

$$D(\mathbf{x},\mathbf{y}) = \frac{1}{n}\sum_i \left| \log\left(\frac{x_i}{y_i}\right) - mean \right|,$$

where **x** and **y** are n vectors, and mean is the arithmetic mean of the terms

$$\log\left(\frac{x_i}{y_i}\right).$$

In the rest of this chapter, when it is required to calculate a measure of distance between price vectors, it is this MAD distance measure which is used. Note also that the chapter by Diewert (this volume) contains a more formal and extended treatment of similarity indices.

7.5   THE RESULTS OF THE DIFFERENT AGGREGATION METHODS

The aggregation methods defined in section 7.2 were applied to the data set of 136 items and 57 countries, to give volume estimates for each method and country (the USA was taken as base country). International price factors and expenditure deflators for each method were, of course, also obtained.

It is useful to obtain a first impression of the relationships between the different indices by deriving a simple measure of distance between any pair of indices. If $v_1(j)$ and $v_2(j)$ represent the volume estimates for country j produced by indices 1 and 2, then a simple measure of distance between indices 1 and 2 is defined as the larger of $\max\{v_1(j)/v_2(j) - 1\}$ or $\max\{v_2(j)/v_1(j) - 1\}$, where in both cases the maxima are taken over all countries j.[3]

Table 7.1 shows the volume distances between the different indices using the above measure. For convenience, the indices have been ordered with the less 'democratic' indices, the GK and SRK, coming first, and the more democratic indices later. Also included in the table in the final column is the Gini Eltetö Köves Schultz (GEKS) index: this is not an additive index, so it is not considered in detail in this chapter. But since it is a standard index used in international comparisons, it is useful to have this indication of how it compares with the other indices.

The first point to note about Table 7.1 is that the distances between the indices are typically large. For example, the distance of 0.65 between the Iklé and the GK means that for one country, there is a 65 per cent difference between these two indices: (in fact, this country is SLE, the larger of the two indices in this case being the GK). This is an important point: it means that, for as heterogeneous a set of data as considered here, choice of aggregation method matters a great deal, at least for some countries.

The second point to notice about Table 7.1 is that the 'democratic/non–democratic' dimension has a big effect on the distances between the different

---

[3]   Note that this simple distance measure is not an ideal measure – for example, it is not invariant to choice of the base country when the indices are being calculated. But for present purposes it is adequate for giving an initial impression of how the different aggregation methods compare to one another.

indices. The two 'non–democratic' indices, the GK and the SRK, differ by at most 10.8 per cent over all the countries. The group of 'democratic' indices, (Iklé, VY, SS, OW), differ by at most 26.4 per cent for some country. The big differences, however, are between the two groups.

Table 7.1　Volume distances between indices

	GK	SRK	Iklé	Van Ij'n	SS	OW	GEKS
GK	0.000	0.108	0.650	0.499	0.398	0.507	0.829
SRK	0.108	0.000	0.827	0.639	0.514	0.669	1.000
Iklé	0.650	0.827	0.000	0.167	0.264	0.158	0.225
Van Yzerin	0.499	0.639	0.167	0.000	0.083	0.113	0.248
SS	0.398	0.514	0.264	0.083	0.000	0.155	0.353
OW	0.507	0.669	0.158	0.113	0.155	0.000	0.388
GEKS	0.829	1.000	0.225	0.248	0.353	0.388	0.000

Finally, bringing in the GEKS index, the table shows that there are substantial differences between the GEKS and all the additive indices considered. The GEKS is closest to the Iklé (but there is still a difference of 22.5 per cent for one country, BGD, the larger of the two indices in this case being the Iklé). The distance from the GEKS to the other indices is much larger for the non–democratic rather than the democratic indices (in fact, the largest distance in the table is between the SRK and the GEKS: this occurs for NPL, where the SRK estimate of volume is double the GEKS estimate). This last feature is predictable, in that the GEKS, while non–additive, is nevertheless based on a 'democratic' weighting system.

After this initial exploratory work, we now want to consider in a rather more formal fashion the differences between the volume estimates produced by the different aggregation methods. We can imagine the volume estimates produced by the different methods arranged in an array of dimension 6 by 57, denoted by **V**, with the rows corresponding to the different aggregation methods, and the columns to the different countries. Since the USA has been (arbitrarily) taken as base country, each row has been scaled so that the column corresponding to the USA is constant. What we want to do is to examine the structure of this 'method by country' array **V**, but using a technique which is invariant under multiplicative scaling of the rows of the array, (and so is independent of choice of base country): and also which is independent of scale effects in the columns, (that is, we do not want our analysis of the structure of **V** to be affected by the fact that some countries are bigger than others).

The following procedure has been adopted for examining the structure **V** in a way which is independent of row and column scaling effects, namely:

(a) Take logs: i.e., define $y_{jk} = \log(v_{jk})$

(b) Consider the residuals, r_{jk}, on fitting a 'main effects' model to these quantities: that is

$$r_{jk} = y_{jk} - \bar{y}_{.k} - \bar{y}_{j.} + \bar{y}_{..}$$

(where, in an obvious notation, $\bar{y}$ represents arithmetic mean over the dotted subscript).

(c) Then analyse the principal components of the covariance matrix of the matrix **R** of residuals: (effectively, this means extracting the leading eigen values and associated eigenvectors of **R'R** , since the columns of **R** sum to zero and hence are already centred on their means).

Table 7.2 shows the first three principal components of the matrix **R'R** and their associated eigenvalues. Effectively, almost all (over 98 per cent) of the variability in the **R** matrix is accounted for by the first two principal components – with the first principal component alone accounting for 93 per cent of the variability. We concentrate, therefore, on explaining these two principal components. There is a clear pattern to the coefficients of the first principal component: most of the countries which we have described as falling in the 'advanced' group have positive coefficients on the first principal component, and most countries in the 'Africa' and 'non–advanced Asia' groups have negative coefficients. The first principal component, therefore, effectively represents a difference between the advanced and other groups. There is no obvious pattern to the coefficients of the second principal component.

The next step was to calculate the scores of the different aggregation methods on these two principal components and to plot the scores: this plot is shown in Figure 7.1. The picture which emerges from Figure 7.1 is interesting. Looking at the first principal component, (the horizontal axis), it can be seen that the two 'non–democratic' indices, the GK and the SRK, have large negative scores, while the other more 'democratic' indices have positive scores on this component. Referring back to the coefficients of the first principal component in Table 7.2, this implies that countries like LUX, USA, CAN, JPN, DEU, NDR, IRL, FRA, FIN, which have large positive coefficients on the first principal component, do relatively better under the more democratically weighted indices than countries with large negative coefficients, (like SLE, COG, NPL, ZMB, BGD, SEN): and vice versa under the 'non–democratic' indices. Since the former group of countries contains the larger, advanced economies, the first principal component appears to be describing a classic Gerschenkron effect.

Table 7.2   *Principle components of covariance matrix*

	Principle Components of Covariance Matrix				Principle Components of Covariance Matrix		
	1	2	3		1	2	3
DEU	0.145	−0.132	−0.018	PHL	0.025	0.202	−0.078
FRA	0.142	−0.102	0.017	BWA	−0.087	0.088	0.003
ITA	0.125	−0.059	−0.054	EGY	−0.124	0.229	−0.025
NLD	0.149	−0.148	−0.008	ETH	−0.144	−0.001	−0.075
BEL	0.116	−0.033	−0.059	KEN	−0.095	0.220	−0.110
LUX	0.181	−0.121	0.108	MWI	−0.125	−0.020	0.032
GBR	0.090	−0.025	−0.114	MUS	−0.121	0.045	−0.044
IRL	0.145	−0.047	0.066	NGA	−0.152	−0.196	−0.280
DNK	0.129	−0.039	−0.123	SLE	−0.269	−0.435	−0.189
GRC	0.074	0.067	−0.023	SWZ	−0.050	0.002	0.013
ESP	0.090	0.069	−0.017	TZA	−0.072	0.238	0.046
PRT	0.014	0.127	0.038	ZMB	−0.211	0.068	0.077
AUT	0.122	0.006	0.045	ZWE	−0.058	0.031	−0.067
FIN	0.138	0.036	−0.119	BEN	−0.109	0.041	−0.142
NOR	0.162	−0.111	0.066	CMR	−0.135	0.000	−0.141
SWE	0.116	0.078	−0.222	COG	−0.253	−0.109	0.183
AUS	0.181	−0.184	0.114	CIV	−0.144	−0.196	−0.094
NZL	0.144	−0.084	0.120	MDG	−0.125	0.029	−0.034
JPN	0.157	−0.132	0.199	MLI	−0.146	0.081	0.033
CAN	0.168	−0.079	−0.017	MAR	−0.079	0.243	−0.077
USA	0.169	−0.088	−0.055	RWA	−0.186	−0.262	−0.002
TUR	0.106	0.087	0.000	SEN	−0.173	−0.143	−0.145
HKG	0.044	−0.069	−0.132	TUN	−0.060	0.149	−0.094
KOR	0.133	0.039	0.110	POL	0.118	0.055	0.104
THA	−0.021	0.069	0.062	HUN	0.079	0.057	−0.001
IND	0.064	0.284	0.044	YUG	0.080	−0.032	0.140
IRN	0.010	0.123	−0.199	BGD	−0.169	−0.020	0.348
LKA	−0.009	0.104	0.096	NPL	−0.221	−0.050	0.511
PAK	−0.077	0.048	0.186	eigenvalue	0.237	0.014	0.003
				% var	93.1	5.4	1.2

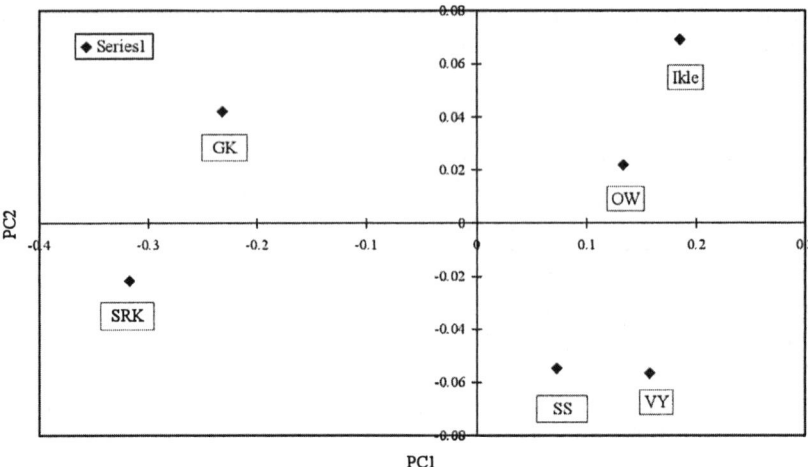

*Figure 7.1   Scores of first two principal components of covariances of
residuals*

Looking at the vertical axis in Figure 7.1, relating to scores on the second
principal component, what we see is that the two GGK indices, (the GK and
the Iklé), have positive scores: the three van IJzeren indices have negative
scores: and the OW (which does not fall into either the GGK or van IJzeren
sub–classes), falls in the middle. This suggests that underlying the second
principal component is the fact that some countries do relatively better under
GGK as compared with van IJzeren indices: and vice versa.

7.6   UNDERSTANDING THE EFFECT UNDERLYING
PRINCIPAL COMPONENT 1

To illustrate how the effect underlying principal component 1 arises, we
concentrate on two particular indices, one non–democratic (the GK), and the
other democratic (the Iklé), and consider what factors explain the relative
variation between these two indices. As we have already noted from section
7.3, there is strong negative price quantity correlation for each individual
country in the data set. So countries for which country prices are relatively
close to GK international prices are likely to have relatively small GK
volumes: and countries which have country prices relatively close to Iklé
prices are likely to have relatively small Iklé volumes. If we consider the
ratio of the Iklé to GK volumes for each country, we could hypothesise that

this ratio will be related to a measure of the relative closeness of that country's prices to GK as compared with Iklé prices.

To measure the distance between country prices and international prices, we use the MAD distance measure described in section 7.4. Figure 7.2 shows, for each country, the distance from that country's prices to GK international prices, and Iklé international prices. The ordering of the countries on the horizontal axis of the chart corresponds to the ordering of the countries derived from the *logIP* correlation dendrogram. Countries up to YUG correspond to what may be called the 'advanced' group: the next set up to TZA, corresponds to the Africa group: and the last set to non–advanced Asia.

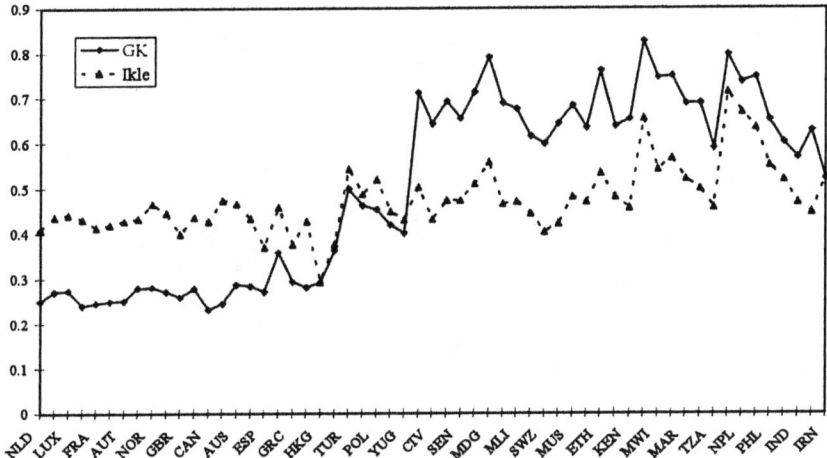

Figure 7.2   Distances from international prices to country price vectors

Figure 7.2 shows some interesting features:

• Most 'advanced' countries are closer to the GK than to the Iklé: African and non–advanced Asian countries are the other way round, and there is a group of intermediate countries, (in the tail of the advanced block, from HKG to YUG) where distances from the Iklé and GK are about the same. This overall pattern is much as we might expect – we would expect GK prices to be heavily dominated by the 'advanced' block, which contains not just the largest economies, but a large number of economies with similar price structures. Nevertheless, it is fascinating to see this confirmed so strikingly in the chart and also that the turnover point, where the GK becomes further from country prices than the Iklé, occurs exactly at the boundary of the 'advanced' grouping that emerged from the *logIP* dendrogram.

• As expected, the Iklé is much closer to equidistance from all countries than the GK, reflecting its more 'democratic' nature. But note that the Iklé is still closer to most advanced countries than to most African countries – and that most non–advanced Asian countries are even further distant from Iklé prices. Again, this is a feature which could have been predicted – but one that it is nevertheless interesting to see working through in practice. Although the Iklé is 'democratic' in that it is not affected by individual country scale effects, nevertheless it will reflect the relative numbers of countries in the different country groups – and the relative homogeneity of the price structures within these groups. Hence Iklé international prices will reflect both the size and homogeneity of the advanced grouping of countries. This is an important point.

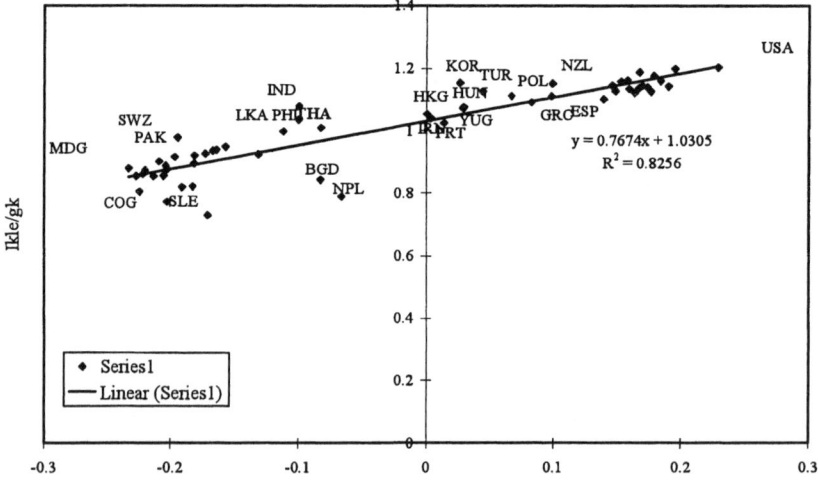

Figure 7.3   Iklé/GK, (normalised to product of 1), against D(Iklé price, country price)–D(GK price, country price)

We can now examine the question raised at the beginning of Section 7.6 namely, how do the relative values of the Iklé and GK for a country relate to the relative closeness of that country's prices to GK and Iklé international prices respectively. This question is examined in Figure 7.3.

As a measure of relative closeness of country prices to GK as compared with Iklé prices, I have taken D(Iklé prices, country prices)–D(GK prices, country prices). This measure is plotted on the horizontal axis in Figure 7.3, against the Iklé/GK ratio on the vertical axis.

The figure shows a striking picture. Note first of all how the country groupings of advanced, intermediate, non–advanced Asia, and Africa are spread out almost perfectly along the x–axis (with some anomalies, like PAK lying with the African countries).

But above all, note the very strong linear relationship: in other words, almost all, (83 per cent), of the variability in the Iklé/GK ratio is explained by a linear relationship with the measure of the relative closeness of country prices to the GK as compared with the Iklé. The fact that there is such a relationship is not unexpected: but the fact that it is of such a simple form, and so strong, is interesting.

What this section has illustrated, therefore, is how it is the distance from international prices to country prices (interacting with the observed negative price quantity correlation in the data set), which drives the type of effect underlying the first principal component: and, moreover, how the distance from country prices to international prices reflects the interaction of the particular aggregation method being used with the underlying structure of price and quantity data. An important ancillary point to remember is the point made earlier in this section: even a 'democratic' index like the Iklé may have international prices which are consistently closer to one group of countries than another, depending on the group structure of the data. Hence, given negative price quantity correlation, there will be some consistent group effects even with democratic indices like the Iklé.

7.7　UNDERSTANDING THE EFFECT UNDERLYING PRINCIPAL COMPONENT 2

As already noted in section 7.5, the second principal component can be interpreted as implying that some countries (those with large positive coefficients for this principal component) do relatively better under indices in the GGK class compared with the van Ijzeren class: and vice versa for indices with large negative coefficients.

We can formulate an intuitive hypothesis to suggest what sort of features in the data might account for this effect. It will be recalled from equation 7.3 that GGK international prices are formed by summing the following terms over countries, namely:

$$\frac{e_j p_{ij} \beta_j q_{ij}}{\sum_j \beta_j q_{ij}}.$$

Now suppose that, for a given item, prices and quantities were, (in some sense), negatively correlated over countries. Then, as the terms in the above expression are summed over countries, countries which have large weights, (large q_{ij}), will tend to be associated with relatively low prices: and conversely, low prices will tend to be associated with high weights. So, (although this argument is loose and intuitive), we might expect GGK international prices to be relatively low for those items for which there is strong negative price quantity correlation, compared to a weighting scheme which did not depend directly on q_{ij}.

This intuitive argument suggests the following hypothesis: namely that, if a particular country has a high proportion of its expenditure on items which have high negative price quantity correlation, then that country will tend to have relatively low volumes under GGK compared to, say, van IJzeren type aggregation methods.

To test this hypothesis, the indicators *IP* and *IQ* were used to calculate, for each item *i*, the covariance $Cov(IP_{ij}, IQ_j)$. It is interesting that, for almost all items, these covariances were negative (in fact, the covariances were negative for 131 out of the 136 items in the data set).

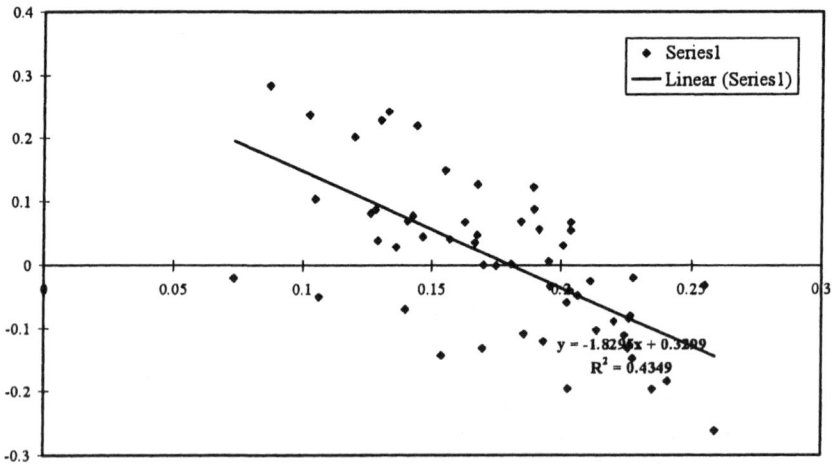

Figure 7.4   PC2 coefficients (y-axis), against proportion of expenditure on items with high negative covariance between p and q (x-axis)

For any chosen cut–off value, those items can be selected where the price quantity covariance is less than the cut–off, and for each country, the proportion of expenditure in that country on selected items was computed. Figure 7.4 shows the result (for cut–off value −0.9) of plotting the country coefficients on the second principal component, (vertical axis), against the proportion of expenditure on selected items (SLE was omitted from the plot as an outlier). This particular cut–off value was chosen because it is around this value that the strongest effect was observed: so there is an element of data dredging going on here. Nevertheless, the strength of the linear relationship in Figure 7.4 is striking, with a correlation coefficient of -0.66 between the coefficient in principal component 2, and the proportion of expenditure on selected items.

There is therefore strong evidence that the above hypothesis is consistent with the data. What seems to be underlying the second principal component is that there are differences between items in the degree of negative price quantity correlation: and that countries which have a high proportion of expenditure on highly negatively correlated items will tend to have relatively smaller volumes under GGK indices compared with indices in the van Ijzeren class.

7.8   CONCLUSIONS

In conclusion, (and without restating the results in detail), this chapter has shown (a) that there is a good deal of structure in the data set considered, with negative correlation between prices and quantities (both for countries and for items) and with countries grouped into natural country blocks on the basis of their price (and also quantity), characteristics; and (b) it has been shown that there are two main effects which describe the relative values of the group of additive indices considered here: first of all, a Gerschenkron type effect, accounting for 93 per cent of the residual variability in the method by country volume matrix: and secondly, a consistent difference between GGK and van Ijzeren class indices, accounting for 5.4 per cent of the residual variability. It has been shown how the effects observed at (b) relate to the features of the data set described at (a).

REFERENCES

Cuthbert, J.R. (1999), 'Categorisation of Additive Purchasing Power Parities', *Review of Income and Wealth*, **45 (2)**, 235-249.
Cuthbert, J.R. (2000), 'Theoretical and Practical Issues in Purchasing Power Parities, Illustrated with Reference to the 1993 Organisation for Economic Co–operation and Development Data', *Journal of Royal Statistical Society, Series A*, **163**, 421-444.

Cuthbert, J.R. (2001), 'Using Price and Quantity Indicators to Explore Data Structure', World Bank/OECD Seminar on Recent Advances in Purchasing Power Parities: Washington, DC.

Diewert, E. (this volume), 'Similarity Indices and Criteria for Spatial Linking'.

Dikhanov, Y. (1997), 'Sensitivity of PPP–Based Income Estimates to Choice of Aggregation Procedures'. mimeographed, Washington DC: The World Bank.

Geary, J. (1958), 'A Note on the Comparison of Exchange Rates and Purchasing Power between Countries'. *Journal of Royal Statistical Society*, **121**, 97–99.

Iklé, D.M. (1972), 'A New Approach to Index Number Theory.' *Quarterly Journal of Economics*, **86**, 188–211.

IJzeren, J van. (1987) *Bias in International Index Numbers: a Mathematical Elucidation*, Dissertation, Hungarian Academy of Sciences (private edition).

Sakuma, I., D.S. Prasada Rao, ,Y. Kurabayashi (this volume), 'Additivity, Matrix Consistency, and a New Method for International Comparisons of Real Income and Purchasing Power Parities'.

Sergeev, S. (this volume), 'Aggregation Methods Based on Structural International Prices'.

PART III

Methods for Spatial Linking and Analysis of
Price Structures

8. Similarity Indexes and Criteria for Spatial Linking

Erwin Diewert

8.1 INTRODUCTION[1]

One of the most difficult problems in economics from both a theoretical and applied point of view is the problem of making international comparisons of prices and quantities (or volumes) between countries.

Three broad approaches to this problem have been followed in the literature:

- Use the star system where each country in the comparison group is compared to a 'star' country using normal bilateral price and quantity indexes;[2]
- Use a symmetric multilateral system where every country's data enter the multilateral formula in a completely symmetric manner;[3] or
- Use spatial or geographic linking of similar countries and eventually find a 'tree' that compares all countries using a bilateral index number formula to link each pair of countries.[4] This is the spatial linking method.

If there are incomplete price and quantity data for the countries in the comparison, then it is likely that the third approach is the most promising since the other two approaches require a substantial degree of overlap

---

[1] The author would like to thank the SSHRC of Canada and the World Bank for financial support and Bert Balk, Jim Cuthbert, Yuri Dikhanov, Kevin Fox, Robert Hill, Prasada Rao, Abhijit Sengupta, Sergey Sergeev and Alan Woodland for helpful comments and discussions. None of the above are responsible for any opinions expressed in this chapter. The present chapter is a slightly revised version of Diewert (2002).
[2] Kravis (1984, p 10) seems to have introduced this terminology.
[3] See Balk (1996, this volume) and Diewert (1999) for surveys of these methods.
[4] Fisher (1922, p 271–276) hinted at the possibility of using spatial linking; that is, of linking countries that are similar in structure. However, the modern literature has grown due to the pioneering efforts of Robert Hill (1995, 1999a, 1999b, 2001).

between prices and quantities of each country. The third method offers the possibility of making comparisons between countries that have the most 'similar' price and quantity structures.

However, an essential input into the spatial linking method is a criterion for determining which pair of countries have the most 'similar' price or quantity structures. Hill (1995) used the spread between the Paasche and Laspeyres price indexes as an indicator of similarity.[5] Thus let $p^i \equiv [p_1^i,...,p_N^i]$ and $q^i \equiv [q_1^i,...,q_N^i]$ be the price and quantity[6] vectors for country i for $i = 1,2$. The Laspeyres and Paasche price indexes comparing the prices between the two countries are P_L and P_P defined as follows:

$$P_L(p^1,p^2,q^1,q^2) \equiv p^2 \cdot q^1/p^1 \cdot q^1 ; \qquad (8.1)$$

$$P_P(p^1,p^2,q^1,q^2) \equiv p^2 \cdot q^2/p^1 \cdot q^2 ; \qquad (8.2)$$

where $p^i \cdot q^j \equiv \sum_{n=1}^{N} p_n^i q_n^j$ is the inner product of the vectors p^i and q^j. Hill defined the price structures between the two countries to be more dissimilar the bigger is the spread between P_L and P_P; that is, the bigger is max $\{P_L/P_P, P_P/P_L\}$. The problem with this measure of dissimilarity in the price structures of the two countries is that we could have $P_L = P_P$ (so that the Hill measure would register a maximal degree of similarity) but p^1 could be very different than p^2. Thus there is a need for a more systematic study of similarity (or dissimilarity) measures in order to pick the 'best' one that could be used as an input into Hill's (1999a, 1999b, 2001) spanning tree algorithm for linking countries.

The present chapter will take an axiomatic approach to both relative and absolute indexes of price and quantity dissimilarity.[7] An *absolute index of price dissimilarity* regards p^1 and p^2 as being dissimilar if $p^1 \neq p^2$ whereas a *relative index of price dissimilarity* regards p^1 and p^2 as being dissimilar if $p^1 \neq \lambda p^2$ where $\lambda > 0$ is an arbitrary positive number. Thus the relative index regards the two price vectors as being dissimilar only if *relative prices* differ in the two countries.

The relative index concept seems to be the most useful for judging whether the structure of prices is similar or dissimilar across two countries. However, assuming that the quantity vectors being compared are per capita quantity vectors, then the absolute concept seems to be more appropriate for judging the degree of similarity across countries. If per capita quantity

---

[5] It turns out that this criterion gives the same results as a criterion that looks at the spread between the Paasche and Laspeyres quantity indexes.

[6] Typically, the quantity vectors will be per capita quantity vectors.

[7] Allen and Diewert (1981, p 433) made a start on such an axiomatic approach. Sergeev (2001) also pursued an axiomatic approach to similarity indexes.

vectors are quite different, then it is quite likely that the rich country is consuming (or producing) a very different bundle of goods and services than the poorer country and hence big disparities in the absolute level of q^1 versus q^2 are likely to indicate that the components of these two vectors are really not very comparable. In any case, it is of some interest to develop the theory for both the absolute and relative concepts.

In addition to being an essential building block for the third approach to making international comparisons listed above, relative indexes of price and quantity similarity or dissimilarity are very useful in deciding how to aggregate up a large number of price and quantity series into a smaller number of aggregates.[8] Finally, absolute indexes of dissimilarity can be useful in deciding when an observation in a large cross sectional data set is an outlier.[9]

In section 8.2 below, we study absolute dissimilarity indexes when the number of commodities being compared is only one. We offer what we think are a fairly fundamental set of axioms or properties that such an absolute dissimilarity index should satisfy and characterize the set of indexes which satisfy these axioms. In section 8.3, we take a somewhat different approach to the determination of a functional form for a dissimilarity index in the case where N = 1. In section 8.4, we add some additional axioms in an attempt to pin down the exact functional form of the absolute index in the case where N = 1. In section 8.5, we extend the axioms to cover the case where the number of commodities is arbitrary. Section 8.6 modifies the previous analysis relating to absolute indexes to relative dissimilarity indexes. Section 8.7 looks at the properties of some of the relative dissimilarity indexes that have been suggested in the literature by using measures of the angle between the vectors *x* and *y*. Sections 8.8 and 8.9 extend the analysis to weighted absolute and relative dissimilarity indexes. Section 8.10 concludes with a discussion of which of the many functional forms for dissimilarity indexes that are exhibited that we think might be most useful in the spatial linking context. An Appendix has proofs of the Propositions.

8.2 FUNDAMENTAL AXIOMS FOR ABSOLUTE DISSIMILARITY INDEXES: THE CASE WHERE N EQUALS ONE

We denote an *absolute dissimilarity index* as a function of two variables, $d(x,y)$, where *x* and *y* are restricted to be positive scalars. The two variables *x*

---

[8] For applications along these lines, see Allen and Diewert (1981).
[9] See Fox et al. (2004) for examples of this use for a dissimilarity index.

and y could be the two prices of the first commodity in the two countries, $p_1{}^1$ and $p_1{}^2$, or they could be the two per capita quantities of the first commodity in the two countries, $q_1{}^1$ and $q_1{}^2$. It is obvious that $d(x,y)$ could be considered to be a distance function of the type that occurs in the mathematics literature. However, it turns out that the axioms that we impose on $d(x,y)$ are somewhat unconventional as we shall see.

The six fundamental axioms or properties that we think an absolute dissimilarity index should satisfy are the following ones:[10]

A1: *Continuity*: $d(x,y)$ is a continuous function defined for all $x > 0$ and $y > 0$.
A2: *Identity*: $d(x,x) = 0$ for all $x > 0$.
A3: *Positivity*: $d(x,y) > 0$ for all $x \neq y$.
A4: *Symmetry*: $d(x,y) = d(y,x)$ for all $x > 0$ and $y > 0$.
A5: *Invariance to Changes in Units of Measurement*: $d(\alpha x, \alpha y) = d(x,y)$ for all $\alpha > 0$, $x > 0$, $y > 0$.
A6: *Monotonicity*: $d(x,y)$ is increasing in y if $y \geq x$.

Some comments on the axioms are in order. The continuity assumption is generally made in order to rule out indexes that behave erratically. The identity assumption is a standard one in the mathematics literature; that is, the absolute distance between two points x and y is zero if x equals y. A3 tells us that there is a positive amount of dissimilarity between x and y if x and y are different.[11] The symmetry property is very important: it says that the degree of dissimilarity between x and y is independent of the ordering of x and y. A5 is another important property from the viewpoint of economics: since units of measurement for commodities are essentially arbitrary, we would like our dissimilarity measure to be independent of the units of measurement. Finally, A6 says that as y gets bigger than x, the degree of dissimilarity between x and y grows. This is a very sensible property.

It turns out that there is a fairly simple characterization of the class of dissimilarity indexes $d(x,y)$ that satisfy the above axioms; in other words, we have the following Proposition:

Proposition 1: Let $d(x,y)$ be a function of two variables that satisfies the axioms A1–A6. Then $d(x,y)$ has the following representation:

---

[10] Counterparts to Axioms A2–A6 in the context of relative dissimilarity indexes were proposed by Allen and Diewert (1981, p.433). Sergeev (2001, p 4) also proposed counterparts to A2, A4 and A6 in the context of similarity indexes (as opposed to dissimilarity indexes).

[11] It can be shown that A3 is implied by the other axioms.

$$d(x,y) = f[\max\{x/y, y/x\}] \qquad (8.3)$$

where $f(u)$ is a continuous, monotonically increasing function of one variable, defined for $u \geq 1$ with the following additional property:

$$f(1) = 0. \qquad (8.4)$$

Conversely, if $f(u)$ has the above properties, then $d(x,y)$ defined by (8.3) has the properties A1–A6.

A proof of this Proposition (and the other Propositions which follow) may be found in the Appendix.

Example 1: The asymptotically linear dissimilarity index. Let $f(u) \equiv u + u^{-1} - 2$ for $u \geq 1$. Note that $f'(u) = 1 - u^{-2} > 0$ for $u > 1$, which shows that $f(u)$ is increasing for $u \geq 1$. Note that as u tends to infinity, $f(u)$ approaches the linear function $u - 2$. Hence $f(u)$ is asymptotically linear. Since $f(1) = 0$, we see that $f(u)$ satisfies the required regularity conditions and the associated absolute dissimilarity index is[12]

$$d(x,y) = (x/y) + (y/x) - 2 = [(x/y) - 1] + [(y/x) - 1] ; \qquad (8.5)$$
$$x > 0 ; y > 0$$

and it satisfies the axioms A1–A6.

Example 2: The asymptotically quadratic dissimilarity index. Let $f(u) \equiv [u - 1]^2 + [u^{-1} - 1]^2$ for $u \geq 1$. Note that $f'(u) = 2[u - 1] + 2[u^{-1} - 1](-1)u^{-2} > 0$ for $u > 1$, which shows that $f(u)$ is increasing for $u \geq 1$. Since $f(1) = 0$, we see that $f(u)$ satisfies the required regularity conditions and the associated absolute dissimilarity index is

$$d(x,y) = [(x/y) - 1]^2 + [(y/x) - 1]^2 ; \quad x > 0 ; y > 0 \qquad (8.6)$$

and it satisfies the axioms A1–A6.

Note that for both of these examples, the resulting $d(x,y)$ is infinitely differentiable.

In the following section, we show how a large class of one variable dissimilarity indexes can be defined. Then in section 8.4, we will add some

---

[12] If $x \geq y$, then max $\{x/y, y/x\}$ is x/y and $d(x,y) = f[\max\{x/y, y/x\}] = f[x/y] = (x/y) + (y/x) - 2$. If $y \geq x$, then max $\{x/y, y/x\}$ is y/x and $d(x,y) = f[\max\{x/y, y/x\}] = f[y/x] = (y/x) + (x/y) - 2 = (x/y) + (y/x) - 2$.

additional axioms in an attempt to narrow down the choice of a particular index to be used in applications.

8.3   AN ALTERNATIVE APPROACH FOR GENERATING ABSOLUTE DISSIMILARITY INDEXES

Let g and h be continuous monotonically increasing functions of one variable with $g(0) = 0$ and consider the following class of dissimilarity indexes:

$$d_{g,h}(x,y) \equiv g\{|h(y/x) - h(1)|\}. \tag{8.7}$$

Thus we first transform y/x and 1 by the function of one variable h, calculate the difference, $h(y/x) - h(1)$, take the absolute value of this difference and then transform this difference by g.

It is easy to verify that the d defined by (8.7) satisfies all of the axioms A1–A6 with the exception of A4, the symmetry axiom, $d(x,y) = d(y,x)$. However, this defect can be readily overcome. Note that $d_{g,h}(y,x) \equiv g\{|h(x/y) - h(1)|\}$ also satisfies A1–A6 with the exception of A4. Thus, if we take a *symmetric mean*[13] of these two indexes,[14] we will obtain a new index which satisfies axiom A4. Hence, let m be a symmetric mean function of two variables and let g and h be continuous monotonically increasing functions of one variable with $g(0) = 0$ and consider the following class of *symmetric monotonic transformation dissimilarity indexes*:

$$d_{g,h,m}(x,y) \equiv m[g\{|h(y/x) - h(1)|\}, g\{|h(x/y) - h(1)|\}. \tag{8.8}$$

Proposition 2: Let g and h be continuous monotonically increasing functions of one variable with $g(0) = 0$ and let $m(a,b)$ be a symmetric mean. Then each member of the class of symmetric monotonic transformation indexes $d_{g,h,m}(x,y)$ defined by (8.8) satisfies the axioms A1–A6.

Let us try and specialize the class of functional forms defined by (8.8). The simplest symmetric mean m of two numbers is the arithmetic mean and

---

[13] Diewert (1993, p 361) defined a *symmetric mean* of a and b as a function $m(a,b)$ that has the following properties: (1) $m(a,a) = a$ for all $a > 0$ (mean property); (2) $m(a,b) = m(b,a)$ for all $a > 0$, $b > 0$ (symmetry property); (3) $m(a,b)$ is a continuous function for $a > 0$, $b > 0$ (continuity property); (4) $m(a,b)$ is a strictly increasing function in each of its variables (increasingness property).

[14] Our method for converting a measure that is not symmetric into a symmetric method is the counterpart to Irving Fisher's (1922) *rectification* procedure, which is actually due to Walsh (1921). A rectified index number formula satisfies the time reversal test; in other words, it is symmetric in its treatment of time.

so let us set $m(a,b) = (1/2)a + (1/2)b$. It is also convenient to get rid of the absolute value function in (8.8) (so that the resulting dissimilarity index will be differentiable) and this can be done in the most simple fashion by setting $g(u) = u^2$.[15] This leads us to following class of *simple symmetric transformation dissimilarity indexes*, which depends only on the continuous monotonic function h:

$$d_h(x,y) \equiv (1/2)[h(y/x) - h(1)]^2 + (1/2)[h(x/y) - h(1)]^2. \qquad (8.9)$$

The two simplest choices for *h* are $h(u) \equiv u$ and $h(u) \equiv \ln u$.[16] These two choices for *h* lead to the following concrete dissimilarity indexes:

Example 3: The linear quadratic dissimilarity index:

$$d(x,y) \equiv (1/2)[(y/x) - 1]^2 + (1/2)[(x/y) - 1]^2. \qquad (8.10)$$

Note that this example is essentially the same as example 2.

Example 4: The log quadratic dissimilarity index:

$$\begin{aligned} d(x,y) &\equiv (1/2)[\ln(y/x) - \ln(1)]^2 + (1/2)[\ln(x/y) - \ln(1)]^2 \qquad (8.11) \\ &= (1/2)[\ln y - \ln x]^2 + (1/2)[\ln x - \ln y]^2 \\ &= [\ln y - \ln x]^2 \\ &- [\ln(y/x)]^2. \end{aligned}$$

Our conclusion at this point is that even in the one variable case, there are a large number of possible measures of absolute dissimilarity that could be chosen. Hence, in the following section, we add some additional axioms to our list of axioms, A1–A6, in an attempt to narrow down this large number of possible choices.

---

[15] There is another good reason for this choice of *g*. In most applications, we want the slope of $g(u)$ to be zero at $u = 0$ and then increase as *u* increases. This means the amount of dissimilarity between *x* and *y* will be close to zero in a neighbourhood of points where *x* is close to *y* but the degree of dissimilarity will grow at an increasing rate as *x* diverges from *y*. We will formalize these properties as axioms A7 and A8 in the next section. Hence if we want the slope of $g(u)$ to increase at a constant rate as *u* increases, then $g(u) = u^2$ is the simplest function which will accomplish this task.

[16] Bert Balk in a comment on an earlier version of this chapter suggested the following choice for *h*: $h(u) \equiv u^{1/2}$.

8.4   ADDITIONAL AXIOMS FOR ONE VARIABLE ABSOLUTE DISSIMILARITY INDEXES

Consider the following axiom:

A7: *Convexity*: $d(x,y)$ is a convex function of y for $y \geq x > 0$.

The meaning of this axiom is that we want the amount of dissimilarity between x and y to grow at a constant or increasing rate as y grows bigger than x. Put another way, we do not want the rate of increase in dissimilarity to *decrease* as y grows bigger than x. Although this property seems to be a reasonable one for many purposes, it must be conceded that this property is not as fundamental as the previous six properties.

Proposition 3: The asymptotically linear dissimilarity index defined by (8.5) and the linear quadratic dissimilarity index defined by (8.10) satisfy the convexity axiom A7 but the log quadratic dissimilarity index defined by (8.11) does *not* satisfy A7.[17]

How can we choose between the asymptotically linear dissimilarity index defined by (8.5) and the asymptotically quadratic dissimilarity index defined by (8.6) or (8.10)? Both indexes behave similarly for x close to y but as y diverges from x, the amount of dissimilarity between x and y will grow roughly quadratically in y for the index defined by (8.10) whereas for the index defined by (8.5), the amount of dissimilarity will tend towards a linear in y rate. Hence the choice between the two indexes depends on how fast one wants the amount of dissimilarity between x and y to grow as y grows bigger than x. It should be noted that the index defined by (8.10) will be much more sensitive to outliers in the data so perhaps for this reason, the index defined by (8.5) should be used when there is the possibility of errors in the data.[18]

Another axiom which is also not fundamental but does seem reasonable is the following one:

A8: *Differentiability*: $d(x,y)$ is a once differentiable function of two variables.

---

[17] If $d(x,y)$ is defined by (8.11) so that $d(x,y) = [\ln y - \ln x]^2$, then note that this function is a convex function of $\ln y$ for $\ln y \geq \ln x$. In other words, the failure of convexity of the log quadratic dissimilarity index is not too severe since it is convex in $\ln y$ rather than in y.

[18] If there are possible outliers in the data, then again the index defined by (8.5), the asymptotically linear index, should be preferred to the log quadratic dissimilarity index defined by (8.11).

The real impact of the axiom A8 is along the ray where $x = y$. If we look at the proof of Proposition 1, we see that if we add A8 to the list of axioms, the effect of the differentiability axiom is to force the derivative of $f(u)$ at $u = 1$ to be 0; that is, under A8, we must have $f'(1) = 0$. In many applications, this will be a very reasonable restriction on f since it implies that the amount of dissimilarity between x and y will be very small when x is very close to y. All of our examples 1 to 4 above satisfy the differentiability axiom.

We now consider another axiom for $d(x,y)$, which is more difficult to justify, but it does determine the functional form for d:

A9: *Additivity*: $d(x,y + z) = d(x,y) + d(x,z)$ for $x>0$, $y \geq 0$ and $z \geq 0$.

Proposition 4: Suppose $d(x,y)$ satisfies the axioms A1–A6 and A9. Then d has the following functional form:[19]

$$d(x,y) = \alpha[\max\{x/y, y/x\} - 1] \tag{8.12}$$
$$\text{where } \alpha > 0.$$

Let us set $\alpha = 1$ in (8.12) and call the resulting $d(x,y)$, *example 5, the linear dissimilarity index*. It can be seen that for large y, the dissimilarity indexes defined by examples 1 and 5 will approach each other. The big difference between the two indexes is along the ray where $x = y$: the linear dissimilarity index will not be differentiable along this ray, whereas the asymptotically linear dissimilarity index will be differentiable everywhere. Also for x close to y, the linear dissimilarity index will be greater than the corresponding asymptotically linear dissimilarity measure.

We conclude this section by indicating a simple way for determining the exact functional form for $d(x,y)$: we need only consider the behavior of $d(1,y)$ for $y \geq 1$. This behavior of the function d determines the underlying generator function $f(u)$ that appeared in Proposition 1. Hence consider the following 'axioms'[20] for d:

A10: $d(1,y) = (y - 1)^\beta$ $y \geq 1$, where $\beta > 0$;
A11: $d(1,y) = \ln y$; $y \geq 1$;
A12: $d(1,y) = e^y$; $y \geq 1$.

---

[19] The $f(u)$ that corresponds to this functional form is $f(u) \equiv \alpha[u - 1]$ where $\alpha > 0$. The $d(x,y)$ defined by (8.12) also satisfies the convexity axiom A7 but it does not satisfy the differentiability axiom A8.

[20] Obviously, these 'axioms' are properties that are very close to specifying the functional form for d and hence have less force than the previous axioms.

It is straightforward to show that if $d(x,y)$ satisfies A1–A6 and A10, then d is equal to the following function: (*example 6*):

$$d(x,y) \equiv [\max\{x/y,\ y/x\} - 1]^\beta\ ;\ \beta > 0. \tag{8.13}$$

Of course, if $\beta = 1$, then example 6 reduces to example 5.[21]

Similarly, it is straightforward to show that if $d(x,y)$ satisfies A1–A6 and A11, then d is equal to the following function: (*example 7*):[22]

$$d(x,y) \equiv \ln\ [\max\{x/y,\ y/x\}]. \tag{8.14}$$

Finally, if $d(x,y)$ satisfies A1–A6 and A12, then d is equal to the following function: (*example 8*):[23]

$$d(x,y) \equiv e^{\max\{x/y,y/x\}} - e. \tag{8.15}$$

The functional forms for the dissimilarity indexes defined by (8.13)–(8.15) are all relatively simple but they all have a disadvantage: namely, *they are not differentiable along the ray where $x = y$*. Hence, they are probably not suitable for many economic applications.

We turn now to N variable measures of absolute dissimilarity.

8.5   AXIOMS FOR ABSOLUTE DISSIMILARITY INDEXES IN THE N VARIABLE CASE

We now let $x \equiv [x_1,...,x_N]$ and $y \equiv [y_1,...,y_N]$ be strictly positive vectors[24] (either price or quantity) that are to be compared in an absolute sense. Let $D(x,y)$ be the absolute dissimilarity index, defined for all strictly positive vectors x and y.[25] The following six axioms or properties are fairly direct

---

[21] The $d(x,y)$ defined by (8.13) satisfies the convexity axiom A8 if and only if $\beta \geq 1$.

[22] This $d(x,y)$ does not satisfy A8.

[23] This $d(x,y)$ does satisfy the convexity axiom A8.

[24] Notation: $x \gg 0_N$ means that each component of x is positive; $x \geq 0_N$ means that each component of x is non–negative.

[25] The restriction to strictly positive vectors is a problem in the context of international comparisons because it is frequently the case that items (and even entire classes of expenditures) are not present in all countries in the comparison. Our inclination is to restrict bilateral comparisons to items or classes that are present in *both* countries and hence this leads us to set up the axioms for strictly positive vectors: basically, one cannot compare the incomparable. However, alternative points of view are

counterparts to the six fundamental axioms that were introduced in section 8.2 above.

B1: *Continuity*: $D(x,y)$ is a continuous function defined for all $x \gg 0_N$ and $y \gg 0_N$.

B2: *Identity*: $D(x,x) = 0$ for all $x \gg 0_N$.

B3: *Positivity*: $D(x,y) > 0$ for all $x \neq y$.

B4: *Symmetry*: $D(x,y) = D(y,x)$ for all $x \gg 0_N$ and $y \gg 0_N$.

B5: *Invariance to Changes in Units of Measurement*: $D(\alpha_1 x_1,..., \alpha_N x_N;$ $\alpha_1 y_1,..., \alpha_N y_N) = D(x_1,...,x_N;y_1,...,y_N) = D(x,y)$ for all $\alpha_n > 0$, $x_n > 0$, $y_n > 0$ for $n = 1,...,N$.[26]

B6: *Monotonicity*: $D(x,y)$ is increasing in the components of y if $y \geq x$.

The above axioms or properties can be regarded as fundamental. However, they are not sufficient to give a nice characterization Proposition like Proposition 1 in section 8.2. Hence we need to add additional axioms to determine D.

Possible additional properties are the following ones:

B7: *Invariance to the ordering of commodities*: $D(Px,Py) = D(x,y)$ where Px denotes a permutation of the components of the x vector and Py denotes the same permutation of the components of the y vector.

B8: *Additive Separability*: $D(x,y) = \sum_{n=1}^{N} d_n(x_n,y_n)$.

The N functions of two variables, $d_n(x_n,y_n)$, are obviously absolute dissimilarity measures that give us the degree of dissimilarity between the components of the vectors x and y.

Proposition 5: Suppose $D(x,y)$ satisfies B1–B8. Then there exists a continuous, increasing function of one variable, $f(u)$, such that $f(1) = 0$ and $D(x,y)$ has the following representation in terms of f:

$$D(x,y) \equiv \sum_{n=1}^{N} f[\max\{x_n/y_n, y_n/x_n\}]. \qquad (8.16)$$

Conversely, if $D(x,y)$ is defined by (8.16) where f is a continuous, increasing function of one variable with $f(1) = 0$, then D satisfies B1–B8.

Thus adding the axioms B7 and B8 to the earlier axioms B1–B6

---

possible; Hill and Timmer (2006) take a stochastic approach to making comparisons across countries and are able to deal with the incomparability problem in their framework.

[26] Note that this axiom implies that D has the homogeneity property $D(\lambda x, \lambda y) = D(x,y)$. To see this, let each $\alpha_n = \lambda$.

essentially reduces the N dimensional case down to the one dimensional case.

In applications, it is sometimes useful to be able to compare the amount of dissimilarity between two N dimensional vectors x and y to the amount of dissimilarity between two M dimensional vectors u and v. If we decide to use the function of one variable f to generate the dissimilarity index defined by (8.16), then we can achieve comparability across vectors of different dimensionality if we modify (8.16) and define the following family of dissimilarity indexes (which depend on N, the dimensionality of the vectors x and y):

$$D_N(x,y) \equiv \sum_{n=1}^{N} (1/N) f[\max\{x_n/y_n, y_n/x_n\}]. \qquad (8.17)$$

Recall examples 1 and 2 in section 8.2. We now use the generating functions $f(u)$ for these examples to construct N variable measures of absolute dissimilarity between the positive vectors x and y. Using the generating function $f(u) \equiv [u - 1] + [u^{-1} - 1]$ in (8.16) gives us the following *N dimensional asymptotically linear index of absolute dissimilarity*, which is the N dimensional generalization of Example 1 above, which we now label as *example 9*:

$$D_{AL}(x,y) \equiv (1/N)\sum_{n=1}^{N} [(y_n/x_n) + (x_n/y_n) - 2]. \qquad (8.18)$$

Using the generating function $f(u) \equiv [u - 1]^2 + [u^{-1} - 1]^2$ in (8.16) gives us the following *N dimensional asymptotically quadratic index of absolute dissimilarity*, which is the N dimensional generalization of Example 2 above, which we now label as *example 10*:

$$D_{AQ}(x,y) \equiv (1/N)\sum_{n=1}^{N} [(y_n/x_n) - 1]^2 + (1/N)\sum_{n=1}^{N} [(x_n/y_n) - 1]^2. \qquad (8.19)$$

The indexes defined by (8.18) and (8.19) are our preferred indexes of absolute dissimilarity.

It is possible to obtain an axiomatic characterization of a larger class of absolute dissimilarity indexes by dropping the additive separability assumption B8 and replacing it by the following weaker separability assumption:

B9: *Componentwise Symmetry*: $D(x_1,...,x_N;y_1,...,y_N) = D(y_1,x_2,...,x_N;x_1,y_2,...,y_N)$.

What is the meaning of property B9? Suppose that we are comparing the vectors x and y and we have calculated the dissimilarity measure $D(x,y) = D(x_1,...,x_N;y_1,...,y_N)$. Now suppose we interchange the first component of the x vector with the first component of the y vector and we calculate the dissimilarity measure for these new vectors, which will be

$D(y_1,x_2,...,x_N;x_1,y_2,...,y_N)$. The axiom B9 says that we get our original dissimilarity measure, $D(x,y)$. Using B7, it can be seen that if we interchange component n of both the x and y vectors and compute the dissimilarity measure for the interchanged vectors, then B9 says that we get the original dissimilarity measure, $D(x,y)$. With the help of this last axiom, we can now derive the following counterpart to Proposition 1.

Proposition 6: Let $D(x,y)$ be a function of 2N variables that satisfies the axioms B1–B7 and B9. Then $D(x,y)$ has the following representation:

$$D(x,y) \equiv f[\max\{x_1/y_1, y_1/x_1\},\max\{x_2/y_2, y_2/x_2\},...,\max\{x_N/y_N, y_N/x_N\} \quad (8.20)$$

where $f(u)$ is a symmetric continuous, monotonically increasing function of N variables, $u \equiv [u_1,...,u_N]$ defined for $u \geq 1_N$ with the following additional property:

$$f(1_N) = 0. \quad (8.21)$$

Conversely, if $f(u)$ has the above properties, then $D(x,y)$ defined by (8.20) has the properties B1–B7 and B9.

Thus absolute dissimilarity functions satisfying properties B1–B7 and B9 can all be generated (using formula (8.20) above) by a symmetric, continuous, increasing function of N variables $f(u)$ defined for $u \geq 1_N$ which also satisfies (8.21). Examples 11 and 12 below satisfy all of the properties B1–B7 and B9. These examples show that the class of dissimilarity indexes defined by (8.20) in Proposition 6 is indeed larger than the class defined by (8.16) in Proposition 5.

Example 11: Define $f(u) \equiv \{\sum_{n=1}^N (1/N)[u_n - 1]^2\}^{1/2}$ for $u_n \geq 1$ for n = 1,...,N. The resulting $D(x,y)$ is

$$D(x,y) = \{\sum_{n=1}^N (1/N)[\max\{x_n/y_n, y_n/x_n\} - 1]^2\}^{1/2}. \quad (8.22)$$

Example 12: Define $f(u) \equiv \prod_{n=1}^N [u_n - 1]^{1/N}$ for $u_n \geq 1$ for n = 1,...,N. The resulting $D(x,y)$ is

$$D(x,y) = \prod_{n=1}^N [\max\{x_n/y_n, y_n/x_n\} - 1]^{1/N}. \quad (8.23)$$

We turn now to a discussion of relative dissimilarity indexes in the case of N commodity prices or quantities that must be compared.[27]

---

[27] The case N = 1 is not relevant in the case of relative dissimilarity indexes (since in this case, any two positive numbers are relatively similar). Hence we assume that N $\geq$ 2 when discussing relative dissimilarity indexes.

8.6   AXIOMS FOR RELATIVE DISSIMILARITY INDEXES IN THE N VARIABLE CASE

In making relative comparisons, we regard x and y as being similar if x is proportional to y or if y is proportional to x; that is, if $y = \lambda x$ for some scalar $\lambda > 0$. We denote the relative dissimilarity index between two vectors x and y by $\Delta(x,y)$. The earlier axioms B1–B7 for absolute dissimilarity indexes are now replaced by the following axioms:

C1: *Continuity*: $\Delta(x,y)$ is a continuous function defined for all $x >> 0_N$ and $y >> 0_N$.

C2: *Identity*: $\Delta(x, \lambda x) = 0$ for all $x >> 0_N$ and scalars $\lambda > 0$.

C3: *Positivity*: $\Delta(x,y) > 0$ if $y \neq \lambda x$ for any $\lambda > 0$.

C4: *Symmetry*: $\Delta(x,y) = \Delta(y,x)$ for all $x >> 0_N$ and $y >> 0_N$.

C5: *Invariance to Changes in Units of Measurement*: $\Delta(\alpha_1 x_1,..., \alpha_N x_N ; \alpha_1 y_1,..., \alpha_N y_N) = \Delta(x_1,...,x_N; y_1,...,y_N) = \Delta(x,y)$ for all $\alpha_n > 0$, $x_n > 0$, $y_n > 0$ for n = 1,...,N.

C6: *Invariance to the Ordering of Commodities*: $\Delta(Px, Py) = \Delta(x,y)$ where Px is a permutation or reordering of the components of x and Py is the same permutation of the components of y.

C7: *Proportionality*: $\Delta(x, \lambda y) = \Delta(x,y)$ for all $x >> 0_N$, $y >> 0_N$ and scalars $\lambda > 0$.

The last axiom says that the degree of relative dissimilarity between the vectors x and y remains the same if y is multiplied by the arbitrary positive number λ.

The above axioms all seem to be fairly fundamental in the relative dissimilarity index context.[28] We have not developed a counterpart to the absolute monotonicity axiom B6 for relative indexes of dissimilarity because it is not clear what the appropriate relative axiom should be. This is a topic for further research. Also, we do not have any nice characterization theorems for relative dissimilarity indexes that are analogous to the results in Propositions 5 and 6 in the previous section. However, we do have a strategy for adapting the absolute dissimilarity indexes to the relative context.

Our suggested strategy is this. First, find a *scale index* $S(x,y)$ that is essentially a price or quantity index between the vectors x and y and that has the property $S(x, \lambda x) = \lambda$ for all $\lambda > 0$.[29] Second, find a suitable absolute dissimilarity index, $D(x,y)$. Finally, use the scale index S and the absolute

---

[28] Axioms C2–C7 were proposed by Allen and Diewert (1981, p 433).

[29] This property means that $S(x,y)$ is to be interpreted as an index of the size of y relative to x; that is, $S(x,y)$ is to be interpreted as an index of y relative to x.

dissimilarity index D in order to define the following relative dissimilarity index Δ:

$$\Delta(x,y) \equiv D(S(x,y)x, y). \tag{8.24}$$

Thus in (8.24), we scale up the base vector x by the index number $S(x,y)$ which makes it comparable in an absolute sense to the vector y. We then apply an absolute index of dissimilarity D to the scaled up x vector, $S(x,y)x$, and the vector y. Naturally, in order for the Δ defined by (8.24) to satisfy the axioms C1–C7, it will be necessary for D and S to satisfy certain properties. We will assume that the absolute dissimilarity index D satisfies B1–B5 and B7 in the previous section. We will also impose the following properties on the scale index $S(x,y)$:[30]

D1: *Continuity*: $S(x,y)$ is a continuous function defined for all $x \gg 0_N$ and $y \gg 0_N$.

D2: *Identity*: $S(x,x) = 1$ for all $x \gg 0_N$.

D3: *Positivity*: $S(x,y) > 0$ for all $x \gg 0_N$ and $y \gg 0_N$.

D4: *Time or Place Reversal*: $S(x,y) = 1/S(y,x)$ for all $x \gg 0_N$ and $y \gg 0_N$.

D5: *Invariance to Changes in Units of Measurement*: $S(\alpha_1 x_1,...,\alpha_N x_N ; \alpha_1 y_1,...,\alpha_N y_N) = S(x_1,...,x_N; y_1,...,y_N) = S(x,y)$ for all $\alpha_n > 0$, $x_n > 0$, $y_n > 0$ for $n = 1,...,N$.

D6: *Invariance to the Ordering of Commodities*: $S(Px,Py) = S(x,y)$ where Px is a permutation or reordering of the components of x and Py is the same permutation of the components of y.

D7: *Proportionality*: $S(x, \lambda y) = \lambda S(x,y)$ for all $x \gg 0_N$, $y \gg 0_N$ and scalars $\lambda > 0$.

Proposition 7: If the scale index $S(x,y)$ satisfies D1–D7 and the absolute dissimilarity index $D(x,y)$ satisfies B1–B5 and B7 listed in the previous section, then the relative dissimilarity index $\Delta(x,y)$ defined by (8.24) satisfies properties C1–C7.

The above Proposition can be used in order to generate a wide class of relative dissimilarity indexes. Obviously, more work needs to be done in order to obtain characterization results that are similar to the Propositions in the previous section.

We conclude this section by giving some examples of how Proposition 7 could be applied in order to define some indexes of relative dissimilarity.

---

[30] Note that $S(x,y)$ can be interpreted as an elementary quantity index; that is, an index that compares y to x when price weights are not available. For a discussion of the analogous elementary price index, see Diewert (2004a).

Example 13: Recall the N variable index of dissimilarity $D_{AL}(x,y)$ defined by (8.18) above. It can be verified that this absolute index of dissimilarity satisfies axioms B1–B9. We need to choose a scale index $S(x,y)$ that satisfies the axioms D1–D7. The simplest choice for such an S is:

$$S_J(x,y) \equiv \Pi_{n=1}^{N} (y_n/x_n)^{1/N}. \tag{8.25}$$

Thus $S(x,y)$ is the geometric mean of the y_n divided by the geometric mean of the x_n. This functional form (for a price index) is due to Jevons (1865) and it is still used today as a functional form for an elementary price index. It can be verified that S_J satisfies the axioms D1–D7. It should be noted that the following scale indexes do *not* satisfy the time reversal test, D4:

$$S_A(x,y) \equiv \sum_{n=1}^{N} (1/N)(y_n/x_n) \,; \tag{8.26}$$

$$S_H(x,y) \equiv [\sum_{n=1}^{N} (1/N)(y_n/x_n)^{-1}]^{-1}. \tag{8.27}$$

Note that S_A is the arithmetic mean[31] of the ratios y_n/x_n and S_H is the harmonic mean of the ratios y_n/x_n.

Inserting S_J defined by (8.25) into formula (8.24) where D is defined by (8.18) leads to the following *asymptotically linear index of relative dissimilarity* (which satisfies C1–C7):

$$\Delta_{AL}(x,y) \equiv D_{AL}(S_J(x,y)x, y) = \sum_{n=1}^{N}(1/N)[(S_J(x,y)x_n/y_n) + (y_n/S_J(x,y)x_n) - 2] \tag{8.28}$$

Example 14: Recall the N dimensional asymptotically quadratic index of absolute dissimilarity, $D_{AQ}(x,y)$ defined by (8.19) above. It can be verified that this absolute index of dissimilarity satisfies axioms B1–B8. Inserting S_J defined by (8.25) into formula (8.24) where D is defined by (8.19) leads to the following *asymptotically quadratic index of relative dissimilarity* (which also satisfies C1–C7):

$$\Delta_{AQ}(x,y) \equiv D_{AQ}(S_J(x,y)x, y)$$
$$=\sum_{n=1}^{N}(1/N)[(S_J(x,y)x_n/y_n) - 1]^2 + \sum_{n=1}^{N}(1/N)[(y_n/S_J(x,y)x_n) - 1]^2. \tag{8.29}$$

Example 15:   Recall the log squared single variable measure of absolute dissimilarity defined by (8.11) above. The additively separable extension of

---

[31] S_A is known in the price index literature as the Carli (1804) index (originally published in 1764); see Diewert (2004a). Note that the geometric mean of S_A and S_H does satisfy the axioms D1–D7 and hence could be used in place of the Jevons scale index S_J. $S_{AH}(x,y) \equiv [S_A(x,y)S_H(x,y)]^{1/2}$ has been suggested as the functional form for an elementary price index by Carruthers et al. (1980).

this measure to the N variable case is the following *log squared index of absolute dissimilarity*:

$$D_{LS}(x,y) \equiv \sum_{n=1}^{N} (1/N)[\ln(y_n/x_n)]^2. \qquad (8.30)$$

It can be verified that this absolute index of dissimilarity satisfies axioms B1–B9. Inserting S_J defined by (8.25) into formula (8.24) where D is defined by (8.30) leads to the following *log squared index of relative dissimilarity* (which also satisfies C1–C7):

$$\begin{aligned}
\Delta_{LS}(x,y) \equiv D_{LS}(S_J(x,y)x, y) &= \sum_{n=1}^{N} (1/N)[\ln(y_n/S_J(x,y)x_n)]^2 \\
&= (1/N)\sum_{n=1}^{N} [\ln(y_n/x_n) - \ln S_J(x,y)]^2 \\
&= (1/N)\sum_{n=1}^{N} [\ln(y_n/x_n) - \ln\{\Pi_{n=1}^{N} (y_n/x_n)^{1/N}\}]^2.
\end{aligned}$$
$$(8.31)$$

The last line of (8.31) shows that $\Delta_{LS}(x,y)$ is equal to a constant times the Allen Diewert (1981, p.433) measure of nonproportionality between the vectors x and y. Allen and Diewert derived their measure by regressing the N logarithmic ratios, $\ln(y_n/x_n)$, on a constant, obtaining $(1/N)\sum_{n=1}^{N} \ln(y_n/x_n) = \ln\{\Pi_{n=1}^{N} (y_n/x_n)^{1/N}\}$ as the least squares estimator of this constant. They then used the sum of squared residuals from their regression as their measure of nonproportionality, which is N times the last line of (8.31).

Example 16: For this example, we again start off with the absolute dissimilarity index D_{AQ} defined by (8.19) but instead of using the geometric scale function $S_J(x,y)$, we use the harmonic scale function $S_H(x,y)$ defined by (8.27) in the following way:

$$\begin{aligned}
\Delta_A(x,y) \equiv &\sum_{n=1}^{N} (1/N)[(S_H(x,y)x_n/y_n) - 1]^2 \qquad (8.32) \\
&+ \sum_{n=1}^{N} (1/N)[(S_H(y,x)y_n/x_n) - 1]^2 \\
= &\sum_{n=1}^{N} (1/N)[(x_n/y_n S_A(y,x)) - 1]^2 \\
&+ \sum_{n=1}^{N} (1/N)[(y_n/S_A(x,y)x_n) - 1]^2
\end{aligned}$$

since $S_H(x,y) = [S_A(y,x)]^{-1}$. Note that $S_A(x,y)$ is the arithmetic mean of the N ratios y_n/x_n and $S_A(y,x)$ is the arithmetic mean of the N ratios x_n/y_n. Thus in the first summation on the right-hand side of (8.32), we divide each x_n/y_n by the arithmetic mean of these N ratios[32] and in the second summation, we divide each y_n/x_n by the arithmetic mean of these N ratios. Using (8.32), it can be shown that $\Delta_A(x,y) \neq D_{AQ}(S_H(x,y)x,y)$, since the x_n are multiplied by $S_H(x,y)$ in the first summation of terms in (8.32) and by $S_A(x,y)$ in the second summation

---

[32] Note that $S_H(x,y)x_n/y_n = (x_n/y_n)/S_A(y,x) = (x_n/y_n)/[\sum_{i=1}^{N} (1/N)(x_i/y_i)]$

of terms in (8.32). Nevertheless, the index of relative dissimilarity $\Delta_A(x,y)$ defined by (8.32) *does* satisfy all of the axioms C1–C7. The only axiom which requires a bit of computation to check is the symmetry axiom, namely that $\Delta_A(x,y) = \Delta_A(y,x)$. We have, using definition (8.32):

$$
\begin{aligned}
\Delta_A(y,x) &\equiv \sum_{n=1}^{N} (1/2N)[(S_H(y,x)y_n/x_n) - 1]^2 \qquad\qquad (8.33)\\
&\quad + \sum_{n=1}^{N} (1/2N)[(S_H(x,y)x_n/y_n) - 1]^2 \\
&= \sum_{n=1}^{N}(1/2N)[(S_H(x,y)x_n/y_n) - 1]^2 \\
&\quad + \sum_{n=1}^{N}(1/2N)[(S_H(y,x)y_n/x_n) - 1]^2
\end{aligned}
$$

interchanging the two sums

$$
= \Delta_A(x,y)
$$

using definition (8.32).

  We turn now to a rather different approach that has been used to derive measures of relative dissimilarity.

8.7   ANGULAR AND LEAST SQUARES MEASURES OF RELATIVE DISSIMILARITY

In this section, we consider a somewhat different approach to obtaining relative dissimilarity measures between two vectors. These methods rely on the Cauchy Schwarz inequality or on the theory of correlation coefficients and they were pioneered by Kravis, Heston and Summers (1982) and Sergeev (2001, this volume).

  Let us start with an approach based on the Cauchy Schwarz inequality, which states that for two nonzero vectors x and y, $(x \cdot y)^2 \leq (x \cdot x)(y \cdot y)$, with a strict inequality unless $x = \lambda y$ for some number $\lambda \neq 0$. In economic applications, x and y will be positive vectors in which case, the inequality can be rewritten as follows:

$$
0 < (x \cdot y)^2/(x \cdot x)(y \cdot y) \leq 1 \qquad\qquad (8.34)
$$

with the upper bound holding as an equality if and only if $x = \lambda y$. Hence we can define *the Cauchy Schwarz relative dissimilarity index* as

$$
\Delta_{CS}(x,y) \equiv 1 - (x \cdot y)^2/(x \cdot x)(y \cdot y). \qquad\qquad (8.35)
$$

What are the properties of Δ_{CS}? It can be verified that Δ_{CS} satisfies all of the axioms C1–C7 except axiom C5, the invariance to changes in the units of measurement property. This is a fatal flaw so we conclude that Δ_{CS} is not suitable as an index of relative dissimilarity.

Let us attempt to overcome this difficulty. Thus define the components of the vectors $r \equiv [r_1,...,r_N]$ and $s \equiv [s_1,...,s_N]$ as follows:

$$r_n \equiv y_n/x_n \;;\; s_n \equiv x_n/y_n \;;\; n = 1,...,N. \tag{8.36}$$

Thus the r_n are just the ratios y_n/x_n and the s_n are the reciprocals of these ratios. Now apply the Cauchy Schwarz inequality to the vector r and the vector of 1's, 1_N. We obtain the following counterpart to (8.34):

$$0 < (r \cdot 1_N)^2/(r \cdot r)(1_N \cdot 1_N) \le 1 \tag{8.37}$$

with the upper bound holding if and only if $\lambda r = 1_N$ or $x = \lambda y$.[33] Hence we can define a *new Cauchy Schwarz relative dissimilarity index* as

$$\Delta_r(x,y) \equiv 1 - \{(r \cdot 1_N)^2/(r \cdot r)(1_N \cdot 1_N)\}. \tag{8.38}$$

It can be verified that Δ_r satisfies all of the axioms C1–C7 except axiom C4, the symmetry property. This is a fatal flaw so we conclude that Δ_r is also not suitable as an index of relative dissimilarity.

We can also define another *new Cauchy Schwarz relative dissimilarity index* using the vector s instead of r as

$$\Delta_s(x,y) \equiv 1 - (s \cdot 1_N)^2/(s \cdot s)(1_N \cdot 1_N). \tag{8.39}$$

Of course, Δ_s also satisfies all of the axioms C1–C7 except axiom C4, the symmetry property. This is a fatal flaw so we again conclude that Δ_s is not suitable as an index of relative dissimilarity.[34]

Now let $m(a,b)$ be a symmetric mean of a and b. Use this mean function to define yet *another class of relative dissimilarity indexes* (example 17):

$$\Delta_m(x,y) \equiv m[\Delta_r(x,y), \Delta_s(x,y)] \tag{8.40}$$

where $\Delta_r(x,y)$ and $\Delta_s(x,y)$ are defined by (8.38) and (8.39).

It is straightforward to verify that the class of *symmetric mean relative*

---

[33] Taking into account the positivity of r, the lower bound in (8.37) is $1/N$, which can be approached as r tends to e_n, the nth unit vector.

[34] Note that both $\Delta_r(x,y)$ and $\Delta_s(x,y)$ satisfy the inequalities $0 \le \Delta(x,y) < 1 - (1/N)$, where we have used the positivity of x and y in deriving these bounds.

dissimilarity indexes defined by (8.38)–(8.40) satisfies all of the axioms C1–C7.[35] If we let $m(a,b)$ be the arithmetic mean, then (8.40) becomes the following *arithmetic mean relative dissimilarity index* (example 18):

$$\Delta_a(x,y) \equiv 1 - \{(1/2)(r \cdot 1_N)^2/(r \cdot r)(1_N \cdot 1_N)\} - \{(1/2)(s \cdot 1_N)^2/(s \cdot s)(1_N \cdot 1_N)\}. \quad (8.41)$$

We conclude that Δ_a defined by (8.41) is a perfectly acceptable index of relative dissimilarity.[36]

There is another way to derive an index of relative dissimilarity that follows the regression approach pioneered by Allen and Diewert (1981, p.433) and also utilized by Sergeev (2001, 2005). Let us regress the ratios r_n on a constant and then calculate the resulting sum of squared residuals in order to obtain the following relative dissimilarity index:

$$\Delta_{r*}(x,y) \equiv r \cdot r - (r \cdot 1_N)^2/(1_N \cdot 1_N) \quad (8.42)$$
$$= \sum_{n=1}^{N} (r_n)^2 - N r^{*2}$$

where $r^* \equiv (1/N) \sum_{n=1}^{N} r_n$ is the arithmetic mean of the r_n

$$= \sum_{n=1}^{N} (r_n - r^*)^2$$

$$\geq 0.$$

In a similar manner, we can regress the ratios s_n on a constant and then calculate the resulting sum of squared residuals in order to obtain the following relative dissimilarity index:

$$\Delta_{s*}(x,y) \equiv s \cdot s - (s \cdot 1_N)^2/(1_N \cdot 1_N) \quad (8.43)$$
$$= \sum_{n=1}^{N} (s_n)^2 - N s^{*2}$$

where $s^* \equiv (1/N) \sum_{n=1}^{N} s_n$ is the arithmetic mean of the s_n

$$= \sum_{n=1}^{N} (s_n - s^*)^2$$

$$\geq 0.$$

It is straightforward to verify that the relative dissimilarity indexes $\Delta_{r*}(x,y)$ and $\Delta_{s*}(x,y)$ satisfy all of the axioms C1–C7 except the symmetry axiom C4 and the proportionality axiom C7. The failure of the symmetry axiom can be cured if we take a symmetric mean m of $\Delta_{r*}(x,y)$ and $\Delta_{s*}(x,y)$. The failure of

---

[35] In addition, $\Delta_m(x,y)$ will satisfy the inequalities $0 \leq \Delta_m(x,y) \leq 1 - (1/N)$.

[36] The relative dissimilarity indexes defined by (8.46)–(8.49) can be termed *angular measures of dissimilarity* since $x \cdot y/[x \cdot x \, y \cdot y]^{1/2}$ can be interpreted as a measure of the angle between the vectors x and y.

test C7 can be cured in at least two ways by dividing $\Delta_{r*}(x,y)$ and $\Delta_{s*}(x,y)$ by appropriate normalizing factors. Thus for our first method of curing the problem, we divide $\Delta_{r*}(x,y)$ by the positive number $r \cdot r$ and we divide $\Delta_{s*}(x,y)$ by the sum of squares $s \cdot s$. This leads to the following *class of relative dissimilarity indexes for each symmetric mean function m:*

$$m[\Delta_{r*}(x,y)/r \cdot r, \Delta_{s*}(x,y)/s \cdot s] = \Delta_m(x,y) \equiv m[\Delta_r(x,y), \Delta_s(x,y)] \quad (8.44)$$

where $\Delta_r(x,y)$ and $\Delta_s(x,y)$ were defined by (8.38) and (8.39). Thus this first method leads back to the class of relative dissimilarity indexes, $\Delta_m(x,y)$, already defined by (8.40).[37] For the second method of curing the defects of (8.42) and (8.43), divide $\Delta_{r*}(x,y)$ by the positive number r^{*2} and divide $\Delta_{s*}(x,y)$ by the positive number s^{*2} and take a symmetric mean of these two numbers. This leads to the following *class of relative dissimilarity indexes for each symmetric mean function m* (example 19):

$$m[\Delta_{r*}(x,y)/r^{*2}, \Delta_{s*}(x,y)/s^{*2}] \quad (8.45)$$
$$= m[\{\sum_{n=1}^{N} (r_n - r^*)^2\}/r^{*2}, \sum_{n=1}^{N} (s_n - s^*)^2/s^{*2}]$$
using (8.42) and (8.43)
$$= m[\sum_{n=1}^{N} (\{r_n/r^*\} - 1)^2, \sum_{n=1}^{N} (\{s_n/s^*\} - 1)^2].$$

Let m be the arithmetic mean function and (8.45) becomes (example 20):

$$(1/2)[\Delta_{r*}(x,y)/r^{*2}] + (1/2)[\Delta_{s*}(x,y)/s^{*2}] \quad (8.46)$$
$$- (1/2)\sum_{n=1}^{N} (\{r_n/r^*\} - 1)^2 + (1/2)\sum_{n=1}^{N} (\{s_n/s^*\} - 1)^2$$
$$= (1/2)N \Delta_A(x,y)$$

where $\Delta_A(x,y)$ is the relative dissimilarity index defined by (8.32) in example 16 above.

Thus, in this section, we have related both the Cauchy Schwarz and least squares regression type relative dissimilarity indexes to the relative dissimilarity indexes that were studied in Section 6 above.

Sergeev (2001) did not actually propose any of the above angular measures of *dissimilarity*. In fact, Sergueev preferred to work with *similarity* measures and his preferred (unweighted) *measure of relative similarity* was (example 21):

$$S_S(x,y) \equiv [r \cdot 1_N s \cdot 1_N/r \cdot r \, s \cdot s]^{1/2}$$

---

[37] This shows that our earlier class of angular relative dissimilarity indexes $\Delta_m(x,y)$ is in fact closely related to the radial or circular type dissimilarity indexes defined by (8.40) and (8.41).

$$=[r \cdot 1_N/(r \cdot r \ 1_N \cdot 1_N)^{1/2}]^{1/2} \times [s \cdot 1_N/(s \cdot s \ 1_N \cdot 1_N)^{1/2}]^{1/2}[N/(r \cdot r)]^{1/4}[N/(s \cdot s)]^{1/4}$$

$$(8.47)$$

Using the positivity of r and s and the Cauchy Schwarz inequality, it can be seen that the first two terms on the right-hand side of (8.47) are between $1/N$ and 1. Since the s_n are the reciprocals of the r_n, it can be verified by solving a minimization problem that:

$$(r \cdot r)^{1/2} \ (s \cdot s)^{1/2} \geq N \qquad\qquad (8.48)$$

which shows that the last two terms on the right–hand side of (8.47) are bounded from above by 1 (and the positivity of r and s implies that the last two terms are also bounded from below by 0). Hence Sergeev's similarity measure is bounded from above by 1 (maximum similarity of the two vectors being compared) and bounded from below by 0 (minimum similarity).[38] Hence $1 - S_S(x,y)$ is a dissimilarity index.[39] It is straightforward to show that it satisfies the axioms C1–C7.

We turn now to weighted absolute and relative dissimilarity indexes.

8.8   WEIGHTED ABSOLUTE DISSIMILARITY INDEXES

The analysis up to this point has implicitly assumed (using the axioms B7 or C6) that the amount of dissimilarity between each component of the x and y vectors is equally important and hence gets an equal weight in the overall index of dissimilarity. In many applications, this assumption is not justified, which suggests that the individual component measures of dissimilarity should be weighted according to the *economic importance* of that commodity. However, there are several ways that this economic importance could be measured. If we are constructing an index of price dissimilarity, then it might be natural to weight by either the *quantities transacted* in the two situations or by the *expenditures* pertaining to that component. However,

---

[38] Sergeev (2001) argues that the fact that his measure is bounded from both above and below by a finite number is an advantage of his relative similarity measure over the relative dissimilarity measures that follow along the Allen and Diewert (1981) analysis where there is a finite lower bound but an infinite upper bound. However, if *m* is an Allen–Diewert type measure of dissimilarity that takes on values between zero and plus infinity, then $m/(1+m)$ is a transformation of the original measure that takes on values between 0 and 1. A more important consideration is to obtain dissimilarity measures that are comparable across situations where N differs. Hence, in the present version of this chapter, we have tried to suggest measures that are comparable across varying N.

[39] Note the relationship of $1 - S_S(x,y)$ to the dissimilarity indexes defined by (8.38) and (8.39).

if the prices of a large country are being compared to those of a small country, then using either of these two methods of weighting will perhaps give too much weight to the large country. Hence, we will follow the example of Theil (1967, pp.136–137) and weight the importance of commodities by their *expenditure shares* in the two countries.[40] Thus define the *expenditure share* of commodity n in country i as

$$s_n^i \equiv p_n^i q_n^i / p^i \cdot q^i \; ; \; i = 1,2 \; ; \; n = 1,...,N. \tag{8.49}$$

Let $m(a,b)$ be a symmetric mean of the positive numbers a and b and let $f(u)$ be an increasing continuous function of one variable, defined for $u \geq 1$ with the property that $f(1) = 0$. Then we can use the functions m and f in order to define the following *weighted absolute indexes of price and quantity dissimilarity*, D_P and D_Q:

$$D_P(p^1,p^2,q^1,q^2) \equiv \sum_{n=1}^{N} m(s_n^1,s_n^2) f[\max\{p_n^1/p_n^2, p_n^2/p_n^1\}] \tag{8.50}$$

$$D_Q(p^1,p^2,q^1,q^2) \equiv \sum_{n=1}^{N} m(s_n^1,s_n^2) f[\max\{q_n^1/q_n^2, q_n^2/q_n^1\}] \tag{8.51}$$

It can be seen that we have just used the characterization of $D(x,y)$ in the unweighted case given by Proposition 5 and weighted the commodities according to their economic importance, which is reflected in the weights $m(s_n^1,s_n^2)$.[41]

It will be necessary to make concrete choices for the mean function m and the generator function f in empirical examples. As in the earlier sections, on the grounds of simplicity, we choose the arithmetic mean so that

$$m(a,b) = (1/2)a + (1/2)b. \tag{8.52}$$

Our two preferred choices for f were made at the end of section 8.2 and in examples 9 and 10 in section 8.5. With the first preferred choice, (8.50) and (8.51) become the *weighted asymptotically linear index of absolute dissimilarity* (example 22):

$$D_{PAL}(p^1,p^2,q^1,q^2) \equiv \sum_{n=1}^{N} (1/2)(s_n^1 + s_n^2) [(p_n^1/p_n^2) + (p_n^2/p_n^1) - 2] \; ; \tag{8.53}$$

$$D_{QAL}(p^1,p^2,q^1,q^2) \equiv \sum_{n=1}^{N} (1/2)(s_n^1 + s_n^2)[(q_n^1/q_n^2) + (q_n^2/q_n^1) - 2] \tag{8.54}$$

---

[40] Recent papers that also pursue this weighted approach are Heston et al. (2001) and Sergeev (2001).

[41] In (8.17), we used the normalizing factor $(1/N)$ in place of our present normalizing factor, $m(s_n^1,s_n^2)$. It can be seen that the dissimilarity measures defined by (8.50) and (8.51) are comparable for differing N.

With the second preferred choice, (8.50) and (8.51) become the *weighted asymptotically quadratic index of absolute dissimilarity* (example 23):

$$D_{PAQ}(p^1,p^2,q^1,q^2) \equiv \sum_{n=1}^{N} (1/2)(s_n^1 + s_n^2)\,[\{(p_n^1/p_n^2) - 1\}^2 + \tag{8.55}$$
$$\{(p_n^2/p_n^1) - 1\}^2]\,;$$

$$D_{QAQ}(p^1,p^2,q^1,q^2) \equiv \sum_{n=1}^{N} (1/2)(s_n^1 + s_n^2)\,[\{(q_n^1/q_n^2) - 1\}^2 + \tag{8.56}$$
$$\{(q_n^2/q_n^1) - 1\}^2].$$

We can follow Theil (1967, p 138) and give the following statistical interpretation of the right-hand side of (8.50) when *m* is defined by (8.52). Define *the absolute dissimilarity of the nth price ratio* between the two countries, r_n, by:

$$r_n \equiv f[\max\{p_n^1/p_n^2,\; p_n^2/p_n^1\}] \quad \text{for n} = 1,\ldots,N. \tag{8.57}$$

Now define the discrete random variable, *R* say, as the random variable which can take on the values r_n with probabilities $\rho_n \equiv (1/2)[s_n^0 + s_n^1]$ for n = 1,...,N. Note that since each set of expenditure shares, s_n^0 and s_n^1, sums to one, the probabilities ρ_n will also sum to one. It can be seen that the expected value of the discrete random variable *R* is:

$$E[R] \equiv \sum_{n=1}^{N} \rho_n\, r_n \tag{8.58}$$
$$= \sum_{n=1}^{N} (1/2)(s_n^0 + s_n^1)\, f[\max\{p_n^1/p_n^2,\; p_n^2/p_n^1\}]$$
$$= D_P(p^1,p^2,q^1,q^2)$$

using (8.50) and (8.57). Thus $D_P(p^1,p^2,q^1,q^2)$ can be interpreted as *the expected value of the absolute dissimilarities of the price ratios between the two countries*, where the N discrete price dissimilarities are weighted according to Theil's probability weights, $\rho_n \equiv (1/2)[s_n^0 + s_n^1]$ for n = 1,...,N.

A similar interpretation can be given to $D_Q(p^1,p^2,q^1,q^2)$ defined by (8.51) when *m* is defined by (8.52). Thus $D_Q(p^1,p^2,q^1,q^2)$ can be interpreted as *the expected value of the absolute dissimilarities of the quantity ratios between the two countries*, where the N discrete absolute quantity dissimilarities, $f[\max\{q_n^1/q_n^2,\; q_n^2/q_n^1\}]$, are weighted according to Theil's probability weights, $\rho_n \equiv (1/2)[s_n^0 + s_n^1]$ for n = 1,...,N.

We note that it is not clear how to define weighted (for economic importance) absolute dissimilarity indexes in the non-separable case. This is a topic for further research.

8.9 WEIGHTED RELATIVE DISSIMILARITY INDEXES

Let $P(p^1,p^2,q^1,q^2)$ and $Q(p^1,p^2,q^1,q^2)$ be the 'best' bilateral price and quantity indexes that one could choose.[42] We want the index number formulae P and Q to satisfy counterparts to the axioms D1–D7 listed above.[43] Adapting the strategy outlined in section 8.6 above, we again use the functions m and f in order to define the following *weighted relative indexes of price and quantity dissimilarity*, Δ_P and Δ_Q:

$$\Delta_P(p^1,p^2,q^1,q^2) \equiv \sum_{n=1}^{N} m(s_n^1,s_n^2) \tag{8.59}$$
$$\times f[\max\{P(p^1,p^2,q^1,q^2)p_n^1/p_n^2,\ p_n^2/P(p^1,p^2,q^1,q^2)p_n^1\}]\ ;$$

$$\Delta_Q(p^1,p^2,q^1,q^2) \equiv \sum_{n=1}^{N} m(s_n^1,s_n^2) \tag{8.60}$$
$$\times f[\max\{Q(p^1,p^2,q^1,q^2)q_n^1/q_n^2,\ q_n^2/Q(p^1,p^2,q^1,q^2)q_n^1\}].$$

As in the previous section, we specialize m to be the arithmetic mean. With this choice, (8.59) and (8.60) become the following *weighted relative indexes of price and quantity dissimilarity*:

$$\Delta_P(p^1,p^2,q^1,q^2) \equiv \sum_{n=1}^{N} (1/2)(s_n^1 + {}_n^2) \tag{8.61}$$
$$\times f[\max\{P(p^1,p^2,q^1,q^2)p_n^1/p_n^2,\ p_n^2/P(p^1,p^2,q^1,q^2)p_n^1\}]\ ;$$

$$\Delta_Q(p^1,p^2,q^1,q^2) \equiv \sum_{n=1}^{N} (1/2)(s_n^1 + s_n^2) \tag{8.62}$$
$$\times f[\max\{Q(p^1,p^2,q^1,q^2)q_n^1/q_n^2,\ q_n^2/Q(p^1,p^2,q^1,q^2)q_n^1\}]$$

where $f(u)$ is an increasing continuous function of one variable, defined for $u \geq 1$ with the property that $f(1) = 0$.

Example 24: Consider the following special case where we choose $f(u) \equiv [\ln u]^2$. The resulting *weighted log quadratic index of relative price dissimilarity* using the bilateral index number formula P is:

$$\Delta_{PLQ}(p^1,p^2,q^1,q^2) \equiv \sum_{n=1}^{N} (1/2)(s_n^1 + s_n^2)\ \ln(p_n^2/P(p^1,p^2,q^1,q^2)p_n^1)]^2\ . \tag{8.63}$$

The above formula is a generalization of the Allen–Diewert (1981) unweighted formula (8.31) above. The Törnqvist–Theil bilateral index (Theil, 1967) number formula $P_T(p^1,p^2,q^1,q^2)$ seems to be the appropriate generalization of the unweighted Jevons formula to use in (8.63) for

---

[42] Diewert (1992) argued that the Fisher (1922) price and quantity indexes are 'best' from the axiomatic point of view but Balk (1995), Von Auer (2001) and Diewert (2004b) argue for some other choices as well.

[43] The Fisher ideal indexes satisfy these properties.

$P(p^1,p^2,q^1,q^2)$ but any superlative price index formula $P(p^1,p^2,q^1,q^2)$ could be used in (8.63).[44]

Example 25: Consider the following special case of (8.59) where $f(u) \equiv [u + u^{-1} - 2]$ for $u \geq 1$. The resulting *weighted asymptotically linear index of relative price dissimilarity* using the bilateral index number formula P is:

$$\Delta_{PAL}(p^1,p^2,q^1,q^2) \equiv \sum_{n=1}^{N} (1/2)(s_n^1 + s_n^2) \qquad (8.64)$$
$$\times \{(p_n^2/P(p^1,p^2,q^1,q^2)p_n^1) + P(p^1,p^2,q^1,q^2)(p_n^1/p_n^2) - 2\}.$$

The above formula is the weighted generalization of the unweighted relative formula (8.28) above.

Example 26: Consider the following special case of (8.59) where $f(u) \equiv (1/2)[u - 1]^2 + (1/2)[u^{-1} - 1]^2$ for $u \geq 1$. The resulting *weighted asymptotically quadratic index of relative price dissimilarity* using the bilateral index number formula P is:

$$\Delta_{PAQ}(p^1,p^2,q^1,q^2) \equiv \sum_{n=1}^{N} (1/2)(s_n^1 + s_n^2) \qquad (8.65)$$
$$\times \{[(p_n^2/P(p^1,p^2,q^1,q^2)p_n^1) - 1]^2$$
$$+ [(P(p^1,p^2,q^1,q^2)(p_n^1/p_n^2) - 1]^2\}.$$

The above formula is the weighted generalization of the unweighted relative formula (8.29) above.

Our preferred index of relative dissimilarity when there is the possibility of outliers in the data is the weighted asymptotically linear index of relative price dissimilarity defined by (8.64). If the data are regarded as being quite reliable, then the weighted log quadratic and the weighted asymptotically quadratic indexes of relative price dissimilarity defined by (8.63) and (8.65) could be used. Of course, analogous indexes can be defined for quantities rather than prices

8.10 CONCLUSION

Our tentative conclusion is that linking between countries should be based on the sum of a *weighted absolute dissimilarity index of quantities* and a *weighted relative dissimilarity index of prices*.

---

[44] See Diewert (1976) for examples of superlative indexes. Our preferred superlative index is the Fisher (1922) ideal index.

We have exhibited many different functional forms for these two dissimilarity indexes but until more theoretical and empirical research becomes available, we recommend the use of the *asymptotically linear* or *asymptotically quadratic* functional forms. Both of these functional forms are differentiable when the price vectors being compared are proportional and when the quantity vectors being compared are equal but the asymptotically quadratic functional form penalizes large deviations between the two vectors much more heavily than does the asymptotically linear functional form.[45] Thus we are specifically recommending either the *weighted asymptotically linear index of relative price dissimilarity* $\Delta_{PAL}(p^1,p^2,q^1,q^2)$ defined by (8.64) where the price index $P(p^1,p^2,q^1,q^2)$ is the Fisher (1922) ideal formula or the *weighted asymptotically quadratic index of relative price dissimilarity* $\Delta_{PAQ}(p^1,p^2,q^1,q^2)$ defined by (8.65) as our preferred measures of relative price dissimilarity.[46] Similarly, we are specifically recommending either the *weighted asymptotically linear index of absolute quantity dissimilarity* $D_{QAL}(p^1,p^2,q^1,q^2)$ defined by (8.54) or the *weighted asymptotically quadratic index of quantity dissimilarity* $D_{QAQ}(p^1,p^2,q^1,q^2)$ defined by (8.56) as our preferred measures of absolute quantity dissimilarity. These indexes satisfy all of the important axioms that we have discussed.

REFERENCES

Allen, R.C. and W.E. Diewert (1981), 'Direct versus Implicit Superlative Index Number Formulae', *Review of Economics and Statistics*, **63**, 430–435.

Balk, B.M. (1995), 'Axiomatic Price Index Theory: A Survey', *International Statistical Review*, **63 (1)**, 69–93.

Balk, B.M. (1996), 'A Comparison of Ten Methods of Multilateral International Price and Volume Comparisons', *Journal of Official Statistics*, **12**, 199–222.

Balk, B.M. (this volume), 'Aggregation Methods in International Comparisons: an Evaluation'.

Carli, Gian–Rinaldo (1804), 'Del Valore e Della Proporzione de' Metalli Monetati', 297–366 in *Scrittori Classici Italiani di Economia Politica*, Volume 13, Milan: G.G. Destefanis (originally published in 1764).

Carruthers, A.G., D.J. Sellwood and P.W. Ward (1980), 'Recent Developments in the Retail Prices Index', *The Statistician*, **29**, 1–32.

Diewert, W.E. (1976), 'Exact and Superlative Index Numbers', *Journal of Econometrics*, **4**, 114–145.

---

[45] Researchers who prefer the sum of absolute deviations as a measure of dispersion will probably be comfortable with the asymptotically linear functional form whereas researchers who prefer the variance as a measure of dispersion will probably be more comfortable using the asymptotically quadratic functional form.

[46] An alternative to the use of (8.65) is the use of (8.63) with the use of the Törnqvist–Theil (1967) bilateral index number formula $P_T(p^1,p^2,q^1,q^2)$ as the price index.

Diewert, W.E. (1992), 'Fisher Ideal Output, Input and Productivity Indexes Revisited', *Journal of Productivity Analysis* **3**, 211–248; reprinted in W.E. Diewert and A.O. Nakamura (eds), (1993), *Essays in Index Number Theory, Volume 1*, Amsterdam: North–Holland, 317–353.

Diewert, W.E. (1993), 'Symmetric Means and Choice under Uncertainty'', W.E. Diewert and A.O. Nakamura (eds), *Essays in Index Number Theory, Volume 1*, Amsterdam: North–Holland, 355–433.

Diewert, W.E. (1999), 'Axiomatic and Economic Approaches to International Comparisons', in A. Heston and R.E. Lipsey (eds), *International and Interarea Comparisons of Income, Output and Prices, Studies in Income and Wealth*, **61**, NBER, Chicago: University of Chicago Press, 13–87.

Diewert, W.E. (2002), 'Similarity and Dissimilarity Indexes: an Axiomatic Approach', Discussion Paper 02–10, Department of Economics, University of British Columbia, Vancouver, B.C., Canada, V6T 1Z1.

Diewert, W.E. (2004a), 'Elementary Indices', chapter 20 in P. Armknecht (ed.), *Producer Price Index Manual: Theory and Practice*, Washington DC: International Monetary Fund.

Diewert, W.E. (2004b), 'A New Axiomatic Approach to Index Number Theory', Discussion Paper 04–05, Department of Economics, University of British Columbia, Vancouver, B.C., Canada, V6T 1Z1

Eichhorn, W. (1978), *Functional Equations in Economics*, Reading, MA: Addison–Wesley Publishing Company.

Fisher, I. (1922), *The Making of Index Numbers*, Boston, MA: Houghton Mifflin.

Fox, K.J., R.J. Hill and W.E. Diewert (2004), 'Identifying Outliers in Multi–Output Models', *Journal of Productivity Analysis*, **22**, 73–94.

Heston, A., R. Summers and B. Aten (2001), 'Some Issues in Using Chaining Methods for International Real Product and Purchasing Power Comparisons', Paper presented at the Joint World Bank and OECD seminar on Purchasing Power Parities, January 30–February 2, Washington D.C.

Hill, R.J. (1995), 'Purchasing Power Methods of Making International Comparisons', Ph. D. dissertation, Vancouver: The University of British Columbia.

Hill, R.J. (1999a), 'Comparing Price Levels across Countries Using Minimum Spanning Trees', *Review of Economics and Statistics* **81**, 135–142.

Hill, R.J. (1999b), 'International Comparisons using Spanning Trees', in A. Heston and R.E. Lipsey (eds), *International and Interarea Comparisons of Income, Output and Prices, Studies in Income and Wealth*, **61**, NBER, Chicago: University of Chicago Press, 109–120.

Hill, R.J. (2001), 'Measuring Inflation and Growth Using Spanning Trees', *International Economic Review*, **42**, 167–185.

Hill, R.J. and M.P. Timmer (2006), 'Standard Errors and Weights in Multilateral Price Indexes', *Journal of Business and Economic Statistics*, **24** (3), 366–377.

Jevons, W.S. (1865), 'The Variation of Prices and the Value of the Currency since 1782', *Journal of the Statistical Society of London* **28**, 294–320; reprinted in *Investigations in Currency and Finance* (1884), London: Macmillan and Co., 119–150.

Kravis, I.B. (1984), 'Comparative Studies of National Incomes and Prices', *Journal of Economic Literature*, **22**, 1–39.

Kravis, I.B., A. Heston and R. Summers (1982), *World Product and Income: International Comparison of Real Gross Product*, Baltimore, MD: Johns Hopkins University Press.

Pexider, J.V. (1903), 'Notiz über Funktionaltheoreme', *Monatshefte Mathematische Physik*, **14**, 293–301.

Sergeev, S. (2001), 'Measures of the Similarity of the Country's Price Structures and their Practical Application', Conference on the European Comparison Program, U.N. Statistical Commission, Economic Commission for Europe, Geneva, November 12–14, 2001.

Sergeev, S. (this volume), 'Aggregation Methods Based on Structural International Prices.

Theil, H. (1967), *Economics and Information Theory*, Amsterdam: North–Holland Publishing.

von Auer, L. (2001), 'An Axiomatic Checkup for Price Indices', Working Paper No. 1/2001, Faculty of Economics and Management, Otto von Guericke University Magdeburg, Postfach 4120, 39016 Magdeburg, Germany.

Walsh, C.M. (1921), 'Discussion of the Best Form of Index Number', *Journal of the American Statistical Association*, **17**, 537–544.

APPENDIX

PROOFS OF PROPOSITIONS

Proof of Proposition 1: Using A5 with $\alpha = x^{-1}$, we have:

$$d(x,y) = d(1,y/x). \qquad (A1)$$

Now use A5 with $\alpha = y^{-1}$ and we find:

$$
\begin{aligned}
d(x,y) &= d(x/y,1) \\
&= d(1,x/y) \quad \text{using A4} \\
&= d(1,y/x) \quad \text{using A1 and A2.}
\end{aligned}
\qquad (A2)
$$

For $u \geq 1$, define the continuous function of one variable, $f(u)$ as

$$f(u) \equiv d(1,u) \,; u \geq 1. \qquad (A3)$$

Using A1 and definition (A3), we have

$$f(1) = d(1,1) = 0. \qquad (A4)$$

Using A6, we deduce that $f(u)$ is an increasing function of u for $u \geq 1$. Now if $x \geq y$, then from (A2) and definition (A3), we deduce that $d(x,y) = f(x/y)$. If however, $y \geq x$, then from (A2) and (A3), we deduce that $d(x,y) = f(y/x)$. These two results can be combined into the following result:

$$d(x,y) = f[\max\{x/y, y/x\}] \qquad (A5)$$

which completes the first part of the Proposition. Going the other way, if $f(u)$ is an increasing, continuous function for $u \geq 1$ with $f(1) = 0$, then if we define $d(x,y)$ using (A5), it is easy to verify that $d(x,y)$ satisfies the axioms A1–A6.

Proof of Proposition 2: Straightforward computations except for axiom A6, which we now verify. Let $y'' > y' \geq x > 0$. Then

$$d_{g,h,m}(x,y'') \equiv m[g\{|h(y''/x) - h(1)|\}, g\{|h(x/y'') - h(1)|\}] \qquad (A6)$$
$$= m[g\{h(y''/x) - h(1)\}, g\{h(1) - h(x/y'')\}]$$

using $y'' > x$ and the monotonicity of h

$$> m[g\{h(y'/x) - h(1)\}, g\{h(1) - h(x/y'')\}]$$

using $y'' > y'$, $x > 0$ and the monotonicity of h, g and m

$$> m[g\{h(y'/x) - h(1)\}, g\{h(1) - h(x/y')\}]$$

using $y'' > y'$, $x > 0$ and the monotonicity of h, g and m

$$= m[g\{|h(y'/x) - h(1)|\}, g\{|h(x/y') - h(1)|\}]$$

using $y' > x$ and the monotonicity of h

$$\equiv d_{g,h,m}(x,y'). \qquad \text{Q.E.D.}$$

Proof of Proposition 3: Let $y \geq x > 0$ and define $f(y) \equiv d(x,y)$. For the $d(x,y)$ defined by (8.5), we find that $f'(y) = 2x/y^3 > 0$ and so the asymptotically linear dissimilarity index defined by (8.5) is convex in y.

For the $d(x,y)$ defined by (8.11), we find that $f'(y) = 2(x/y)^2[1 - x^{-1}\ln(y/x)]$ which is negative for y large enough and hence the log quadratic dissimilarity index defined by (8.11) does not satisfy A7.

For the $d(x,y)$ defined by (8.10), we find that:

$$f'(y) = x^{-2} + 3x^2 y^{-4} - 2xy^{-3} \equiv g(y). \qquad (A7)$$

Let us attempt to minimize $g(y)$ defined in (A7) over $y \geq x$. We have:

$$g'(y) = -12x^2 y^{-5} + 6xy^{-4} = 0. \qquad (A8)$$

The positive roots of (A8) are $y^* = 2x$ and $y^{**} = +\infty$. We find that $g(y)$ attains a strict local minimum at $y = 2x$ and this turns out to be the global minimum of $g(y)$ for $y \geq x$. Thus we have for $y \geq x$:

$$f'(y) \geq f'(2x) = x^{-2} + 3x^2 (2x)^{-4} - 2x (2x)^{-3} > 0 \qquad \text{(A9)}$$

and hence the linear quadratic dissimilarity index defined by (8.10) satisfies A7. Q.E.D.

Proof of Proposition 4: If $d(x,y)$ satisfies A1–A6, then by Proposition 1, $d(x,y) = f[\max\{x/y, y/x\}]$ where $f(u)$ is continuous, increasing for $u \geq 1$ with $f(1) = 0$. Substitute this representation for $d(x,y)$ into A9 and letting $x > 0, y \geq 0$ and $z \geq 0$, we find that f satisfies the following functional equation:

$$f(1 + (y/x) + (z/x)) = f(1 + (y/x)) + f(1 + (z/x)) \; ; x > 0, y \geq 0, z \geq 0. \quad \text{(A10)}$$

Define the variables u and v as follows:

$$u \equiv y/x \; ; \; v \equiv z/x . \qquad \text{(A11)}$$

Substituting A11 into A10, we find that f satisfies the following functional equation:

$$f(1 + u + v) = f(1 + u) + f(1 + v) \; ; \; u \geq 0, v \geq 0. \qquad \text{(A12)}$$

Define the function g as follows:

$$g(u) \equiv f(1 + u) . \qquad \text{(A13)}$$

Using A13, A12 can be rewritten as follows:

$$g(u + v) = g(u) + g(v) \; ; \; u \geq 0, v \geq 0. \qquad \text{(A14)}$$

But A14 is Cauchy's first functional equation or a special case of Pexider's (1903) first functional equation[47] and has the following solution:

$$g(x) = \alpha x \; ; \; x \geq 0 \qquad \text{(A15)}$$

where α is a constant. Using A13 and A15,

$$f(u) = \alpha(u - 1) \; ; \; u \geq 1. \qquad \text{(A16)}$$

Equation A16 implies that d is equal to the right–hand side of (8.12). However, in order that $f(u)$ be increasing for $u \geq 1$, we require that $\alpha > 0$,

---

[47] See Eichhorn (1978, p.49) for a more accessible reference.

which completes the proof.   Q.E.D.

Proof of Proposition 5: Using B2 and B8, we have

$$D(1_N, 1_N) = \sum_{n=1}^{N} d_n(1,1) = 0. \tag{A17}$$

Thus

$$D(x,y) = D(x,y) - D(1_N, 1_N) \tag{A18}$$

using (A17)

$$= \sum_{n=1}^{N} d_n(x_n, y_n) - \sum_{n=1}^{N} d_n(1,1)$$

using B8

$$= \sum_{n=1}^{N} d_n^*(x_n, y_n)$$

where the $d_n^*(x_n, y_n)$ are defined for $n = 1, 2, \ldots, N$ as:

$$d_n^*(x_n, y_n) \equiv d_n(x_n, y_n) - d_n(1,1). \tag{A19}$$

It is easy to check that the d_n^* functions satisfy the following restrictions for $n = 1, \ldots, N$:

$$d_n^*(1,1) = 0 . \tag{A20}$$

Using (A18), we have:

$$D(x_1, 1_{N-1}, y_1, 1_{N-1}) = d_1^*(x_1, y_1) + \sum_{n=2}^{N} d_n^*(1,1) \tag{A21}$$
$$= d_1^*(x_1, y_1) \quad \text{using (A20).}$$

Properties B1–B6 on D imply that $d_1^*(x_1, y_1)$ will satisfy properties A1–A6 listed in section 8.2 above. Hence, we may apply Proposition 1 and conclude that $d_1^*(x_1, y_1)$ has the following representation:

$$d_1^*(x_1, y_1) = f[\max\{x_1/y_1, \ y_1/x_1\}] \tag{A22}$$

for some continuous, increasing function of one variable $f(u)$ defined for $u \geq 1$ with $f(1) = 0$:
Using B7, we deduce that

$$d_n^*(x_n, y_n) = d_1^*(x_n, y_n) \tag{A23}$$
$$= f[\max\{x_n/y_n, \ y_n/x_n\}];$$

for n = 2,...,N using (A22) and this establishes (8.16). The second half of the Proposition is straightforward. Q.E.D.

Proof of Proposition 6: Using B5 with $\alpha_n \equiv (x_n)^{-1}$ for n = 1,...,N, we deduce that

$$D(x,y) = D(1_N, y_1/x_1,...,y_N/x_N). \qquad (A24)$$

For $u \geq 1_N$, define the continuous function of N variables $f(u)$ as follows:

$$f(u) \equiv D(1_N, u_1,...,u_N). \qquad (A25)$$

Using B7, we deduce that $f(u)$ is symmetric in u. Using B6, we deduce that $f(u)$ is increasing in the components of u for $u \geq 1_N$. Using B2, we deduce that

$$f(1_N) = 0. \qquad (A26)$$

Using (A24), (A25) and B9, it is straightforward to verify that D and f satisfy equation (8.20) above. Note that we required only properties B1, B2, B5, B6, B7 and B9 to establish the first half of Proposition 3.[48] The converse part of the Proposition is also straightforward. Q.E.D.

Proof of Proposition 7: Properties C1 and C5 are obvious. Now check property C2:

$$
\begin{aligned}
\Delta(x, \lambda x) &\equiv D(S(x, \lambda x)x, \lambda x) && \text{using definition (8.24)} &&(A27)\\
&= D(\lambda S(x,x)x, \lambda x) && \text{using D7}\\
&= D(\lambda x, \lambda x) && \text{using D2}\\
&= 0 && \text{using B2.}
\end{aligned}
$$

Check property C3:
Given x and y, suppose that $y \neq \lambda x$ for any $\lambda > 0$. Using definition (8.24), we have:

$$
\begin{aligned}
\Delta(x,y) &\equiv D(S(x,y)x, y) && &&(A28)\\
&= D(\mu x, y) && \text{where } \mu = S(x,y) > 0 \text{ using D3}\\
&> 0 && \text{using B3 since } y \neq \mu x.
\end{aligned}
$$

Check property C4:

---

[48] Property B3 is implied by properties B2 and B6 and property B4 is implied by Property B7 and B9.

$$\Delta(x,y) \equiv D(S(x,y)x, y) \qquad \text{using definition (8.24)} \qquad \text{(A29)}$$
$$= D(1_N, y_1/x_1 S(x,y),...,y_N/x_N S(x,y)) \qquad \text{using B5}$$
$$= D(1_N, S(y,x)y_1/x_1,...,S(y,x)y_N/x_N) \qquad \text{using D4}$$
$$= D(x, S(y,x)y) \qquad \text{using B5 again}$$
$$= D(S(y,x)y,x) \qquad \text{using B4}$$
$$\equiv \Delta(y,x) \qquad \text{using definition (8.24) again.}$$

Property C6 follows from Properties B7 and D6.

Finally, check Property C7.

Let $x \gg 0_N$, $y \gg 0_N$ and $\lambda > 0$. Then by definition (8.24),

$$\Delta(x,\lambda y) \equiv D(S(x,\lambda y)x, \lambda y) \qquad\qquad\qquad\qquad\qquad \text{(A30)}$$
$$= D(\lambda S(x,y)x, \lambda y) \qquad \text{using D7}$$
$$= D(S(x,y)x, y) \qquad \text{using B5 with all } \alpha_n = \lambda$$
$$= \Delta(x,y) \qquad \text{using definition (8.24).} \qquad \text{Q.E.D.}$$

9. Comparing Per Capita Income Levels Across Countries Using Spanning Trees: Robustness, Prior Restrictions, Hybrids and Hierarchies

Robert Hill

9.1 INTRODUCTION

The use of chaining has the potential to considerably simplify, and cut the cost of, multilateral international comparisons of per capita income, while at the same time increasing characteristicity. Nevertheless, although now widely used in time–series comparisons, chaining has not made much impact on the international comparisons literature. This is because an international comparison lacks a natural ordering of countries analogous to the chronological ordering of a time series. This study shows how this problem can be resolved using spanning–tree methods. Minimum–spanning trees defined on a suitable metric provide such an ordering. Minimum–spanning trees, however, tend not to be very robust over time. That is, the minimum–spanning tree for one period may differ significantly from that in another. This study assesses the extent of this robustness problem, and considers ways of increasing the temporal stability of a minimum–spanning tree and its resulting price indexes through the imposition of prior restrictions or by combining spanning trees with other multilateral methods to form new hybrid methods. These issues are investigated using ICP and OECD data sets.

9.2 THE UNDERLYING STRUCTURE OF MULTILATERAL PRICE INDEXES

Graph Theory provides a useful framework for analysing the underlying structure of multilateral price indexes. A graph consists of a collection of vertices linked by edges. In the context of international comparisons, each vertex represents one of the countries in the comparison, while each edge represents a bilateral comparison between a pair of countries. Two particularly important graphs are the *star graph* and the *complete graph*. Both are depicted in Figure 9.1, for the case of five vertices. The star graph has one central vertex to which all other vertices are connected. In contrast, in a complete graph, all pairs of vertices are connected.

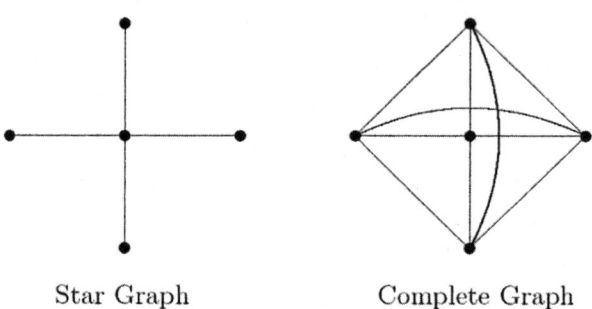

Star Graph   Complete Graph

Figure 9.1   Examples of graphs

Two broad classes of multilateral methods have been proposed in the index number literature.[1] The first class compares each country with an artificially constructed average country. By implication, the underlying structure of such methods is a star graph, with the artificial average country at the center of the star. For this reason, methods of this class are referred to here as *star methods*. Each bilateral comparison in the star is usually made using the Paasche price index formula, with the artificial country as the base. That is, the price index of country k, P_k, is calculated as follows:

$$P_k = P_{Xk}^P = \frac{\mathbf{p}_k \cdot \mathbf{q}_k}{\mathbf{p}_X \cdot \mathbf{q}_k}, \qquad (9.1)$$

where $\mathbf{p}_k$ and $\mathbf{q}_k$ denote, respectively, the price and quantity vector of country k; $\mathbf{p}_X$ denotes the price vector of the artificially constructed average country, and P_{Xk}^P denotes a Paasche price index comparison between countries X and k. Star methods that use the Paasche formula are sometimes also called *average price* methods. The most widely used average price method is Geary (1958)–Khamis (1972). In particular, it has been used by the International

---

[1]   See Hill (1997) for a more general taxonomy of multilateral methods.

Comparison Program (ICP) and to construct the Penn World Table.[2] The Geary–Khamis average price vector, $\mathbf{p}_X$, is computed as follows:

$$p_{Xi} = \sum_{k=1}^{K} \left(\frac{q_{ki}}{\sum_{j=1}^{K} q_{ji}} \frac{p_{ki}}{P_{Xk}^P} \right) \quad \forall i = 1,...,N , \tag{9.2}$$

where $k = 1,...,K$ indexes the set of countries and $i = 1,...,N$ the set of headings over which the comparison is made. The average price vector, $\mathbf{p}_X$, and Paasche price indexes, P_{Xk}^P, are obtained by solving the system of $N+K$ simultaneous equations in (9.1) and (9.2).

The second class, which includes EKS (see Eltetö and Köves, 1964; Szulc, 1964) and CCD (see Caves et al., 1982), makes bilateral comparisons between all possible pairs of countries. This means that the underlying structure of such methods is a complete graph. Hence methods of this class are referred to here as complete–graph methods. However, to obtain an internally consistent set of multilateral price indexes from a complete graph, the bilateral price indexes must be transitivized using a formula first proposed by Gini (1931). The price index of country k, P_k is calculated as follows:

$$P_k = \prod_{j=1}^{K} [(P_{jk})^{1/K}],$$

where P_{jk} denotes the result of a bilateral comparison between countries j and k. The EKS and CCD methods use the Fisher and Törnqvist formulae respectively to make each bilateral comparison. The EKS method is the most widely used complete–graph method. In particular, it is used by the OECD and Eurostat.

Both star methods and complete–graph methods become increasingly problematic as the sample of countries in a comparison rises, since they require all countries to provide price and expenditure data on the same set of basic headings. The more diverse the set of countries, the harder it becomes to construct a list of commodities within each basic heading that are representative of all the countries in the comparison.

A related problem faced by average–price star methods is that the price vector of the artificial country at the center of the star becomes increasingly

---

[2] See Summers and Heston (1991) and World Bank (1993).

unrepresentative of the prices faced by many of the countries in the comparison for very heterogeneous groupings of countries such as those included in the Penn World Table. This can cause substitution bias which may seriously distort estimates of both per capita income differentials at a point in time and convergence rates over time (see Nuxoll, 1994; Dowrick and Quiggin, 1997; Hill 2000). Geary–Khamis, in particular, will tend to underestimate per capita income differentials across countries, since its average price vector usually approximates more closely the price vectors of the richer countries in the comparison. Hence the substitution bias tends to be larger for poorer countries. This tendency is sometimes referred to as the *Gerschenkron effect* (see Gerschenkron, 1951).

The main problem with complete–graph methods is that, in a comparison between K countries, there are $K(K-1)/2$ possible bilateral comparisons. This means that, as the number of countries rises, the number of bilateral comparisons that must be made soon becomes rather large. For example, Heston et al. (2001) make comparisons over 115 countries. If the EKS method was used this would require 6555 bilateral comparisons. Inevitably, some of these comparisons are more reliable than others. For example, there may be very little overlap between the goods and services consumed in the United States and Tanzania, making a meaningful direct comparison very difficult. Largely for these reasons, Heston et al. consider alternative approaches including the minimum–spanning–tree method. Also, as noted above, a comparison between the United States and Canada will not be as good as it could be if the commodities within each basic heading, and the basic headings themselves, have to be the same as those used in all other 6554 bilateral comparisons. Thus it is tempting to conclude that the overall results could be improved by excluding bilateral comparisons between countries with very different consumption patterns. Later sections of this study discuss some ways in which this can be done.

9.3   SPANNING–TREE METHODS

The two classes of multilateral methods outlined in the previous section are not the only options. In fact, a multilateral comparison between K countries can be made by simply chaining together $K-1$ bilateral comparisons, as long as the underlying graph is a *spanning tree*. A spanning tree is a connected graph that does not contain any cycles. In other words, any pair of vertices in the graph are connected by one and only one path of edges. The reason why there must be no cycles in the graph is to ensure that the multilateral price indexes are transitive and hence internally consistent. Otherwise, the Gini transitivization formula must be used. A total of K^{K-2} different spanning trees are defined on a set of K vertices. Three examples of spanning trees defined on the set of five vertices are shown in Figure 9.2.

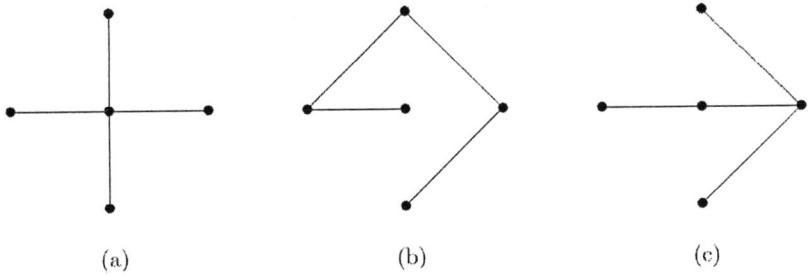

(a)   (b)   (c)

Figure 9.2   Examples of spanning trees

The resulting set of multilateral price indexes depends both on the choice of formula used for making the bilateral comparisons and on the choice of spanning tree. The bilateral comparisons should be made using a superlative formula such as Fisher or Törnqvist.[3] Since superlative formulae satisfy the country reversal test (i.e., $P_{jk} = 1/P_{kj}$), there is no need for directional arrows on the edges in the spanning tree to identify the base country in each bilateral comparison.

The choice of spanning tree is more problematic. A criterion is needed for deciding which edges (bilateral comparisons) to include and which to exclude. Ideally, we should use whichever bilateral comparisons are most reliable. Reliability in this context is measured by the sensitivity of a bilateral comparison to the choice of index number formula. The less sensitive a bilateral comparison is to the choice of formula, the more confidence we can have in the result. Two possible criteria for measuring sensitivity are discussed in the next section.

9.4   MEASURING THE SENSITIVITY OF A BILATERAL COMPARISON TO THE CHOICE OF INDEX NUMBER FORMULA

9.4.1   Relative Price Variability

One possible metric for measuring the distance, D_{jk}, between the price vectors of countries j and k is the standard deviation of the logarithm of the

---

[3] See Diewert (1976, 1978) and Hill (2006) for a definition and discussion of the properties of superlative indexes.

price relatives, p_{ki}/p_{ji}, defined over the set of goods and services indexed by $i=1,\ldots,N$.[4]

$$D_{jk} = \sqrt{\frac{1}{N} \sum_{i=1}^{N} \left[\ln\left(\frac{p_{ki}}{p_{ji}}\right) - \frac{1}{N} \sum_{n=1}^{N} \ln\left(\frac{p_{kn}}{p_{jn}}\right) \right]^2}$$ (9.3)

There is no index number problem if the price data of the two countries satisfy the conditions for Hicks's (1946) composite commodity theorem (i.e. $\mathbf{p}_k = \lambda \mathbf{p}_j$), since, under this scenario, all bilateral price index formulae will give the same answer λ. In this case, the distance metric $D_{jk}=0$. Conversely, if the data are not consistent with Hicks's composite commodity theorem, then $D_{jk}>0$. This is the basis for the claim that the distance metric, D_{jk}, measures the sensitivity of a bilateral comparison to the choice of index number formula. A larger value of D_{jk} implies greater sensitivity.

9.4.2 Paasche–Laspeyres Spread

The Paasche and Laspeyres price indexes are defined as follows:

Paasche: $P_{jk}^P = \dfrac{\mathbf{p}_k \cdot \mathbf{q}_k}{\mathbf{p}_j \cdot \mathbf{q}_k}$,   Laspeyres: $P_{jk}^L = \dfrac{\mathbf{p}_k \cdot \mathbf{q}_j}{\mathbf{p}_j \cdot \mathbf{q}_j}$.

Following Hill (1999), the Paasche–Laspeyres spread (PLS) between countries j and k is defined here as

$$PLS_{jk} = \left| \ln\left(\frac{P_{jk}^L}{P_{jk}^P}\right) \right|.$$

Like the distance metric, D_{jk}, the Paasche–Laspeyres spread, PLS_{jk} equals zero if the price data satisfy the conditions for Hicks's composite commodity theorem (i.e., $\mathbf{p}_k = \lambda \mathbf{p}_j$). However, unlike D_{jk}, the Paasche–Laspeyres spread also equals zero if $\mathbf{q}_k = \mu \mathbf{q}_j$. In this case, the quantity data satisfy the conditions for Leontief's (1936) aggregation theorem, and hence all quantity index formulae will give the same answer, μ. Even though our focus here is price indexes, Leontief's aggregation theorem is still directly relevant. This is because price and quantity indexes are not independent of each other. A price index, P_{jk}, and quantity index, Q_{jk}, are linked by the factor test as follows:

---

[4] This distance metric is also used by Allen and Diewert (1981), Debelle and Lamont (1997) and Hill (2000) to measure relative price variability.

$$P_{jk}Q_{jk} = \frac{\mathbf{p}_k \cdot \mathbf{q}_k}{\mathbf{p}_j \cdot \mathbf{q}_j} \, .$$

Using the factor test, a price index can be derived implicitly from a quantity index. In other words, if all quantity indexes give the same answer, then so should all price indexes, i.e.

$$Q_{jk} = \mu \Rightarrow P_{jk} = \frac{\mathbf{p}_k \cdot \mathbf{q}_k}{\mu(\mathbf{p}_j \cdot \mathbf{q}_j)} \, .$$

For this reason, PLS_{jk} is probably a better measure than D_{jk} of the sensitivity of a bilateral comparison to the choice of index number formula, since it is consistent with both Hicks's and Leontief's aggregation theorems.

9.5   THE MINIMUM–SPANNING TREE METHOD

A total of $K(K-1)/2$ distinct bilateral comparisons can be made over a set of K countries. The minimum–spanning tree method for computing multilateral price indexes requires a weight to be placed on each of these bilateral comparisons.[5] The weights could be given by D_{jk}, PLS_{jk}, or some other measure of the sensitivity of a bilateral comparison to the choice of formula. However, for the reasons discussed in the previous section, here we will use the Paasche–Laspeyres spreads, PLS_{jk}, as weights. The minimum–spanning tree is the spanning tree with the smallest sum of weights on its edges. (Each edge corresponds to a bilateral comparison.) The minimum–spanning tree can be computed using Kruskal's algorithm. Kruskal's algorithm selects sequentially the edges (bilateral comparisons) with the smallest weights, subject to the constraint that adding each edge does not create a cycle. The program terminates once $K-1$ edges have been selected, since at this point it is no longer possible to select any more edges without creating a cycle. The resulting graph is the minimum–spanning tree.[6]

If the Paasche–Laspeyres spreads are used as weights, a reasonable case can be made for arguing that the resulting minimum–spanning tree is the spanning tree that minimizes the sensitivity of the *multilateral* price indexes to the choice of bilateral index number formula. This is because it is

---

[5] See Hill (1999) for a more detailed analysis of the minimum–spanning tree method.

[6] A proof of this result can be found in Wilson (1985). More detailed explanations of Kruskal's algorithm and the concept of a minimum–spanning tree can be found in any introductory book on graph theory.

constructed from the bilateral comparisons that are least sensitive to the choice of formula.

The minimum–spanning tree (MST) method is illustrated below using four cross–sections of data. The first two cross–sections are drawn from the ICP database used to construct the Penn World Table, and cover the years 1980 and 1985. The first cross–section consists of price and quantity data on 30 countries defined over 151 goods and services headings. The second cross–section consists of price and quantity data for the same 30 countries defined over 139 goods and services headings. The countries in the sample consist of ten from Western Europe, three from Eastern Europe, two from North America, seven from Asia and eight from Africa.[7]

The second two cross–sections use OECD data for 1993 and 1996, respectively. The 1993 cross–section consists of price and quantity data for 34 countries defined over 147 goods and services headings. The 1996 cross–section consists of price and quantity data for the same 34 countries defined over 162 goods and services headings. The countries included are the European countries and some former Soviet republics.

The minimum spanning trees for 1980 and 1985 are depicted respectively in Figures 9.3 and 9.4.[8] The minimum spanning trees for 1993 and 1996 are depicted respectively in Figures 9.5 and 9.6.[9] Multilateral (transitive) price indexes are obtained by chaining a superlative price index such as Fisher or Törnqvist across the minimum–spanning tree. The resulting per capita income rankings are discussed below.

---

[7] A total of 42 countries were present in both the 1980 and 1985 ICP data sets. To make the regional groupings of countries more balanced, 5 smaller European countries and 7 African countries were removed from the sample.

[8] The country codes in Figures 9.3 and 9.4 are DEU – Germany, DNK – Denmark, ESP – Spain, FIN – Finland, FRA – France, GBR – Great Britain, GRC – Greece, HUN – Hungary, ITA – Italy, NOR – Norway, POL – Poland, PRT – Portugal, YUG – Yugoslavia, CAN – Canada, USA – United States of America, HKG – Hong Kong, IND – India, JPN – Japan, KOR – Korea, LKA – Sri Lanka, PAK – Pakistan, PHL – Philippines, CIV – Ivory Coast, CMR – Cameroon, KEN – Kenya, MAR – Morocco, NGA – Nigeria, TUN – Tunisia, TZA – Tanzania, ZWE – Zimbabwe.

[9] The country codes in Figures 9.5 and 9.6 are AUT – Austria, BEL – Belgium, DNK – Denmark, FRA – France, FIN – Finland, GER – Germany, GRC – Greece, IRE – Ireland, ITA – Italy, LUX – Luxembourg, NLD – Netherlands, PRT – Portugal, SPA – Spain, SWE – Sweden, UK – United Kingdom, ICE – Iceland, NOR – Norway, POL – Poland, SWI – Switzerland, CZE – Czech Republic, HUN – Hungary, TUR – Turkey, SLK – Slovak Republic, RUS – Russia, ROM – Romania, BLR – Belarus, BGR – Bulgaria, HRV – Croatia, SVN – Slovenia, UKR – Ukraine, MDA – Moldova, EST – Estonia, LVA – Latvia, LTU – Lithuania.

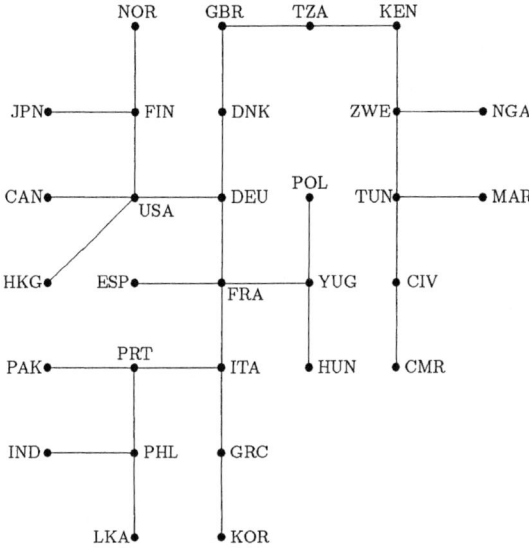

Figure 9.3   Minimum–spanning tree for 1980

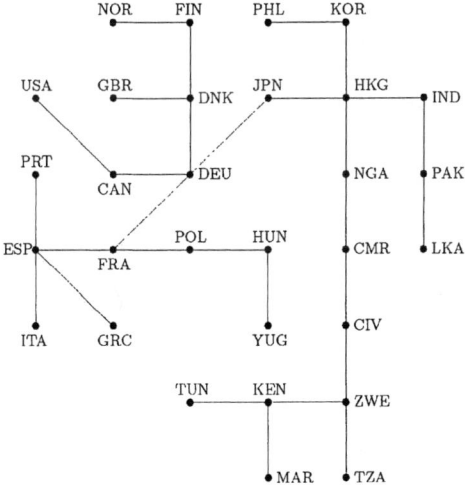

Figure 9.4   Minimum–spanning tree for 1985

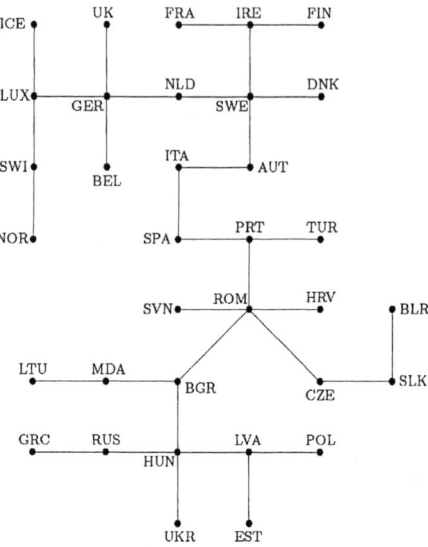

Figure 9.5   Minimum–spanning tree for 1993

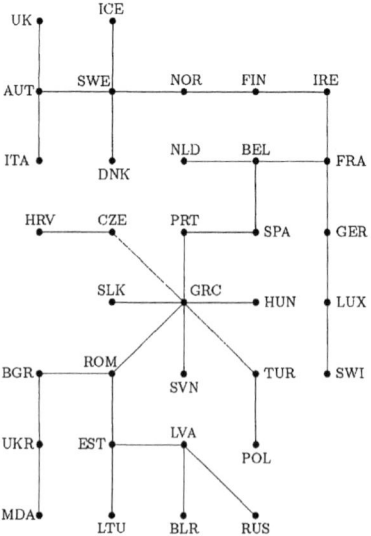

Figure 9.6   Minimum–spanning tree for 1996

9.6   AN EMPIRICAL COMPARISON OF MULTILATERAL METHODS

Tables 9.1–9.4 show the per capita income rankings for each cross–section obtained using five different multilateral methods. In Tables 9.1 and 9.2, PWT denotes the Penn World Table rankings which were computed using Geary–Khamis for 1980, and separate regional Geary–Khamis comparisons in 1985 which were then linked by bilateral comparisons between core countries.[10] The MST80 rankings are obtained by chaining Fisher price indexes across the 1980 minimum–spanning tree depicted in Figure 9.3. Likewise, the MST85 rankings are obtained by chaining Fisher price indexes across the 1985 minimum–spanning tree depicted in Figure 9.4. (Note that we use the 1980 minimum–spanning tree to compute multilateral price indexes in 1985 as well as 1980, and the 1985 minimum–spanning tree to compute multilateral price indexes in 1980 as well as 1985). Finally, the EKS and ExR results were computed, respectively, using the EKS method and market exchange rates. In Tables 9.3 and 9.4, GK denotes Geary–Khamis, while MST93 and MST96 rankings are obtained, again, by chaining Fisher price indexes across the respective minimum–spanning tree.[11]

One important reason for making international comparisons is to determine the level of inequality across countries. This can be measured by the standard deviation of the logarithm of per capita income, x_k, across the set of countries $k=1,\ldots,K$.

$$I = \sqrt{\frac{1}{K} \sum_{k=1}^{K} \left[\ln(x_k) - \frac{1}{K} \sum_{j=1}^{K} \ln(x_j) \right]^2} \qquad (9.4)$$

---

[10] See World Bank (1993) for more details.

[11] For technical reasons, mainly due to the difficulty of comparing public consumption between OECD countries and former Eastern–block countries, a few headings were not available in 1993. Hence the 1993 per capita incomes in Table 9.3 do not cover the whole of GDP and the rankings may be somewhat distorted.

Table 9.1   Per capita income rankings in 1980 (US dollars)

PWT		MST80		MST85		EKS		ExR	
CAN	11 615	USA	11 448	USA	11 448	USA	11 448	NOR	14 110
USA	11 448	CAN	10 838	CAN	10 837	CAN	10 708	DEU	13 306
NOR	11 325	NOR	10 251	DEU	10 178	DEU	9 858	DNK	12 964
DEU	10 200	DEU	9 961	NOR	10 066	NOR	9 822	FRA	12 137
DNK	9 831	DNK	9 696	DNK	9 906	FRA	9 637	USA	11 448
FRA	9 780	FRA	9 652	FRA	9 861	DNK	9 447	CAN	10 817
FIN	8 641	JPN	8 787	JPN	8 661	GBR	8 008	FIN	10 479
JPN	8 414	GBR	8 311	GBR	8 491	JPN	7 999	GBR	9 345
GBR	8 253	FIN	8 124	FIN	7 977	FIN	7 665	JPN	8 910
ITA	7 788	ITA	7 476	ITA	7 527	ITA	7 545	ITA	6 899
HKG	7 136	HKG	6 294	HKG	6 428	HKG	6 171	ESP	5 635
ESP	6 353	ESP	5 918	ESP	6 046	ESP	6 043	HKG	5 445
GRC	5 097	HUN	4 273	GRC	4 277	GRC	4 337	GRC	4 192
HUN	4 632	GRC	4 255	HUN	3 771	YUG	3 782	YUG	3 150
POL	4 322	POL	3 940	POL	3 542	HUN	3 767	PRT	2 429
YUG	4 042	YUG	3 760	YUG	3 319	POL	3 616	POL	2 247
PRT	3 932	PRT	3 188	PRT	3 184	PRT	3 403	HUN	1 917
KOR	2 583	KOR	1 966	KOR	2 140	KOR	2 030	KOR	1 528
TUN	1 993	TUN	1 614	TUN	1 988	TUN	1 596	TUN	1 366
PHL	1 740	PHL	1 324	PHL	1 461	PHL	1 387	CIV	1 282
CIV	1 368	CIV	1 056	CIV	1 276	CIV	1 013	NGA	997
LKA	1 226	MAR	959	MAR	1 118	MAR	900	MAR	878
MAR	1 200	LKA	911	PAK	1 007	LKA	890	CMR	830
PAK	1 097	PAK	809	LKA	968	PAK	850	PHL	736
CMR	911	ZWE	769	ZWE	933	ZWE	773	ZWE	724
ZWE	894	CMR	734	CMR	887	CMR	734	KEN	423
NGA	894	NGA	716	NGA	780	NGA	675	PAK	347
KEN	637	KEN	573	KEN	694	KEN	571	LKA	280
IND	570	IND	479	IND	544	IND	497	TZA	257
TZA	361	TZA	312	TZA	359	TZA	303	IND	244

Table 9.2   Per capita income rankings in 1985 (US dollars)

PWT		MST80		MST85		EKS		ExR	
USA	16 494	USA	16 494	USA	16 494	USA	16 494	USA	16 494
CAN	15 258	CAN	14 753	CAN	14 753	CAN	14 540	NOR	14 066
NOR	13 913	NOR	13 322	NOR	13 558	NOR	13 453	CAN	13 634
DNK	12 234	DNK	12 201	DNK	11 995	DNK	12 097	DNK	11 404
DEU	12 169	DEU	11 887	DEU	11 687	DEU	11 929	FIN	11 125
JPN	11 795	FRA	11 432	ITA	11 262	FRA	11 353	JPN	11 064
FIN	11 464	ITA	11 379	FRA	11 239	ITA	11 059	DEU	10 334
FRA	11 434	FIN	10 987	FIN	11 181	FIN	10 782	FRA	9 333
GBR	10 905	GBR	10 760	GBR	10 578	GBR	10 495	GBR	8 020
ITA	10 827	JPN	10 169	JPN	9 995	JPN	10 146	ITA	7 431
HKG	10 204	HKG	9 701	HKG	9 859	HKG	9 768	HKG	6 130
ESP	7 589	ESP	6 602	ESP	6 489	ESP	6 558	ESP	4 275
GRC	5 861	GRC	5 791	GRC	5 693	GRC	5 605	GRC	3 271
PRT	5 568	PRT	4 413	PRT	4 130	PRT	4 199	PRT	2 160
HUN	5 140	HUN	4 018	HUN	3 867	YUG	4 096	KOR	2 102
YUG	4 810	YUG	4 007	YUG	3 856	HUN	3 984	YUG	2 021
POL	4 039	POL	3 410	KOR	3 396	POL	3 360	POL	1 928
KOR	3 979	KOR	3 209	POL	3 248	KOR	3 284	HUN	1 788
TUN	3 446	TUN	2 220	TUN	2 628	TUN	2 400	TUN	1 138
CMR	2 724	CMR	1 895	CMR	1 931	CMR	2 043	CMR	989
MAR	2 371	PHL	1 733	PHL	1 657	PHL	1 611	NGA	948
LKA	1 852	LKA	1 415	MAR	1 447	MAR	1 481	CIV	712
PHL	1 791	CIV	1 401	CIV	1 428	CIV	1 447	PHL	602
CIV	1 710	MAR	1 368	ZWE	1 343	LKA	1 405	ZWE	600
ZWE	1 684	ZWE	1 267	LKA	1 295	ZWE	1 303	MAR	542
PAK	1 342	PAK	1 100	PAK	1 136	PAK	1 020	LKA	360
KEN	995	NGA	806	NGA	856	NGA	870	PAK	317
NGA	980	IND	795	KEN	688	IND	652	TZA	295
IND	749	KEN	649	IND	681	KEN	640	KEN	294
TZA	418	TZA	331	TZA	302	TZA	314	IND	283

Table 9.3 Per capita income rankings in 1993 (Deutschmarks)

GK		MST93		MST96		EKS	
LUX	54 742	LUX	49 957	LUX	49 957	LUX	52 233
SWI	44 531	SWI	45 883	SWI	45 883	SWI	44 597
AUT	35 802	FRA	35 180	BEL	35 306	BEL	35 751
ICE	35 318	AUT	34 833	ICE	35 068	DNK	34 201
BEL	35 154	ICE	34 774	FRA	34 826	ICE	34 190
GER	34 149	BEL	34 657	AUT	34 593	AUT	34 156
NOR	33 998	GER	34 149	GER	34 149	GER	34 149
FRA	33 318	NOR	34 111	DNK	33 626	NOR	34 044
DNK	32 994	DNK	33 860	NOR	32 958	FRA	33 393
ITA	32 889	ITA	32 747	ITA	32 521	ITA	32 550
NLD	30 435	NLD	30 355	NLD	30 995	NLD	31 237
UK	29 178	SWE	29 583	SWE	29 379	SWE	29 045
SWE	28 650	UK	29 475	UK	28 900	UK	28 308
FIN	27 301	FIN	28 032	FIN	27 750	FIN	27 443
IRE	25 260	IRE	26 354	IRE	26 089	IRE	26 457
SPA	24 475	SPA	23 717	SPA	23 877	SPA	22 755
PRT	21 906	PRT	20 968	PRT	21 110	PRT	19 481
GRC	20 463	GRC	18 878	GRC	19 859	GRC	17 726
SVN	17 597	SVN	17 614	SVN	17 695	SVN	16 265
CZE	14 960	CZE	15 760	CZE	16 691	CZE	14 516
HUN	12 123	BLR	10 552	HUN	11 551	HUN	10 069
BLR	11 484	HUN	10 402	SLK	11 386	SLK	9 809
SLK	11 276	SLK	9 920	TUR	10 155	TUR	9 092
TUR	10 341	US	9 754	RUS	9 651	RUS	8 340
RUS	9 723	TUR	9 254	POL	9 329	POL	8 153
BGR	9 528	POL	328	BGR	8 183	BLR	7 529
POL	9 336	BGR	7 982	ROM	7 756	BGR	7 380
LTU	9 314	LTU	7 665	BLR	7 560	ROM	6 714
ROM	8 377	ROM	7 565	EST	7 419	EST	6 634
EST	8 176	EST	6 963	LTU	7 296	LTU	6 565
UKR	971	UKR	6 778	HRV	6 996	HRV	6 306
HRV	7 120	HRV	6 742	UKR	6 898	UKR	5 741
MDA	981	LVA	5 612	LVA	5 980	LVA	5 338
LVA	5 617	MDA	4 666	MDA	4 267	MDA	3 743

Table 9.4   Per capita income rankings in 1996 (Deutschmarks)

GK		MST93		MST96		EKS		ExR	
LUX	64 204	LUX	63 656	LUX	63 656	LUX	66 193	SWI	62 623
NOR	52 114	SWI	51 610	NOR	52 585	NOR	53 806	LUX	61 456
SWI	51 005	NOR	51 493	SWI	51 610	SWI	50 441	NOR	54 208
ICE	45 541	DNK	47 568	DNK	48 678	DNK	47 190	DNK	50 008
DNK	45 013	BEL	44 928	ICE	47 247	ICE	45 820	SWE	43 292
AUT	43 484	ICE	44 885	AUT	45 875	BEL	45 513	GER	43 235
GER	43 235	AUT	44 828	BEL	45 302	AUT	44 553	AUT	42 716
BEL	42 952	GER	43 235	GER	43 235	NLD	44 030	ICE	40 598
NLD	41 554	NLD	42 369	ITA	43 075	GER	43 235	BEL	39 737
FRA	39 952	ITA	42 093	NLD	42 599	ITA	42 110	FRA	39 419
ITA	39 863	FRA	41 723	FRA	41 761	FRA	41 135	NLD	38 407
UK	38 700	SWE	40 171	SWE	41 109	SWE	40 539	FIN	36 741
SWE	38 670	UK	39 400	UK	40 634	UK	39 618	ITA	31 848
FIN	36 883	FIN	39 141	FIN	39 177	FIN	39 273	UK	29 518
IRE	34 082	IRE	36 868	IRE	36 901	IRE	38 129	IRE	29 300
SPA	30 066	SPA	31 366	SPA	31 130	SPA	30 636	SPA	22 424
PRT	28 374	PRT	28 567	CZE	29 306	PRT	27 630	GRC	17 664
CZE	27 308	CZE	28 101	PRT	28 352	SVN	25 948	PRT	16 493
GRC	26 669	SVN	28 032	SVN	27 477	CZE	25 842	SVN	14 255
SVN	25 558	GRC	24 926	GRC	27 146	GRC	25 308	CZE	8 238
HUN	20 276	SLK	19 979	HUN	21 369	HUN	18 937	HUN	6 668
SLK	19 945	HUN	19 031	SLK	21 291	SLK	18 222	HRV	6 227
EST	15 354	POL	13 831	POL	15 269	POL	13 805	SLK	5 352
POL	14 474	EST	13 075	RUS	14 767	EST	13 547	POL	5 243
ROM	14 147	RUS	13 017	ROM	14 625	RUS	12 905	EST	4 475
RUS	14 026	ROM	13 000	EST	14 554	TUR	12 254	RUS	4 377
HRV	13 214	TUR	12 683	TUR	13 451	ROM	12 035	TUR	4 356
LTU	13 146	HRV	11 828	HRV	13 008	HRV	12 001	LTU	3 203
TUR	13 053	LTU	11 528	LTU	12 593	LTU	11 261	LVA	3 106
LVA	12 562	BLR	11 437	BLR	11 277	LVA	10 434	ROM	2 339
BLR	12 452	LVA	9 961	LVA	11 088	BLR	9 739	BLR	1 962
BGR	11 714	BGR	9 855	BGR	11 086	BGR	9 550	BGR	1 769
UKR	8 805	UKR	6 367	UKR	7 512	UKR	6 466	UKR	1 312
MDA	5 262	MDA	3 437	MDA	3 839	MDA	3 493	MDA	579

As a measure of inequality, I has the advantage that it is invariant to changes in the currency units in which per capita income is measured. The results are shown in Table 9.5.

Table 9.5   Average per capita income differentials

	1980	1985		1993	1996
PWT	1.058	1.015	GK	0.6505	0.6064
MST80	1.129	1.100	MST93	0.7041	0.7017
MST85	1.060	1.102	MST96	0.6999	0.6631
EKS	1.121	1.105	EKS	0.7524	0.7111
ExR	1.332	1.364	EXR	—	1.8621

The most striking result that emerges from Table 9.5 is that exchange rates clearly overestimate inequality across countries.[12] The fact that the Penn World Table (based on Geary–Khamis) in 1980 and 1985 and Geary–Khamis in 1993 and 1996 generate the smallest per capita income differentials is consistent with the so–called Gerschenkron effect. In contrast, EKS, and the minimum–spanning tree results should tend neither to overestimate nor underestimate inequality across countries, since they are all constructed from superlative Fisher indexes. It is not surprising, therefore, that these methods generate similar per capita income differentials.

Determining whether or not income levels are converging or diverging across countries has, in the last decade, become a research industry in the economics profession (for example, see Barro and Sala–i–Martin, 1992; Quah, 1996). The results in Table 9.5 for the period 1980–85 provide a sobering insight into the measurement problems faced by this literature. According to three of the five methods, some convergence occurred over this period, while according to the other two there was divergence. However, over the period 1993–96 all four methods show some convergence, although this result should not be taken too seriously given the problems with the underlying data for 1993 alluded to earlier.

It is also informative to compare the similarity of the per capita income levels generated by the five methods. An ideal measure of dissimilarity between the results of two methods a and b must also be invariant to changes in the currency units in which per capita income is measured.[13] One such measure, S_{ab}, is the standard deviation of the logarithm of the per capita income relatives, x_{ak}/x_{bk}, across the set of countries $k=1,\ldots,K$.

---

[12] For an explanation of this result, see for example, Kravis and Lipsey (1983).

[13] See Diewert (2002) for a detailed discussion on the properties of dissimilarity measures.

$$S_{ab} = \sqrt{\frac{1}{K}\sum_{k=1}^{K}\left[\ln\left(\frac{x_{bk}}{x_{ak}}\right)-\frac{1}{K}\sum_{j=1}^{K}\ln\left(\frac{x_{bj}}{x_{aj}}\right)\right]^2} \tag{9.5}$$

The results are shown in Tables 9.6 – 9.9.

Table 9.6   Dissimilarity of per capita income levels in 1980

	PWT	MST80	MST85	EKS	ExR
PWT	0.0000	0.0982	0.0877	0.0921	0.4287
MST80	0.0982	0.0000	0.0962	0.0432	0.3734
MST85	0.0877	0.0962	0.0000	0.0905	0.3902
EKS	0.0921	0.0432	0.0905	0.0000	0.3818
ExR	0.4287	0.3734	0.3902	0.3818	0.0000

Table 9.7   Dissimilarity of per capita income levels in 1985

	PWT	MST80	MST85	EKS	ExR
PWT	0.0000	0.1526	0.1351	0.1315	0.4864
MST80	0.1526	0.0000	0.0581	0.0532	0.4037
MST85	0.1351	0.0581	0.0000	0.0413	0.3993
EKS	0.1315	0.0532	0.0413	0.0000	0.3935
ExR	0.4864	0.4037	0.3993	0.3935	0.0000

Table 9.8   Dissimilarity of per capita income levels in 1993

	GK	MST93	MST96	EKS
GK	0.0000	0.0785	0.1061	0.1313
MST93	0.0785	0.0000	0.0630	0.0676
MST96	0.1061	0.0630	0.0000	0.0643
EKS	0.1313	0.0676	0.0643	0.0000

Table 9.9   Dissimilarity of per capita income levels in 1996

	GK	MST93	MST96	EKS	ExR
GK	0.0000	0.1138	0.0806	0.1151	1.4265
MST93	0.1128	0.0000	0.051	0.0441	1.3883
MST96	0.0806	0.0510	0.0000	0.0621	1.4063
EKS	0.1151	0.0441	0.0621	0.0000	1.3760
ExR	1.4265	1.3883	1.4063	1.3760	0.0000

Not surprisingly, all the results obtained using price indexes are much closer to each other than they are to the results of an exchange rate comparison. Also, with the exception of 1980, the minimum–spanning tree and EKS results are rather closer to each other than to the Penn World Table/Geary–Khamis results. These results have significant implications. A spanning tree comparison requires only $K–1$ bilateral comparisons. In contrast, EKS requires $K(K–1)/2$. In other words, EKS requires a factor of $K/2$ more bilateral comparisons. For the case of $K=34$ considered here for 1993 and 1996, the factor is 17. Inspection of Tables 9.6–9.9 strongly suggests that switching from EKS to a minimum–spanning tree would dramatically simplify the process and reduce the cost of making a multilateral comparison without having much impact on the price index estimates. Furthermore, by no longer requiring all countries to provide price and expenditure data on the same set of headings, the characteristicity of each bilateral comparison in the spanning tree could be improved. To obtain these benefits, however, it is necessary that the same spanning tree is used for a number of years. The attractiveness of the minimum–spanning–tree method therefore depends partially on how robust it is over time. This issue of robustness is investigated in the next section.

9.7   THE PROBLEM OF ROBUSTNESS

The minimum–spanning trees in Figures 9.3 and 9.4 each have 29 edges. Only nine edges are common to both spanning trees. The minimum–spanning trees in Figures 9.5 and 9.6 have 33 edges of which only 10 are common to both. Hence clearly the minimum–spanning tree is not stable over time. Neither is it likely to be robust to slight changes in the data. This can be seen from Kruskal's algorithm. Any change in the ranking of the PLS_{jk} measures may alter the minimum–spanning tree. The PLS_{jk} measures whose rankings are most likely to change, if the data are perturbed, are the smallest ones since they will tend to differ only very slightly. At the same time, as far as Kruskal's algorithm is concerned, these are also the most important PLS_{jk} measures, since the algorithm selects sequentially edges with the smallest weights (subject to the constraint that adding each additional edge does not create a cycle). By implication, the minimum–spanning tree will tend not to be very robust.

   Nevertheless, both pairs of minimum–spanning trees generate similar clusters of countries. For 1980 and 1985, the clusters coincide closely with the regional clusters used by Summers and Heston in the 1985 ICP comparison. Notably, in both spanning trees, the eight African countries form a cluster, as do the three Eastern European and five Southern European countries. Also, in both minimum–spanning trees, France forms a bridge between Northern, Southern and Eastern Europe, while the United States and Canada are linked to Europe through Germany. The remaining countries are somewhat dispersed in Figure 9.3. However, in Figure 9.4, the Asian and Northern European countries also form separate clusters. Hence when viewed from the perspective of clusters of countries, the minimum–spanning tree is quite stable over the period 1980–85. In the 1993 and 1996 minimum–spanning trees, the countries are arranged in two easily discernible clusters. The first consists of the member countries of the European Community (excluding Greece), while the second consists of the countries of Eastern Europe and former Soviet Republics. In both cases, the link country for the EC is Portugal.

In 1993 the link country for the second cluster is Romania, while in 1996 it is Greece. Indeed, Greece plays a pivotal role in the 1996 minimum–spanning tree, as does Romania in 1993. In principle, the second cluster in 1996 could itself be subdivided into two parts, the first of which would consist of primarily central European countries (Czech Republic, Slovakia, Slovenia, Croatia, Hungary, Poland, Greece and Turkey). Again, although the links within clusters are not robust, the clusters themselves are. The only country that switches cluster from 1993 to 1996 is Turkey, which in 1993 is linked to Portugal, while in 1996 it is linked to Greece.

The maximum–spanning tree for each data set is also of interest, since it provides the upper bound on the summed PLS measures. The maximum–spanning tree is the spanning tree whose multilateral price indexes will be most sensitive to the choice of bilateral index number formula. In this sense it is the worst possible way of linking countries. The maximum spanning trees for both ICP data sets are remarkably similar. Both closely resemble the star spanning tree with Sri Lanka at the center. For the 1980 data set, 25 out of 29 countries are linked directly to Sri Lanka, while for the 1985 data set, 20 countries are linked directly to Sri Lanka. The structure of the maximum–spanning tree is somewhat more complicated for the OECD data sets. In 1993, it consists of four star spanning trees linked together. The countries at the centers of the stars are Luxembourg, Belarus, Norway and Lithuania, which are linked together in that order. Former Eastern block countries are linked to either Luxembourg or Norway, while EC countries are linked to either Belarus or Lithuania. In 1996, the maximum–spanning tree consists of two star spanning trees linked together. The countries at the center of the stars are Luxembourg and Moldova. All the EC countries are linked to Moldova, while the former Eastern–block countries are linked to Luxembourg, with the exception of Croatia which is linked to Switzerland.

The summed PLS measures of the minimum and maximum–spanning trees for all four data sets are shown in Table 9.10. The summed PLS measures of the minimum and maximum–spanning trees provide a useful point of reference when evaluating the performance of other spanning trees. The results in Table 9.10 indicate that MinST85 performs reasonably well in

1980, as does MinST80 in 1985 (that is., the summed PLS measures of both are far closer to the lower bound than to the upper bound). Likewise, MinST93 and MinST96 also perform reasonably well in 1996 and 1993, respectively. These results suggest that, once a minimum–spanning tree has been constructed, it is not unreasonable to use it again in subsequent comparisons.

Table 9.10   Summed PLS measures

	MinST 1980	MinST 1985	MaxST 1980	MaxST 1985
1980 data	5.288	8.609	31.513	27.808
1985 data	6.78	4.447	30.633	32.893
	MinST 1993	MinST 1996	MaxST 1993	MaxST 1996
1993 data	1.326	3.61	30.531	20.923
1996 data	4.251	1.506	26.317	36.671

Of course, with regard to robustness, what really matters is the robustness of the multilateral price indexes, not the robustness of the minimum–spanning tree. The results in Tables 9.6–9.9 indicate that the multilateral price indexes are rather less sensitive to the choice of spanning tree than one might suspect (at least as long as the Fisher index is used to make the bilateral comparisons). For example, in Tables 9.8 and 9.9, the dissimilarity measure S_{jk} between MST93 and MST96 is less than half that between Geary–Khamis and EKS. In other words, multilateral price indexes constructed using a spanning tree are less sensitive to the choice of spanning tree than multilateral price indexes constructed using more traditional methods are to the choice of multilateral formula.

9.8   IMPOSING PRIOR RESTRICTIONS ON THE MINIMUM–SPANNING TREE

Using the same spanning tree for a number of years would dramatically simplify multilateral international comparisons. Each country would only have to compare itself with its immediate neighbors in the spanning tree, thus reducing the cost and increasing the timeliness of international comparisons. Furthermore, by construction, each country's immediate neighbors in the minimum spanning tree will tend to have similar consumption patterns. This may substantially increase the characteristicity of the comparisons. Geary–Khamis by contrast, compares all countries using a single average price vector. In a comparison over rich and poor countries the average price vector may bear little resemblance to the actual price vectors of many of the countries in the comparison. Conversely, EKS uses all possible combinations of bilateral comparisons. This also requires all countries to provide price and expenditure data on the same set of basic headings, thus reducing the characteristicity of each comparison.

Of course, to compute a minimum–spanning tree also requires all countries to provide price and expenditure data on the same set of basic headings. Therefore, the minimum–spanning tree method is only useful if the same spanning tree is used for more than one period. This is why determining the robustness of the minimum–spanning tree over time is important. Although it is robust over clusters of countries, the fact that it is not at the level of individual countries implies that the minimum–spanning–tree method should not be used blindly. This conclusion is reinforced by the fact that, in the real world, there are other considerations that must be taken into account apart from the sensitivity of the results to the choice of bilateral index number formula. In particular, some countries have better-resourced national statistical offices than others. It would make little sense to put a country with an under-resourced national statistical office at the center of a regional star even if so specified by the minimum–spanning tree.

What is required is some way of combining prior knowledge with the minimum–spanning tree methodology. It turns out that prior restrictions can easily be imposed on the minimum–spanning tree. Suppose, for example, in Figure 9.4 we do not want India to be linked directly with Hong Kong. This *exclusion* restriction can be imposed by replacing the PLS measure between India and Hong Kong, in the $K \times K$ PLS matrix, by a large dummy value, that is, by a value larger than the largest PLS measure in the matrix. This ensures that the corresponding edge is not selected by Kruskal's algorithm. Similarly, suppose we want Korea to be linked directly with Japan. This *inclusion* restriction can be imposed by replacing the PLS measure between Korea and Japan with a small dummy value, that is, a value smaller than the smallest PLS measure in the matrix (excluding the terms on the lead diagonal), but still strictly positive. This ensures that the corresponding edge is selected.

One approach for choosing a spanning tree would be to first compute the minimum–spanning tree. Then one or more prior restrictions of either the exclusion or inclusion variety are placed on the minimum–spanning tree, which is then recomputed. If necessary, subsequent rounds of prior restrictions are imposed. After each round, the impact of the prior restrictions on the performance of the restricted minimum–spanning tree can be checked by computing the sum of its PLS measures. Ultimately the decision as to whether or not to include a particular prior restriction involves a trade–off between the conviction with which the prior belief is held and its impact on the summed PLS measures. Inevitably, this means that the final spanning tree is somewhat subjective. Nevertheless, the presence of an underlying methodology, should make it easier to justify to users.

9.9　HYBRID METHODS: LINKING REGIONAL COMPARISONS USING SPANNING TREES

The minimum–spanning–tree method can also be combined with other multilateral methods using a two–stage procedure. First, the world is broken up into regions using cluster algorithms, and a method such as Geary–Khamis or EKS is used to make comparisons within each region. Then, the minimum–spanning–tree method is used to link the regions. A major attraction of this approach is that, by construction, the countries in each regional block should be fairly homogeneous, thus significantly increasing the characteristicity of the comparison within each region. In other words, when used in combination with the minimum–spanning–tree method, the Geary–Khamis and EKS methods are likely to perform rather better.

Here we consider three different methods of grouping countries into regions.

9.9.1　Regional Subtrees

Regional groupings of countries can be formed from subtrees of the minimum–spanning tree. For example, consider the minimum–spanning tree for 1996 in Figure 9.6. One possible decomposition of this minimum–spanning tree would group the countries as follows:

Region 1: UK, ICE, AUT, SWE, NOR, FIN, IRE, ITA, DNK, NLD, BEL, FRA, PRT, SPA, GER, LUX, SWI

Region 2: HRV, CZE, SLK, GRC, HUN, SVN, TUR, POL

Region 3: BGR, ROM, UKR, EST, LVA, MDA, LTU, BLR, RUS

These regions are formed by simply removing the PRT–GRC and GRC–ROM edges from the minimum–spanning tree in Figure 9.6. Table 9.11 shows the resulting per capita income rankings obtained if separate EKS comparisons are made for each of the three regions, and then, as specified by the minimum–spanning tree, Regions 1 and 2 are linked by a bilateral comparison between Portugal and Greece, and Regions 2 and 3 by a bilateral comparison between Greece and Romania. Both bilateral comparisons are made using the Fisher formula.

Table 9.11   Per capita income rankings in 1996 (Deutschmarks)

GK		MST93		MST96		EKS		ExR	
LUX	64204	LUX	63656	LUX	63656	LUX	66193	SWI	62623
NOR	52114	SWI	51610	NOR	52585	NOR	53806	LUX	61456
SWI	51005	NOR	51493	SWI	51610	SWI	50441	NOR	54208
ICE	45541	DNK	47568	DNK	48678	DNK	47190	DNK	50008
DNK	45013	BEL	44928	ICE	47247	ICE	45820	SWE	43292
AUT	43484	ICE	44885	AUT	45875	BEL	45513	GER	43235
GER	43235	AUT	44828	BEL	45302	AUT	44553	AUT	42716
BEL	42952	GER	43235	GER	43235	NLD	44030	ICE	40598
NLD	41554	NLD	42369	ITA	43075	GER	43235	BEL	39737
FRA	39952	ITA	42093	NLD	42599	ITA	42110	FRA	39419
ITA	39863	FRA	41723	FRA	41761	FRA	41135	NLD	38407
UK	38700	SWE	40171	SWE	41109	SWE	40539	FIN	36741
SWE	38670	UK	39400	UK	40634	UK	39618	ITA	31848
FIN	36883	FIN	39141	FIN	39177	FIN	39273	UK	29518
IRE	34082	IRE	36868	IRE	36901	IRE	38129	IRE	29300
SPA	30066	SPA	31366	SPA	31130	SPA	30636	SPA	22424
PRT	28374	PRT	28567	CZE	29306	PRT	27630	GRC	17664
CZE	27308	CZE	28101	PRT	28352	SVN	25948	PRT	16493
GRC	26669	SVN	28032	SVN	27477	CZE	25842	SVN	14255
SVN	25558	GRC	24926	GRC	27146	GRC	25308	CZE	8238
HUN	20276	SLK	19979	HUN	21369	HUN	18937	HUN	6668
SLK	19945	HUN	19031	SLK	21291	SLK	18222	HRV	6227
EST	15354	POL	13831	POL	15269	POL	13805	SLK	5352
POL	14474	EST	13075	RUS	14767	EST	13547	POL	5245
ROM	14147	RUS	13017	ROM	14625	RUS	12905	EST	4475
RUS	14026	ROM	13000	EST	14554	TUR	12254	RUS	4377
HRV	13214	TUR	12683	TUR	13451	ROM	12035	TUR	4356
LTU	13146	HRV	11828	HRV	13008	HRV	12001	LTU	3203
TUR	13053	LTU	11528	LTU	12593	LTU	11261	LVA	3106
LVA	12562	BLR	11437	BLR	11277	LVA	10434	ROM	2339
BLR	12452	LVA	9961	LVA	11088	BLR	9739	BLR	1962
BGR	11714	BGR	9855	BGR	11086	BGR	9550	BGR	1769
UKR	8805	UKR	6367	UKR	7512	UKR	6466	UKR	1312
MDA	5262	MDA	3437	MDA	3839	MDA	3493	MDA	579

9.9.2   Regional Stars

Suppose instead that a representative country is chosen *ex ante* for each
region. Then, for each country in the comparison, the Paasche–Laspeyres
spread between it and each of the representative countries are compared in
turn. Each country is linked to the representative country with the smallest
Paasche–Laspeyres spread. For example, using again the 1996 data set,
suppose Germany (GER), Greece (GRC) and Russia (RUS) are chosen as the
representative countries. Now taking the example of the UK, the following

Paasche–Laspeyres spreads are obtained: $PLS_{UK,GER}$=0.0297, $PLS_{UK,GRC}$=0.1248, $PLS_{UK,RUS}$=0.5199. Hence the UK is placed in the same region as Germany.[14] Using this approach, the following regions are obtained:

Region 1: UK, ICE, AUT, SWE, NOR, FIN, IRE, ITA, DNK, NLD, BEL,
          FRA, **GER**, LUX, SWI

Region 2: PRT, SPA, CZE, SLK, **GRC**, HUN, SVN, TUR, POL, ROM

Region 3: HRV, BGR, UKR, EST, LVA, MDA, LTU, BLR, **RUS**

These regions differ from those obtained using the regional subtree method in that PRT and SPA have moved from Region 1 to 2, HRV has moved from Region 2 to 3, and ROM has moved from Region 3 to 2.

The regions can be linked using Kruskal's minimum–spanning–tree algorithm. By imposing K–3 inclusion prior restrictions on the matrix of PLS measures, Kruskal's algorithm can be forced to select the three star subtrees corresponding to Regions 1, 2 and 3. In fact, the subtrees can take any form as long as each country is placed in the right region. Since, in this case, Kruskal's algorithm is used simply to determine how the three regions are linked, this means that, in practice, only two edges are selected. Although this may seem to leave the algorithm little choice, there are in fact 45 900 different ways to link the three regions. The link edges selected by Kruskal's algorithm for the 1996 data set are BEL–SPA and ROM–BGR. The resulting per capita income rankings are shown in Table 9.11. Again, the comparisons within each region are made using EKS, and the comparisons between BEL–SPA and ROM–BGR are made using the Fisher formula.

9.9.3 Regional Hierarchies

The hierarchical approach selects the same edges as the minimum–spanning tree. However, unlike the minimum–spanning tree, the order in which the edges are selected matters. The hierarchical approach forms the countries into regions based on the order in which edges are selected by Kruskal's algorithm.

---

[14] Although this prior selection of representative countries seems to introduce an element of arbitrariness to the method, this is in some sense also an advantage. It allows the international organization coordinating the comparison to ensure that each region contains at least one country with a well–resourced national statistical office. In cases where many of the national statistical offices in a region lack adequate funding, it may be preferable to use the star method rather than EKS to make comparisons within the region.

Figure 9.7 depicts the hierarchical tree derived from the 1996 data set. A more complicated grouping of countries is suggested by Figure 9.7.[15]

Region 1: UK, ICE, AUT, SWE, NOR, FIN, IRE, ITA, DNK, NLD, BEL, FRA, PRT, SPA, GER, LUX, SWI
Region 2: CZE, SLK, GRC, HUN, BGR, ROM, UKR, EST, LVA, LTU, RUS
Region 3: TUR, POL
Region 4: SVN
Region 5: HRV
Region 6: MDA
Region 7: BLR

In this case, EKS could be used to make separate comparisons in Regions 1 and 2, and the Fisher formula to compare Turkey and Poland in Region 3. The seven Regions are then linked by imposing $K–7$ inclusion prior restrictions on Kruskal's algorithm. The edges selected by Kruskal's algorithm are as follows: PRT–GRC, GRC–TUR, GRC–SVN, CZE–HRV, UKR–MDA, LVA–BLR. These bilateral comparisons are made using the Fisher formula. Again, the resulting per capita income rankings are shown in Table 9.11.[16]

Table 9.11 compares the per capita income rankings obtained from the minimum–spanning–tree and EKS methods with those obtained from the three regional hybrid methods. All five methods seem to generate remarkably similar results. This impression is confirmed by Table 9.12, which shows the matrix of dissimilarity measures computed using the formula in (9.5).

Table 9.12   Dissimilarity of per capita income levels in 1996

	MST96	EKS	Reg. Subtree	Reg. Star	Reg. Hierarchy
MST96	0.0000	0.0631	0.0176	0.0596	0.0180
EKS	0.0631	0.0000	0.0568	0.0296	0.0694
Reg. Subtree	0.0176	0.0568	0.0000	0.0522	0.0203
Reg. Star	0.0596	0.0296	0.0522	0.0000	0.0672
Reg.Hierarchy	0.018	0.0694	0.0203	0.0672	0.0000

---

[15] Note that Region 1 here is the same as for the regional subtree method.
[16] This hierarchical approach was suggested to the author by Yuri Dikhanov in his comments on the earlier draft of this chapter at the joint World Bank/OECD conference in January 2001 in Washington. For a more detailed discussion of ways of grouping data see Kaufman and Rousseeuw (1990).

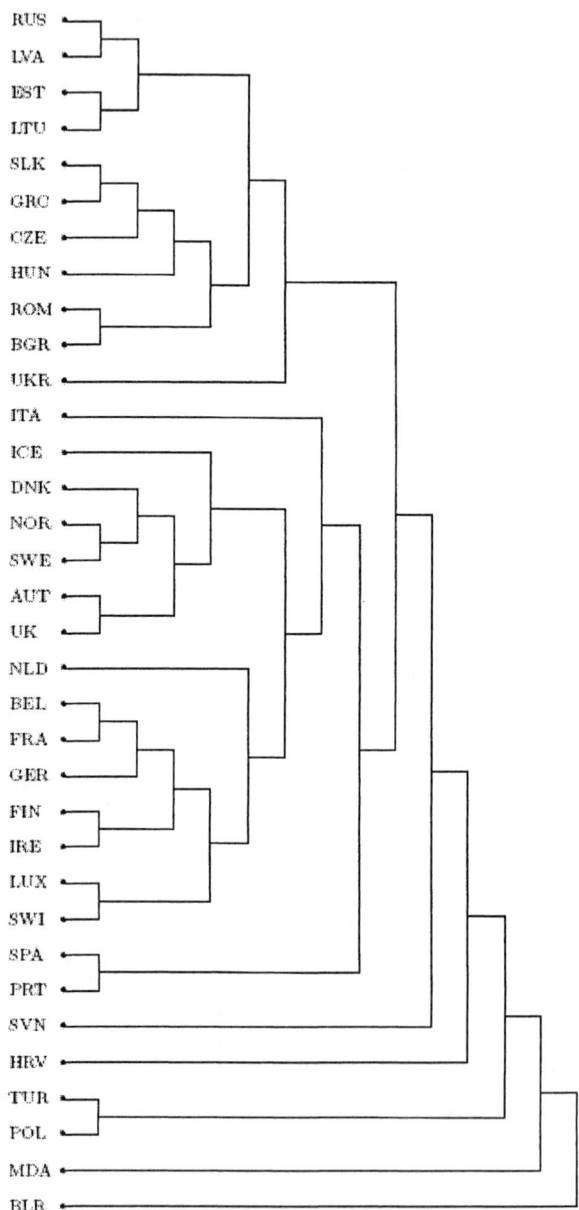

Figure 9.7   Hierarchical tree for 1996

9.10 CONCLUSION

It has been shown how the minimum–spanning–tree method provides a key for unlocking the benefits of chaining in the context of international comparisons. These benefits include considerably simplifying the comparison process, reducing the cost and improving characteristicity. Although the minimum–spanning tree is not particularly robust from year to year, it does tend to group countries into the same regional clusters. The versatility of the minimum–spanning–tree method is demonstrated by the fact that prior restrictions can easily be imposed on it to improve robustness. In addition, the method can be used to link regional blocks as well as individual countries, and hence it can be combined with other multilateral methods such as EKS or Geary–Khamis. Such hybrids methods warrant further investigation.

REFERENCES

Allen, R.C. and W.E. Diewert (1981), 'Direct versus Implicit Superlative Index Number Formulae', *Review of Economics and Statistics*, **63**, 430–435.

Barro, R.J. and X. Sala–i–Martin (1992), 'Convergence', *Journal of Political Economy*, **100** (2), 223–251.

Caves, D.W., L.R. Christensen and W.E. Diewert (1982), 'Multilateral Comparisons of Output, Input and Productivity using Superlative Index Numbers', *Economic Journal*, **92**, 73–86.

Debelle, G. and O. Lamont (1997), 'Relative Price Variability and Inflation: Evidence from U.S. Cities', *Journal of Political Economy*, **105** (1), 132–152.

Diewert, W.E. (1976), 'Exact and Superlative Index Numbers', *Journal of Econometrics*, **4**, 115–145.

Diewert, W.E. (1978), 'Superlative Index Numbers and Consistency in Aggregation', *Econometrica*, **46**, 883–900.

Diewert, W.E. (2002), 'Similarity and Dissimilarity Indexes: an Axiomatic Approach', Discussion Paper 02–10, Department of Economics, University of British Columbia.

Dowrick, S. and J. Quiggin (1997), 'True Measures of GDP and Convergence', *American Economic Review*, **87**, 41–64.

Eltetö, O. and P. Köves (1964), 'On a Problem of Index Number Computation Relating to International Comparison', *Statisztikai Szemle*, **42**, 507–518.

Geary, R.G. (1958), 'A Note on the Comparison of Exchange Rates and PPPs between Countries', *Journal of the Royal Statistical Society, Series A*, **121**, 97–99.

Gerschenkron, A. (1951), *A Dollar Index of Soviet Machinery Output', 1927–28 to 1937*, Santa Monica, CA: Rand Corporation.

Gini, C. (1931), 'On the Circular Test of Index Numbers', *International Review of Statistics*, **9** (2), 3–25.

Heston, A., R. Summers and B. Aten (2001), 'Price Structures, the Quality Factor and Chaining', Paper Presented at the Joint World Bank–OECD Seminar on Purchasing Power Parities in Washington DC, 30 Jan–2 Feb 2001.

Hicks, J.R. (1946), *Value and Capital*, 2nd Edition, Oxford: Clarendon Press.
Hill, R.J. (1997), 'A Taxonomy of Multilateral Methods for Making International Comparisons of Prices and Quantities,' *Review of Income and Wealth*, **43** (1), March, 49–69.
Hill, R.J. (1999), 'Comparing Price Levels Across Countries using Minimum Spanning Trees', *Review of Economics and Statistics*, **81** (1), 135–142.
Hill, R.J. (2000), 'Measuring Substitution Bias in International Comparisons Based on Additive Purchasing Power Parity Methods', *European Economic Review*, **44**, 145–162.
Hill, R.J. (2006), 'Superlative Index Numbers: Not All of Them are Super', *Journal of Econometrics*, **130** (1), 25–43.
Kaufman, L. and P. J. Rousseeuw (1990), *Finding Groups in Data: an Introduction to Cluster Analysis*, New York: John Wiley & Sons.
Khamis, S.H. (1972), 'A New System of Index Numbers for National and International Purposes', *Journal of the Royal Statistical Society, Series A*, **135**, 96–121.
Kravis, I.K. and R. Lipsey (1983), *Toward an Explanation of National Price Levels*, Princeton: Princeton Studies in International Finance, No. 52.
Leontief, W. (1936), 'Composite Commodities and the Problem of Index Numbers', *Econometrica*, **4**, 39–59.
Nuxoll, D.A. (1994), 'Differences in Relative Prices and International Differences in Growth Rates', *American Economic Review*, **84**, 1423–1436.
Quah, D.T. (1996), 'Twin Peaks, Growth and Convergence in Models of Distribution Dynamics', *Economic Journal*, **106**, July, 1045–1055.
Summers, R. and A. Heston (1991), 'The Penn World Table (Mark 5): an Expanded Set of International Comparisons, 1950–1988', *Quarterly Journal of Economics*, **106**, 327–368.
Szulc, B. (1964), 'Indices for Multiregional Comparisons' [translated from Polish], *Przeglad Statystyczny*, **3**, *Statistical Review*, **3**, 239–254.
Wilson, R.J. (1985), *Introduction to Graph Theory*, 3rd Edition, New York: Longman.
World Bank (1993), *Purchasing Power of Currencies: Comparing National Incomes Using ICP Data*, Washington, DC: International Economics Department, World Bank.

10. Chaining Methods for International Real Product and Purchasing Power Comparisons: Issues and Alternatives

Bettina Aten and Alan Heston[1]

Finally the Chain Method is statistically laborious and inconvenient to apply in practice – so much so that it has been very seldom employed, in spite of the many years which have passed by since it was first recommended and the general approval (more than it deserves in my opinion) which it has received from theorists.

John Maynard Keynes (*A Treatise on Money*, 1930, p. 119)

10.1 INTRODUCTION

The above quotation from Keynes is primarily in the context of temporal chaining. However, it is in a chapter on *Comparisons of Purchasing Power* and his remarks on chaining would equally have been applied to spatial comparisons, which are also discussed.[2] Whether one accepts Keynes's views, it is worth reminding ourselves that many of the issues of concern in this and other chapters in this volume have been around for some time.

In the past few years there has been a renewed interest in using binary links between countries to build up multilateral comparisons. One reason for this increasing interest is that more and more countries have taken to chaining their temporal price indexes and real product accounts. Another reason is that as the number of countries participating in benchmark comparisons grows, there has been increasing concern about the reliability of the various multilateral methods of aggregation. This has led to increased interest in spatial chaining methods with parallel efforts to find more satisfactory multilateral methods of aggregation.

[1] Support of the National Science Foundation (SES99–11377) for Heston's part of this work is gratefully acknowledged.
[2] Keynes's own recommendation would be to choose those parts of the expenditures in two positions (time or space) that are identical, 'supplementing this by a list of the expenditures discarded and added (so as to enable a general judgment to be made as to the extent of improved opportunities)' (1930, volume 1, p. 119).

Despite strong support for spatial chaining, it is fair to say that the profession is not close to agreement yet on whether or how to do it. Temporal chaining has the advantage that one year follows the next, and this provides a natural, though not the only possible, sequence for linking over time.[3] Not so across space. There are natural sequences by which to chain countries, like total population, total area, geographical contiguity, total GDP, or GDP per person. However, only the last would have any economic appeal. But it has a circular character since the whole process of spatial chaining is to arrive at a plausible cardinal order of the per capita GDPs of countries. So, one needs an answer before beginning the search.[4]

Early work on international comparisons of real product began with binary comparisons that often involved a star or node country. However, as multilateral methods of comparison evolved they were given center stage. Robert Hill has spurred a revival of interest in spatial chaining, particularly his minimum spanning tree approach on which he has done considerable experimentation. This approach to chaining involves several dimensions (Hill, 1999a, 1999b) and results in a path by which to chain over space that involves the minimum number of binary comparisons to link all countries in a comparison. There are two elements in obtaining this chain. One is a minimization procedure that is used in conjunction with the second element, a plausible measure of economic similarity for each pair of countries. In Hill's spanning tree approach this second element is the Paasche–Laspeyres Spread (PLS) between each possible pair of countries.

In this chapter we will focus on the first element, namely alternatives to the minimization procedure for obtaining the chain. It should be noted that other chapters in this volume focus on the second element, measuring similarity of prices and quantities of pairs or groups of countries (for example, Diewert's chapter in this volume). Also, an earlier paper (Heston et al., 2001) looked at chaining using price similarity indexes as an alternative to the PLS used by Hill. Section 10.2 of the chapter summarizes some of the results and issues arising from past studies. Section 10.3 puts forward some

---

[3]   A well–known problem with temporal chaining is that a disturbance in relative prices, like the recent oil price blip, may return to its original position after some time. However, a chain index will not return to its original position in its recording of the phenomenon. This may be less of a problem for chaining over space.

[4]   In an earlier paper (Kravis, Heston and Summers (KHS), 1978) KHS had used the ranking from the multilateral results for the 16 benchmark countries for 1973 as a basis for a chain binary and compared it with the results from a star system binary with the United States. The results were not encouraging in the sense that the resulting Paasche–Laspeyres Spread tended to be much larger than for the direct binaries with the United States. However, we did not use nodes in our chain, each country entering the chain twice except for the lowest and highest countries that entered only once.

alternative approaches to chaining that might be considered. In addition to the usual pleas for more research, the chapter concludes in section 10.4 that development of world comparisons in the future will very likely involve some binary links. However, it seems likely that only some of these links will involve pairs of individual countries, while the most important will involve groups of countries.

10.2   THE PRESENT POSITION OF SPATIAL CHAINING

10.2.1   Background

Because international comparisons were first carried out as binary exercises between two countries there was an initial move to make multilateral comparisons as a special type of spatial chaining, sometimes called the star method. The early work of Gilbert and Kravis (1954) used the United States as the centre of a star involving the UK, France, Germany and Italy. Direct binary comparisons between the four European countries were not carried out, so the only way their relative per capita GDP could be derived was through binary comparisons with the United States. This use of one country as a node, or center for a star, has been employed in a number of other studies since that time.

For example, most member countries of the Council of Mutual Economic Assistance (CMEA) did very detailed price comparisons from the 1960s until 1990, though usually the results were not published. However, the method built up multilateral comparisons through binary comparisons of each member country with the USSR. The United Nations Economic Commission for Latin America (UNECLA, 1963) carried out a study in the 1960s where the possibility of the United States playing a significant role was considered but rejected.[5] A star set of comparisons did take place with Austria as the center of Group 2 in Europe (Group 1 being the EU). During various benchmark comparisons beginning with 1980, Austria was the center of a star that included Hungary, Poland, Finland, Bulgaria, and Romania. A characteristic of each of the star comparisons mentioned above is that the criteria for a country to be the node or center of a star was some combination of their willingness to do the work or their political and/or economic

---

[5]   For the period 1960–62 the Economic Commission for Latin America carried out a study of capital cities in 19 Latin American countries and in Houston and Los Angeles. In the end, the study only carried out purchasing power comparisons excluding the United States cities. The method of weighting was to choose a representative basket for all 19 countries so that no country within the region played a larger role than another (UNECLA, 1963).

centrality to the comparisons being carried out. From the standpoint of economic similarity, comparing Hungary and Poland through Austria, or Italy and France through the United States, does not have great merit.

Another form of spatial linking has been between groups of countries. For example, Japan has been a link between ESCAP and OECD countries. Again, this has not been a very satisfactory method from an economic standpoint since Japan is at the high end of the ESCAP countries. This method was also used in the linking the 1985 results for Africa to the world, but here some of the links, like Pakistan and Kenya, were more plausible. Whatever the merit of past linking of regions, this is likely to be an increasingly important feature of any future world comparisons.

10.2.2   The Spanning Tree Method

In the Hill version, one country may also become a star for several other countries. However, there is an important difference between this type of star country and those described above. In the spanning tree version there is a similarity in economic structure of the countries linked to a star country, whereas that has usually not been characteristic of links in the ICP in the past.

10.2.3   Why not use Multilateral Links?

As multilateral comparisons have developed from binary beginnings it seemed logical to try to develop methods that dealt with the fact that binary comparisons between A/B, A/C, and B/C do not lead to a transitive result. That is the direct comparison of B/C will not generally equal the indirect comparison obtained by dividing A/C by A/B. Many investigations have been carried out on how to do this and many of the commonly used methods have been discussed by Erwin Diewert (1999) and Rao (this volume). The broad results of all the methods support the most important finding of the ICP, namely that the price level (purchasing power divided by the exchange rate) of GDP systematically rises with per capita GDP, sometimes referred to as the Balassa–Samuelson effect (Heston et al., 1994).

However, there are differences between the methods with respect to the total disparity of incomes between rich and poor countries, it being typically less with the GK method using total country GDP as weights, and larger for the commonly used Elteto–Koves–Szulc (EKS) method. However, the differences between the two methods are much less than are the differences between either of the methods and the result one would get using exchange rates (Kravis, Heston and Summers, 1982 – hereafter KHS, 1982). Another issue between methods is how the sub–components of GDP are calculated; in

Geary–Khamis (GK) they are a by–product of the method while for EKS they have to be estimated directly by EKS, or indirectly.[6]

One further point needs to be emphasized about the aggregations, namely that weighting is really the crucial element. Balk (this volume) reviews a number of aggregation methods and tests their performance in the context of volume comparisons. If the GK method is used with the same weighting system as EKS, namely each country receives the same weight, then the differences between the two methods is slight. Or if EKS is weighted in the same way as is typical for the GK method, namely total GDP of each country, the differences are also substantially reduced. A further point is that in most of the comparisons of methods for the world as a whole, China and India have not been included, so when weights have been used they have been skewed towards the price structure of the OECD countries. If China and India were both included in the comparisons, the international prices used would be closer to a country like Korea or Mexico, than to Italy or Belgium.

Another issue with multilateral methods is that as the number of countries in a comparison increases or decreases, the estimates for individual countries may change. Since the number of countries usually differs from one ICP regional benchmark to another, this does introduce potential variations in results across benchmark years that is regrettable and may be less than transparent to ordinary users of the results. When spatial chaining is used additional countries may be linked in without affecting the results of other countries, at least as a first approximation.

10.2.4   The Quality and Technology Problems

There is still a more fundamental difficulty in comparing countries, namely holding the quality of goods and services constant between countries at very different income levels. One important influence on the quality of data and its comparability across countries in all benchmarks is the fact that the number of products and services and their quality are changing more rapidly than in the past. As is discussed in Heravi et al., (2001), this has typically been handled by choosing items for comparisons that are of somewhat dated technology because they will be the common denominator across the countries, not obviously a good choice. What was demonstrated in this chapter was that it is possible to make comparisons for items with many

---

[6] When sub–components are directly estimated by EKS then the sum of the sub–components may be less or more than GDP as estimated by EKS, and the discrepancy may be 10 per cent or more. It is also possible to distribute the EKS total by shares of sub–components at national prices but this means that the sub–components are not strictly comparable across countries. More discussion of this point is presented in Section 10.3.

leading edge features using hedonic regressions across space. If the comparisons were limited to exact matches the range of qualities would have been greatly restricted.   This was across fairly homogeneous countries, France, the Netherlands and the UK. Across less homogeneous countries, the use of hedonics for complex items like producer durables, including information technology items, has great potential for handling the range of technologies that are used in rich and poor countries.

A related quality problem concerns comparing like with like and a key notion of the ICP framework, namely, the use of national average prices. The concept of a national average price deserves re–examination, along with a related working rule developed early in the ICP, namely that 'a potato is a potato'. The 'potato is a potato' rule says that whether purchased in a village market or a gourmet grocery, the goal is to compare the weighted average price of a kilogram of potatoes in each country. In the late 1960s when the ICP methods were developed, it was important to have a framework that would permit comparisons, and at the time the national average price seemed a reasonable concept. But is it still a satisfactory approach?[7]

In his evaluation of the ICP for the United Nations Statistical Commission, Jacob Ryten (1998, sec. 7.3) discussed several dilemmas facing future ICP work, of which one is geographical coverage. In our potato is a potato rule, what if 90 per cent of the potatoes are purchased in rural markets and 10 per cent in supermarkets in one country, and in another country, the ratios are reversed. Does it make sense to compute a national average price?

By going to a national average price much of the underlying market information is lost on where the item is purchased, whether from rural outdoor markets, small shops, and supermarkets in various regions of a country. A major concern is that the quality of the item and associated shopping experience may not be the same as we move from outlets with few amenities to those with much better physical facilities. This is a common problem in services, like transport and health, but it is also very important in commodities too. In fact the 'new good' problem so common in time–to–time indexes has its direct counterpart in spatial comparisons. There are many instances where items are common in some countries and not others, usually because markets are income sensitive, or factor price differences lead to the prevalence of lower-tech items being used in poorer countries for the same purposes that higher-tech items are used in more affluent countries. Despite rapid globalization, differences in income and size of markets mean that new or technologically more sophisticated products will be more common in some

---

[7]   In drawing up these methods the views of Irving Kravis, who had participated with Milton Gilbert (Gilbert and Kravis, 1954) and others in the OEEC comparisons, and the views of several individuals who had worked in the CMEA comparisons of the USSR and Eastern Europe were influential.

countries and less common in others. Again, the potential to handle these problems through hedonics is only beginning to be exploited. It turns out that the very simple procedure that Robert Summers (1973) proposed, the Country–Product–Dummy method or CPD, can be extended to other features of an item, size of package, type of outlet, and so on, to effectively deal with the problem of finding exact matches for very common items, like cereal or potatoes. And if weights are known they can also be handled within a CPD framework.

Typically the variety of goods will be larger, their average quality higher and the amenities associated with outlets will be more in more affluent countries. This will show up in both consumer goods and services and also producer durables, especially in small countries that may only have one or two distributors. Thus far, hedonics has not been used to handle the variety problem. A related issue is that a characteristic of many outlets of the Wal–Mart type that have large variety, also offer only limited customer service. If type of outlet can be held constant, this latter problem can be sorted out.

Services are especially difficult to match across different countries; for example, a hospital bed involves very different facilities even if private and shared rooms are distinguished. While hedonics might play a role here, services are not covered well in national statistics in time–to–time indexes, even though they are an increasing share of consumption. The problems of comparing non–priced services over time or across space are even greater. If more resources were available it would be possible to overcome some of these comparison problems, but even if the budgets of statistical offices in participating countries went up, it is unlikely that ICP would receive high priority. Most countries have trouble doing an adequate job of comparing priced services over time, let alone across space. We argue below that another reason for considering spatial chaining is that it may serve to overcome several of these quality issues in making comparisons.

10.2.5   The Role of Chaining

Many differences in quality and proportion of high tech items discussed above are likely to be more pronounced between countries with very different economic structures. If criteria can be developed to identify countries with similar economic structure and they are compared only with each other, then it may overcome many of the issues of quality and lowest common denominator item comparisons. Economically similar countries are likely to have outlet types in similar proportions carrying the same types of goods and services. So direct comparisons between such countries will do a better job of holding constant the quality of the items than comparisons across more diverse countries.

What criteria should be used to identify economically similar countries? As mentioned above, Hill (1999a and 1999b) has used the ratio of the Paasche to the Laspeyres index to obtain the spread (PLS) for prices or quantities as his criterion. (He in fact uses the logarithm of the absolute value of the spread so that it does not matter which country is in the numerator.) His spanning tree approach minimizes the sum of the spread subject to the constraint that all countries must be in the chain and that no country can appear more than once. As we noted in the introduction, Keynes thought that comparisons of two countries or two times would be more clear–cut the greater the overlap of goods purchased in the two countries or time periods. This might be another criterion for economic similarity.

Another criteria is the price similarity index first discussed in Kravis et al., (1982, Ch. 4). An empirical application of this index is described in detail in Heston et al., (2001). We draw from some of the results to illustrate our discussion below.

The price similarity index is defined as,

$$S_{jk} = \sum_{i=1}^{m} w_{ijk} pp_{ij} pp_{ik} \Bigg/ \sqrt{\sum_{i=1}^{m} w_{ijk} \overline{pp_{ij}^2 pp_{ik}^2}} \qquad (10.1)$$

where S_{jk} is the price similarity index between country j and k, and pp_{ij} is the price–parity in price level form for the ith heading in country j, expressed as a deviation from the average value for the heading.[8] The weight for each of the m headings, w_{ijk}, is defined

$$w_{ijk} = \frac{(\exp_{ij} + \exp_{ik})}{2} \qquad (10.2)$$

---

[8] We are indebted to Erwin Diewert and Jim Cuthbert for pointing out that in our earlier work, the definition of the similarity index was not base–country invariant. In that version, the parity for each heading was expressed as the national currency units per US dollar, with the entry for the US for each heading being 1.0. However, because changing base country does affect the spanning tree path and the resulting multilateral comparisons, it is important to go with a definition of the similarity index that is base country invariant. In the present version each country's price level for a heading is expressed relative to that of the simple average of all the countries. As discussed by Diewert in Chapter 8, there are alternative measures of price, and or price and quantity similarity that might be used as criteria for spanning trees. An area for further research is to see how sensitive the chaining results are to alternative similarity measures.

where $\exp_{ij}$ is expenditure share of i–th basic heading in j–th country.[9] For each pair of countries, the average of their expenditure shares is used as the heading weight so there will be as many w_i's as there are country pairs. In the case of the price similarity index, the spanning tree method can be applied where the sum of the price similarity indexes is maximized.

Figures A.10.1 and A.10.2 in the Appendix show the spanning trees from the PLS and the similarity index respectively as applied to 32 heading parities and expenditure shares that had been put together by the World Bank for 115 countries from various regional comparisons that took place between 1993 and 1996. There are 6555 (115*114/2) possible links for each chain, that is, half the matrix of possible binaries. The first 114 links to join all countries without creating a closed loop form the minimum spanning tree or chain based on the PLS and price similarity indexes. The algorithm required going to the 2114th ranked pair (out of the 6555 possible pairs) for the PLS index and to the 2208th pair for the price similarity index.[10]

An essential feature of the trees is that each country must be linked to at least one other country, but there is no limit (short of that set by the total country sample) to the number of countries to which a node may be linked. In practice, however, a node country will not have more than four to six links out of a total of 115 countries. In addition, nodes may cluster so that one can see if geography emerges as an important feature of the chain. In both Figures A.10.1 and A.10.2 there are typically several branches or clusters of countries, with a few countries serving as nodes to link these clusters.

---

[9] This definition of the weight is different from the one used in KHS (1982). Previously we had used the world average real expenditure share for each heading that came from total world expenditures from a GK aggregation. We believe now that the average shares of each pair of countries at their national prices is a more appropriate weight. Also in KHS (1982) we did not use the heading parities, but rather the heading parities divided by the overall parity of the country so that it was a relative price that depended upon an overall PPP. We did this to provide an easy way for the US, the numeraire, to also have a similarity index with each country. And each country would have a similarity index with the world average, or Earthea, as we termed the world price structure. This was not done in the present chapter, however. As noted in the previous footnote, some earlier versions of our similarity index were not base–country invariant.

[10] In the PLS tree, the pair with the lowest Paasche–Laspeyres spread is Peru and Ecuador, while the highest spread is between Georgia and Barbados, the latter being likely candidates to have very different price and quantity relationships. Using the similarity index tree, the highest and lowest pairs in the tree are Spain and Greece and Belize and the Bahamas. The latter is somewhat surprising given that these countries are not from the same region.

10.2.6   Some Anomalies of Spanning Tree Results

Robert Hill and others have noted that the spanning tree approach can produce results that are not totally satisfactory. For example, Hill (1999a) has found that the particular chain used to link countries is not robust across benchmarks. This may not be surprising, but it would be much nicer if the results were stable over time. Hill (1999a) has suggested that the spanning tree could be implemented as a resource–saving device if one knew in advance the binary comparisons that were required. Thus, if Cambodia were only linked to Thailand, there would be no need for Cambodia to collect prices for items other than those relevant to Thailand. However, because the spanning tree will not necessarily be stable over time, resource savings may not be great.

Another aspect of the results that gives rise to questions is the particular structure of the chains that tend to emerge when the spanning tree approach is applied to either the PLS or price similarity criteria. What is troublesome in the procedure is that often countries can take a pivotal position in the estimation, even when it is known that their database is not strong. In his work for the 1996 OECD benchmark countries for example, Hill (this volume) found using the PLS that several countries had three links but that the country with the most links, six, was Greece. On many criteria, including overlap of items with other countries, Greece is not obviously the country to play a central role.

The same is true when the PLS is applied to all 115 countries, with Greece acting as the pivotal link or star between most of the OECD countries, Africa and the rest of the world (Figure A.10.1). Albania is also critical in linking the Middle East, Russia and Central Asia to the rest of the world. However, the quality of the statistical base of Albania, for example, is not as strong as Hungary's, which only links the Czech Republic and Slovakia.

Unfortunately the situation is not necessarily better using price similarity indexes as the criteria for chaining. In Figure A.10.2, Chile has seven links, linking diverse countries such as Canada, the Cameroon, the Czech Republic, Morocco, Mongolia, New Zealand and Turkmenistan to the rest of the world. The good news is that many of the branches are geographically close, with Caribbean countries clustered in the lower–left, and Western Europe in the top branch.

Another aspect of the spanning tree approach is that it cannot make the claim that it only links one country with another because they are highest in price similarity or lowest in PLS. Any pair of countries will probably have considerable similarity but the following situation may well emerge. The closest link of Belize may be with Jamaica. However, if Jamaica is closer to say, Peru and Brazil, than are Peru and Brazil to each other, Jamaica may not be directly linked to Belize. This could happen regardless of which criteria is used to chain.

The above are some of the less attractive attributes of chaining using the spanning tree technique on two candidate measures of economic similarity. Perhaps other measures of economic similarity will produce better results; certainly this is an area for future research. However, having indicated some reservations about spatial chaining, it should be pointed out that the actual results of chaining are quite plausible. What do we mean by this?

The spatial chain provides a path between any two countries. Thus to compare Norway and Great Britain in Figure A.10.2, a simple binary comparison suffices. But to compare Norway with the United States, the product of 21 additional binaries are needed: Great Britain with Ireland, Ireland with Finland, Finland with Sweden and so forth down the tree.

Table A.10.1 in the Appendix shows the per capita income estimates for each country relative to the United States for both the PLS and the similarity index spanning trees.[11] As a basis for judging how sensible the chains performed they were compared with three alternatives, namely (1) Fisher indexes with the USA as the only node or star country; (2) EKS; (3) supercountry–weighted GK. A well–known result is that EKS tends to give lower estimates than GK for low income countries. Using either the PLS or price similarity criteria, the spatial chains tended to be closer to EKS than to GK for low–income countries, with a number of individual variations. However, overall the chaining results were plausible, and displayed a number of characteristics similar to the multilateral methods.

We conclude that although there are limitations on the present state of the art with respect to spatial chaining, the overall results are encouraging. This leads us to consider in Section10.3 whether there are ways that spatial chaining might be improved and whether it is better in some types of applications versus others.

10.3   DIRECTIONS FOR FUTURE RESEARCH ON SPATIAL CHAINING

Hill (1999b) found that between the 1980 and 1985 ICP benchmark comparisons, the spatial chain was not stable. This does not mean that the ranking of countries by per capita income would necessarily be different using a chain from 1980 and one from 1985, but only that the actual links between countries that would be used to obtain the result would differ

---

[11] In the empirical work the actual measure of income was, for technical reasons, per capita domestic absorption.

between the two benchmarks. It would be a tidier world if this were not the case, but this does not strike us as a major limitation of chaining.

However, another limitation on the spanning tree approach is that some countries with weak statistical systems may be pivotal in the chains, and that is worrisome. Therefore it does seem important to see if other approaches to chaining might produce both more plausible chains and sets of final product estimates. A very desirable feature of the spanning tree approach is that it requires the user to use minimum judgment in arriving at the chain. In the discussion below, we will in fact make the distinction between more and less judgmental methods of deriving a spatial chain.

10.3.1   Less Judgmental Approaches

There are other techniques that might also be employed in deriving the chain. In Kravis, Heston and Summers (KHS, 1982, Ch. 4) both the criteria discussed above, the PLS and price similarity were used, employing cluster analysis to achieve groupings of countries, but not an explicit chain.[12] In this exercise the results of using cluster analysis were compared with those using a strictly geographical criterion or no grouping at all. These results are discussed in some detail because they are suggestive of still other ways that chaining might be carried out in the future.

In applying the spanning tree approach there is some latitude in specifying the path. We have discussed the Hill criterion of minimizing the sum of the log of the absolute values of the price level spreads subject to constraint that no country is omitted or included more than one time. The parallel criterion for the price similarity index would be to maximize the sum of the similarity indexes. One practical constraint would be require that spanning trees be first generated within pre–designated regions (or even sub–regions). Only then would a spanning tree between regions be established. The fact that some political regions like the OECD extend from East Asia to Oceania, Europe and to North America, would require more *ad hoc* treatment. The case for

---

[12] It should be pointed out that the PLS may be expressed in the way we have described it up to now, namely a number that as it takes on larger values for pairs of countries that are less similar economically. In KHS (1982, Ch. 7) the measure of the PLS was the ratio of the per capita income of the lower income country to that of the higher income country; consequently, more similar pairs of countries took on a value of the PLS closer to 1, and less similar pairs of countries had lower values. The advantage of this formulation versus the absolute value of the log of the ratio used by Hill, is that it was parallel in direction with the price similarity index. For the 34 countries in KHS (p.109) the regression of the PLS on the price similarity index across the 561 pairs of countries was $0.45 + 0.37 *$ price similarity with $R^2 = 0.47$.

constraining spanning trees or other methods of linking techniques sequentially from within regions to beyond appears strong.

For the 561 possible pairs of countries in the 1975 benchmark comparison the average value of the price similarity index was 0.754 with a standard deviation of 0.096. If one divided the 34 countries into six geographical regions, there would be 165 pairs of countries, with an average price similarity of 0.803 and a standard deviation of 0.082. Using cluster analysis yielded six groups with 134 pairs where the average price similarity index was 0.840 and the standard deviation 0.050. Clearly cluster analysis yields groups of more similar countries and also improves upon a strict geographical division.[13] That is, the cluster analysis increases the average price similarity index from 0.754 to 0.850, or 0.086 while the straight geographical coverage from 0.754 to 0.803, or 0.049, or 57 per cent of the total (0.049/0.086 * 100).

This same point about regions is elaborated in the discussion of Table 10.1 where calculations of similarity ratios and PLSs has been done for the 1996 benchmark of 115 countries. The fact that location accounts for a great deal of the differences in price similarity raises another possible line of research. Aten (1996) presented evidence of substantial spatial autocorrelation of price structures, which would be expected on the basis of transport costs, alone. One could well define a measure of similarity that was the product of say distance and price similarity, perhaps with different weights. This would produce a composite criteria for chaining that could also be used in a spanning tree approach.

This review of previous results concludes with a major practical limitation on the use of such methods, including the minimum spanning tree approach. The issue is that the organization of the benchmark work may substantially limit the options that can actually be carried out. To illustrate with a case that turned up in the 1975 benchmark, one fairly important link that emerged from cluster analysis based upon the PLS was between Uruguay and Iran. Even if such a result between Uruguay and Iran were replicated in other studies, it is unlikely that either country or any international organization would see much merit in these countries engaging in an intensive binary

---

[13] A similar exercise was carried out for the PLS and the pattern was similar. However, whereas a straight geographical division of countries accounted for 57 per cent of the reduction in the average price similarity index as discussed above, for the PLS the same division into regions accounted for 87 per cent of the reduction in the PLS. (KHS, 1982, p. 109) To anticipate later discussion, the average values of the similarity indexes (PLS) for the 1975 benchmark were lower (higher) than the exercise we have reported for 1996. This is most likely due to the fact that the 1975 benchmark involved over 150 common detailed headings, and the 1996 exercise only 32 headings.

comparison. This leads into our discussion of methods of using chains that blend both objective methods with some consideration of the practical issues in carrying out the comparisons.

10.3.2   More Judgmental Approaches

One great advantage of multilateral methods is that the actual estimation procedure does not require discretion on the part of those producing the results. There are still a great many judgments made in the process of preparing the inputs, including item and outlet choice, the handling of non–priced services and the like, but once that is done, the computations can be mechanically carried out. However, while this has been true for benchmark comparisons within regional groups like ESCAP and other groups like the OECD, the joining of comparisons across groups has always required a number of judgments.

Spatial chaining begins with the same basic inputs as multilateral comparisons (a few exceptions are noted below) and requires several judgments along the way. Given the regional structure of benchmark comparisons, a goal in putting together world comparisons should be to reduce the need for discretionary judgments as much as possible. With this background in mind a discussion of the next round of the ICP benchmarks is given below, indicating what is being done, and also where this departs from what it would be desirable to do with more time and resources.[14]

10.3.3   ICP 2005 Benchmark Organization

The organization of the ICP into regions began with the 1980 round when the world was divided into the EU, the OECD, the Group 2 countries in Europe, Africa, ESCAP and South America. In the 1980 round the proposed method of linking was to have suitable binary comparisons that would join regions. The overlap of the EU and OECD was one link, Austria as the star in Group II within Eastern Europe linked with the OECD , and Japan in the OECD and ESCAP was a third link. This left Africa and South America to be done. It was agreed to try to link several African countries with EU countries (Kenya and the UK and France with Senegal) as well as Kenya and Pakistan. In addition, Germany and Argentina and France and Brazil were to provide a link with South America. We have already discussed one major drawback to most of these linkages, namely that the pivotal countries were often not

---

[14] The contributors to this volume have all taken part in preliminary meetings about the current round of the ICP that is being coordinated by a Global Office at the World Bank. This discussion is informed by the experience of Heston on the Technical Advisory Group of the Bank.

economically similar to the group they were linking. And there was the further issue for countries like Austria and Japan. Did they want their position in the world comparisons to reflect the results obtained in the Group 2 or OECD comparisons in the case of Austria, or in the ESCAP or OECD comparisons in the case of Japan?

What happened in the 1980 benchmark was that the links with Africa and the OECD and South America and the OECD were never satisfactorily realized so that a compromise had to be reached. This compromise involved matching as well as possible the prices from 20 countries representing the various world regions.[15] The lesson derived from this experience was that it is necessary to have some core list of items that are priced in all regions by at least some of the countries so that there can be overlap for most basic headings.

What has emerged in the 2005 round of the ICP is an outward structure not too different from 1980, but with a very much improved framework and program of implementation. This can be seen by the interested reader on the ICP website of the World Bank that contains a number of technical papers, chapters of a new ICP manual and a wealth of background and explanatory information. Several features of the 2005 round deserve special mention, beginning with the Structured Product Description or SPD, which has been used in other countries, including price collection in São Paulo.[16] In the United States the SPD is similar to the worksheet associated with the Entry Level Item or ELI of the Bureau of Labor Statistics.

10.3.4 The SPD Framework

The consumer price index tradition of very detailed item specifications was carried over to spatial comparisons from the beginning. An SPD is simply another way of specifying a product, sometimes called the checklist approach. It is an integral part of the US CPI where for example, collectors are provided an outlet for soft drinks. At the outlet the collector will ask the manager what is the volume seller, and checks off the characteristics of that item, including size, type of container, brand, whether flavored or plain, aerated or not, and the like. The outlet characteristics and location are also

---

[15] This compromise is described in the UN report on the comparisons (United Nations and Eurostat, 1986). Essentially, item prices were obtained from 20 of the 60 countries in the benchmark comparisons This allowed estimation of parities across the world regions.

[16] SPD and other terms are defined in the glossary of the final report of the 2005 benchmark (World Bank, 2008), which is published and online. More detailed discussions are in the online ICP Handbook: http://go.worldbank.org/MW520NNFK0.

known. The SPD is basically a check list for determining in the case of the US, what was priced, and in the case of the ICP what can be priced in a country.

A major accomplishment of the 2005 round has been to develop SPDs that are based on the United Nations COICOP (Classification of Individual Consumption by Purpose) classification system of expenditures that countries are gradually adopting as their national system. However, for the 2005 round, countries will continue to match a particular product, which is one combination of characteristics of a structured product description. For the 2005 round, this has required finding out in the regions what is priced and representative in their countries. The process has been iterative with some new SPDs developed along the way. For the 2005 round, the world is divided into the EU–OECD, the CIS (Commonwealth of Independent States) countries, Asia, Western Asia, Africa, and Latin America, six groups. The EU–OECD and CIS already had their own classification system and set of specifications that they will map into the SPD system. Learning what countries can price has been a major investment in resources that will improve the quality of the global comparisons, though much of the practical gain from this investment will be in subsequent rounds of the ICP. Once the SPD framework is developed it will automatically conform to a standard for expenditure classifications, and will likely be matched by the systems of many countries.

10.3.5   Representative Items

Another development with respect to item matching is that the 2005 round has adopted a weighting system that the EU developed in their comparisons over the last 25 years. First the basic heading is a level of expenditures below which expenditure weights were typically unavailable. For each of the items specified, Eurostat asked countries to indicate whether a given item could be priced in a country and if so whether it was representative. The OECD came to adopt this system too, and based on this experience, the 2005 ICP sought this information of other countries in other regions, but in fact, it did not prove useable.

The EU method has been to build up binary comparisons within a basic heading based on match prices using only items that are representative in at least one of the countries. It is also possible to include items that both countries can price, which is under review. In either approach the binary comparisons at the basic heading level are used as inputs to the EKS procedure to obtain transitive parities. Information on representative items can also be used within the CPD framework and Chapters 10 and 11 of the

ICP Handbook that have been drafted by Peter Hill discuss this. This procedure has been termed the CPRD method.

In the future, the SPD framework may be used in an hedonic framework, but it was felt that for the 2005 benchmark this was not really feasible. For example, countries in the future may be able to provide individual prices within their country with market characteristics, like region, urban or rural, and type of outlet, as well as item characteristics like unit of purchase, capacity, brand or similar information. This would permit estimation of a hedonic regression either by the country or by a coordinating group for the items in a basic heading using an extended CPRD approach. The authors believe that this would be a preferable approach in future ICP rounds to traditional matching.

10.3.6   How to Build up World Comparisons

The likely reality of future comparisons is that they are initiated at a regional or country group level. And it is unlikely that a regional group will want an intermediary country from another group playing a role in their comparisons which was the type of chaining model discussed in Section 10.2. These country groups might be thought to be fairly homogeneous, but typically that is not the situation. The case we have made for spatial chaining to overcome problems of holding constant the quality and range of goods compared apply within most country groups. The OECD core countries are fairly diverse across space and economic structure. The CIS and Eastern European countries have also undertaken comparisons with the assistance of the OECD and this greatly increases the heterogeneity of the total group of 50 countries. ESCAP includes Hong Kong, Singapore and Japan at the top and Nepal, Bhutan and Laos at the low–income end. Western Asia is equally diverse.

Our conclusion is not to give up spatial chaining altogether but to suggest that generating a chain across all countries of the world in a benchmark is not a likely or necessarily desirable outcome. It is not likely given the way that ICP benchmark comparisons are organized. And it may not be desirable because existing algorithms to generate chains produce results that are only marginally better than chains built up from the regions.

Consider the following results from the 1996 comparisons. We have examined measures of the average price similarity and the average PLS for various combinations of pairs of countries. First we consider in column (2) of Table 10.1 all pairs of countries, and in column (3) the minimum spanning tree of 115 countries. In columns (4) and (5) the pairs involved with 15 regional groups based solely on geography, and finally a set of seven groups of countries that have in the past actually implemented regional comparisons.

Table 10.1   Spanning trees versus regional groupings

	All Pairs	Tree	Regional Groupings	
# Groups	1	1	15	7
# Pairs	6551	114	744	1044

Average Similarity Index				
mean	0.9251	0.9939	0.9606	0.9580
std. dev	0.0668	0.0060	0.0469	0.0452
cv	7.2%	0.6%	4.9%	4.7%

Average PLS				
mean	1.8677	1.0445	1.2836	1.1947
std. dev	0.9122	0.0667	0.4021	0.3135
cv	48.8%	6.4%	31.3%	26.2%

The results in Table 10.1 show that the minimum spanning tree increases the average similarity index and greatly reduces the average PLS compared with what is achieved over all possible pairs of countries. As EKS uses all possible pairs of countries, this does provide some indication of why EKS over all countries may introduce noise in the quest for transitivity.

The main point that we wish to make about Table 10.1 however, is the degree to which breaking the countries into regions substantially reduces the average PLS and increases the average similarity index. Consider first the PLS. Using all pairs the average is 1.8677 which is reduced to 1.0445 when the minimum spanning tree is used, a reduction of 0.8232. However, most of this reduction can be achieved by moving to regional groups. Thus moving to 15 geographic groups reduces the average PLS by 0.5841 or by 71 per cent of 0.8232. When we go to the 7 implementing groups, it accounts for 82 per cent (0.673/0.8232*100) of the reduction in the PLS achieved by the minimum spanning tree.[17]

But this only tells a part of the story. Suppose that within the geographical regions a minimum spanning tree were constructed. We have not done this for all 15 regions, but it will be enough to illustrate with one region, East Asia where there are only four countries. The average PLS using the minimum path is 1.2772, while using all 10 pairs in the region it is 1.4422.

---

[17] The fact that division of the countries into the seven groups does more to reduce the average PLS than the division into 15 groups is a comment on the degree to which implementing groups of countries tend to be more homogeneous in putting together the basic data for the benchmark comparisons. However, this pattern does not hold for the price similarity indexes in Table 10.1.

So that if one chose to work with pairs of countries within regions one would reduce much of the PLS and going to the minimum tree within the region would reduce it still more. Put another way, these results suggest that not much is lost by applying the minimum spanning tree technique only within regions rather than across all countries.

For price similarity indexes the increase in the average is also improved by going to regions, though the percentage effect is somewhat smaller. That is, the improvement in Table 10.1 from all pairs to the minimum spanning tree is 0.0688. Of this 0.0355 or 52 per cent of the increase in average similarity index is obtained by going to 15 regions and 0.0329 or 48 per cent by going to seven country groups. This is not as large as for the PLS but there is also less differences between the similarity indexes than the PLS.[18] As with the PLS there is a further reduction of the average similarity indexes if one were to apply the minimum spanning tree within regions.

As an illustration for Africa and the Middle East, a group of 11 countries and 55 possible pairs, the minimum spanning tree with the region yields an average similarity index of 0.9803 versus 0.8929 for the 55 pairs. So as with the PLS, much of the gain in economic similarity can be obtained from regional groupings of countries, and applying chaining within the country groups.

While multilateral techniques have been and can be applied at a regional level, binary chains within regions should seriously be examined as an alternative. First, there is substantial diversity within regions so it may be very useful to build up regional comparisons on the basis of binary comparisons of economically similar countries. This also might allow some countries with less diverse markets and modest statistical capabilities to carry out benchmark comparisons for fewer basic headings by linking to similar countries that are slightly higher on the economic and statistical ladder. The choice of such pairings could be based upon criteria like the PLS spread, though in many regions there may be consensus in a region on where to begin the chain.

Another version of chaining within regions does not rely on algorithms like the minimum spanning or particular criteria for chaining. Rather it deals with a realistic issue that arises in carrying out benchmark comparisons especially for countries taking part in the ICP for the first time. What frequently happens is that countries can only provide their data long after other countries in a region; or their data are incomplete; or both. But the country and region would like to make some use of the efforts by the country.

---

[18] For example, the lowest similarity index observed in Table 10.1 is 0.398 with average of 0.925. If the PLS were also constrained to be between 0 and 1 across all pairs, the lowest value (biggest spread) would be 0.306 and the average would be 0.530.

One way to do this is that the region goes ahead with its comparison not including the country with late and/or insufficient data. In part this would be done because they want to complete a regional comparison which in turn is needed for a world comparison. And in part because there may be concern that including the data of that country would reduce the reliability of the regional comparison. Because late countries tend to be poor countries and/or countries with weak statistical offices, the latter is a real concern.

The late country can then be added using a chaining procedure that might link it through a binary comparison to a similar country using the type of criteria discussed earlier in the paper. An alternative is to compare the prices of the late country to the average prices of the region, which does not leave the late country as subject to the chance errors and limitations on item prices of the country chosen as its binary counterpart. On the other hand, use of averages does not eliminate the problem of likely quality differences across the countries of the region.

10.3.7   Chaining Between Regions

The issue of how one chains between regions has hitherto been dealt with on an ad hoc basis, the most important factor usually being the fact that countries like Japan and Austria have taken part in multilateral benchmark comparisons in each of two separate country groups. In the 2005 round the equivalent of what were core countries in the 1980 comparison, are now termed Ring countries and these 18 countries were chosen in advance of the completion of the regional comparisons. Linking of sub–regions was considered for 2005 but was not carried except in the OECD–CIS region where this has been the practice in the past.

This has already been done in the EU and OECD comparisons where candidate countries to the EU and associate countries of the OECD form separate sub–regions whose comparisons are linked to the main comparisons. Within the EU–OECD comparisons the principle of *fixity* is applied, meaning that the results for the EU comparisons among the member countries must be maintained when it is linked to the OECD. Similarly the candidate countries of the EU and the associate members of OECD are linked in such a way as to not change the results for the member OECD countries.

All regions in the 2005 benchmarks also chose *fixity*. Most economists would follow Yogi Berra's maxim, *when you come to a fork in the road, take it*; meaning that they would prefer to present results for regions based on just regional data and in addition results involving countries from all regions. A case can be made for both approaches and the interested reader may consult Kravis (1984, pp. 35–37).

In the 2005 round it is recognized that the role of a Ring country is basically to provide quality price comparisons with countries in different regions. If a country is 'representative' of its region, all the better. But the more important criteria adopted for Ring countries are willingness to participate, a good statistical office, and an open economy with markets selling a wide variety of goods. If a country has an expenditure distribution that is not typical of its region this is not a problem because weights of the Ring countries do not enter into the global results. Rather the Ring country comparison is used to produce for each of the 150 basic expenditure headings a parity expressing its currency relative to the world numeraire. The procedure to do this was developed within the Technical Advisory Group and formalized in a paper by Erwin Diewert (2008) on the World Bank website.[19] However, one new insight has been developed in the technical deliberations that will play a pivotal role and will be briefly described.

In the 1980 comparisons and in most discussions of linking through Ring countries, the problem was how do you join the Ring comparisons with the regional comparisons at the basic heading level? In the Ring comparison the relationship between two Ring countries in the same region at the basic heading will usually be different than it is in within the regional comparison, the exception being if both countries price the identical items in both comparisons. How will these be linked into the regional comparison was the question?

The method set out in Diewert (2008) basically normalizes the prices of each Ring country to the average prices in its region. In effect, the prices entering into the Ring comparison are converted to regional prices so that what results is a parity for each region for each basic heading. This heading parity can then be multiplied by the regional heading parities to express them relative to the world numeraire currency. Because there are a different number of Ring countries in each region and the number of items priced by each Ring country may differ, there is a remaining question of what weight the Ring country prices should have in the estimation of the heading parities for each region. Several acceptable methods were considered and in the final calculations the edited prices of all Ring countries were used to obtain the linking factors at the basic heading level.

It is possible in future benchmark comparisons that it will be more feasible to use chaining methods than in the 2005 benchmark. In fact, as the 2005 benchmark information for the approximately 145 countries is analysed it will be possible to investigate the potential use of spanning trees and other methods much more fully than has been possible before.

---

[19] http://go.worldbank.org/HLM9CVSX60

10.4   CONCLUSION

This chapter argues that use of binary–based chains to build up world comparisons is not obviously the wave of the future. It is not the way the world is organized; most benchmark comparisons are now developed by country groups, with an overall world expenditure distribution and item list providing some guidelines. And empirically, examination of spanning tree chains suggest that in terms of being based upon measures of economic similarity between pairs of countries, little will be lost by beginning with regional groups of countries.

We have suggested that a more useful approach may be to examine chains within regions, where approaches like the spanning tree method may be quite fruitful. Also, when there are some countries within a region that supply less than the minimum necessary for a full benchmark and/or are late in their provision of data, some type of binary approach may be useful for linking such countries to the rest of the region. To link regions, a separate exercise will be required and several methods have been developed as part of the 2005 benchmark that should improve past practice. The linking would be carried out at the basic heading level involving about 130 expenditure groups within GDP.

One issue not discussed in this chapter relates to the level of aggregation. Most experiments with the spanning tree approach have constructed spatial chains at the level of GDP. Probably real GDP and associated PPP are the most frequently used numbers coming out of the ICP, but for many purposes we are interested in the structure of GDP and it is not clear that the chain resulting from applying spanning tree techniques would be the best for examination of any sub–aggregate. In fact, any of the multilateral methods would appear to have some advantage over chaining methods as they have been applied. However, there is no reason a spatial chain might not be used to generate heading parities that could also be used as inputs to multilateral aggregations.

We conclude that chaining of individual countries at the world level seems of doubtful merit. And that while feasible, it may be some time before an acceptable method of chaining within regions is developed. The two areas where some type of linking procedure will continue to be required are adding countries with more limited data to a regional comparison and bridging regional comparisons. Recent efforts to define economic similarity of countries, which has been a parallel development with chaining, have been important though there remain a number of areas of study. Some methods being tested in the 2005 benchmark appear to make the process of linking regions more transparent than past practice, an encouraging development. There remain issues in how to present the final results of the ICP exercise and there is ample scope for further research on improving the underlying price comparisons including more use of hedonics.

REFERENCES

Aten, B.H. (1996), 'Evidence of Spatial Autocorrelation in International Prices', *Review of Income and Wealth,* **42** (2), 149–163.
Balk, B.M (this volume), 'Aggregation Methods in International Comparisons: an Evaluation'.
Diewert, W.E (1999), 'Axiomatic and Economic Approaches to International Comparisons', in A. Heston and R.E. Lipsey (eds), *International and Interarea Comparisons of Income, Output and Prices,* NBER and CRIW, *Studies in Income and Wealth,* **61**, 13–109. Chicago: University of Chicago Press.
Diewert, W.E (2008), 'Similarity Indexes and Criteria for Spatial Linking' and 'On the Stochastic Approach to Linking the Regions in the ICP', both at http://go.worldbank.org/HLM9CVSX60, World Bank, Washington DC.
Gilbert, M. and I.B. Kravis (1954), *An International Comparison of National Products and the Purchasing Power of Currencies: a Study of the United States, the United Kingdom, France, Germany and Italy,* Paris: OEEC.
Heravi, S., A. Heston and M. Silver (2001), 'Using Scanner Data to Estimate Country Price Parities,' World Bank–OECD Seminar on Purchasing Power Parities, Washington, D.C., http://www.oecd.org/dataoecd/24/3/2424651.pdf.
Heston, A., R. Summers and D. Nuxoll (1994) 'The Differential Productivity Hypothesis and Purchasing Power Parities: Some New Evidence', *Review of International Economics,* **2** (3), 227–43.
Heston, A., R. Summers and B. Aten (2001), 'Price Structures, the Quality Factor, and Chaining,' *Statistical Journal of the United Nations Economic Commission for Europe',* **18** (1), 77–101.
Hill, R.J. (1999a), 'Comparing Price Levels Across Countries Using Minimum Spanning Trees,' *Review of Economics and Statistics,* **81**, 135–142.
Hill, R.J. (1999b), 'International Comparisons Using Spanning Trees' in A. Heston and R.E. Lipsey (eds), *International and Interarea Comparisons of Income, Output, and Prices,* NBER and CRIW, *Studies in Income and Wealth,* **61**, 109–120, NBER, Chicago: University of Chicago Press.
Hill, R.J. (this volume), 'Comparing Per Capita Income Levels Across Countries Using Spanning Trees: Robustness, Prior Restrictions, Hybrids and Hierarchies'
Keynes, J.M. (1930). 'A Treatise on Money, Volume 1'. New York: Harcourt and Brace.
Kravis, I.B. (1984), 'Comparative Studies of National Incomes and Prices,' *Journal of Economic Literature,* XXII, March.
Kravis, I.B., A. Heston and R. Summers (1978), 'Aggregation Methods in International Comparisons of Real Product', Eurostat News, Special Number, Eurostat, Luxembourg.
Kravis, I.B., A. Heston and R. Summers (1982), World Product and Income, Baltimore, MD: Johns Hopkins University Press.
Rao, D.S. Prasada (this volume), 'Generalised Elteto–Koves–Szulc and Country–Product–Dummy Methods for International Comparisons'.

Ryten, J. (1998), *The Evaluation of the International Comparison Project (ICP): Summary of a Report*, Consultant's Report to the Thirteenth Session of the Statistical Commission, E/CN.3/1998/8, United Nations, New York.

Summers, R. (1973), 'International Comparisons with Incomplete Data', *Review of Income and Wealth,* **19**, 1–16.

United Nations and Eurostat, 1986, 'World Comparisons of Purchasing Power and Real Product for 1980', ST/ESA/STAT/SER F/42, New York.

UNECLA (United Nations Economic Commission for Latin America) (1963), 'A Measurement of Price Levels and the Purchasing Power of Currencies in Latin America, 1960–1962', Mar del Plata Argentina, May, E/CN.12/653, a more accessible summary is available in Stanley Braithwaite (1968). 'Real Income Levels in Latin America', *Review of Income and Wealth,* **14(2)**, 113-182.

World Bank (2008), 'Global Purchasing Power Parities and Real Expenditures: 2005 International Comparison Program', http://go.worldbank.org/VMCB80AB40, (accessed on 12 May, 2009) Washington DC.

APPENDIX

Table A.10.1   Per capita DA (domestic absorption) relative to the United States of America

ISO code	Fisher (1)	EKS (2)	GK (3)	PLS Tree (4)	Similarity Tree (5)	Country name
LUX	102.7	106.8	108.3	99.9	102.7	Luxembourg
USA	100.0	100.0	100.0	100.0	100.0	USA
JPN	85.3	84.4	87.6	79.6	84.5	Japan
CHE	83.5	83.9	86.2	80.7	83.5	Switzerland
HKG	83.1	87.6	101.2	114.4	83.0	Hong Kong
DNK	80.6	82.2	82.8	78.1	80.8	Denmark
NOR	79.9	81.9	82.6	77.0	79.6	Norway
ISL	79.7	79.5	79.3	77.6	79.5	Iceland
CAN	77.8	75.8	77.5	76.0	77.8	Canada
AUT	77.7	79.5	79.3	75.8	77.5	Austria
AUS	77.5	78.4	77.4	76.3	80.6	Australia
BEL	72.4	72.6	71.9	70.5	72.1	Belgium
GER	72.1	72.8	73.7	69.1	71.2	Germany
FRA	70.9	70.1	70.1	67.8	70.4	France
SGP	70.0	78.5	91.7	94.3	67.5	Singapore
ITA	69.0	69.0	69.5	67.0	68.5	Italy
GBR	68.7	69.0	68.0	66.2	69.2	United Kingdom
NLD	68.6	69.0	69.0	65.4	67.2	Netherlands
ISR	65.3	64.6	64.9	62.0	63.7	Israel
SWE	64.2	63.6	63.5	61.1	63.2	Sweden
BMU	61.8	64.6	76.3	68.1	65.5	Bermuda
NZL	60.8	61.7	61.0	59.3	63.5	New Zealand
FIN	60.6	61.1	60.8	58.6	60.3	Finland
IRL	55.2	55.9	55.3	54.1	55.6	Ireland
ESP	52.9	54.2	53.4	52.9	54.9	Spain
PRT	51.9	53.2	52.8	51.7	48.3	Portugal
GRC	49.8	50.5	50.1	49.5	50.6	Greece
KOR	49.6	52.9	58.3	48.3	48.8	Korea
CZE	48.4	48.0	50.2	47.5	45.9	Czech Republic
QAT	48.2	47.7	56.7	56.4	44.8	Qatar
BHS	48.2	47.2	56.4	47.4	45.5	Bahamas
SVN	46.4	46.7	46.2	45.4	46.8	Slovenia
BRB	42.0	40.1	67.0	29.4	39.3	Barbados
MUS	38.3	37.1	46.8	32.6	37.9	Mauritius
ARG	34.9	36.6	39.3	38.7	35.9	Argentina
KNA	34.9	33.2	37.8	36.0	33.3	St. Kitts & Nevis
HUN	34.6	33.9	35.8	33.3	30.5	Hungary
SVK	34.0	34.2	36.5	33.3	31.8	Slovakia

Continued

Table A.10.1   Per capita DA (domestic absorption) relative to the United States of America – continued

ISO code	Fisher (1)	EKS (2)	GK (3)	PLS Tree (4)	Similarity Tree (5)	Country name
URY	30.6	29.3	31.9	30.8	28.3	Uruguay
OMN	30.1	31.8	43.7	33.8	26.9	Oman
ATG	29.9	29.0	34.8	29.9	27.7	Antigua & Barbuda
CHL	28.5	29.7	31.1	31.4	29.8	Chile
EST	27.6	27.1	29.1	24.3	26.9	Estonia
BHR	25.1	26.1	31.9	36.7	28.0	Bahrain
BRA	24.7	24.5	26.9	25.9	23.8	Brazil
POL	24.6	24.8	26.9	23.5	23.8	Poland
MEX	24.6	25.0	25.2	26.8	24.6	Mexico
THA	23.3	25.0	28.9	25.8	23.7	Thailand
HRV	22.8	21.8	23.8	19.2	21.8	Croatia
TTO	22.5	22.4	27.4	21.8	21.7	Trinidad & Tobago
TUR	22.0	23.1	24.1	20.5	22.5	Turkey
TUN	21.9	21.2	26.2	19.8	23.3	Tunisia
RUS	21.8	20.9	23.2	19.6	21.5	Russia
LTU	21.1	20.7	23.0	18.5	20.7	Lithuania
GRD	20.6	20.1	25.8	19.8	18.8	Grenada
ROM	20.3	21.1	22.9	20.4	26.3	Romania
GAB	19.6	17.9	23.0	16.2	20.4	Gabon
BWA	19.3	19.2	19.9	18.7	19.9	Botswana
LCA	19.1	18.7	21.5	19.7	18.7	St. Lucia
LVA	18.9	17.9	20.6	15.9	18.0	Latvia
PAN	18.8	19.2	19.9	20.0	21.5	Panama
IRN	18.5	17.4	18.3	15.4	19.2	Iran
DMA	18.1	17.1	23.2	18.3	17.4	Dominica
VEN	17.6	17.8	20.4	19.7	17.4	Venezuela
BLR	17.3	16.9	20.8	16.1	17.1	Belarus
BLZ	17.3	17.7	21.1	18.0	17.3	Belize
SWZ	16.9	16.4	19.5	16.3	16.3	Swaziland
VCT	16.7	15.0	20.0	15.8	15.0	St. Vincent & Grenadines
FJI	16.4	15.9	16.7	16.2	16.0	Fiji
PER	15.5	15.3	16.2	15.9	14.5	Peru
BGR	15.4	15.7	18.3	14.6	18.3	Bulgaria
KAZ	15.4	15.1	18.4	13.3	14.0	Kazakhstan
MKD	14.2	13.9	14.9	13.1	13.9	Macedonia
MAR	14.2	13.4	15.5	12.3	14.7	Morocco
JAM	12.1	12.1	14.2	12.7	11.8	Jamaica
PHL	11.9	13.0	13.6	13.6	17.5	Philippines
LBN	11.9	13.5	20.1	15.2	13.7	Lebanon
UKR	11.8	11.1	13.8	9.8	9.7	Ukraine
EGY	11.7	12.3	14.8	11.3	13.9	Egypt
GEO	11.7	10.7	13.8	10.0	9.5	Georgia

Continued

Table A.10.1   Per capita DA (domestic absorption) relative to the United States of America – continued

ISO code	Fisher (1)	EKS (2)	GK (3)	PLS Tree (4)	Similarity Tree (5)	Country name
TKM	11.6	12.1	14.3	12.5	11.9	Turkmenistan
JOR	11.5	11.9	15.0	16.1	11.9	Jordan
IDN	11.4	11.9	13.6	13.9	10.9	Indonesia
LKA	11.3	11.0	11.4	10.9	11.6	Sri Lanka
ECU	10.6	11.0	11.8	11.6	10.6	Ecuador
ZWE	10.3	10.2	11.6	9.6	9.9	Zimbabwe
SYR	10.2	10.7	12.7	9.5	9.9	Syria
ALB	10.1	11.1	12.5	10.5	11.4	Albania
KGZ	8.5	8.0	9.6	7.3	9.2	Kyrgyzstan
ARM	8.1	8.2	10.2	7.2	8.2	Armenia
UZB	7.9	6.9	8.9	5.9	7.9	Uzbekistan
BOL	7.9	8.0	8.8	8.2	7.8	Bolivia
AZE	7.9	7.7	9.1	7.2	7.1	Azerbaijan
GIN	7.0	7.3	9.9	6.4	7.0	Guinea
MDA	6.8	6.3	8.2	5.6	5.6	Moldova
PAK	6.5	6.6	7.0	6.6	6.2	Pakistan
CIV	5.8	5.7	7.0	5.2	6.6	Cote d'Ivoire
CMR	5.7	5.7	7.3	5.3	6.4	Cameroon
COG	5.7	5.6	6.1	5.5	7.5	Congo
VNM	5.3	5.5	6.2	5.7	6.4	Vietnam
SEN	5.0	5.0	5.7	4.6	4.7	Senegal
BGD	4.9	4.9	5.2	4.8	5.2	Bangladesh
KEN	4.0	4.0	4.5	3.5	4.0	Kenya
NPL	4.0	4.1	5.4	4.5	3.4	Nepal
MNG	3.9	3.9	4.3	3.9	3.7	Mongolia
BEN	3.5	3.4	3.9	3.2	4.3	Benin
SLE	3.3	2.9	4.2	2.6	3.1	Sierra Leone
ZMB	2.9	2.9	3.1	3.0	3.1	Zambia
YEM	2.9	2.8	3.7	2.4	2.5	Yemen
TJK	2.8	2.6	3.3	2.4	2.4	Tajikistan
MLI	2.7	2.9	3.5	2.9	2.7	Mali
MDG	2.6	2.8	3.0	3.1	3.0	Madagascar
MWI	2.3	2.4	2.9	2.2	2.2	Malawi
NGA	2.2	2.2	2.4	2.3	2.6	Nigeria
TZA	1.7	1.8	1.9	1.8	2.4	Tanzania

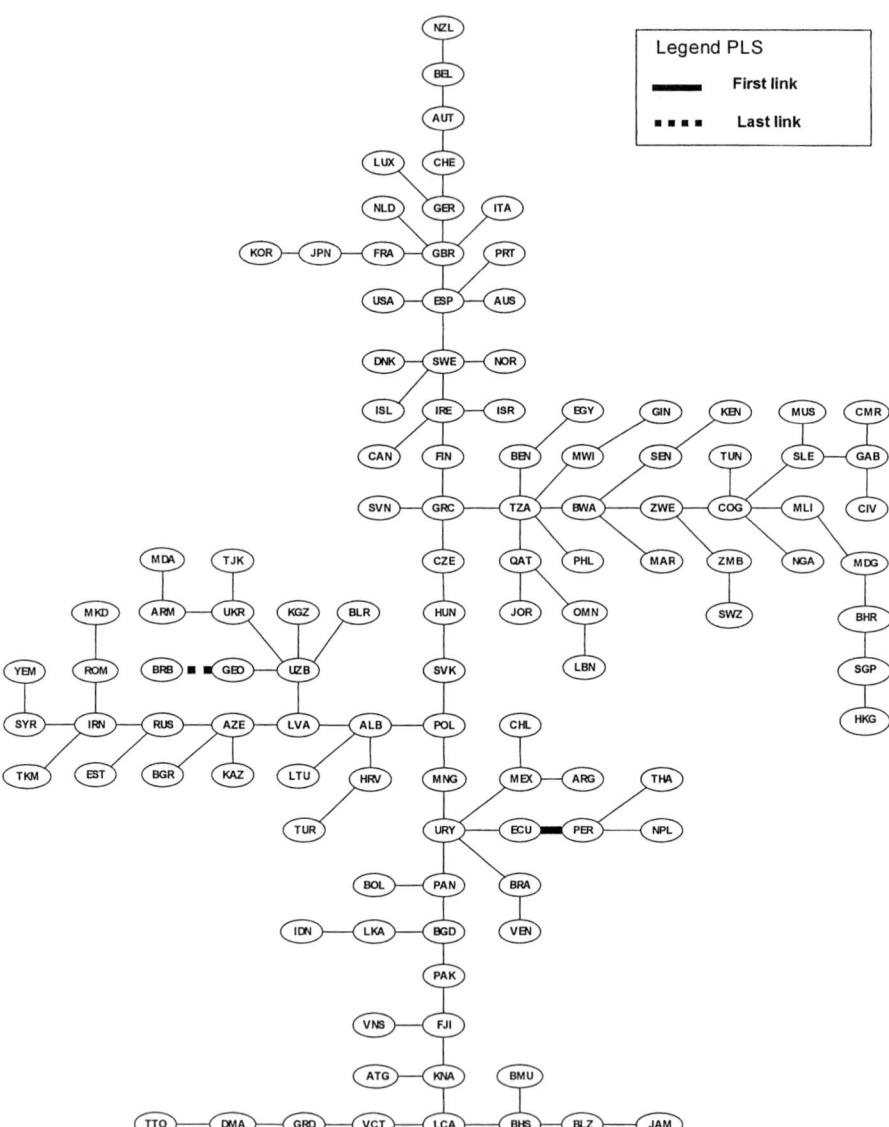

Figure A.10.1   PLS minimum spanning tree

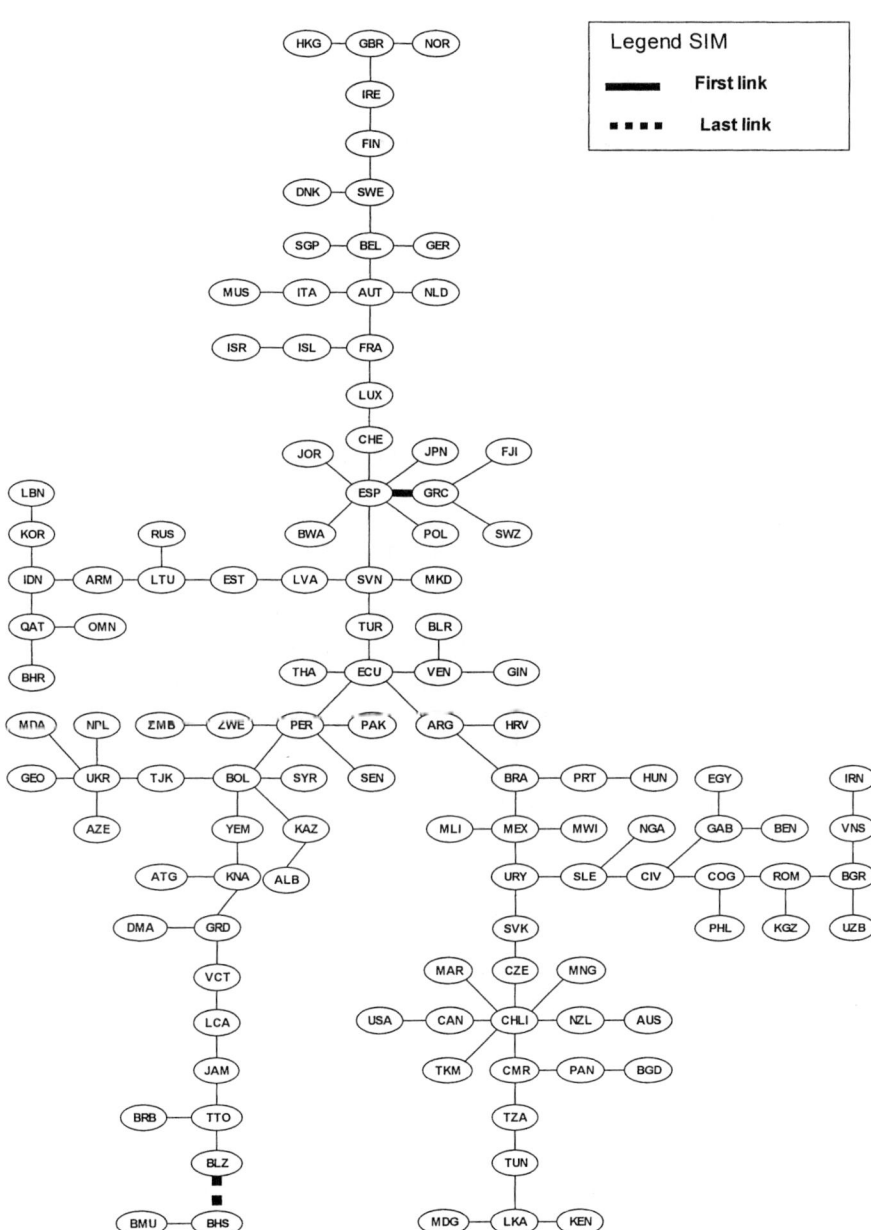

Figure A.10.2   SIM minimum spanning tree

11. Aggregation Methods Based on Structural International Prices

Sergey Sergeev

11.1   INTRODUCTION

The comparability of macroeconomic data is constantly improved due to harmonization work by national statistical offices and international organisations resulting in standardized definitions, classifications, methods of valuation and so on. Consequently, it is possible to focus more attention on the computational procedures within international comparisons, particularly to the aggregation methods of multilateral comparisons of prices and real incomes.

Suppose we are interested in multilateral comparison among N countries of an economic aggregate which covers M commodities (or basic headings[1]). The matrix of national prices, $\mathbf{P} = ((p_{ij}))(i=1,2,...,M; j=1, 2,...,N)$ and the matrix of corresponding quantities $\mathbf{Q} = ((q_{ij}))(i=1,2,...,M; j=1,2,...,N)$ are used as input data. The results of international comparisons in the form of purchasing power parities (PPPs) and volume indices should posses some important analytical properties. These properties are extensively discussed by Balk (1996; this volume), Diewert (1996), and Hill (1997a). Therefore only two following major properties are mentioned here:

Equi–representativity:[2] This property implies that the basket of products (goods and services) priced and weights (or common international prices) used in an international comparison are representative of all participating countries.

---

[1] See Roberts (this volume) for a detailed description of a basic heading.

[2] This property is linked partially with the property 'characteristicity' which was introduced by Drechsler (1973) and it meant that the 'best' bilateral index is obtained on the basis of price and quantity data of the two countries in question only (without the use of any data of the remaining countries).

Additivity:[3] This property, when satisfied, means that the real value aggregates at any level of aggregation can be obtained as the sum of real values of lower level categories of a given aggregate. Additivity requires a method to compare all countries using a common vector of prices (a vector of international prices).[4]

The importance attached to each of the properties varies with the coverage of countries and the uses to which the results of the comparison are put.

The International Comparison Program (ICP) usually covers sets of heterogeneous countries and the choice of aggregation procedure has an impact on the results.[5] The choice of the best multilateral method was broadly discussed at two Experts Group meetings organized jointly by Eurostat, OECD and the Statistical Office of the UN (Luxembourg, June 1988 and Paris, June 1989). A majority of experts expressed an opinion that no single method can be recommended and that different methods should be used for different purposes. A comprehensive review of aggregation procedures used in multilateral comparisons was done by van IJzeren (1983), Diewert (1996), Balk (1996, this volume) and Hill (1997b).

The two aggregation procedures currently in use[6] in ICP are the Geary–Khamis (GK) method and the Elteto–Koves–Szulc (EKS) method[7] (the averaging of bilateral results).[8]

The Geary–Khamis method provides additivity (in terms of international average prices) which is very desirable if international comparisons are made at varying levels of aggregation. The main drawback of GK arises as a result of the fact that the GK common vector of international prices is obtained by

---

[3] The property of additivity is linked with the property of matrix consistency. The relationship between the additivity and matrix consistency is explained in detail by Sakuma, Rao and Kurabayashi (this volume). A categorization of additive methods is given by Cuthbert (1999).

[4] See Sakuma, Rao and Kurabayashi (this volume) for a detailed discussion of additivity and the related property of matrix consistency.

[5] The detailed investigations about the influence of the choice of multilateral method on the results of ICP are the following: Dikhanov (1994) and Hill (1997b).

[6] In the recently completed 2005 round of the ICP, the Iklé aggregation method was used in the African regional comparisons.

[7] Historical research found that the EKS method was first proposed in 1924 by Gini (1931) and it was later rediscovered by three independent researchers in 1964 (Elteto and Koves, 1964 and Szulc, 1964), therefore GEKS is used in some recent papers.

[8] Detailed description of the GK and the EKS methods and a discussion of their advantages and disadvantages are given in many publications: for example Kravis et al. (1975); Kravis et al. (1982) and Eurostat (1983). Short but a clear description of multilateral methods is also provided in the SNA'93 (United Nations, 1993), Chapter XYI, part F.

taking a quantity weighted average of the price vectors of different countries. Hence the vector of the international prices tends to be closer to the price vectors faced by large (or rich) countries than small (or poor) countries. It is well–known that the volume of a country tends to be lower as the prices used in the comparison become relatively closer to its own national prices as compared with the prices of other countries. This bias caused by unequal relative closeness of used prices is usually referred to in literature as the Engel–Gerschenkron effect. The GK average prices calculated for a set of heterogeneous countries are not characteristic of outlying countries (these outliers are usually the poor but sometimes also the rich small countries). This effect may significantly distort the comparative real product levels (especially in the developing countries, which are more sensitive to the choice of aggregation method).

The EKS method ignores the differences in the size of countries compared and attempts to obtain equi–representativity of results (that is to eliminate 'Engel–Gerschenkron' effect[9]). The EKS results have another attractive property, namely that relationships between countries are only marginally influenced by the composition of the group of countries compared due to the minimization procedure that underpins the aggregation method. The main drawback of EKS is the lack of additivity. Therefore, the possibilities of structural analysis are limited. Moreover, the lack of additivity can lead to paradoxical results. The average volume index (or PPP) can be higher (or lower) than each of particular indices (this is the so called 'average test'). Hill gave the comments about multilateral methods that take the Fisher indices as the starting point (EKS and the like) in an aphoristic form:

> The construction of a multilateral set of measurements at a later stage has then to be regarded as a process whereby an initial set of perfectly good binary measures has to be distorted, rather in the manner practiced by Procrustes, in the interests of securing transitivity. (Hill quoted in Kravis et al. 1982, p.77)

Khamis commented on the use of the EKS method within the Eurostat comparisons with the following words:

> In the opinion of the author, the adoption of the EKS(F) results by EUROSTAT is a retrogressive step in comparison with their excellent earlier comparisons including those of 1975 based on the Gerardi UCW method. (Khamis, 1993, p. 2)

---

[9] Some authors believe that there is no a clear evidence that the GK method is influenced by this effect or, at least, the EKS method is also not 'free' from this effect also (for example, Khamis (1998).

The GK method satisfies additivity but fails characteristicity, the EKS method – vice versa. To combine the advantages and to minimize the disadvantages of different methods, it was decided within the Eurostat–OECD PPP Programme to use the EKS–method for volume comparisons (official results) and the Geary–Khamis method for structural analyses (for analytical purposes).

Obviously, use of different methods for the same purpose could be a source of confusion. This raises the question, is it possible to combine advantages of both methods within an unique method? Ahmad (1994, p.2) expressed the following considerations about this problem:

> To reduce the Gerschenkron effect and at the same time retain matrix consistency (additivity) of the results, it is proposed that an unweighted or equal weighted Geary–Khamis be used. Tests show that the results are very similar to EKS but with an added advantage of additivity. Should another aggregation method such as Iklé be used instead?

Several methods were proposed in the literature in pursuit of this aim:

- Iklé–method – Iklé (1972) and Dikhanov (1994).
- 'Implicit price' method (IP method) developed by Eurostat (1983);
- Minimum Spanning Tree method – Köves (1983), Hill (1999).
- Weighted EKS method and Generalized CPD method – Rao (this volume)
- Generalized GK method – Cuthbert (1999).
- CKS method (Commensurable Kurabayashi–Sakuma method) – see Sakuma, Rao, and Kurabayashi (this volume)
- Shared weighted GK–Rao method – Rao (2000).

These methods have some advantages relative to the EKS and the GK methods but they do not directly address the task of obtaining comparisons which are simultaneously additive and equi–characteristic for all the countries in the multilateral comparison. This means that a set of possible multilateral methods should be broader and new ideas and proposals are desirable.

Multilateral aggregation methods currently in vogue can be classified into two types:

1. Averaging of bilateral indices (for example, the EKS method)
2. Use of average international prices – an averaging of national prices recalculated by PPPs into a common currency (for example, Geary–Khamis, Van IJzeren, Iklé and Rao methods)

The methods under (2) are based usually on the simultaneous calculation of the international prices and overall PPPs or overall quantities or volumes within a system of equations.

A new kind of aggregation procedure of type (2) based on the use of structural international prices is proposed in this chapter. It is easy to show that volume index for any pair of countries j and k $(IQ^{j/k})$ can be calculated not only on the basis of a given set of common vector of prices (π) but also on the basis of their ratios (relative to a product M selected as a basis):

$$IQ^{j/k} = \frac{\sum\limits_{i=1}^{M} \pi_i q_{ij}}{\sum\limits_{i=1}^{M} \pi_i q_{ik}} = \frac{\sum\limits_{i=1}^{M} (\pi_i / \pi_M) q_{ij}}{\sum\limits_{i=1}^{M} (\pi_i / \pi_M) q_{ik}} \qquad (11.1)$$

Equation (11.1) leads to the idea not to average national prices, as it is done by the traditional methods of type (2), but to average intra–country national price ratios. The intra–country ratios of prices do not depend on the national currencies. Therefore they are directly comparable and can be averaged between countries without the use of PPPs. These average international price ratios can be named as international structural prices. The corresponding PPPs can be derived indirectly as a ratio between value for a given aggregate at national prices (in national currency) and value in international structural prices. In effect, the methods based on structural prices are strictly additive. This approach was not used yet explicitly in international comparisons. However it is easy to demonstrate that the well-known Gerardi UCW method (Unit–Country–Weight) can be presented in the form of structural international prices (Gerardi, 1982; Hill, 1982; Khamis and Rao, 1989).

The main aim of this chapter is to introduce a new type of international prices – *structural international prices* – into PPP calculations.

11.2   METHOD OF 'MAXIMAL POSSIBLE CHARACTERISTIC PRICES' (MPCP–METHOD)

The approach proposed here tries to achieve representativity and additivity simultaneously using a vector of international prices which are maximally possible characteristic of all the countries involved.

To realize this principle, it is necessary to measure similarity (dissimilarity) of price structures. Several measures of similarity (dissimilarity) of national price structures have been proposed in the literature (Laspeyres–Paasche spread and its modifications (Köves, 1983; Hill, 1999); Kravis–Heston–Summers measure used in ICP 1975 (Kravis et al., 1982); Allen–Diewert measure (1981) and its modification; Heston–Aten measure; Cuthbert measure; van Ark–Monnikhof–Timmer (1999) measure and so on). A detailed discussion on similarity measures can be found in Diewert (this volume). A similar analysis was also undertaken by the author (Sergeev, 2001). To avoid the drawbacks of the methods mentioned, a new measure of similarity (dissimilarity) of price structures was proposed.

Consider a multilateral comparison among N countries of an aggregate which contains M commodities (or basic headings). The aim is to obtain transitive, additive and most possible characteristic (for each country) results. The matrix of national prices $\mathbf{P}$ = (p_{ij}) $(i=1,2,...,M;\ j=1,\ 2,...,N)$ and the matrix of corresponding quantities $\mathbf{Q}$ = (q_{ij}) $(i=1,2,...,M;\ j=1,2,...,N)$ are used as input data.[10]

The structure of national prices for country j can be presented in a compressed form as a vector of scalars p_{ij}/p_{Mj}, where p_{Mj} is price of numeraire product M. If the price data of countries j and k satisfy the conditions for Hicks's composite commodity theorem – $p_{ij} = \lambda * p_{ik}$ – then the price structures are identical. The coefficient of similarity of price structures between countries j and k (τ_{jk}) can be derived in a way similar to that of the deduction a coefficient of linear correlation (as geometric mean from two regression coefficients).[11] It is defined here as:

---

[10] In actual comparisons, input data are not quite those originally envisioned: prices and quantities for individual products. Usually PPPs 'National currency/Numeraire currency' and expenditure in numeraire currency for primary groups (basic headings) are used as notional (fictitious) prices and quantities.

[11] The indicator τ_{jk} is a certain analogy (but not identical) with a coefficient of correlation (the coefficient of the correlation itself is not very appropriate for the measuring of price similarities because it reflects the correlation in the form Y = c*X + b but not in the form Y = c*X as it is necessary) and has some analogous useful analytical properties ($\tau_{jk} = \tau_{kj}$; $0 < \tau_{jk} \le 1$; if $\tau_{jk} = 1$ – price structures in the countries 'j' and 'k' are identical; if $\tau_{jk} \to 0$ – price structures are very different.). The indicator τ_j has some similarities with the Allen–Diewert distance. But τ_j coefficient has an important preference because it has a lower bound as well as an upper bound (it lies between zero and 1), while the Allen–Diewert measure lies between 0 (zero) and infinity, that is, it has only a lower bound.
There are also several other uses of the indicator τ_j:

- Analysis of dynamics of price structures: for example, this indicator can be used as one from the characteristics of the impact of the introduction of the Euro on price convergence.
- Measure of reliability of bilateral comparisons:, the larger the value of this measure, the greater the similarity (weight) and the greater the reliability of bilateral indices.

$$\tau_{jk} = \sqrt{\frac{\sum\limits_{i=1}^{M}\{\left(\dfrac{p_{ij}}{p_{ik}}\right)*s_i^{jk}\}*\sum\limits_{i=1}^{M}\{\left(\dfrac{p_{ik}}{p_{ij}}\right)*s_i^{jk}\}}{\sum\limits_{i=1}^{M}\{\left(\dfrac{p_{ij}}{p_{ik}}\right)^2*s_i^{jk}\}*\sum\limits_{i=1}^{M}\{\left(\dfrac{p_{ik}}{p_{ij}}\right)^2*s_i^{jk}\}}} \qquad (11.2)$$

where

$$s_i^{jk} = (s_i^{j} + s_i^{k})/2$$

is the average share (weight) for basic heading i for countries j and k; and s_i^{j}, s_i^{k} are shares of basic heading i in total expenditure of countries j and k.

A new multilateral aggregation method producing additive and simultaneously the most characteristic results can be derived on the basis of the measure of similarities of price structures described in (11.2) above. This method is termed the **MPCP**–method – the method of 'Maximal Possible Characteristic Prices' (Sergeev, 1982, 1998). The method used in identifying a vector of international prices π which can be considered MPCP is described below.

Suppose there is a positive vector of international prices, $\pi = (\pi_i)$, $(i=1,2,...,M)$. The similarity between the national price structure of country j and the structure of international prices, τ_j, can be measured using the similarity index in (11.2) and, therefore, given by:

$$\tau_{j} = \sqrt{\frac{\sum\limits_{i=1}^{M}\{\left(\dfrac{p_{ij}}{\pi_i}\right)*s_i\}*\sum\limits_{i=1}^{M}\{\left(\dfrac{\pi_i}{p_{ij}}\right)*s_i\}}{\sum\limits_{i=1}^{M}\{\left(\dfrac{p_{ij}}{\pi_i}\right)^2*s_i\}*\sum\limits_{i=1}^{M}\{\left(\dfrac{\pi_i}{p_{ij}}\right)^2*s_i\}}} \qquad (11.3)$$

where

$$s_i = \sum\nolimits_{k=1}^{N}s_i^{k}/N$$

is the average weight for basic heading i across all countries (s_i^{k} are defined earlier).

The term τ_j can be considered as the degree of characteristicity of a given vector of international prices π with respect to the prices observed in country j. Then characteristicity of the vector of international prices π with respect to the observed prices in all the countries is defined as the minimal value among τ_j $(j=1,...N)$.

Then the indicator, τ_{min}, is defined as:

$$\tau_{min} = \min \ (\tau_1, \ \tau_2, \ \tau_3, \ ..., \ \tau_N) \tag{11.4}$$

The indicator τ_{min} can be considered as the degree of general characteristicity of a given vector of international prices, π, with respect to prices in all the countries ($j=1...,N$). The MPCP method, which seeks to identify the international price vector that exhibits maximal characteristicity, consists of searching for the vector π which has the maximal (highest) possible value for the indicator τ_{min}. Thus we consider the following optimization problem:

$$\text{maximize}_\pi \ (\min \ \tau_j) = = \ \max_\pi \ \{\min \ \frac{\sum_{i=1}^{M}\{\left(\frac{p_{ij}}{\pi_i}\right)*s_i\} * \sum_{i=1}^{M}\{\left(\frac{\pi_i}{p_{ij}}\right)*s_i\}}{\sqrt{\sum_{i=1}^{M}\{\left(\frac{p_{ij}}{\pi_i}\right)^2 *s_i\} * \sum_{i=1}^{M}\{\left(\frac{\pi_i}{p_{ij}}\right)^2 *s_i\}}} \ \} \tag{11.5}$$

satisfying the condition $\pi_i > 0$ ($i = 1, 2, 3, ..., M$) and $j=1,2,...,N$.

If a vector π is a solution of (11.5) then any vector of the form $\lambda*\pi$ is also a solution, that is, prices π can be found only with accuracy up to scalar. Therefore, relative structural prices are appropriate for this purpose – these can be derived after selecting a product, say a base product B, as the reference price with its price is set as 1 ($\pi_B=1$) and all other prices are measured to the relation to the price of base product. The indicators τ are invariant to the product selected as base.

By construction, the international prices π_i obtained from (11.5) will have the highest possible degree of characteristicity for all comparing countries ($j=1,..N$). Once these prices are identified, these prices can be used making volume comparisons on the basis of vector π. Such comparisons would be transitive, additive and they have the highest possible degree of characteristicity for all countries.

The MPCP method proposed here has two distinguishing features.

1. The approach here makes use of an indicator of similarity of price structures instead of using distance between values of different kinds of indices. For example, the 'IP' method uses the distance between IP–indices and Fisher (or EKS) indices; and the EKS method uses the

distance between transitive indices and non–transitive Fisher indices (or an other type of bilateral indices like Tornqvist index) in arriving at a multilateral system.

2. The method makes use of maximin of similarity of price structures for searching of international prices, π_i, instead of the minimization of the total sum of distances (for all countries in question) between the national and international prices. The procedure is also different from the methods used by Hill in determining the optimal chains based on the minimum spanning trees (see Hill, 1997b, and also this volume).

The second feature of the MPCP method is very important because there could be situations where total sum of similarity coefficients is high but the similarity indices with respect to some countries may be very small that leading to small magnitudes τ_j for some *i*. As an illustration consider the following case with 3 countries and two different international price vectors.

1st international price vector: $\tau_1 = 0.90$; $\tau_2 = 0.95$; $\tau_3 = 0.40$.
$$\min (\tau_j) = 0.40; \quad \sum \tau_j = 2.25.$$

2nd international price vector: $\tau_1 = 0.70$; $\tau_2 = 0.80$; $\tau_3 = 0.60$.
$$\min (\tau_j) = 0.60; \quad \sum \tau_j = 2.10.$$

If we use the MPCP approach, 2nd international price vector is preferable from the point of view of obtaining the maximal possible characteristic results for all countries. However, if total of similarity indices is used then the first international price vector is preferred. It can be seen that the first vector has more similarity with prices in countries 1 and 2 but low characteristicity when it comes to the third country. In contrast, the 2nd international price vector exhibits a high degree of characteristicy with respect to prices of all the three countries.

For a practical example, consider the results, for example Table IV.2 from the Eurostat 2002 comparison. The average coefficient of similarity between international prices by the GK method and national prices (= 0.8241) is higher than the average for the MPCP method (= 0.8081). However, the minimal value obtained by the MPCP (= 0.6799, CH) is much higher than by the GK method (= 0.4840, Bulgaria).

The computational aspects of MPCP method can be illustrated using a simple imaginary example. Consider a comparison involving three countries (A, B, and C) and the price data are for two commodities only. Let the price data be:

- for country A: $p_{1A} = 2,$ $p_{2A} = 1;$
- for country B: $p_{1B} = 8,$ $p_{2B} = 1;$
- for country C: $p_{1C} = 10,$ $p_{2C} = 1.$

The unweighted version of (11.3) is used here for the simplicity. If there are only two products then the formula (11.3) without weights can be transformed to more simple form (only one unknown variable – π_1 with $\pi_2 = 1$). Then the similarity of the international price vector with the price vectors of each of the countries can be written as:

$$\tau_j = \sqrt{p_{1j} * \pi_1} * \frac{p_{1j} + \pi_1}{p_{1j}^2 + \pi_1^2} \quad ; j = A, B, C \tag{11.6}$$

Then it is possible to plot the values of τ_j (11.7) for countries A, B, C as a function of values π_1. These plots are shown on Figure 11.1.

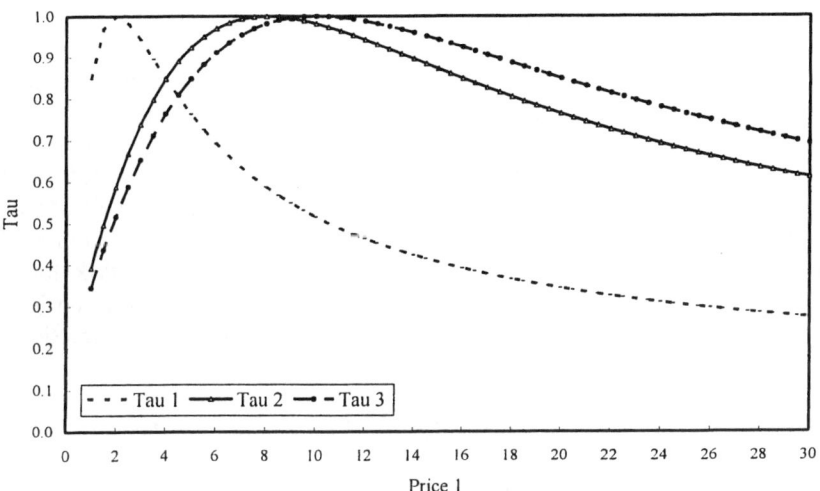

Figure 11.1   Coefficients of similarity with international prices

The function 'min τ_j' with its maximal value is shown on Figure 11.2. From Figure 11.2 it can be see that the max(min τ_j) for given input data is 0.8065 ($\tau_A = 0.8065;$ $\tau_B = 0.8881;$ $\tau_C = 0.8065$) which is obtained with international price $\pi_1 = 4.47$ ($\pi_2 = 1$).[12]

---

[12] In the case with only two products, the initial approximation for π_1 calculated by (11.7) is exactly equal to the optimal solution: $4.47 = (2*10)1/2.$

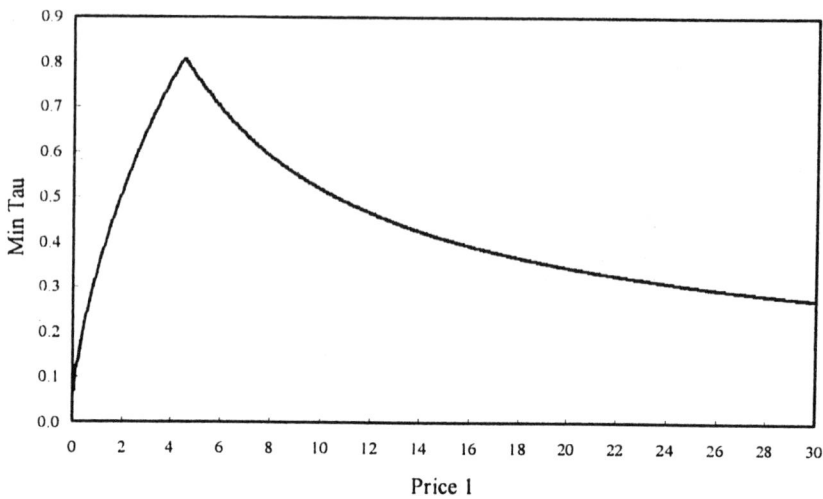

Figure 11.2   Max Min Tau

The actual implementation of the MPCP method is not easy from the computational perspective when a large number of countries and large number of products are involved. For example, most of the OECD–Eurostat comparisons involve the computation of international prices for 150 to 300 basic headings (or products). The objective function given in (11.5) is a highly non–linear function in the unknown international prices. Searching for a vector π that optimizes (11.5) is a difficult computational task for the calculations. It is preferable to use iterative methods starting from an initial vector of the values π_i. Several tests showed that the best approximation of the initial vector π is given by:

$$\pi_i = [\min_j (p_{ij}/p_{Bj}) * \max_j (p_{ij}/p_{Bj})]^{1/2} \; ; \; i=1, 2,..., M; \quad \pi_B=1 \qquad (11.7)$$

p_{Bj} – the price for basic product B $(1 \le B \le M)$ in j^{th} country.

The method of configurations (Hooke's – Jeeves's method) or Nelder's – Mead's method can be used for the optimization of (11.5). The latter method is preferable for practical calculations with a significant number of unknown variables π_i (Himmelblau, 1972).

It is also possible to use a combination of the GK method with the proposed method:

•   Start with an initial vector of PPPs

- Calculate the international prices in accordance with the GK method as quantity–weighted average of the PPPs–adjusted national prices:

$$\pi_i = \sum_{j=1}^{N}(P_{ij} / PPP_j) * q_{ij} / \sum_{j=1}^{N} q_{ij} \, ; \, i = 1,2,...,M \qquad (11.8)$$

- Introduce the GK international prices from (11.8) into equation (11.5).

The optimization (11.5) will be done for the PPP variables which should be further used for the calculation of the resulting set of international prices (11.8). This procedure is a compromise between the weighting procedure (averaging the national prices) which means their gravitation to the prices of large (rich) countries and their characteristicity for all countries. Due to this modification there is a possibility to use only one set of results of a multilateral comparison instead of two sets of results as in Eurostat–OECD PPP Programme (EKS – for volume comparisons where the request of characteristicity has the preference and GK – for structural comparisons where the request of addivity has the preference).

The MPCP method produces additive results with the highest possible characteristicity exhibited by the international prices. Hence the MPCP results can be used for structural analysis as well as for volume comparison.

The MPCP method can also be used for linking results of several comparisons, that is to compile overall (global) ICP results from a set of regional comparisons). One can use a simple generalization of the MPCP method proposed. Apply the MPCP for each region resulting in a set of international price vector for each of the L regions involved. Each regional comparison is based on its own vector of regional international prices π_k ($k=1,...,L$). Once the regional prices are known, we can use equation (11.5) to derive a MPCP international price vector that has maximum characteristicity with the L regional price vectors. The resulting MPCP vector may be considered as the set of world international prices which are characteristic for each region in a maximally possible degree.

11.3 METHOD OF STANDARDIZED STRUCTURE (SS–METHOD)

From the discussion on the MPCP method it is clear that the procedure is computationally intensive and operationally difficult. The search for optimum of a complicated multidimensional function is a difficult task from a computational point of view and, respectively, the obtaining of a meaningful international price vector by an iterative method depends partly on the selection of a good initial approximation. The observations of Cuthbert (1993) concerning the IP method – the absence of uniqueness and possible instability – are valid, in principle, for the MPCP method too.

Therefore, a simpler aggregation method producing additive and simultaneously characteristic results on the basis of using some non-traditional elements of standard elementary indices is proposed in this chapter. This method is labelled the method of Standardized Structure (or SS method).

The basic idea of using an average structure has been used in defining some traditional index number methods like the Tornqvist index or the Walsh index. These methods use geometric averaging of individual indices between countries and, therefore, the resulting indices are non-additive because a geometric mean is additive in logarithmic terms but not in usual linear terms.

To see how the average structure can be used to obtain additive results it is useful to examine the Laspeyres and Paasche quantity index numbers in a non-standard form.

Non-traditional Presentation of Laspeyres and Paasche Indices

Consider the case of with two countries A and B. Input data for an aggregate are sets of national prices (p_A and p_B) and quantities (q_A and q_B).

The Paasche Quantity index $(P_q^{A/B})$ for country A with country B as the base– the index based on the prices of country A can be presented in the following form (subscripts of individual items are omitted for simplicity):

$$P_q^{A/B} = \frac{\Sigma p_A * q_A}{\Sigma p_A * q_B} = \frac{\Sigma[q_A/(q_A+q_B)]*[p_A*(q_A+q_B)]}{\Sigma[q_B/(q_A+q_B)]*[p_A*(q_A+q_B)]} = \qquad (11.9)$$

$$= \frac{\Sigma s_A^Q * e_A^T}{\Sigma s_B^Q * e_A^T} = \frac{\Sigma s_A^Q *[e_A^T/\Sigma e_A^T]}{\Sigma s_B^Q *[e_A^T/\Sigma e_A^T]} = \frac{\Sigma s_A^Q * s_A^T}{\Sigma s_B^Q * s_A^T}$$

$Q = (q_A+q_B)$ – total quantity for a product for countries A and B

$s_A^Q = q_A/Q$; $s_B^Q = q_B/Q$ – the shares of countries A and B in the total quantity for each product

$e_A^T = p_A * Q$ – total value for a product at the prices of country A

$s_A^T = [e_A^T/\Sigma e_A^T]$ – the share of a product in the total value at the prices of country A ($\Sigma s_A^T = 1$)

The Laspeyres Quantity index $(L_q^{A/B})$ – an index that is defined using the prices of country B can be presented in a similar form with expenditure weights at the prices of country B.

There are two new features that can be seen in the non–traditional presentation of Laspeyres and Paasche indices in equation (11.9): (1) the use of the shares of quantities (s_A^Q) instead of the quantity indices; and (2) the use of expenditure weights calculated on the basis of set of total quantities instead of the use on national expenditure shares.

The shares s_A^T and s_B^T, respectively reflect the structure of prices of countries A and B (the vector of quantities $\mathbf{Q}$ is the same in both cases). An arithmetic average of the shares s_A^T and s_B^T (standardized structure) would be equi–characteristic for both countries:

$$s^T = (s_A^T + s_B^T)/2 \ (\textstyle\sum s^T = 1)$$
(11.10)

Now, using the standardized structure s^T, quantity index between countries A and B defined using the method of standardized structure, denoted by $IQ_{SS}^{A/B}$ [13] is obtained as:

$$IQ_{SS}^{A/B} = \frac{\sum s_A^Q * s^T}{\sum s_B^Q * s^T}$$
(11.11)

It is easy to show that index $IQ_{SS}^{A/B}$ is, like the Fisher index, is an average from the Laspeyres and Paasche indices. One can believe that the $IQ_{SS}^{A/B}$ index will be usually very close to the Fisher's index especially if differences between Laspeyres and Paasche indices are not very high. The $IQ_{SS}^{A/B}$ index possesses all properties of the Fisher's index and at the same time the SS index is also additive. [14]

---

[13] This method is named as the method of Standardized Structure = SS method.

[14] The SS method has some similar features with the CKS method (Commensurable Kurabayashi–Sakuma method – see Sakuma, Rao, Kurabayashi (this volume)). Both methods use the total quantities as a basis for the standardization (normalization). There are also some similarities with the Edgeworth–Marshall quantity index which is obtained as the value index divided by EM–PPP).

From Sakuma, Rao and Kurbayashi (this volume) it is clear that the product of CKS and EM indices (it is related to the price as well as to the volume indices) is Fisher index in square. Then the Fisher's index ($Fq^{A/B}$) can be presented as a geometric unweighted average of the CKS and EM indices:

$$F_q^{A/B} = (IQ_{CKS}^{A/B} * IQ_{EM}^{A/B})^{1/2}.$$

It is easy to show that the $IQ_{SS}^{A/B}$ index is an arithmetic average from $IQ_{CKS}^{A/B}$ and $IQ_{EM}^{A/B}$ indices with the specific weights $(1 + L_q^{A/B})$, $(1 + P_q^{A/B})$. Given these two results, it is reasonable to expect that the $IQ_{SS}^{A/B}$ index is a good approximation of

Multilateral version of the SS method

The proposed SS method defined for the bilateral case can be generalized to the multilateral case involving more than two countries.[15] Consider a multilateral comparison with N countries for an aggregate with M primary groups (basic headings = BH). The standard sets prices p_{ij} and quantities q_{ij} (matrices of size M × N) for the basic data for the computation of multilateral index numbers.

The general computational algorithm of the multilateral SS method is the same as in the bilateral case described above. The average standardized structure is calculated on the basis of the sets of standardized structures at the national prices of all participating countries:

$$s_i^T = \sum_{j=1}^{N} s_{ij}^T / N \quad i = 1, 2, ..., M \tag{11.12}$$

where

$$s_i^T = (p_{ij} * Q_i) / \sum_{l=1}^{M} (p_{lj} * Q_l)$$

is the standardized share of i–th basic heading or commodity in total expenditure value of aggregate at prices of country j.

The quantity (volume) index between each pair of countries j and k for the aggregate in question can be obtained as the following:

$$I_{jk}^Q = \frac{\sum_{i=1}^{M} s_{ij}^Q * s_i^T}{\sum_{i=1}^{M} s_{ik}^Q * s_i^T} \tag{11.13}$$

---

the Fisher index. Numerous simulations by simple numerical examples confirm this hypothesis. The bilateral versions of the following methods were tested: Edgeworth–Marshall (EM), Geary–Khamis (GK), Gerardi (G), Tornqvist (T), Commensurable Kurabayshi–Sakuma (CKS) and Standardized Structure (SS). Note that the bilateral Fisher, EM, CKS and SS indices lay strictly between Laspeyres and Paasche indices. The bilateral Tornqvist, Gerardi and Geary–Khamis indices do not possess this property in general cases. The SS method produced, in most cases, the closest results to the Fisher index. The Fisher's index is regarded usually as an 'ideal' ('best') index in a bilateral case.

[15] The main idea of the SS method was proposed firstly in S. Sergeev (1982). See also Sergeev (1983; 1989; 1990; 1998).

where

$Q_i = \sum\limits_{j=1}^{N} q_{ij}$ – total quantity of the ith product (basic heading = BH),

$s_{ij}^{Q} = q_{ij} / Q_i$ – share of country j in total quantity of ith product (BH)

The formula (11.13) allows us to calculate the volume indices for each sub–aggregate but it is much more appropriate to calculate the detailed results using a set of international prices. The following approach is proposed under SS approach. The set of international prices π_i (these prices can be named as the prices of standardized structure) should be determined so that together with total quantities (Q_i) they should reproduce standardized shares (11.12). Therefore, π_i should satisfy the following set of equations:

$$s_i^{T} = \frac{\pi_i * Q_{ij}}{\sum\limits_{i=1}^{M} \pi_i * Q_{ij}} \quad i = 1, 2, ..., M \qquad (11.14)$$

The system of linear equations (11.14) consists of M linear equations in M unknowns. However as the shares sum to unity, one equation is redundant. This system is homogeneous. It is sufficient for the comparison to have the prices determined uniquely up to scalar multiple, that is, relative prices are uniquely determined. If product M, is selected as the base product setting its price as 1 ($\pi_M = 1$) then all the remaining prices are measured as the ratios to the price of base product. By dropping one equation (say, the last equation) and setting $\pi_M = 1$, the system can be solved to yield the remaining π_I's. All that is required is to a system of linear equations (11.14) by the standard methods of linear algebra.

The volume index for each pair of countries (j and k) and for each level of aggregation is obtained on the basis of the prices of standardized structure (SS–prices) in the usual way as:

$$IQ^{j/k} = \frac{\sum\limits_{i=l_1}^{l_2} (\pi_i \cdot q_{ij})}{\sum\limits_{i=l_1}^{l_2} (\pi_i \cdot q_{ik})} \qquad (11.15)$$

where l_1 and l_2 are the bounds for the items included in the definition of the particular sub–aggregate. In the case where we are interested in the full aggregate, we have $l_1 = 1$ and $l_2 = M$.

11.4   EMPIRICAL ILLUSTRATIONS ON THE BASIS OF DATA FROM ACTUAL COMPARISONS

To examine the numerical differences between the results obtained by the traditional and new methods, some experimental calculations were made on the basis of actual data from the Eurostat comparison for 2002 which comprised 282 primary groups (basic headings) for 31 countries. Thus we have $M=282$ and $N=31$. The following methods were used: official EKS, Gerardi (Unit–Country–Weight); Geary–Khamis; CPD–Rao (geometric share weighted GK); arithmetic share weighted GK–Rao; Iklé (harmonic share weighted GK), MPCP method and SS method (Standardized Structure). The comparative results (volume indices per capita) obtained using different methods are presented in Tables 11.1. Table 11.2 contains the coefficients of price similarity between the country's national prices and different international prices. To obtain the full comparability with the official results, a two–stage procedure was applied by all methods to hold the fixity of the results for the 15 EU Members[16] (a standard principle applying within the Eurostat comparisons due to operational considerations relevant for the region).[17]

Tables 11.1 and 11.2 show that the MPCP and SS methods work well within the actual comparisons on the basis of detailed data. In fact the SS results are quite close to the official Eurostat results obtained by the EKS method. This means that the SS method has the numerical properties of the EKS procedure and at the same time it produces additive results which are necessary for the analysis of structures. The SS method can be recommended for the practical applications due to its simplicity and since it possesses the property of characteristicity and additivity simulataneously.

---

[16] It means that the methods were applied firstly to the 15 EU countries, secondly – to all 31 participating countries and the results (volume indices) for 15 EU Members from the first calculation were integrated in the results obtained during the second calculation.

[17] See Roberts (this volume) for a discussion of the fixity principle used in the OECD and Eurostat comparisons.

Table 11.1 GDP volume indices per capita (EU15 = 100): Eurostat 2002 comparison

	EKS official	SS–method	MPCP	Gerardi UCW	GK	CPD–Rao	ShGK–Rao	Iklé	Max Index	Min Index	Max/Min
Germany (D)	99.6	99.2	99.3	99.1	99.3	99.3	99.3	99.3	99.6	99.1	1.004
Belgium (B)	106.5	105.4	107.1	105.5	105.7	105.7	105.6	105.7	107.1	105.4	1.016
Denmark (DK)	112.7	113.1	114.9	113.2	113.5	113.4	113.4	113.6	114.9	112.7	1.020
Greece (EL)	70.9	73.2	72.6	73.1	73.0	72.2	72.5	72.1	73.2	70.9	1.033
Spain (E)	86.1	86.2	85.7	86.2	86.1	85.7	85.8	85.7	86.2	85.7	1.006
France (F)	104.6	104.1	105.0	104.1	104.4	104.6	104.6	104.5	105.0	104.1	1.009
Ireland (IRL)	125.4	127.6	128.7	127.9	129.1	128.1	128.2	128.3	129.1	125.4	1.029
Italy (I)	98.2	97.5	96.7	97.5	97.3	97.0	97.0	97.0	98.2	96.7	1.016
Luxembourg (L)	188.9	196.3	199.0	196.1	197.0	195.1	195.6	195.0	199.0	188.9	1.053
Netherlands (NL)	111.5	111.3	112.8	111.4	111.6	111.3	111.2	111.4	112.8	111.2	1.014
Austria (A)	110.9	109.8	110.2	109.9	110.2	110.1	110.0	110.2	110.9	109.8	1.010
Portugal (P)	70.7	73.5	72.3	73.4	73.6	73.1	73.3	73.0	73.6	70.7	1.040
Finland (FIN)	101.7	102.4	103.1	102.5	103.5	102.7	102.6	102.9	103.5	101.7	1.017
Sweden (S)	104.6	105.8	107.8	106.0	106.2	106.2	106.0	106.4	107.8	104.6	1.031
United K. (UK)	107.5	108.2	107.1	108.2	107.5	108.4	108.3	108.4	108.4	107.1	1.012
Iceland (IS)	109.0	109.4	110.2	109.2	111.4	108.8	108.7	108.9	111.4	108.7	1.025
Norway (NO)	136.3	146.1	154.5	145.9	141.4	144.9	146.6	144.5	154.5	136.3	1.133
Switzerland (CH)	114.1	119.1	122.1	118.7	116.9	119.2	120.3	118.7	122.1	114.1	1.070
Bulgaria (BG)	26.4	30.9	26.9	29.9	32.8	29.9	30.9	29.0	32.8	26.4	1.241

Continued

Table 11.1 GDP volume indices per capita (EU15 = 100): Eurostat 2002 comparison – continued

	EKS official	SS–method	MPCP	Gerardi UCW	GK	CPD–Rao	ShGK–Rao	Iklé	Max Index	Min Index	Max/Min
Cyprus (CY)	76.1	76.5	73.5	77.3	80.9	78.5	77.4	79.5	80.9	73.5	1.101
Czech R. (CZ)	61.9	61.3	59.1	61.2	63.9	61.9	62.0	61.9	63.9	59.1	1.081
Estonia (EE)	40.1	42.3	38.4	41.6	44.8	42.1	42.8	41.5	44.8	38.4	1.166
Hungary (HU)	53.4	53.8	51.0	53.1	55.9	54.0	54.6	53.4	55.9	51.0	1.095
Latvia (LV)	34.8	37.7	34.2	36.9	40.0	37.3	38.1	36.7	40.0	34.2	1.168
Lithuania (LT)	39.1	42.3	39.0	41.3	44.9	42.0	43.0	41.1	44.9	39.0	1.152
Malta (MT)	69.1	69.0	65.3	68.8	71.8	69.4	69.2	69.2	71.8	65.3	1.100
Poland (PL)	41.2	41.8	39.5	41.2	43.7	41.9	42.4	41.4	43.7	39.5	1.107
Romania (RO)	26.5	29.3	26.9	28.6	30.7	28.7	29.4	28.1	30.7	26.5	1.157
Slovak R. (SK)	47.0	49.0	45.8	48.6	51.7	49.1	49.4	48.8	51.7	45.8	1.129
Slovenia (SI)	69.0	68.5	68.3	68.5	69.5	68.8	69.1	68.8	69.5	68.3	1.017
Turkey (TR)	24.6	27.1	24.7	26.5	28.6	26.7	27.3	26.4	28.6	24.6	1.163

Table 11.2 Coefficients of similarity of national prices/international price structures: Eurostat 2002 comparison

	SS prices	MPCP prices	G–UCW prices	G–K prices	CPD–Rao	GK–Rao prices	Iklé prices
Germany (D)	0.8754	0.7618	0.8541	0.9294	0.8650	0.8690	0.8400
Belgium (B)	0.9247	0.8179	0.9073	0.9650	0.9180	0.9205	0.8965
Denmark (DK)	0.8905	0.7794	0.8780	0.9323	0.8822	0.8786	0.8663
Greece (EL)	0.9542	0.9131	0.9530	0.9282	0.9510	0.9504	0.9445
Spain (E)	0.9439	0.8768	0.9361	0.9586	0.9392	0.9368	0.9273
France (F)	0.9289	0.8322	0.9162	0.9664	0.9240	0.9242	0.9084
Ireland (IRL)	0.8787	0.7631	0.8597	0.9187	0.8761	0.8785	0.8567
Italy (I)	0.9299	0.8433	0.9135	0.9511	0.9221	0.9251	0.9010
Luxembourg (L)	0.7958	0.6801	0.7682	0.8523	0.7817	0.7905	0.7487
Netherlands (NL)	0.9119	0.8083	0.8997	0.9548	0.9062	0.9035	0.8913
Austria (A)	0.9275	0.8304	0.9148	0.9612	0.9185	0.9175	0.9011
Portugal (P)	0.8984	0.8717	0.8966	0.8562	0.8858	0.8875	0.8765
Finnland (FIN)	0.8832	0.7696	0.8646	0.9073	0.8743	0.8782	0.8541
Sweden (S)	0.8691	0.7579	0.8574	0.9185	0.8589	0.8556	0.8425
United K. (UK)	0.8941	0.7864	0.8848	0.9317	0.8866	0.8847	0.8735
Iceland (IS)	0.8611	0.7765	0.8576	0.8776	0.8584	0.8514	0.8523
Norway (NO)	0.8672	0.7537	0.8563	0.9005	0.8551	0.8525	0.8399
Switzerland (CH)	0.7976	0.6799	0.7778	0.8664	0.7949	0.7965	0.7721

Continued

Table 11.2 Coefficients of similarity of national prices/international price structures: Eurostat 2002 comparison – continued

	SS prices	MPCP prices	G–UCW prices	G–K prices	CPD–Rao	GK–Rao prices	Iklé prices
Bulgaria (BG)	0.5523	0.6927	0.5864	0.4840	0.5634	0.5498	0.5945
Cyprus (CY)	0.8496	0.8007	0.8476	0.8183	0.8320	0.8295	0.8236
Czech R. (CZ)	0.8626	0.9255	0.8800	0.7828	0.8576	0.8543	0.8680
Estonia (EE)	0.7593	0.8667	0.7950	0.6907	0.7679	0.7518	0.7977
Hungary (HU)	0.8605	0.9309	0.8823	0.7852	0.8533	0.8475	0.8672
Latvia (LV)	0.6320	0.7461	0.6643	0.5540	0.6310	0.6201	0.6560
Lithuania (LT)	0.6657	0.7752	0.6979	0.5856	0.6662	0.6560	0.6915
Malta (MT)	0.8674	0.8770	0.8754	0.8019	0.8603	0.8598	0.8606
Poland (PL)	0.8421	0.9030	0.8636	0.7572	0.8375	0.8330	0.8515
Romania (RO)	0.5923	0.7156	0.6239	0.5202	0.6064	0.5951	0.6340
Slowak R. (SK)	0.7434	0.8504	0.7709	0.6627	0.7465	0.7393	0.7668
Slovenia (SI)	0.9395	0.8848	0.9317	0.9184	0.9258	0.9292	0.9150
Turkey (TR)	0.6895	0.7816	0.7156	0.6099	0.6894	0.6835	0.7085
Max	0.9542	0.9309	0.9530	0.9664	0.9510	0.9504	0.9445
Min	0.5523	0.6799	0.5864	0.4840	0.5634	0.5498	0.5945

11.5   CONCLUSIONS

In this chapter, two new additive methods for international comparisons have been proposed. These methods are designed to maintain the characteristicity of the binary comparisons and at the same time achieve additivity of international comparisons for different sub–aggregates.

The first method, the MPCP method (method of Maximal Possible Characteristic Prices), is an additive method which constructs international prices that reflect in maximal possible degree the price structures of all participating countries, that is, it allows to obtain the maximally possible characteristic results. Therefore this method can be fruitfully used for volume comparisons as well as for structural comparisons for heterogeneous set of countries.

A computational simpler multilateral aggregation method, the standardized structure (SS) method, is proposed and its properties with respect to the Fisher and other binary indexes are discussed. Empirical implementation of the MPCP and the SS methods using Eurostat data for the year 2002 showed that the SS results possess the property of characteristicity and are numerically close to the EKS results and at the same time the SS method produced additive results.

The experience of international comparisons showed that there is no single universally acceptable method and different methods should be used for different aims. However it is desirable to have the methods which combine the advantages and eliminate the disadvantages of different methods. Two such methods, the MPCP and the SS methods, are proposed and illustrated in this chapter.

REFERENCES

Ahmad, S. (1994), '*Reduced Information Initiative*'. Washington, D.C.: World Bank.

Allen, R.C. and Diewert, W.E. (1981), 'Direct versus Implicit Superlative Index Number Formulae', *Review of Economics and Statistics*, **LXIII** (3), 430–435.

Ark, van B., E.J. Monnikhof and M.P. Timmer (1999), 'Prices, Quantities and Productivity in Industry: a Study of Transition Economies in a Comparative Perspective', in R. Lipsey and A. Heston (eds), *International and Interarea Comparisons of Prices, Income and Output*, NBER, Chicago: Chicago University Press.

Balk, B.M. (1996), 'A Comparison of Ten Methods for Multilateral International Price and Volume Comparison', *Journal of Official Statistics*, **12**, 199–222.

Balk, B.M. (this volume), 'Aggregation Methods in International Comparisons: an Evaluation'.

Cuthbert, J.R. (1993), 'IP and EKS Aggregation Methods: Preservation of Price Structure under the IP Method', Eurostat Mimeo, Eurostat, Luxembourg.

Cuthbert, J.R. (1999), 'Categorisation of Additive PPP', *Review of Income and Wealth*, **45**, 235–249.

Cuthbert, J.R. and M. Cuthbert (1988), 'On Aggregation Methods of Purchasing Power Parities', OECD Working Papers.

Diewert, W.E. (1996), 'Axiomatic and Economic Approaches to International Comparisons'. Conference on Research in Income and Wealth, 15–16 March 1996, Arlington, Virginia.

Diewert, W.E. (this volume), 'Similarity Indexes and Criteria for Spatial Linking'.

Dikhanov, Y. (1994), 'Sensitivity of PPP–Based Income Estimates to Choice of Aggregation Procedures' (IARIW session on International Comparison; St.Andrews, New Brunswick, Canada, 21–27 August 1994).

Drechsler, L. (1973), 'Weighting of Index Numbers in Multilateral International Comparisons', *Review of Income and Wealth*, **19**, 17–34.

Eltetö, O. and P. Köves (1964), 'On a Problem of Index Number Computation Relating to International Comparison', *Statisztikai Szemle*, **42**, 507–518 (in Hungarian).

Eurostat (1983), *Comparison in Real Terms of the Aggregates of ESA, 1980*. Luxembourg, Statistical Office of the European Communities.

Gerardi, D. (1982), 'Selected Problems of Inter–Country Comparisons on the Basis of the Experience of the EEC', *Review of Income and Wealth* **28**, 253–259.

Gini, C. (1931), 'On the Circular Test of Index Numbers', *International Review of Statistics*, **9** (2), 3–25.

Hill, P. (1982), *Multilateral Measurements of Purchasing Power and Real GDP*, SOEC, Luxembourg.

Hill, R.J. (1997a), 'A Taxonomy of Multilateral Methods for Making International Comparisons of Prices and Quantities', *The Review of Income and Wealth*, **43** (1), 49–69.

Hill R. J. (1997b). '*Comparing Price Levels and Living Standards across the ESCAP Countries Using Spanning Trees and other Aggregation Methods*', Paper for a UN Seminar on comparison within the ESCAP, Beijing, 16–20, June.

Hill, R.J. (1999), 'Comparing Price Levels Across Countries Using Minimum – Spanning Trees', *Review of Economics and Statistics*, 1999, **81** (1), 135–142.

Hill, R. J. (this volume), 'Comparing Per Capita Income Levels Across Countries Using Spanning Trees: Robustness, Prior Restrictions, Hybrids and Hierarchies'.

Himmelblau, D. (1972), *Applied Nonlinear Programming*. McGraw-Hill.

IJzeren, J. van. (1983), 'Index Numbers for Binary and Multilateral Comparison', *Statistical* Studies, **34**, Netherlands Central Bureau of Statistics.

Iklé, D.M. (1972), 'A New Approach to the Index Number Problem', *Quarterly Journal of Economics*, **86**, 188–211.

Khamis, S.H. (1993), '*On Some Aspects of the Measurement of Purchasing Power Parities*'. Reports of ISI Session, August, Florenz.

Khamis, S.H. (1998) 'Measurement of Real Product: Some Index Number Aspects' presented at the 25th General conference of the IARIW, 23–29 August, Cambridge.

Khamis, S.H. and D.S. Prasada Rao (1989), 'On Gerardi Alternative for the Geary–Khamis Measurement of International Purchasing Powers and Real Product', *Journal of Official Statistics*, **5**, 83–87.

Köves, P. (1983), *Index Theory and Economic Reality*', Akademiai Kiado, Budapest.

Kravis, I.B., Z. Kenessy, A. Heston and R. Summers (1975), '*A System of International Comparison of Gross Product and Purchasing Power*', Baltimore, MD: Johns Hopkins University Press.

Kravis, I.B., A.W. Heston and R. Summers (1982), '*World Product and Income, International Comparison of Real Gross Product*', Baltimore, MD: Johns Hopkins University Press.

Rao, D.S. Prasada (2000), 'Expenditure Share Weighted Size–neutral Geary–Khamis Method for International Comparisons: Specification and Properties', Mimeograph, Washington DC: World Bank.

Rao, D.S. Prasada (this volume), 'Generalised Eltetö–Köves–Szulc and Country–Product–Dummy Methods for International Comparisons'.

Roberts, D. (this volume), 'The Compilation of Purchasing Power Parities: the Eurostat–OECD Purchasing Power Parity Programme'.

Sakuma I., D.S. Prasada Rao and Y. Kurabayashi (this volume), 'Additivity, Matrix Consistency and a New Method for International Comparisons of Real Income and Purchasing Power Parities'.

Sergeev, S. (1982), 'Multilateral Methods for International Comparisons', Ph.D. Dissertation, Moscow: Central Statistical Committee of Soviet Union, (in Russian).

Sergeev, S. (1983) 'The Making of the Indices for International Comparisons'. – *Economic and Mathematical Methods*, **XIX** (6), USSR Academy of Sciences, Central Economic Mathematical Institute. (in co-authorship, in Russian).

Sergeev S. (1989) 'An Improvement of International Comparisons of Main Macroeconomic Indicators of CMEA–Countries' in 'Statistical Cooperation of the CMEA–Countries', **5**, Moscow: CMEA (in co-authorship, in Russian).

Sergeev S. (1990) 'Modern Tendencies in the Cross-country Comparison of the Macroeconomic Indicators.' *Economic and Mathematical Methods*, **XXYI** (4), USSR Academy of Sciences, Central Economic Mathematical Institute (in co-authorship).

Sergeev, S. (1998), *New Methods for International Price and Volume Comparisons* (a Research Project of the Austrian National Bank), Vienna, FGW, **127** (in German with a translation into English).

Sergeev, S. (2001), *Measures of the Similarity of the Country's Price Structures and their Practical Application* – ECE, Joint Consultation on the European Comparison Programme, 12–14 November, Geneva.

Szulc, B. (1964), 'Indices for Multiregional Comparisons', *Przeglad Statystyczny* **3**, *Statistical Review* **3**, 239–254 (in Polish).

United Nations (1992), '*Handbook of the International Comparison Programme*'. ST/ESA/STA/SER:F/62 (UN publications, Sales No. E.92.XVII.12).

United Nations (1993), *A System of National Accounts*, New York.

PART IV

Applications

12. Purchasing Power Parities and their Policy Relevance

Michael Ward[1]

12.1 INTRODUCTION

Four decades have past since *Purchasing Power Parities* were first introduced, initially through the research efforts of the University of Pennsylvania, to the international scene, although an understanding of their relevance has been known for much longer (Cassel). Yet the practical significance of purchasing power parities (PPPs) to policy, as opposed to acknowledgements of their analytical usefulness in academic studies, has still to be properly recognized. They are used by international agencies, mostly at the aggregate level, but few governments pay any real heed to the performance of other countries when concentrating attention on issues of domestic policy concern. Nevertheless, given the avowed intention of most governments in this present day and age to preserve the real purchasing power of people's money, particularly by controlling significant uplifts to domestic price levels, this apparent lack of interest in international buying power is surprising. PPPs provide information on both relative and absolute price levels pertaining to all goods and services falling within GDP. They enable countries to take a hard look at their economic structures and financial systems in an international context. If for no other reason than to manage an efficient allocation of scarce resources and oversee the corresponding distribution of goods and services in real terms, policymakers need to understand why PPPs matter. Governments should know which sorts of goods and services are relatively cheap and which are expensive in international terms. This has specific implications for market organization

---

[1] It is with profound sadness I report here that the author, Michael Ward, suddenly passed away on 18th October, 2008 soon after his return from New Zealand. The version published here is the latest version I received from Michael on 30th September, 2008. He had indicated that he was going to make further revisions to the manuscript after his return to Cambridge. With due respect to Michael, as the editor I have decided to include his latest version without making any changes.

and improving national competitiveness. There are, perhaps, even more important lessons for those agencies engaged primarily in international activities and transactions.

This chapter examines some of the more important uses of PPPs in an operational policy context. It reviews the value of the accompanying new data that have been generated by the latest International Comparisons Program (ICP 2005) results to domestic, international and overall global analysis. By their very nature, as time bound inter–spatial price indices, PPPs are of greatest relevance to international comparisons. But this is not all. The usefulness of PPPs to relative domestic price levels for various commodity groups through a logical link to a uniform, across the board, price level numeraire, is equally valuable. Developments since 1985 have also seen the construction of regional group price levels as well as international average prices. This has considerably widened the scope and relevance of PPPs to potential analysis. The chapter reviews the respective importance of PPPs under four different but inter–related economic headings and their main sub–components:

> *National:* the real domestic structure of GDP; the size of government; relative national competitiveness; and specific price and consumption relationships
>
> *International:* wealth; size of the economy (total GDP); income per head (GNP per capita); poverty; food consumption per head; inequality; growth; and competitiveness
>
> *Global aggregates:* price structures and globalization; PPPs, price distortions and market structures; the real value of aid; global income inequality; and the real value of aid
>
> *Other uses:* true debt and payback burden; energy efficiency; and energy intensity.

Comparisons of performance set against an independent standard show the use of PPP adjusted data provides a relevant if not more accurate assessment of real progress.

12.2   PPPS – THE CONCEPT

This chapter identifies those policy situations where PPP adjusted nominal values serve as a better indicator for determining differences in levels of development than uni–dimensional exchange rates. While PPPs provide a more reliable basis for strengthening economic policies, decisions relating to international asset and portfolio management, financial transactions and debt settlement appropriately continue to rely on exchange rates.

International comparability remains a key objective of the UN statistical system, considered by most as providing the universal standard for compiling data determining what concepts and conventions need to be generally recognized. The core feature of PPPs is that, compared with official exchange rates that determine the international value of a nation's currency, they reflect differences in domestic price levels in countries. PPPs represent the 'shadow' exchange rate that implicitly revalues national quantities expressed in national prices to a common international price basis. Consequently, in equalizing price levels across countries, they allow meaningful direct comparisons of real economic magnitudes in value terms. To understand which countries, overall, may be deemed 'cheap' and those that are 'expensive' according to this 'normalized' international price level, it is necessary to divide the relevant GDP PPP by the corresponding foreign exchange rate with respect to the same specified currency numeraire. If, for example, the PPP between the UK and US is £1 = \$1.95 and the corresponding official exchange rate is £1 = \$1.50 then the price level (1.85/1.50 = 1.23) indicates that, in general, prices in the UK are almost a quarter higher than in the USA. This is simply a reflection of the fact that, in real terms, the \$1.50 converted to £1 at the official exchange rate will not be enough money to buy in Britain what the equivalent dollar sum would command in the US, that is, it buys only 77 per cent (1.50/1.95) of the US basket.

PPPs serve as measures of price levels of specific, well–defined groups of commodities. The further a PPP ratio for a group of products is from one, the higher (or lower) the price level of that GDP sub–aggregate will be as compared with GDP itself. In particular, if in any given country the overall GDP price level in international terms is defined as 1.00, then an expenditure category (say, rents or housing repairs) that exceeds 1.00 will be considered 'expensive' whereas any category below 1.00 (perhaps bread and cereals, for example) will be viewed as 'cheap'.

PPPs are economic status measures relating to differences in price levels at a particular time (spatial indices) whereas conventional price indexes relate to flows and measure the change in price of a given set of goods and services over time and overall inflation. In the case of PPPs, the 'distance' between any two observations is not fixed whereas, in a conventional price index, corresponding measurements are made sequentially at fixed reporting periods that are constrained to refer to regular well–defined chronological intervals. Because disparate and disjoint magnitudes associated with economic size occur in spatial price comparisons, this factor gives rise to potentially greater problems of distortion in PPP price level estimates than might be encountered in conventional time series price indices.

12.3   THE USE OF PPPS IN ECONOMIC ANALYSIS AND POLICY

PPPs create the required unified price basis for conducting international comparisons over a range of meaningful economic aggregates, different commodity groups and strategic sectors.

12.3.1   The National Context

The domestic structure of GDP
In calculating PPPs for participating countries, each successive phase of the ICP) has divided expenditures on GDP into approximately 150 different well–defined categories of consumption called 'basic headings'. In the richer and more complex advanced economies, more than 220 commodity groups belonging to GDP may be identified while in less diversified lower income economies there may be far fewer basic headings. Basic headings represent the approximate expenditure weights for their corresponding respective spending levels. Below this level of national outlay detail, unfortunately, reliable information about weights is generally unavailable. In principle, PPPs can be compiled for every basic heading level, categorized, respectively, to private household consumption, government expenditure and investment expenditure. In the particular case of government (see below), current consumption can be subdivided into those official expenditures incurred collectively, like policing and road repairs, on behalf of the community as a whole and those that are ultimately for the individual benefit of households like medical care and education outlays.

For presentational purposes, as well as to ensure greater reliability across all countries, the detailed basic heading estimates are usually collapsed into some 34 to 52 distinct but more robust common expenditure components. The consolidation of lower level basic headings into higher homogeneous outlay categories helps to reduce the volatility and individual measurement error, as well as potential bias, that may be embedded in the PPP estimates. The basic headings define the sub–components of expenditure for which there is some degree of confidence in the estimates. The availability of data at this level allows comparisons between specific expenditure groupings as well as across spending sectors. Equally important, it allows consistently valued comparisons of the economic structures of each individual country across the whole range of international expenditures. By implication and some extrapolation, certain basic heading expenditures can also be reconstructed to provide rough estimates of output in market prices by their respective producing sectors.

Comparisons of specific final expenditure components

From this detail, analysts can determine how much in real terms is allocated to food (and particularly food purchased per head or per household), or alcohol, tobacco, housing or health care. Because outlays are assessed on a unified price basis this can facilitate a better appraisal of the apparent linear stability of Engels coefficients across income levels (see below). Matched with other non–monetary national data relating to production and import quantities, calorie intake, nutritional standards, housing units, morbidity and so on, these data can provide a much clearer perspective of individual and household command over the basic goods and services they themselves consider necessary (as reflected in their revealed preferences and purchases) for maintaining their well–being. For each expenditure sub–component a separate PPP related to the average underlying international price level in respect of that item or group of items can be calculated. This provides a unique opportunity for governments to determine which goods are relatively expensive in relation to average GDP prices in their respective countries.

Until PPP information became available, when researchers wanted to draw up international comparisons of detailed expenditure outlays and GDP shares, they resorted to calculating price ratios in domestic currency terms or implicit standard exchange rate measures, usually based on the US dollar. The same conversion factor for the nation as a whole was thus applied to the more distinct lower level categories of expenditure where sector prices could be quite different. At these lower levels, outlays tend to be determined by very different domestic (and international) market conditions in each country. The use of an identical single national exchange rate in this context across the whole range of GDP outlays to determine the relative importance of different types of expenditure is thus inappropriate. Furthermore, the underlying valuation basis of, respectively, the numerator and denominator country exchange rates in these cases is different and the derived ratios are therefore inappropriate and evidently unstable over time.

Comparisons of national expenditure structures

It has already been noted that, at the level of GDP, PPP converted values show higher levels of national expenditure for most lower income countries than would be indicated by a conventional exchange rate conversion. These differences are proportionately larger the lower the absolute economic size and average income (GNP per capita) of a country. Similarly, at lower component levels of GDP and its sub–aggregates, PPP converted national expenditures will be different. This means that if an 'additive' aggregation procedure such as the Geary–Khamis (GK) method has been adopted to compile these PPPs, the derived pattern of real outlays in international price terms will not only produce consistent GDP shares but also generate estimates that will be quite different from the structure of an economy as traditionally understood in its own domestic price terms. These differences are sometimes of considerable strategic importance, as in the case of investment and public administration expenditures. The use of official national exchange rates in this context conceals the real 'quantum' differences between the components of GDP being compared. Thus, while the same types of 'money unit' ratios may appear, superficially, 'currency unit free', they are not 'value free' in an international context. Importantly, even when comparing economic change within individual countries over time, such as overall growth rates, it is the use of real outlays at international prices as weights that is relevant. The absolute price levels and price movements underlying the national GDP sector values implicit in these measures are not the same.

Some selected examples
The importance of PPPs for identifying true relative price and quantity structures within a country can be highlighted in several policy relevant cases.

- *Food outlays:* In national price terms, as countries grow richer, the percentage of overall private household consumption going to the purchase of food grows smaller. This parallels the way individual expenditures conform to a recognized 'Engels Law' pattern as personal incomes rise within a country. In international price terms, however, while the trend may be similar, the nature of the baskets typically consumed by the population can be quite different. The whole nature and purpose of food changes with income from being essential to sustenance to being part of conventional social functioning. But the ratios change because the relative price levels are not the same as those implied in a domestic comparison. The price level for food in the US, for example, is relatively low both in comparison with other expenditure categories in the country and in international terms. Hence the real share of expenditure going on food, while low compared with total outlays, is actually greater than that indicated by same consumption shares measured in domestic prices. A more detailed microanalysis of food intakes across countries makes this quite clear. At the other end of the spectrum, researchers (Biru, 1998) have shown that, in several low income African countries, the price level for food as expressed in PPP terms, is higher than the average price level for GDP as a whole. Similar findings have been obtained from studies of food intakes in Indian villages. The real quantities of food acquired in what appears in domestic price terms to be an already large allocation of expenditure for this purpose are thus somewhat smaller in very low income countries.

Nutritionally, therefore, the position of the poor may reveal greater vulnerability than is immediately apparent from a superficial examination of national data. Equally evident, this also indicates that the underlying distribution of income (in its broadest sense) and well–being may be even more skewed than that revealed by a set of values for food consumption that assumes equivalent prices apply across all socio–economic classes.

- *Capital formation:* Conventional measures of the share of capital formation in an economy raise similar concerns of interpretation. It is another example where PPPs rather than exchange rates should be used in interpretative analysis. For many years, those worried about development policy have anguished over why, despite the apparently high proportion of resources devoted to domestic capital formation in low–income economies, many countries have singularly and consistently failed to achieve economic growth and to develop. Apart from all the usual explanations that have been advanced to account for this phenomenon such as, poor policy, absence of effective management and organization skills, weak government and institutional integrity, lack of absorptive capacity, counterpart resource failures, inappropriateness of the investment, the construction of 'white elephants', inadequate repair and maintenance capacity, and so on, the one over–riding factor that analysts have tended to overlook has been the relative high price of capital goods in poor countries. Poorer countries pay more for their investment goods and get less in real terms. Many pieces of plant and equipment, and even for local construction, have to be imported from richer industrial countries. In all phases of the ICP it has been found that the relative price of capital goods compared with the price level for GDP in a country declines progressively as the income of a country grows. At very low per capita GDP levels, the relative price level for investment goods, and particularly for plant equipment and machinery, can often be as much as twice that of the average price level of GDP. Consequently, in international terms, the real investment in these countries is only half of what might have been implied from simply looking at the share of capital formation in local prices. The cost of capital is clearly going to be greater in a low income developing country and this is not just because it is necessary to take account of extra freight, insurance, installation and other fixed overheads. These goods are expensive because they are made in countries where labor costs are high and used in countries where capital is scarce. It is misleading, therefore, to look at comparative investment shares in other than PPP terms to identify real capital formation. The problem is compounded by the fact that, for a variety of reasons, capital destined for lower income countries may not be, technologically, as advanced as that acquired and used in more developed countries. This clearly has further implications for any assessment of the incremental capital–output ratios necessary to achieve a desired economic growth rate and of the estimates of capital that fulfill the requirement for investment models to explain and determine development potential.

• *Official spending on social services:* The general issue of the size of government spending is considered in more detail below but an important area where the calculation of PPPs has thrown up significant differences is in the comparative analysis of the real value of government current expenditures on health and education. This has affected perceptions about the relative real size and effectiveness of the public administration and provisions to the social services sectors. In these cases, a review involving simple direct comparisons of national income shares that are based on domestic prices does not always make sense. In the ICP, because the degree of involvement of various governments in the provision of health and education services varies significantly between countries, official current expenditures need to be re–classified to account for differences between public 'spending' and private 'end–use' and to distinguish between collective official outlays and those made specifically on behalf of households. This then permits the derivation of uniformly comparable PPPs for these sectors that are relevant to public expenditures on the one hand and to personal outlays and actual consumption of households on the other. Countries that have not yet shifted their statistical basis to the new 1993 SNA will not show in their annual national accounts such equivalent expenditure categories. Nevertheless, even where the basis has been changed, comparisons of the share of government in GDP make it clear that domestic price measures of outlays can be quite misleading with respect to the real benefits provided by the government and the services people receive from the public sector.

Not surprisingly, it has been found that the share of government tends to be higher in poor countries in PPP terms. This is primarily a reflection of the dominant role of services, particularly of labor, in government. It occurs despite the relatively lower domestic wage levels that prevail throughout the public sector often because of the limitations imposed in small countries by economies of scale. In evaluating comparative health outlays in OECD countries, on the other hand, it is clear that high domestic costs significantly affect (and can considerably reduce) estimates of the real amount of care and treatment provided by the health sector. Over the years, studies using PPPs have shown that actual health spending secures quite different health benefits in real terms across different countries. For example, in the USA where the basic prices for medical services and health treatment are high, the actual amount of real 'health' services Americans obtain from their national expenditures appears to be much lower than in most other industrial countries for the same outlay, even when assumed quality differences are factored into the equation. Similarly, studies on comparative defense expenditures, policing costs, central administration overheads, public transport services, and so on have all shown significant differences between countries. Such comparisons are complicated, however, by the problem of accounting comprehensively for productivity levels and quality differences. It may well be argued that doctors of similar skills and experience are not the same across countries, not least because of better access to high quality medical back–up services, laboratory analysis, better instruments, good monitoring technologies and well trained support personnel.

12.3.2   Economic Growth and Performance

The analysis of time series relating to comparative growth rates, economic catch–up performance and long run convergence is best understood in PPP terms. At first sight, this may seem surprising. National growth rates are immediately recognized and readily available in implicit national price terms. They clearly have domestic policy relevance but, to determine true international convergence and comparative progress, such growth rates should be re–calculated using standardized weights for expenditures that are valued in equivalent international prices, not in different domestic prices. This is because one key objective is to see whether, with economic progress and global connectivity, countries do converge towards a similar structure of real economic output and behaviour.

12.3.3   Output and Productivity

While growth may be partially explored using internationally comparable expenditure data, a more complete analysis of sector convergence in production (through shared technologies and associated human capital improvement) still needs, additionally, to draw on PPP 'output' estimates based on production data. Output PPPs are also relevant for examining international competitiveness, real productivity differences, and patterns of specialization among industries. Early attempts to study these and similar issues were made by rearranging PPP real expenditure estimates so that they approximately represented particular manufacturing and producing sectors of interest (as defined by their principal products). The major work in this area, however, has approached this question directly from the output side. This research has been undertaken by the Groningen University Growth Group in Holland under the leadership of Professor Angus Maddison. Their studies use national Census of Industry (or Production) figures and other detailed data drawn from enterprise surveys to produce baseline measures of gross output. They produce estimates of net domestic product in comparable terms, using various assumptions about intermediate consumption. There are other statistical issues that have to be taken into account in such analysis, including the qualitative (and perhaps sometimes arbitrary) adjustments that are made for technological changes and other quality improvements. Since these also affect prices they further impact on the value of the deflator applied to derive not only growth rates but estimates of real output and productivity.

12.3.4   PPPs and Development Paths

PPPs are relevant to a better understanding of the overall pattern and change of overall progress. Internal research studies conducted in the World Bank using principal components analysis (Dikhanov 1999) show a more distinct relationship across countries between social outcomes and desired social policy goals (for example, teacher/pupil ratios, average class size and so on) and economic performance when PPPs rather than exchange rates are used to adjust GDP per capita as the measuring standard. Such studies reveal quite dramatic improvements in social well–being around the 'lower middle' and 'middle' income areas of the distribution. The trend in social progress then flattens off onto a distinct plateau as incomes rise proportionately, indicating a movement towards an upper 'asymptotic' limit. A similar 'development path' has been long recognized by UNDP in its Human Development Report. It is implicit in the supporting analysis and results generated by the Human Development Index (HDI). The HDI depends heavily on a national sub–index based on an adjusted logarithmic measure of PPP per capita income.

Other empirical enquiries using cross–sectional regression techniques (Barro and Sala–i–Martin, 1994) show that inter–spatial differences across countries in key social variables, including investment in human and social capital, are better explained by PPP converted GDP measures than by exchange rate converted estimates, reinforcing theoretical expectations. When measured in exchange rate terms or using domestic price shares, the link between investment levels and economic growth has been ambiguous and, at best, tenuous both over time and in cross–country comparisons (Easterly, 1999). Perhaps less surprisingly, the role of the machinery component in capital formation in promoting output improvement and productivity gains appears to be more significant than (by association) private and public construction activity of similar value. Building and construction activity may have a more profound longer–term effect on development progress but this has proved indefinable. In the short run, the impact of construction activity is probably mainly indirect, occurring through the contribution it makes to employment income rather than through use as a capital asset belonging to a particular industrial sector.

12.3.5 Income Spread and Marginalization

By the same token, both PPP and exchange rate information are required to understand the economic significance of marginalization. Marginalization refers mainly to those circumstances where adverse and deteriorating market conditions (as reflected in low price levels and distorted price structures) occur in low–income countries compared with the more conducive trading situations enjoyed by much richer countries. At every phase of the ICP, no matter what countries have been incorporated into the study and what aggregation formula has been selected, PPP converted values have been higher for all low and middle income countries than they are when equivalent exchange rate calculations are made. By the same token, GDP measures and their components have been either similar or somewhat lower for the more closely clustered high income countries. Results obtained for the 1987 (upgraded from 1985) and 1995/6 (mixed with upgraded 1993 data) benchmark studies, for example, show that PPP based estimates of GDP were 3.0 times higher for low income countries and 2.0 times greater for middle income countries than corresponding exchange rate based estimates.

Exchange rates remain the basis of the World Bank's categorizing of low, middle and high income countries according to its own modified 'Atlas' exchange rate methodology it adopts for operational policy purposes. The so–called 'Friends of the Chair' in their report to the Chairman of the Statistical Commission (March 2001) plotted PPP/exchange rate ratios against the Human Development Index (rather than against GDP, or GNP per capita 'Atlas' measures) found that, for the least developed countries, the ratio could be 4.0 or even larger for poor countries. At higher development levels, the ratio became progressively smaller. These dramatic differentials reflect sweeping variations in national price levels. But there is a clear trend from low price countries to high price countries that is highly correlated with GNP per capita (income) as well as with human progress more broadly defined. It suggests that relative factor prices and resource use bear importantly on efficiency and have a lot to do with not only output generation but also overall price levels.

On the surface, it is tempting to conclude that these findings – which clearly compress the macro income distribution between countries when national incomes per head are expressed in real purchasing power – suggest there is a greater integration and perhaps convergence between the world's economies has been taking place than previously thought. But this is not necessarily the case. The results merely follow logically from the fact that the revaluation of all real quantum measures to an average international price level using PPPs raises the GDP values of all countries below the average with low prevailing prices while reducing the income levels, correspondingly, of those countries with high prices. What the measures do show, however, is that there are more poor countries than rich ones, that the 'spread' of countries at the lower and middle income levels is much wider than at the upper income end and that their distance from the 'global' mean income remains considerable.

This finding, as noted above, appears to hold true whatever index formula and aggregation method is used. The adoption of the additive Geary–Khamis formula, or G–K system, rather than some alternative 'equal weighting' methodology, tends to raise the incomes of poorer countries relative to those that are rich to a somewhat greater extent than other aggregation methods. This is because, when using this method, price structures in countries with a large GDP receive more weight in determining average international price structures. For the most part it is the largest and richest advanced industrial countries that – because of their size and diverse economies – exert the greatest influence on the PPP calculations. These countries are also disproportionately represented because they have had the statistical capacity to participate in the PPP surveys while many poor countries have been left out. Thus, the derived structure of international prices tends to be closer to that of the rich countries. Specifically, too, the system will value the cheaper goods and services consumed in large quantities in poor countries at relatively higher average international prices and the more expensive goods (bought in very much smaller quantities) at somewhat lower prices. Consequently, the estimated outlay values in poorer countries will increase significantly in PPP terms.

The use of the G–K formula is consistent with good index number practice in that it derives a single international price structure that appropriately represents the relative importance of different prices in all economic transactions. In an international spatial context, however, diverse economic conditions exist and it can be argued that disparities in levels of development and in growth paths reflect the importance of specific forces applicable in different countries. Potentially, these could lead to quite different price and quantity structures in countries at various stages of economic development. Thus, in making international comparisons, many favor the application of formulae that use 'unweighted' averages based on countries rather than the value of transactions. This approach focuses more on the price levels faced by most of the people in the world and thus produces an international price structure that is less like that of the rich industrial countries.

Unfortunately, in a comparative international GDP context, many of such 'unweighted' procedures preferred by analysts suffer from the major disadvantage that they are not additive. Thus, the values of the separate GDP components of consumption, investment, etc. do not sum to overall GDP and each can only be compared across countries independently. Comparisons between countries taking only one unique aggregate or variable at a time are necessarily more limited when trying to obtain an overview. With all unweighted formulae, the estimated 'average' international price level is lower than when it is derived in the G–K formulation. Hence, the alleged 'distortions' relating to the differences between PPP and exchange rate converted incomes for low–income countries seem considerably smaller. But every form of index number requires some process of averaging. The derivation of average international prices (more accurately, structure of prices) to replace domestic prices to obtain comparable estimates of real quantities inevitably leads to higher income levels for all low income, low price level countries regardless of the formulae chosen if any standard arithmetic, geometric or harmonic averaging procedure is applied. (The MPCP price similarity method [Sergeev, this volume] essentially bypasses this problem by focusing on price structures directly).

Nevertheless, this finding raises some interesting issues regarding the more fundamental nature of marginalization, when taken in a broader economic sense, that goes beyond the simple matter of external trade competitiveness. Marginalization reflects the fact that poorer countries are forced into a global economic environment to survive. When the bulk of output in poor countries flows into domestic consumption and not into world trade there is cause for concern. In most of these countries the size of the overall economy is small. The domestic market, operating at relatively low levels of prices and technology, is rarely large enough to permit the financially sound operation of a firm of technically optimum size if there is little or no external sales focus. The market tends to allow production runs that are usually too short to enable most enterprises to exploit any potential domestic economies of scale on a continuous basis. To move forward economically such poor countries need to export. In the past many have done this by focusing their production effort on mineral exploitation and resource extraction and on plantation agriculture such as sugar, coffee or bananas. But, with weak politico–economic bargaining power and low internal price levels, such countries face the disadvantage of having to acquire, from the world market, various investment goods, input materials, services and so on that are produced by countries with much higher domestic price levels. Thus, the weaker economies encounter more serious discrepancies between their domestic and international trading operations and it is this feature that makes these countries fundamentally 'marginal'. Such small, poor economies also tend to be more open, more exposed to international forces, and less sovereign in the conduct of their own economic affairs. Inevitably, in their export and import trade, they must take the price levels that are embodied in the prices determined by world markets where these are inevitably dominated by more powerful and richer trading economies[2].

This systemic problem goes beyond the traditional historical concern with the terms of trade effects. These effects relate only to traded goods and not to all goods and services produced in the economy. The net barter, or commodity, terms of trade is represented by the ratio of a country's export price index to the import price index measured from a specific benchmark period. If the terms of trade decrease then a country's exports become less valuable or its imports more expensive. Over time, a prolonged downward trend in the terms of trade will merely compound the problem of price level differentials between rich and poor countries.

12.3.6   The Size of Government

Many governments, international lending agencies and donors regularly express a concern about the growing size of government and its encroachment on the economy. There is an implicit, widely held, assumption that 'big' government, per se, is bad. The basic concern, however, should not be with 'size' but with 'responsible' government and the effectiveness of the elected authorities and their officials in maintaining and improving the conditions of general well–being for a country's citizens. While, for taxation reasons and customary budgetary purposes, government accounts are in local currencies because they are designed to serve routine decisions about funding allocations to different departments, it is also useful to have information about real outlays. Even the most prudent management of official funds and judicious financial stewardship will not be sufficient to provide proper insight into the true efficacy of government. PPP adjusted official expenditures are required to determine the more important questions of official operational effectiveness in delivering public goods and services to society. A more informative picture about what governments do emerges only from a clearer understanding of the different price levels underlying private and public spending. Public spending may appear more expensive because it must also take into account legally mandated responsibilities and statutory obligations to the community that require the authorities to spend official funds on activities where a meaningful market does not exist. In many cases, a clear

---

[2] The same competitive disadvantages apply to the broader GATS definition of trade in services and this provides the incentive for legal and illegal labour migration.

social need is indicated on the grounds of the age, physical status, social condition or location of the recipients of government spending.

The issue in which most analysts are interested when assessing the role of government is the distinction between the cost of the so–called 'bureaucracy' (including the military) compared with the relative value of public spending on goods and services that is applied directly to individual household consumption use (as defined in the SNA93). While both areas belong to the 'non–market' expenditure environment (making realistic comparisons with the private market sector unclear), the comparative price levels underlying the administrative functions of government are quite different from those relevant to individual household consumption where market, or full cost pricing, alternatives usually exist but work very imperfectly and favor, in particular, only the highest income groups.

Evidence suggests that an unfortunate outcome of the unwillingness to carry a more in–depth analysis of government outlays has resulted in wide–ranging and a less discriminate across the board cost–cutting of budgets rather than the selective identification of those areas that are seen as socially essential or where potential productivity gains can be made. In many cases where cuts have taken place or alleged 'productivity gains' (measured in current costs) are implemented, they have been secured only at the expense of service quality and delivery, as measured by public reaction and complaints.

12.3.7 Relative National Competitiveness

The calculation of directly observed price ratios provides a suitable basis for assessing, at the final demand stage, what items are competitively priced in the international market (or in comparison with close competitors) and those that are not. This analysis can be further underpinned by reviewing market prices in countries of use compared with countries of origin, in part, to determine the impact of actual tariffs and, in part, to review the possibilities that non–tariff barriers have been put into effect. Research conducted in the World Bank in the latter part of the 1990s used ICP price data to determine the hidden presence of non–tariff barriers and discriminatory trade policies in the East Mediterranean.

Specific Price and Consumption Relationship: The calculation of PPPs allows for some interesting analysis of micro expenditure patterns and their relationship to policy variables. Eurostat and the OECD, having coordinated regular surveys of prices of selected household goods and services that have been undertaken by national statistical offices in their member countries, have published a series of new sheets reporting on purchasing power parities differentials These have indicated the socio–economic significance of specific household expenditures on items like tobacco and household goods.

The analysis relates to derived price levels applying to 31 countries comprising 25 EU member states, the three former EU candidate countries and three Scandinavian EFTA countries; plus the non–European countries of the OECD. The reports so far have covered comparisons for food, beverages and tobacco as well as furniture and household goods. In the case of the first of these groups, a representative bundle of 450 comparable products were identified for pricing. The countries were then grouped according to their respective price levels into:

  a. Those countries where prices were more than 20 per cent above the EU average
  b. Those lying between 100 per cent and 120 per cent of the average
  c. Countries between 80 per cent and 100 per cent of the average
  d. Those below 80 per cent of the average price level for the EU.

For a so–called 'common market', there appears to be a remarkable degree of disparity in prices; but this is mainly the result of adding the EU candidate countries which have much lower prices than those prevailing in the EU in general, as well as the EFTA countries which, on average, have higher prices. Within the EU, for example, the price of the basket of food, beverages and tobacco in Ireland is more than two and half times more expensive than those in the least cost country, Poland. Overall, for this category of goods, the countries of northern Europe are significantly more expensive to live in than in Southern and Eastern Europe. There is, however, some degree of divergence in final consumption prices, depending on the detailed products concerned, which tends to be associated with the prevailing tax policies. This is especially noticeable, as might be expected, in the case of alcoholic beverages and tobacco. For example, the UK and Norway have considerably higher prices for tobacco than most other countries. On the other hand, the prices for fruit, dairy products and mineral waters in both countries, whilst still above the EU average, were less markedly different. This has interesting implications for distinguishing between the general 'autonomous' core price level effects and those that are institutionally influenced or specifically policy determined.

12.4   INTERNATIONAL APPLICATIONS

12.4.1   Measures of Wealth and Total Economic Size

PPPs should be used to make international comparisons of wealth represented by the accumulation of real tangible assets and productive resources. In principle, total wealth should also include portfolio holdings of foreign financial assets where exchange rates should be used. To some observers and commentators like journalists, wealth is more popularly perceived as the total size of the economy, that is, as the gross value added (GDP) of a country and not its overall asset value. PPP converted estimates of GDP (or Gross National Income and so on) when expressed in national currencies, provide an important measure of a country's productive capacity. These estimates, taken across countries, reflect the relative magnitudes of various economies in terms of the real goods and services each produces. It is interesting to note that when GDP is reported in local values it usually refers to an output measure, that is, it relates to the value added by the producing sectors of a country, whereas a PPP converted GDP is associated with the counterpart national expenditure outlays, that is, the respective spending by purchasing sector. Countries like China and India, as well as others such as the Russian Federation, Brazil and Indonesia, turn out to have much larger economies than would be indicated in any current exchange rate comparison.[3]

For the same reason, countries such as Japan and Switzerland with strong exchange rates and thus correspondingly higher domestic price levels according to an international benchmark, appear to have somewhat smaller economies when measured in PPP terms. A similar distortion carries over into potential wealth and capital asset estimates because such measures are built up from perpetual inventory models based on investment flows compiled in the first instance in national currencies.

PPPs clearly challenge long held perceptions about the ranking of countries according to their scale of economic development. Unfortunately, the conventional ordering of countries has become 'institutionalized' in administrative management and international policy thinking. There is some reluctance to change and PPP methodology encounters considerable opposition from agencies that have an entrenched interest in preserving the status quo. At the same time, leading organizations are stressing the need for proper accountability, transparency and, above all equity in the treatment of member countries. This cannot be achieved by applying exchange rates to determine allocations.

12.4.2 Measures of Income

Differences in price levels have similar consequences for the calculation of internationally comparable measures of real income per head. Even allowing for differences in the size of population and age and sex composition, the

---

[3] Internationally comparable measures of capital stocks that refer to productive assets used or acquired in capital formation over time, have been estimated using PPPs. (See Hee and Fok, 1993; and Ward 1996; and the PWT database).

inhabitants of some countries previously understood to be among the very poorest (including China) are now considered in real (PPP) terms not only to be much better off, but also significantly wealthier than other low income countries because of prevailing low price levels. Although such findings appear consistent with what is known about relative differences in growth rates over extended time periods and what has been observed in terms of achievements in social progress as measured by value-free social indicators, the results challenge previously held convictions about country rankings on a development scale based on individual income status. Historically, estimates of relative income levels expressed in US dollars using exchange rate based conversion factors – such as those generated by the World Bank in its annual 'Atlas' GNP per capita figures – have long been recognized as the benchmark measures of comparative development. While the 'Atlas' procedure adopts a modified moving average process to eliminate excessive volatility in existing exchange rates and also adjusts those official rates considered egregious, the approach is still essentially inappropriate for determining real economic development. Politically and economically, however, these numbers have long influenced the way policymakers and analysts have interpreted world development and hence allocated resources accordingly.

The use of PPPs enables countries to be classified in a conceptually more accurate and economically meaningful way both with respect to their overall real size (GNP) and productive potential and their per capita income level, that is, by their international economic status and the individual well-being of their inhabitants.

12.4.3   Measures of Poverty

Following the universal adoption in 2000 of the UN's Millennium Development goals (MDGs), PPPs are now required to generate comparable measures of 'income poverty'. These can be seen as part of a more general assessment of household living standards, individual poverty and global deprivation. Agencies and governments use these threshold measures to assess the degree of need and deprivation. They are intended to help focus and direct policy support to reduce poverty in low-income countries and to allocate international transfers and aid disbursements more fairly. In the area of poverty or basic welfare evaluation, the concept of 'consumption' and its relation to 'disposable income' is considered to be the most valid variable to apply. Actual consumption, seen as revealed expenditures on the goods and services needed to sustain life (thus reflecting a willingness to pay), comes closer to a measure of personal welfare satisfaction than income. At very low levels of income, however, the daily basic food intake takes up most, if not all, of the disposable income of poor households. Of necessity, such consumption will probably include a substantial element of income in kind – particularly the production of crops for own consumption – since this constitutes a distinguishing characteristic of rural subsistence farming. Household consumption has the merit of being easier to measure and to monitor at fairly regular intervals than income. Separately calculated PPPs for 'consumption' rather than for GDP can be applied more meaningfully to the relevant expenditure 'baskets' of the poor to determine a standard internationally comparable poverty line. Even so, it should be noted that patterns of consumption based on overall outlays fall well short of an ideal for poverty analysis because the derived aggregate expenditure shares are strongly influenced by the heavier buying power and revealed spending preferences of richer people, in other words, there is – as in most consumer price index numbers – an acknowledged 'plutocratic' bias in using reported expenditures and so poverty related expenditures and prices are required.

A good example of this class of standard poverty measure is the World Bank's well-known poverty criterion (or, more precisely, low income threshold) of one dollar per head per day (in 1985, 1996 or 2005 PPP terms). Although originally defined in income rather than consumption terms, this indicator fits very neatly into the whole PPP concept, defining the amount of local currency required in each country to purchase the equivalent of what $1 can buy in goods and services in the US. Although the exact contents of each basket may be different reflecting local preferences and buying patterns, the defined poverty basket implicitly represents a similar consumption 'sufficiency' package of desired goods and services. These baskets, although limited as indicators of the true consumption patterns of the poor, are assumed to provide similar welfare across poor countries. The Bank's measure was designed to enable policymakers and analysts to determine how many people in each country fall below a standard low income threshold. It facilitates the derivation of internationally comparable 'poverty counts' and assessments of the size of the poverty gap, that is, the extent to which the incomes of the poor fall below the poverty line. Importantly, by these means, the degree of deprivation that needs to be tackled in each country can be identified. Another relevant example is the Human Development Index (HDI). This uses PPP adjusted measures of income per head to identify the individual economic sovereignty element (personal access to material goods and services) of its annual indicator of human progress at the national level.

Equally, PPPs can be used to convert specific national poverty lines measured in domestic prices into comparable international dollars. Each country's perception of poverty is different and, hence, its defined national poverty line is also different. These lines are mostly consumption based and so the appropriate PPP – which is, in itself, compiled from expenditures – is again for 'consumption' (or, more specifically, 'final household consumption' as it is known in SNA terms). This procedure has been adopted to ensure the Bank's standard criterion does not differ significantly from actual poverty assessments in the poorest countries.

Because the consumption patterns of the poor are usually quite different from the country as a whole, it is appropriate to calculate a specific 'poverty' PPP relevant to the observed consumption basket of the poor in each country. In the absence of any prior information, it might be possible to obtain a good proxy of the consumption of the poor using the outlays of the lowest quintile income or expenditure group as observed from household expenditure surveys. Even this might not be totally adequate because the prices poor people actually pay for their consumption purchases are generally not the same as those that the average person pays for the same goods and services.

The poor live in different areas and they buy goods from different shops. Some evidence suggests that quite often the poor have to pay more for what they need, although this may not be so likely over the longer term. If such were the case, then the real value of an appropriate 'poverty' basket could be even less than what a formal calculation based on price information collected for the regular consumer price index might show. To pursue this approach further, however, would require the compilation of some sort of a common harmonized 'quasi-standard' poverty basket along similar lines to a 'harmonized' CPI.

A more general problem that has not been resolved, however, is whether the adoption of a 'minimum food basket' as a core poverty measure makes much practical sense in itself. George Orwell, in his well-known book, *The Road to Wigan Pier*, draws attention to the irrelevance of a basket of basic necessities to a poor household that also needs uplift, courage and moral support in times of difficulty. As is often recorded in contemporary literature, poor families find they must frequently resort to cigarettes, beer and other alcoholic beverages to see them through a crisis and raise their spirits. These outlays are not incorporated in the minimum list because such consumption is regarded by 'experts' as (physically) unnecessary, to the extent of being a wasteful use of very limited funds.

There are inevitable downsides from the consumption of specific goods when a household is poor. The link between tobacco and poverty across different countries, as well as within each country, has been comprehensively documented by the World Health Organization (WHO). The use of tobacco by the poor is a double-edged sword. Not only are there obvious directly harmful effects to a person's health, affecting his or her ability to work to maximum capacity (especially in physically demanding occupations) day in and day out, but tobacco also impacts adversely on desirable levels of consumption on food. Spending on tobacco reduces appetite and, at the same time, the cost of satisfying these tastes demands a downward shift in other consumption patterns. This results in a regrettable reduction in the actual amount of goods and consumption falls below the desired basic daily food intake level required to sustain life. Food outlays are a flexible element in poor people's regular spending and so they are capable of being squeezed and manipulated – sometimes to the nutritional detriment of the whole family. Among the poorest nations, WHO has calculated that the majority of people who are currently under-nourished could have received a potentially adequate diet if two-thirds of the money spent on tobacco were to have been allocated instead to food expenditures for the family.

Food consumption per head: Nevertheless, since time immemorial, because the crux of concern about household poverty has always been with hunger and malnutrition (and resulting famine), most absolute poverty measures have invariably been based on some objectively defined hypothetical food basket of minimum necessities. Politicians and analysts have seen this as another possible way to assess poverty. In effect, this involves establishing a convenient, internationally recognized independent and objective (although limited) food consumption standard. Such a common standard could be the assumed human need for a minimum nutritional intake of 2 000 calories for each adult working male per day to sustain his life. The cost of this subsistence basket - which would vary in its content according to local dietary preferences, gender and age structures – could then be priced in each country at international prices. Although 'fixed' in its inherent calorie content, such a neutral standard would be configured in international values and this would allow fair comparisons between countries.

There are two main drawbacks to such a measure. One, clearly, is that it is confined to just one (admittedly important) 'flow' dimension of poverty; namely, nutrition or food consumption. This might not reflect the same individual 'utility' or welfare around the globe, even when expressed in similar food consumption terms. Two, a calorie intake standard does not represent similar satisfaction or dietary levels between households in different regions within the same country and because personal requirements are dictated by age and sex and the branch of economic activity in which a person is engaged. Local topographical conditions and environmental circumstances have effects too.

A calorie 'datum' standard is subject to considerable degrees of freedom because the choice of items and the amounts that may be consumed by each person are flexible. Any basic 'nutrition' basket that conforms to the defined calorific standard can be made up in many different ways. While 'hunger' may be the common denominator and a core element of any poverty condition, food consumption indicators of this nature remain quite limited. This is especially so if the composition of the baskets is derived from aggregate output and import estimates and not based on more explicit micro survey data. The measures thus derived may not provide a fair and proper reflection of poverty. They do not incorporate other equally important and often just as critical requirements for human survival such as adequate shelter, fuel for heating and cooking, protective clothing, and clean water. By using expenditure ratios relating to various consumption categories based on historical surveys, it is possible to compile a more comprehensive aggregate poverty line measure that brings into consideration these other crucial elements, but this would be only a very approximate indicator.

Whatever poverty line approach is adopted, all the measures raise questions about the appropriate measurement of individual versus household poverty and whether such measures should be converted into 'adult equivalent units' to improve the basis of comparison. For comparative purposes, however, the issue of using PPPs over exchange rates is never in question.

Assessing inequality: Dikhanov and Ward, (2001) and Prasad Rao, et al. (2005) have shown that standard PPP measures can be used not only for cross-country comparisons but also for global aggregation purposes between expenditure components and countries. PPPs are necessary to combine real variables and spending items in a different way, such as by institutional sectors according to a defined administrative or political unit, by geographical region, or by some other meaningful economic categorization, such as 'low income countries', that groups particular nation states.

12.5   THE GLOBAL EFFECT

12.5.1   Price Structures and Globalization

The ICP data seem to indicate a symbiotic relationship between marginalization on the one hand and the forces of globalization on the other. Both have to do with the existence of non-standard differentials in national price levels. The shifting of the locus of production, involving the fundamental institutional rearrangement of the financing, control and organization of trade, plus changes in the methods of managing corporate operations on a real time basis, have not only encouraged the process of polarization but also facilitated the outsourcing and decentralization of economic activities. The transfer of production bases to lower cost centers and the subsequent re-selling of the resulting output in higher price markets is now a common feature of global corporate activity. Globalization recognizes the existence of lower price levels in low-income 'factor markets' and of higher price levels in high income 'product markets'. It also sees such cost differentials amplified by the lack of enforceable labor legislation that keeps wage costs low and lax environmental controls and safety regulations on production methods and hazardous waste disposal practices suppressing subsidiary costs in many lower income countries.

Structural transformation works only if poor countries already have a foothold in the market and at least an embryonic production base. The level of value added per worker in real terms must also be sufficient to warrant companies shifting their production focus to low cost areas. But the transfer of production bases can reinforce another form of marginalization through raising the potential overhead and infrastructure costs of the host or 'recipient' country. The economic culture absorbed in these poorer countries is inevitably that of a market capitalist system that brings with it a culturally alien product choice and externally oriented consumerism. Furthermore, despite the shift in the locus of production to lower cost and price level countries, if output decisions remain under foreign control, sovereignty is put under question. Corporate headquarters management may also be geared to such issues as global tax incidence, the minimization of output costs, the development of new markets, or reflect efforts to evade more stringent and enforced environmental and labor regulations in their own domestic markets rather than the concerns of host countries.

To avoid a damaging loss of sovereignty, economically weaker nations must keep under review the benefits of local production from a PPP perspective. There can clearly be an associated decline in the economic and financial independence of the host countries concerned. Unless there are adequate and effective provisions for associated technology and knowledge transfers, the establishment of foreign enterprises could lead to a weakening of a genuine domestic production capability and of a country's independent capacity to compete individually in the international economy.

12.5.2   PPPs, International Price Distortions and Market Structures

In addition to the calculated PPPs, the detailed item specific information on prices, basic level price ratios and corresponding expenditure category data collected under the ICP can prove useful in providing fresh inter-country perspectives on comparative market distortions. 'Raw' inequalities measured by selected price ratios for luxury goods versus necessities offer a potentially different insight into market structures. As indicated above, the basic price data also allow assessments of competitiveness and of the impact of non-tariff barriers on observed price differentials between identical products in different retail markets.

In principle, such observed market distortions within countries can be investigated in at least three different dimensions:

- By comparing the size differences in price ratios for specific goods and services typically bought on the one hand, by rich people and, on the other, by poor households. The price of luxuries versus necessities, particularly serving similar needs, should be monitored to check changes in these differentials over time.
- Reviewing the detailed relationships between market prices and corresponding changes in the real command over actual goods and services at the basic heading level, that is, where similar consumption preferences prevail.
- Maintaining surveillance of expenditures and outlet types (and their location) and reviewing how outlays relate to different socio-economic groups as reflected by income levels (where known), density and quality of housing, floor space availability, and other socio-economic characteristics.

The outward manifestation of various concentrations of purchasing power across different geographical regions and social dimensions is assumed to lie in people's revealed expenditure patterns and observed price ratios. Such comparisons might be expected to draw out both the income effect and substitution effects of price changes. They may also reflect the fact that, at low levels of income, evidence suggests that prices matter most to households that struggle to make ends meet whereas, at higher levels of income where there exists some possibility of choice, primary concern is with obtaining better quality. While little analysis has yet been undertaken in this interesting area, the PPP base level data permit such micro level cross-country research of inter-household inequality and behavior.

Comparisons of the extent of price distortions across countries can be viewed from three separate but inter-related perspectives:

1. Differences in national (GDP) price levels.
2. Differences in sector and expenditure category price levels between countries, and between outlays that can be tracked consistently over time in the same country (in PPP terms).
3. Differences in the relative prices of individual items of equivalent quality within the same country and compared with others.

The intent of items (1) and (2) is clear and straightforward. Some of these issues were taken up in the report of 'The Friends of the Chair' of the UN Statistical Commission (2001). In bilateral comparisons between 14 pairs of countries the report noted that for necessities like food, where prices are generally inelastic, the ratio of per capita consumption in PPP terms is relatively close to 1.0 with richer countries having slightly higher consumption levels. But, when the comparison was extended to hi-tec consumer durables where individual demand is far more responsive to price change and purchases demand access to much greater disposable income, the consumption ratios were found to be significantly larger.

12.5.3 Global Income Inequality

The establishment of internationally comparable economic magnitudes at the national level allows analysts to aggregate variables into other coherent socioeconomic categories in a logical manner. Thus international (or rather, inter-country) data can serve, in particular, as a basis for establishing meaningful regional and global aggregates.

The measurement of the world's distribution of income is fundamentally a question of aggregating in ascending order individual incomes across consistent units irrespective of where they originate. PPP adjusted income allows assessments of how the real quantum of goods and services available globally is shared between people ranked from the lowest to the highest level of income taking account of both within and between country variations.

Differences in intra-country inequality as well as inter-country inequality need to be integrated but they make the measurement of the global income distribution that much more complex. The problem is both conceptual and empirical. The internal distribution of income is measured in national currencies and local transactions prices whereas that 'between' countries comparison needs to be assessed using a common international currency and standardized prices. National studies of domestic inequality are also heavily dependent on (mostly) household rather than individual incomes. The former data tend to be based on sample survey information, whereas the latter are more often derived from administrative sources such as tax files.

Cross-country inequality analysis is currently reported mostly in GNP per capita terms and it relies dominantly on the comprehensive national accounts estimates and population profiles of a country. In many cases, the data available from household surveys will relate solely to consumption and not to income. Income data usually have to be derived indirectly on the basis of calculated quintile or decile shares of spending. It is widely acknowledged that household surveys provide an inappropriate and inadequate basis for collecting information about total individual income accruing from different sources. Survey sources often tend to ignore both realized and unrealized capital gains, informal and illegal income, income in kind and other real holding gains. The national accounts, which compile income data primarily from those economic units that pay out income are better at providing a comprehensive picture of incomes generated by source.

Previous use of exchange rates to compile reported national distributions obfuscates the real nature of inequality. Over time, it also confuses the distinction between actual changes in inequality in real terms and other value adjustments that have invariably come about as a result of domestic price level changes and bilateral exchange rate movements.

PPPs allow little to be said about the distribution of wealth which may be more important in the context of inequality since this has to do with the ownership of productive assets and, ultimately, the control of production. Nor do such measures of income disparity represent the distribution of well-being and living standards. Well-being necessarily embraces more intangible social, cultural, political and environmental factors. It also reflects the differential provision by various national governments of non-market goods and services to different socio-economic groups and to the population as a whole. The use of PPPs at two different benchmark periods raises some questions of interpretation because the purchasing capacity over the same quantum of goods and services will change during the intervening time.

For any given reference year, PPP expenditure based calculations of global income inequality – even when applied at lower income levels to proxy the disposable income estimates – will tend to compress the overall distribution of incomes compared with exchange rate measures. The overall shape of this distribution compiled over successive decades appears to remain much the same. This may be less true, however, for exchange rate based comparisons where exchange rate volatility can affect, sometimes significantly, the ordering of countries, that is, the 'between' inequality which has been shown to account for at least two-thirds of observed total inequality.

For the time being, both PPP and exchange rate based income distributions suffer from the disadvantage that, within a country, the actual prices that various socio-economic groups and households in different parts of the country face in making their consumption decisions, differ. In countries like Brazil, India, China and the USA, they have been shown to differ substantially.

If, in addition, as some studies have suggested, poor people pay more for the same commodities as purchased by higher income groups, this would modify the resulting distribution and inequality measures making them even more skewed in real terms. Evidence over time suggests economic growth tends to benefit the rich proportionately more than the poor and this widens the disparities between the top income decile and the median rather than closing the gap between the median income and bottom decile. If, at the same time, population growth adds relatively more to the number of people who are poor – as in the case of most low income countries – then the per capita income distribution will become progressively more distorted.

12.5.4   The Real Value of Aid

The notion of purchasing power also has significance in the area of financial transfers and particular relevance when assessing the real value of aid. Most people could not have failed to note that every request that comes through the mail from a non–government organization asking for a personal donation stresses how much that individual contribution will buy in terms of child feeding programmes, actual medical attention, schooling, books, clean water supplies and the like. The accompanying leaflets point out what little is required to do something useful to raise living standards in low income countries. This is for the familiar reason that aid receiving countries are not only very poor but their price levels are significantly lower than those in the economically developed countries from whom the donations are collected. This means that if, as is often the declared intention, such aid is spent acquiring goods and services produced within a these countries, the dollar donated will buy a lot more than it does in the USA or Europe.

Spending aid money inside the country is what most NGOs at least set out to do but it is not always what happens because the essential requirements are not available locally. In the case of official bilateral transfers where the funds are often destined to support capital outlays and infrastructure projects, most end up being spent on machinery and equipment in donor countries or on overseas consultancy contracts. When development assistance is provided by international donors, it is usually statutorily incumbent on them to put the contract out to tender in these cases, contracts and purchases have to be agreed with outside suppliers who will tend to be paid in US dollars. (The potential risk of 'moral hazard' and related diversion of funds from their intended purpose is another issue.)

The World Bank's World Development Indicators 2002 (WDI 2002), for example, shows (Table 5.6, page 301) that in India only 9 rupees are needed to buy the equivalent of 'a dollar's worth' of goods and services in local markets. Since every US dollar received by India is converted at the official rates into 45 rupees, India's receipts of aid would be worth, in equivalent local terms, around five times as much if it could be spent domestically. This clearly puts a somewhat different complexion on the aid figures released each year in the UNDP Human Development Report (HDR 2003). A summary of aid flows between 1990 and 2001 from the perspective of both donor and beneficiary countries reveals that, although the respective totals do not tally (mainly because disbursements by multilateral agencies are excluded from the donors' side and receipts of aid by countries ignore the regional and joint country aid programs), in 2002, China and Indonesia were the recipients of the largest amounts of aid with Viet Nam close behind. The Russian Federation and India were also major recipients. These are large, populous countries and aid, to have any significant effect, must be correspondingly substantial or spent mostly in the domestic economy.

The real differences and imbalances become far more apparent if the purchasing power equivalence of aid in local goods and services is taken into account. Aid provided goes much further in the poorest countries and the ordering of recipients by their potential ability to gain real benefits by buying locally changes significantly. Viet Nam becomes, in real terms, the largest recipient of aid getting five times more international assistance 'for its buck'. China falls to second place and India moves up to third. But the $1487 millions India received in net official development assistance in 2002 could have been translated into the equivalent of $7665 million in local buying power. By contrast, the value of aid to Israel, because of its high local price level, was only 15 per cent greater than the nominal amount it received in US dollars.

For many reasons, most aid, nor even a significant proportion of it, is disbursed and spent locally. The shift away in recent years from large prestigious development projects and major sector investments designed to promote economic growth to a greater emphasis on poverty reduction and human development programs has probably led to more aid being spent locally, partially compensating for the declining relative share of aid support to poor countries. This 'softer' socially focused aid usually implies a greater degree of local ownership of programmes and involves the creation of active domestic partnerships. In targeting directly people at risk, this process should mean there is a more extensive spending of aid in the local economy. The ability to assess, a priori, the 'real' value of aid using PPPs should not only influence primary allocation decisions but also better inform procurement and disbursement procedures.[4]

12.5.5   International Price Levels and Global Inflation

While little official or academic interest has been shown in the topic of global inflation, it is an issue of growing concern and one that, since it demands

---

[4] In March 2002, the United Nations Conference on Financing for Development held in Monterrey, Mexico, presented a broad consensus on aid effectiveness. Beyond the political rhetoric, the hard evidence shows that aid volumes have fallen by 8 percent over the previous decade (2002 World Bank Atlas, page 16) while only half now goes to the poorest countries. The current value of total aid is trivial both in relation to the needs that should be addressed and the capacity of the donors to provide that support. Housing only 16 per cent of the world's population, the 27 principal aid donors control $25 billion of global national income compared with the $6 billion owned by the other 190 countries who, together, account for more than five times as many people.

aggregative consistency, can only be measured properly using PPP adjusted expenditure weights (Ward, 2001, 2002, 2008). Although much depends on the particular perspective taken by the individual investigator and the objective of enquiry, global inflation in its simplest term measures the average aggregate rate of increase of national prices or of consumer prices across all countries. What analysts would really like to get at, however, is a measure of the inexorable and autonomous core component of international inflation brought about mostly by substantial increases in the prices of basic commodities, heavily mortgaged private and public consumption expenditures and imbalances between rapidly rising debt obligations and falling collateral values. A universal rise in prices has taken place since at least the beginning of the 20th century. Almost no research has been carried out to try and determine what have been the fundamental global forces at work that have brought this about.

In the private sector, interest in such international price changes is growing. PPP adjusted values serve many operational purposes and support routine business management decisions other than those related to inflation (O'Connor, 2008). Greater knowledge about international price levels and price movements has become increasingly relevant to global product marketing and corporate investment decisions. Given the globalization of trade and production, not only the monitoring of prices but also of changes in relative price structures in the international economy has become essential to an understanding of different market situations and relative competitive performance at both the corporate and national level. Large enterprises operating internationally also need to establish salary standards for their overseas staff as well as set appropriate global product prices. The relevance of benchmarking national and regional price changes against some standard numeraire is an important concern to international entrepreneurs.

12.6   OTHER RESOURCE USE

12.6.1   True Debt and Payback Burden

International financial transactions involve legal commitments to conduct business and settle accounts in exchange rate terms. The real 'payback burden', however, can only be understood by examining the inter-relationship between PPP values and the legal obligation to repay loans and credit advanced. This has been implicitly recognized in the recent rapid growth in 'forward' markets and hedging options. If business contracts are secured through formal payments in foreign currencies at existing exchange rates, then the true outcome of the transaction could turn adverse when realized in terms of the real quantity of goods and services required to complete the deal. Weaker economies with lower price levels must necessarily face higher opportunity costs in domestic factor and product markets if they are to keep abreast with the international economy. This applies equally to the repayment of debt and to the costs, if borne locally, of maintaining nationally staffed offices in international organizations that must necessarily be based in New York, London, Washington, Geneva, Tokyo, Vienna and other high price cities.

12.6.2   Energy Efficiency

PPPs are also useful in providing comparable measures of GDP per unit of energy use that serves as an indicator of energy efficiency. The ratio of PPP GDP per kilogram of oil equivalent of commercial energy use (unlike other measures showing the money value of fuel consumption by households and enterprises as a share of GDP) is a measure of real output to inputs. Alleged efficiency measures, employing US dollar converted estimates of GDP produced per kilogram of oil equivalent or per US dollar cost of energy used are not meaningful. Given their primary use in environmental and energy monitoring, such indicators are not comparable over time within the same country, nor across countries, because the derived so-called 'efficiency' measures will be affected by changes in the exchange rate relative to the US dollar.

12.6.3   Energy Intensity

For the same reason, the overall intensity of energy use defined as the oil equivalent in kilograms divided by real GDP in PPP terms – which is essentially the inverse of the previous measure – is often used as an indicator of the future demand for fuel and energy. The demand for energy is associated with a country's level of economic activity and rate of sector output growth. The projected growth patterns, therefore, have likewise to be calculated using both PPPs (rather than own domestic prices) and a corresponding physical 'oil equivalent' rather than in shifting value terms.

12.7   SOME CONCLUDING OBSERVATIONS

In practice, and at a superficial level, selected comparisons between countries are feasible and tangible. In the absence of differences in currencies and the various (and varying) exchange rates between countries, a traveller could pass readily from one contiguous country to the next throughout much of the world and simply observe and note how differently people live. Such differences are often manifested in physically distinct characteristics as architectural styles, religious edifices and institutions, private and public transportation systems, shops and markets, personal clothing and diets, and so on. These features reflect a variety of national factors, including income differences, relative factor endowments and cultural heritage. Once a country's border has been crossed, however, travellers are confronted by another unavoidable but artificial distinction that is reflected in prices made manifest by the national currency unit in which the value of the country's goods and services is denominated. The existence of a local currency adds another dimension to exchanges between countries and visual comparisons based on observed physical differences. Official (and unofficial) exchange rates directly impact local price levels and the potential living standards that the traveller can enjoy in each country.

To preserve a measure of the equivalent real goods and services available to people, irrespective of the currency differences, an estimate of the purchasing power parity is required even if this is seen to be only a hypothetical statistical artefact.

This chapter describes some instances where PPPs should be used. In most financial transactions, however, only exchange rates continue to matter. The chapter suggests where these two different conversion factors should be respectively applied. In certain contexts, however, to gain a full appreciation of what economic issues are at stake and to mine the potential richness of the socio economic analysis that can be undertaken, the use of both PPPs and exchange rates in conjunction is required.

BIBLIOGRAPHY[5]

Ahmad, S. (1996), 'Harmonization of CPI and PPP: Problems and Prospects', *Improving the Quality of Price Indices: CPI and PPP,* EUROSTAT Seminar 18–20 December, 1995.

Balk, B. (1996), 'A Comparison of Ten Methods for Multilateral International Price and Volume Comparison', *Journal of Official Statistics,* **12**, 199–222.

Biru, Y. (1998), 'The Purchasing Power of the Poor in Zambia', World Bank Seminar on Prices and Purchasing Power Parities, Washington, D.C.

---

[5] *Note from the Editor*: The list published here came with the last version of the chapter I received from Michael on 30th September, 2008. His intention was to work on the chapter and fix up the list of references. But sadly he passed away suddenly on 18th October, 2008. I have decided to include the full list even though there are several papers in this list that were not referred to in the text. Similarly, there are some works referred to in the text but not included in this list.

Castles, I. (1997), *The OECD–EUROSTAT PPP Program: Review of Practice and Procedures*, Paris: OECD.

Cuthbert, J.R. (1999), 'Categorization of Additive Purchasing Power Parities', *Review of Income and Wealth*, **45** (2), 235–250.

Decoster, R. (1999), 'Proposal for Comparative Poverty Assessment Using Purchasing Power Parities for Low Income Households', Paper Prepared for the DECDG, World Bank.

Diewert, E.W. (1986), *Microeconomic Approaches to the Theory of International Comparisons*, Technical Working Paper No. 53, Cambridge, MA: National Bureau of Economic Research.

Drechsler, L. (1973), 'Weighting of Index Numbers in Multilateral International Comparisons', *Review of Income and Wealth*, **19**, 17–24.

Eltetö, O. and P. Köves (1964), 'On an Index Number Computation Problem in International Comparison (in Hungarian), *Statisztikai Szemle* **42**, 507–518.

Forsyth, F. and R. Fowler (1982), 'The Theory and Practice of Chain Price Index Numbers', *Journal of Royal Statistical Society*, Series A, **144** (2).

Geary, R.C. (1958), 'A Note on Comparison of Exchange Rates and Purchasing Power Parities Between Currencies', *Journal of Royal Statistical Society*, **121** (1).

Gilbert, M. and I. Kravis (1954), *Comparative National Products and Price Levels*, Paris: OEEC.

Gilbert, M. et al., (1958), *Comparative National Products and Price Levels*, Paris: OEEC.

Hee, Michael and Raquel Fok (1993), 'Physical Capital Stock: Estimates for Developing Economies', Socio-economic Data Division Working Paper, Washington, D.C.: The World Bank.

Heston, A.W. (1996), 'Some Problems in Item Price Comparisons with Special Reference to Uses of CPI Prices in Estimating Spatial Heading Parities' in *Improving the Quality of Price Indices: CPI and PPP*, EUROSTAT Seminar 18–20 December 1995.

Heston, A.W. and R. Summers (1991), 'The Penn–World Table (Mark 5): an Expanded Set of International Comparisons', *Quarterly Journal of Economics*, **106**, 327–68.

Hill, R.J. (1999), 'Chained PPPs and Minimum Spanning Trees' in Lipsey and Heston (eds) *International and Interred Comparisons of Prices, Income and Output*, NBER, Chicago: Chicago University Press, 327–364.

Kenessey, Z. (1996),'International Comparison Program in the 1980s and 1990s', in Rao and Salazar-Carrillo (eds) *International Comparisons of Prices, Output and Productivity*, Amsterdam: North-Holland.

Khamis, S.H. (1984), 'On Aggregation Methods for International Comparisons', *Review of Income and Wealth*, **30**, 185–205.

Kokoski, M., B.R. Moulton and K.D. Zieschang (1999), 'Interred Price Comparisons for Heterogeneous Goods and Several Levels of Commodity Aggregation', in Lipsey and Heston (eds) *International and Interarea Comparisons of Prices, Income and Output*, NBER, Chicago: Chicago University Press, 327–364.

Kravis, I.B., Z. Kenessey and A.W. Heston (1975), *A System of International Comparisons of Gross Product and Purchasing Power*, Baltimore, MD: Johns Hopkins University Press.

Kravis, I.B., A.W. Heston and R. Summers (1978), *International Comparisons of Real Product and Purchasing Power*, Baltimore, MD: Johns Hopkins University Press.

Kravis, I.B., A.W. Heston and R. Summers (1982), *World Product and Income: International Comparisons of Real Gross Domestic Products,* Baltimore, MD: Johns Hopkins University Press.

Rao, D.S. Prasada (1997), 'Aggregation Methods for International Comparison of Purchasing Power Parities and Real Income: Analytical Issues and Some Recent Developments', *Proceedings of the International Statistical Institute,* 51st Session, 197–200.

Rao, D. S. Prasada and J. Salazar-Carrillo (eds) (1996), *International Comparison Of Prices, Output And Productivity,* Amsterdam: North-Holland (Contributions to Economic Analysis Series), 325.

Ryten, J. (1998), *The Evaluation of the International Comparison Project (ICP),* Washington, D.C.: IMF.

Sakuma, I., Y. Kurabayashi and D.S. Prasada Rao (2000), 'Additivity, Matrix Consistency and a New Method for International Comparisons of Real Income and Purchasing Power Parities', Paper presented at the *26th* General Conference of IARIW, Cracow, Poland.

Salazar-Carrillo, J. (1978), 'Prices and Purchasing Power Parities in Latin America, 1960–1972', Rio de Janeiro, ECIEL: published by the OAS, Washington, D.C.

Sergeev, S. (this volume), 'Aggregation Methods Based on Structural International Prices'.

Szulc, B. (1964), 'Index Number of Multilateral Regional Comparisons' (in Polish), *Przeglad Statysticzny,* **3,** 239–254.

Szulc, B. (1989), 'Price Indices Below the Basic Aggregation Level', in Turvey et al., (eds) *Consumer Price Indices: An ILO Manual,* Geneva: International Labor Office.

Turvey, R. (1996), 'Elementary Aggregate (Micro) Indexes', in *Improving the Quality of Price Indices: CPI and PPP,* EUROSTAT Seminar 18–20 December, 1995.

United Nations (1992), *Handbook of the International Comparison Program,* F (62), New York: United Nations.

Ward, M. (1985), 'The Measurement of Real Expenditures and GDP in OECD Countries', Paris: OECD.

Ward, M. (1996), 'Internationally Comparable Measures of Capital Stocks' in Rao and Salazar-Carillo (eds), *International Comparisons of Prices, Output and Productivity,* Amsterdam: North-Holland.

Ward, M (2001), 'International Price Levels and Global Inflation', *Statistical Journal of the UN Economic Commission for Europe,* **18** (1).

Ward, M (2002), 'Purchasing Power Parities vs Exchange Rates in International Comparisons', *Statistical Journal of the UN Economic Commission for Europe,* **19** (4).

Ward, M (2003), 'Does Size Matter? Assessing the Real Importance of Government', *CEIES 2003 Seminar of the European Union on the Size of the Government Sector,* Vienna, 23–4 October.

WHO (2004), 'Tobacco is Bad Economics all Around', Press Release WHO/36, 28 May 2004, Geneva, Switzerland.

13. Purchasing Power Parity Adjustments for Productivity Level Comparisons

Bart van Ark and Marcel Timmer

13.1 INTRODUCTION[1]

International comparisons of productivity levels by industry are a key measure of economic performance next to comparisons of per capita income and other aggregate measures at the economy-wide level. Comparisons of manufacturing productivity have received most attention and are now frequently quoted in the media. Despite greater methodological problems, comparisons of service productivity are also of increasing interest. Recently international organizations, including the International Labour Office (ILO) and the World Bank, have also begun to report industry-based productivity measures on a regular basis.[2]

Industry comparisons contribute to the understanding of the determinants of differences in economic performance across countries and regions. The relative productivity standing in agriculture, industry and services is considered of fundamental importance in structural growth analysis. These comparisons contribute to a sharper analysis of the causes of economic growth and of patterns of divergence between nations in growth accounts, catch up and convergence analysis and the exploration of lead country–follower country phenomena. It also strengthens the analysis of the locus of technical progress, in particular when supplemented by micro-oriented investigation of variance in performance between industries and between average and best practice firms. Finally these studies shed further light on the relation between productivity and competitiveness (Dollar and Wolff, 1993; Bernard and Jones, 1996; Pilat 1996, Scarpetta et al., 2000; Baily and Solow,

---

[1] The authors would like to thank participants at the Joint World Bank–OECD seminar on Purchasing Power Parities, 30 January–2 February 2001, Washington D.C. and the expert group that discussed a preliminary extended draft for helpful comments and suggestions. We are particularly grateful to Dirk Pilat for his advice and to Prasada Rao for editorial comments.

[2] Chapter 17 in ILO (2001) and World Bank (2000), Table 2.6, pp. 58–61.

2001; Maddison and van Ark, 2002). Recent studies have shown that the impact of growth-determinants such as R&D, university education, international trade and market regulation depend crucially on the distance to the technology frontier. A country's distance from the technology frontier is used as a direct measure of the potential for technology transfer, where the frontier is defined for each industry as the country with the highest level of total factor productivity (TFP). Recent applications include Griffith, et al. (2004) on the effects of R&D; Vandenbussche et al. (2006) for the effects of university education; Cameron et al. (2005) for the effects of international trade and Inklaar et al. (2008) for the effects of market services regulation.

Traditionally, productivity comparisons were made on the basis of two methods: the industry-of-origin approach and the expenditure approach. Even though they were originally developed in parallel fashion, ultimately the expenditure approach was adopted as the main approach by the international organizations. The main reason for this was that the expenditure approach could move forward faster through the design of a specific price survey to obtain PPPs that could be aggregated to the GDP level. It has been spelt out in earlier papers that the use of expenditure PPPs for international comparisons by industry can introduce serious errors. The fact that this approach is still widely practised in productivity research, is probably due to the large methodological and data issues in computing PPPs by industry of origin. In 1983 the International Comparisons of Output and Productivity (ICOP) project was set up at the University of Groningen under the direction of Angus Maddison to pursue research on industry-of-origin comparisons of output and productivity. Van Ark and Maddison (1994) and Maddison and van Ark (2002) provide an overview of the progress made over the past twenty years through the research input of a dozen of scholars and work on about 30 countries. Building upon this work, Inklaar and Timmer (2008) construct the GGDC Productivity Level database. This database provides comparisons of output, inputs and productivity at a detailed industry level for a set of 30 OECD countries for the year 1997.

This chapter provides an overview of the various issues and problems involved when making international comparisons of productivity using both the industry-of-origin approach and the expenditure approach. It starts from the main idea that these two approaches are complements rather than substitutes as each approach has its advantages and disadvantages. We will argue that a combination of the two approaches is the most promising way forward to further improve research in this area. This idea is not new (Pilat, 1996; van Ark, 1996; O'Mahony, 1996) and has also been applied by Inklaar and Timmer (2008). But so far it has not been spelled out in a systematic and detailed manner. In this chapter we focus exclusively on the purchasing power parity adjustments needed for output and productivity level comparisons. We will not deal here with equally important issues of international consistency in output, labour and capital input measures. We start with an outine of the basic concepts and methodologies for PPPs in section 13.2 and the application in comparisons of aggregate GDP in section 13.3. The next three sections deal with the advantages and disadvantages of the industry-of-origin approach and the expenditure approach for making industry comparisons. Section 13.7 covers alternatives for deriving intermediate input PPPs and section 13.8 concludes.

13.2   CONCEPTS AND APPROACHES

For comparisons of productivity levels across countries (or regions) one will mostly be interested in comparisons of physical (or volume) productivity. In practice, however, the basic data that can be relied upon for comparisons of productivity levels are not physical quantities of output, but value measures of output and inputs, such as the value of gross output, value added and intermediate inputs. There will be a difference between the measure of volume and value productivity when the relative price level between countries differ. For example, while the average value productivity of a hairdresser in Mexico (for example) turnover per working day in US$ using the peso/$ currency exchange rate) may be 25 per cent of that of his colleague in the US, his physical productivity (for example the number of haircuts per day) may be as much as 75 per cent compared to the US This is because the price of a haircut in Mexico is only one third of that in the US For comparisons of productivity levels across space, value measures need to be corrected for these differences in relative prices between countries. This correction can be made by using purchasing power parities (PPPs).

Purchasing power parity is defined as the ratio of the price of a product or a bundle of products between two countries, with prices expressed in each country's own currency.[3] The relative price level is defined as the (average) price of one country relative to the (average) price of the other country, with

---

[3] A few terminological issues are important to keep in mind for the remainder of this chapter. 'Product' may refer to a good or a service. 'Country' may also refer to a region (for example, an US state) or a group of countries (for example, the European Union) as the PPP adjustment will be necessary for any comparison of geographical units when relative price levels differ. Finally, the term 'purchasing power parity' essentially refers to comparisons of expenditure prices, indicating that with a unit of purchasing power, say one US dollar, one can purchase the same bundle of products in one or more countries. Although this terminology may be less appropriate for comparisons of output or income, it is in practice used in more general terms for any comparison of relative prices across space.

prices expressed in a common currency. When countries have different currencies, the relative price level is obtained as the ratio of the PPP to the currency exchange rate. So the relative price level of a haircut in Mexico compared to the US is obtained by comparing the PPP of the haircut (for example 33 pesos in Mexico to 10 US$ in the US, or a PPP of 3.3 pesos per dollar) to the currency exchange rate (for example 10 pesos to one US$). The relative price level of Mexico relative to the US is then (3.3/10 =) 33 per cent. When two countries have the same currency, (for example, the euro), the relative price level can be directly derived from the PPP. For example, when the ex-factory price of a ton of flat steel of identical quality is 2 000 euro in Portugal against 2 500 euro in Germany, the Portuguese price level is 80 per cent of that in Germany. As a result, the output and productivity in flat steel manufacturing in Portugal relative to the Germany would be understated by (2 500/2 000 –1 =) 25 per cent if directly compared without the PPP adjustment.

The previous discussion implies that when using the currency exchange rate for the purpose of output and productivity comparisons, one does not adjust for international price differences between countries. The comparison is then a value comparison, not a volume comparison. Only when the PPP equals the currency exchange rate, value productivity equals volume productivity. Similarly, for a comparison between countries or regions using the same currency, an adjustment for relative price differences is required to obtain a volume comparison. Refraining from an adjustment for relative prices (for example) by using the currency exchange rate instead of the PPP) will be particularly a problem when comparisons are made at the level of industries or sectors of the economy. Even in sectors which are open to international trade, and for which it may be assumed that relative price levels converge to one in the long run (that is, the PPP equals the exchange rate), different degrees of monopoly power, lags in response to exchange rate movements, and so on, make this assumption unlikely to be fulfilled in practice. For non-traded sectors, there is in fact no reason at all to suppose price ratios will equal the exchange rate. Finally, it is well recognized that the exchange rate is also influenced by short-term capital movements, which should not be reflected in comparative volume measures of output and productivity (Taylor and Taylor 2004).

Parallel to the distinction made in the national accounts framework for deflating current expenditure, output and income over time, there are essentially three methods to construct PPPs for deflation across space.[4] The

---

[4] In the remainder of this chapter we apply, for the sake of convenience, the term 'deflation' also to comparisons across space, instead of something like 'adjustment for differences in relative prices', even though the former of course primarily

first method, the expenditure approach, consists of constructing expenditure-based purchasing power parities (hereafter to be called E–PPPs), which provide PPPs for expenditure categories, such as private consumption, gross fixed capital formation and government consumption (see Table 13.1). E–PPPs refer to purchase prices for final expenditure categories (food, clothing, rent, machinery, education, and so on). Alternatively one can develop purchasing power parities on the basis of the industry-of-origin approach (hereafter to be named O–PPPs). These PPPs are based on basic prices and provide PPPs for gross output and intermediate inputs for individual industries. Finally, one can develop PPPs for comparisons of factor income, that is, for income from labour and capital. These are not extensively used in international comparisons and will not be discussed further in this chapter.

Table 13.1   Various PPP concepts

Expenditure approach (E–PPP)	Industry-of-origin approach (O–PPP)
PPP of C (private consumption)	PPP of GO (gross output)
PPP of I (gross fixed capital formation)	PPP of II (intermediate inputs)
PPP of G (government consumption)	PPP of VA (value added)
PPP of (X–M) (trade balance)	

Aggregate comparisons of productivity levels for the total economy are usually based on gross domestic product (GDP) and deflated on the basis of expenditure-based purchasing power parities (E–PPPs). E–PPPs have originally been compiled within the framework of the International Comparisons Project (ICP). Nowadays E–PPPs are based on a regular survey which is specifically designed for this purpose, and carried out under the auspices of Eurostat and the OECD (see section 13.3). E–PPPs are primarily used for comparative studies of GDP, per capita income and expenditure, but OECD and Eurostat also publish E–PPP-based measures of labour

---

relates to comparisons over time. The use of the term 'deflation' indicates that any comparison of output and productivity, either over time or across space, requires an adjustment for changes or differences in prices.

productivity.[5] This is also done by several academic outlets such as the Penn World Tables (Summers and Heston, 1991) and the Total Economy Database of the Groningen Growth and Development Centre (GGDC) and The Conference Board.[6]

Comparisons of productivity levels by industry are less easily made. Ideally, one requires PPPs of gross output, intermediate inputs and value added derived on the basis of the industry-of-origin approach. However, as O–PPPs are not as readily available as E–PPPs, some scholars have resorted to using selective expenditure PPPs, so-called 'component' E–PPPs, which are based on an allocation of individual E–PPPs to separate industries. Some scholars have gone a step further by adjusting the component PPPs from expenditure to producer price level by taking account of differences in margins and taxes (see section 13.4). Despite the lack of specific surveys for O–PPPs, some scholars have exploited the wide availability of production censuses and industry surveys to compile O–PPPs on the basis of the industry-of-origin approach (section 13.5). The advantages and disadvantages of both approaches, which differ by industry and sector, are discussed in section 13.6.

When making comparisons of levels of value added, which is a common output concept for productivity studies, one must either develop separate PPPs for gross output and intermediate inputs from which the PPP for value added can be implicitly derived, or one must assume that the average PPP for gross output at industry level equals the PPP for intermediate inputs. In the latter case value added is based on, what is called, single deflation, whereas in the former case one obtains a double-deflated value added-measure. Just like PPPs for gross output, intermediate input PPPs can also be based on E–PPPs or O–PPPs (see section 13.7). Table 13.2 provides an overview of the various PPPs commonly used to obtain volume measures for comparisons of output and productivity level for the aggregate economy or by industry. The advantages and disadvantages of the alternative PPP measures are discussed in depth in the remainder of this chapter. For practical applications at the level of individual industries, the reader is referred to Timmer et al. (2007).

---

[5] For OECD Productivity Database, see http://www.oecd.org/topicstatsportal /0,2647,en_2825_30453906_1_1_1_1_1,00.html and for Eurostat Structural Indicators, see http://europa.eu.int/comm/eurostat/.

[6] For Penn World Tables, see http://datacentre2.chass.utoronto.ca/pwt/. For GGDC, see http://www.ggdc.net/dseries.

Table 13.2   Alternative volume measures for output and productivity level comparisons

---

Aggregate GDP (Section 13.3)
- *Expenditure approach*: based on expenditure components (C, I, G) deflated by corresponding E–PPPs and with:
  - deflation of (X–M) by exchange rate, or
  - deflation of (X–M) by aggregate PPP of C, I and G, or
  - deflation of (X–M) by PPP of X and PPP of M
  - *Industry-of-origin approach*: based on aggregation of industry value added

Industry value added
- *Industry-of-origin approach*:
  - single deflation: industry value added deflated by PPP of GO
  - double deflation: industry value added deflated by PPP of VA, which is based on PPP of GO and PPP of II
- *Expenditure approach*:
  - single deflation: industry value added deflated by (adjusted) component E–PPP
  - double deflation: industry value added deflated by PPP of VA, which is based on E–PPP for gross output and E–PPP for intermediate inputs

Industry gross output (Section 13.4–13.5)
- *Industry-of-origin approach (Section 13.4)*:
  - physical quantity comparison
  - deflation of gross output by PPP of GO:
    - based on unit value ratios for product categories
    - based on producer prices for specified products
- *Expenditure approach (Section 13.5)*:
  - deflation of gross output by E–PPP:
    - for aggregate GDP
    - based on allocation of component E–PPPs (for specific items or expenditure categories) to individual industries (= component E–PPP)
    - adjustment of component E–PPP (= adjusted component E–PPP) for:
      - ✓ transport and distribution margins
      - ✓ taxes less subsidies
      - ✓ import and export price relatives

Continued

Table 13.2   *Alternative volume measures for output and productivity level comparisons – Continued*

Intermediate input (Section 13.7)
- *Industry-of-origin approach*: deflation of purchases of intermediate energy, materials and services by:
  - ○   PPP of Intermediate Inputs (II)
  - ○   allocation of PPP of GO for specific products or industries
  - ○   adjustment of allocated PPP of GO from basic price to purchaser price level by:
    - ✓   transport and distribution margins
    - ✓   taxes less subsidies
    - ✓   import and export price relatives
- *Expenditure approach*: deflation of purchases of intermediate energy, materials and services by component E–PPP for specific products or industries

---

13.3   PRODUCTIVITY COMPARISONS AT THE AGGREGATE LEVEL

Expenditure PPPs are well known for their use in comparisons of GDP per capita (Maddison, 1995, 2001; Heston, Summers and Aten, 2006). They can also be applied to comparisons of productivity, notably labour productivity (van Ark and McGuckin, 1999, 2004; Scarpetta et al., 2000; Pilat, 2004). Expenditure comparisons were pioneered by Gilbert and Kravis (1954) and Gilbert and Associates (1958). Since then, the International Comparisons Program (ICP) has developed the systematic construction of E–PPPs under the auspices of the United Nations and the World Bank. A major standard work on ICP was provided by Kravis et al. (1982). Since the early 1980s OECD has regularly published estimates of E–PPPs, derived from its joint programme with Eurostat. Benchmark estimates of E–PPPs for OECD countries are currently available for 1980, 1985, 1990, 1993, 1996, 1999, 2002 and 2005.

Expenditure PPPs are based on prices mostly collected through specific surveys in the various countries participating in the comparisons (see the chapter by Robert Hill in this volume). These are purchase prices for a common basket of products, which cover the whole range of goods and services included in the final expenditure on GDP. The products in the basket are deemed comparable between countries through detailed product specifications. In some cases the specifications are brand and model specific but in many instances generic specifications were used which only describe the relevant characteristics of the product without mentioning of a particular brand and model.[7] The product prices are used to calculate price relatives between countries, which are aggregated to the so-called basic heading level. A basic heading consists of a group of similar well-defined products from which a sample can be selected that are both representative of their type and of the purchases made in the participating countries. In the OECD PPP round of 1999 there were 221 of such basic headings. It is at the level of the basic heading that expenditure categories are defined and PPPs are calculated.[8]

Expenditure PPPs reflect the relative price ratios for private consumption, investment and government expenditure. They can be directly used for comparisons of levels of expenditure (gross domestic expenditure), but some caution is required when using them for comparing levels of output and productivity. To move from PPPs for expenditure to PPPs for gross domestic product, a correction is required for the net foreign trade balance (X–M), that is, for relative prices of exports (X) and imports (M). Currently, the E–PPPs from Eurostat and OECD make an adjustment for the net balance of imports and exports on the basis of the actual exchange rate. In the Penn World Tables the adjustment is made with the overall expenditure PPP. Ideally a correction for differences in terms of trade is required. For this purpose one needs to develop separate export and import PPPs for internationally traded goods. Such PPPs are not yet available on a wide scale. Feenstra et al. (2009) provide a first attempt and show that terms of trade effects can be quite substantial for small open economies.

A GDP PPP can also be built up from the production side by aggregation of PPPs on the basis of the industry-of-origin approach (O–PPPs). An attempt to develop an estimate of comparative output and productivity for the aggregate economies of the UK and the US was pioneered by Paige and Bombach (1959). Subsequently the industry-of-origin approach was more or less abandoned in favour of the E–PPP approach because of the difficulties in obtaining relative prices for outputs as well as inputs by industry.[9] However, conceptually the O–PPP approach should give the same results at the E–PPP approach for GDP, but only with a proper adjustment for the terms-of-trade effect. With current data availability there is potential for a revival of the O–PPP approach, also for aggregate comparisons, in particular when properly combined with the 'adjusted component' E–PPP approach.

---

[7] Brand and model specific PPPs are mainly for consumer goods and primarily for European countries.

[8] The ICP Handbook provides further detail and discussions of the ICP methodology (World Bank 2002).

[9] See Maddison and van Ark (2002) for a review.

13.4 E–PPPs FOR INDUSTRY GROSS OUTPUT

Expenditure-based PPP comparisons are based on purchase prices of final goods and services with a detailed product specification. Hence, to apply them to output and productivity comparisons by industry, the E–PPPs need to be re-allocated from expenditure categories to industry groups (see, for example, Hooper and Vrankovich, 1995; Kuroda and Jorgenson, 2001; Lee and Tang, 2001; van Biesebroeck, 2004).[10] This method may be called the 'component' E–PPP method. The method is best applied by using E–PPPs from the detailed basic heading level and apply those to 3- or 4-digit level industries (using the NACE, NAICS or ISIC industry classification). To obtain a component E–PPP for aggregate industry output, the E–PPPs can be aggregated in translog forms by using nominal output shares of the commodity mix as weights (see, for example, Kuroda and Jorgenson, 2001):

$$\ln EPPP_j^{BA} = \sum_{i=1}^{I_j} \bar{v}_{ij} \ln EPPP_{ij}^{BA} \qquad (13.1)$$

with $E-PPP_j^{BA}$ the component E–PPP for industry j between countries A and B, $E-PPP_{ij}^{BA}$ the E–PPP for expenditure category i and $\bar{v}_{ij}$ the weight of expenditure category i in industry j output, averaged over the two countries.[11] Note that these are output, and not expenditure weights. Ideally detailed industry-by-product (supply) tables are needed to indicate the output value of products originating from each industry. However, in the absence of a detailed supply table, other business statistics (for example, the annual business survey or a production census) can be used to obtain output weights. It is also possible to use the expenditure shares from ICP as a proxy for output weights. These are relatively easy to acquire but do not necessarily reflect output shares as they include imported goods, and exclude production for export. Moreover, they need to be adjusted for sales out of stock and for price differences.

The use of component E–PPPs at industry level has several significant drawbacks (see also section 13.6). Firstly, a complete correspondence between expenditure categories and industries is not possible since, by definition, prices of goods produced as intermediate input for other industries

---

[10] Aggregate E–PPPs are sometimes used at industry level (see, for example, Dollar and Wolff, 1993; Bernard and Jones, 1996). This implies the very strict assumption of identical relative price levels across industries. This method is not recommended to be used for industry–level comparisons.

[11] Of course, other weighting schemes like Laspeyres or Fisher type can also be used. The latter type is often used for industry–of–origin PPPs (see section 13.5).

are not covered by E–PPPs. In an industry like chemicals, production for intermediate consumption can make up more than 70 per cent of output. To bridge the gap, some studies have included close substitutes for a given industry's intermediate deliveries based on its deliveries to final demand. Secondly, E–PPPs are based on a different price concept than the output value to which it is applied. Expenditure PPPs not only reflect the ratio of prices received by the producer, but also cross-country differences in wholesale and retail distribution margins and transportation costs. For example, a comparison of output in the shoe manufacturing industry should be based on the prices received by the manufacturer of shoes and should not include the transport margin of the transportation company and the retail margin gained by the shoe retailer. Expenditure prices also include indirect taxes and subsidies, which often vary across countries. Therefore the use of E–PPPs at industry level requires an adjustment from purchaser price level to basic price level.[12]

The adjusted component E–PPP approach has been pioneered by Jorgenson and associates through 'peeling off' indirect taxes and transport and distribution margins from the expenditure prices (see for example Jorgenson et al., 1987; Timmer et al., 2007):

$$EPPP(ADJ)_j^{BA} = \frac{1+T_j^A}{1+T_j^A}EPPP_j^{BA} \qquad (13.2)$$

Hence the PPP between country A and B for output in a particular industry is proxied by the adjusted E–PPP, calculated as the component E–PPP for this industry multiplied by the industry-specific ratio of tax, transportation and distribution margins (T) in country A over those in country B. Input-output tables are often used to calculate indirect taxes and transport and distribution margins (see Pilat, 1996 and Timmer et al., 2007).

As the expenditure PPPs are based on final consumption rather than on domestic output a third step is needed, namely the adjustment for the foreign trade effect. Relative prices for import goods need to be excluded from the E–PPPs, whereas those for export goods need to be added back in. This adjustment is important insofar as domestic, import and export price relatives for the same product differ and a significant amount of international trade takes place. This is particularly the case for commodities, such as

---

[12] Prices received by manufacturers are sometimes measured as producer prices, i.e. including net taxes (taxes minus subsidies) on products. It is desirable, however, to exclude those and use the basic price. In any case it is crucial that the output and the PPP use the same price concept be it producer or basic prices.

agricultural, mining and manufacturing goods. Hooper (1996) proposes a solution to this problem for deriving manufacturing sector E–PPPs, adjusting domestic prices for import and export price effects. He assumes that import and export prices in manufacturing are set according to 'world' prices (P_{world}). The world price, P_{world}, for each item is obtained as an output-weighted average of each country's item price. This formulation relies heavily on a number of assumptions, in particular that for each country exports and imports are priced at the world price level for the goods in question. It also does not take account of tariffs and non-tariff barriers. Moreover, the average world price level is obviously based only on the prices of the countries which are included in the comparison.[13] Since the pioneering work of Hooper (1996) and Hooper and Vrankovich (1995), this method has not been pursued further. A study of PPPs for exports and imports in combination with weights derived from trade data by industry would be needed to continue this work, along the lines of Feenstra et al. (2009).

Making the adjustments for component E–PPPs at industry level to take account of taxes, margins and the foreign trade effect is empirically important. Table 13.3 shows for a number of countries the step-by-step adjustments when moving from a component expenditure PPP for manufacturing to an adjusted E–PPP. The steps are as follows: first adjusting the E–PPP for wholesale and retail distribution margins, then for net taxes and subsidies, and finally an adjustment for import and export prices following equation (13.3). The results are only shown for aggregate manufacturing. At a lower level of aggregation, differences due to the various adjustments become much more pronounced.

In conclusion, the main drawbacks of the expenditure-based PPP method for comparisons of output and productivity at industry level, is that the adjustment of the PPPs from a purchaser price to basic price concept and the correction for foreign trade are complicated. Furthermore, by definition E–PPPs only cover prices for final expenditure and do not reflect relative prices of intermediate goods.

---

[13] See Hooper and Vrankovich (1995) and Hooper (1996) for details. A practical problem of this method is the ad–hoc definition of the world price, for which Hooper has chosen the average price level for the G7 countries normalized to US dollar price level by using the ratio of the adjusted component PPP relative to the exchange rate. Also, the adjustment is made at the industry, rather than the product level.

Table 13.3   Bilateral manufacturing PPPs derived from expenditure PPPs (units of local currency per dollar), 1990

	US	Japan	West Germany	France	Italy	UK	Canada
E–PPP	1.00	198.32	2.25	7.78	1794	0.71	1.41
Plus adjustment for distribution margins	1.00	221.61	2.36	7.75	1888	0.77	1.41
Plus adjustment for taxes	1.00	208.51	2.33	7.70	1957	0.77	1.42
Plus adjustment for international trade	1.00	217.86	2.36	8.07	2005	0.79	1.43

Source: Hooper and Vrankovich (1995, Table 2)

13.5   O–PPPs FOR GROSS OUTPUT: THE INDUSTRY OF ORIGIN APPROACH

The theoretically most appropriate approach for international comparisons of output and productivity levels is to apply PPPs that are based on the industry-of-origin approach (O–PPPs). These PPPs are specifically designed for making comparisons of output and productivity by industry rather than comparisons of expenditure patterns. The industry-of-origin approach was pioneered by Paige and Bombach (1959) in a comparison of the United Kingdom and the United States. The earlier work was conveniently summarized by Kravis (1976). Since 1985, the O–PPP method was further developed and used in the ICOP project (International Comparisons of Output and Productivity) at the University of Groningen (Maddison and van Ark, 2002; Timmer et al., 2007), at the National Institute of Economic and Social Research (O'Mahony, 1992, 1999) and at the Centre d'études prospectives et d'informations internationales (Freudenberg and Ünal–Kesenci, 1994; Nayman and Ünal–Kesenci, 2000).

In contrast to the E–PPP-method, there is no internationally co-ordinated survey for collecting information on specified output or producer prices from which detailed O–PPPs can be calculated. There are various alternative ways to obtain O–PPPs for gross output, partly depending on the data availability for individual industries. One way is to make use of producer or basic prices for specified products which are collected for alternative purposes.[14] For example, the Food and Agriculture Organization (FAO) collects prices of agricultural commodities for a large set of countries. The most widely used approach to obtain O–PPPs is the unit-value-ratio (UVR) method. This method makes use of production statistics (censuses or business statistics surveys) that record the output values and quantities for product items. By dividing the output value by the corresponding quantities, one obtains unit values, which can then be used for calculating unit value ratios (UVRs) for matched items between countries. As the UVR method is mostly applied to manufacturing industries, the methodological presentation below focuses on that sector. However, the unit value ratio can also be used for several other sectors of the economy.

Below we present the methodology recently used by Timmer et al. (2007). They derive unit value ratios on the basis of unit values for matched product items. As a first step, unit values (*uv*) are derived by dividing ex-factory output values (*o*) by produced quantities (*q*) for each product *i* in each country:

$$uv_i = \frac{o_i}{q_i} \qquad (13.3)$$

The unit value can be considered as an average price, averaged throughout the year for all producers and across a group of nearly similar products. Subsequently, in a bilateral comparison, broadly defined products with similar characteristics are matched. For each matched product, the unit value ratio (UVR) is given by:

$$UVR_i^{AB} = \frac{uv_i^A}{uv_i^B} \qquad (13.4)$$

with *A* and *B* the countries being compared, *B* being the base country. The product *UVR* indicates the relative producer price of the matched product in the two countries.

---

[14] In principle producer price data can be obtained from the national statistical programmes on producer price indices, but in practice it is very difficult to obtain comparable data due to a lack of harmonisation across countries. Moreover, such producer price measures would require an adjustment to basic price level, in case the output concept used is at basic prices.

Table 13.4 Product matching in the meat processing industry (ISIC 151), US and Germany 1997

Product name	Quantity		Value (own currency)		Unit value		Value (other currency)		Unit value ratio
	US (1000 ton) (1)	Germany (1000 ton) (2)	US (mil. USD) (3)	Germany (mil. DEM) (4)	US USD/kg (5)=(3)/(1)	Germany DEM/kg (6)=(4)/(2)	US (mil. DEM) (7)=(1)*(6)	Germany (mil. USD) (8)=(2)*(5)	DEM/USD (9)=(4)/(3)
Fresh and frozen beef	4757	498	15621	2069	3.28	4.16	19779	1634	1.27
Fresh and frozen boneless beef	1448	222	3429	1076	2.37	4.84	7011	526	2.04
Fresh and frozen variety meats	650	263	951	342	1.46	1.30	846	384	0.89
Fresh and frozen veal	85	19	334	146	3.92	7.59	647	75	1.94
Fresh and frozen lamb and mutton	30	3	140	28	4.72	9.79	290	13	2.07
Fresh and frozen pork	647	1615	1276	5163	1.97	3.20	2068	3186	1.62
Cattle hides, skins, and pelts	933	42	1961	125	2.10	2.96	2764	88	1.41
Edible tallow and stearin	710	201	492	162	0.69	0.81	572	139	1.16
Lard	79	122	43	102	0.55	0.83	65	67	1.51
Boiled ham, barbecue pork, and bacon	1530	382	5788	3047	3.78	7.97	12191	1447	2.11
Sausages	2105	1256	7547	10485	3.59	8.35	17576	4502	2.33
Jellied goods	1635	336	6391	1954	3.91	5.82	9523	1312	1.49
Broilers and fryers	9607	398	12373	1186	1.29	2.98	28658	512	2.32
Fryer roaster turkeys	1868	222	3768	858	2.02	3.86	7216	448	1.92
Cooked or smoked turkey	385	38	1403	279	3.64	7.26	2797	140	1.99
Cooked or smoked chicken	1343	91	4125	661	3.07	7.26	9751	279	2.36
Cooked or smoked poultry hams	454	103	1838	1049	4.05	10.22	4646	415	2.53
Total value			67480	28731			126400	15169	
Paasche PPP of GO (4)/(8)									1.89
Laspeyres PPP of GO (7)/(3)									1.87
Fisher PPP of GO									1.88

Source: Based on US Dept. of Commerce, US Census of Manufactures 1997; Statistisches Bundesamt, Produktion im Produzierendes Gewerbe, 1997.

Table 13.4 gives an example of how UVRs are derived, which is drawn from a comparison of output prices for the meat processing industry between the United States and Germany in 1997. In this industry 17 product matches were made. The unit values in national currency are given columns 5 and 6. The item-specific unit value ratios are given in the last column.

Product UVRs need to be aggregated to derive O–PPPs for gross output for individual industries or for the aggregate sector. This can be done in one step from product to aggregate manufacturing, but also in various steps. Given the fact that mostly only a selected number of products are matched, the latter is recommended. The UVRs are then reweighted several times, first according to their output share in the industry, then according to the industry share in the branch and finally according to the branch share in aggregate manufacturing. For example, following the latest version of the International Standard Industrial Classification (ISIC rev 3) product UVRs can be aggregated up 101 three-digit manufacturing industries (following ISIC rev 3), then to 22 two-digit manufacturing branches and finally to aggregate manufacturing. As a result, the aggregate O–PPP better reflect the actual share of each underlying product item for which UVRs are available in total output. The aggregation from product level to the 3-digit industry level can be compared to the practice of aggregating expenditure prices of individual goods first to basic headings. The difference is that product UVRs have weights attached, while expenditure PPPs below the basic heading level have not.

The O–PPP for industry j based on the industry-of-origin approach is given by

$$OPPP_j^{BA} = \sum_{i=1}^{I_j} w_{ij}^{BA} UVR_{ij}^{BA} \qquad (13.5)$$

with

1. $i=1,..,I_j$ the matched products in industry j;

2. $w_{ij} = o_{ij}/o_j$ the output share of the ith commodity in industry j;

3. $o_j = \sum_{i=1}^{I_j} o_{ij}$ the total matched value of output in industry j.

In bilateral comparisons the weights of either the base country (B) or the other country (A) can be used, which provide a Laspeyres and a Paasche type PPP respectively. The use of base country value weights leads to the Laspeyres index. For the Paasche index, weights of the other country quantities valued at base country prices are used in formula (13.5). As the output shares are consistent with the quantities that are used to derive the unit values, the weights and unit value ratios in (13.5) are consistent. This is an important advantage over the use of specified item prices as for the E–PPP approach.

The bottom lines in Table 13.4 show the calculation of industry-level O–PPPs for gross output. The geometric average of the Laspeyres and Paasche indices, the Fisher index, is often used when a single currency conversion factor is required.[15] The next aggregation step can be made by using either the gross output or the value added of each 3-digit industry to obtain an industry-weighted mean of all industry PPPs in a 2-digit branch. Again weights from base country B or the other country A can be used to arrive at Laspeyres and Paasche indices of the branch PPPs respectively. The latter step is repeated for the final aggregation step from branch level to the level of total manufacturing. Columns 4 to 6 in Table 13.5 provides an example of the various branch level O–PPPs for gross output (weighted at gross output) for the Germany–US comparisons for 1997.

As mentioned above, because of the increased variety and complexity of products not all products in an industry j can be matched, not even in a comparison between two countries. This is because of missing value or quantity data, difficulties in matching corresponding products between countries, and because of products that are unique for a specific country. Indeed the composition of output tends to differ much more across countries than the composition of expenditure, which is a complicating factor for industry-of-origin comparisons. Information on the number of product matches made and the output covered by these matched products can be used to assess the reliability and possible biases of the UVRs (see last columns of Table 13.5). The reliability of the O–PPP of gross output for a given industry or sector can also be evaluated on the basis of the coefficient of variation of the UVRs. On the assumption that relative price levels should not vary too much within homogeneous industries, large variations in unit value ratios within an industry or branch signal a lower reliability of the measures. Other indicators of reliability include a measure of the Paasche/Laspeyres spread between O–PPPs, which indicate differences in production structure between countries.

---

[15] Alternatively a Törnqvist aggregation can be made which yields values which are numerically almost identical. So far Fisher indices have been mostly been used for industry–of–origin comparisons.

Table 13.5 Aggregation of unit value ratios from industry, to branch, to sectoral level, US and Germany, 1997

Product name	ISIC	No. of Product Matches (1)	Coverage ratio (%) United States (2)	Germany (3)	Laspeyres (4)	O-PPP Paasche (5)	Fisher (6)	Coefficient of variation Laspeyres (7)	Paasche (8)
Food products, beverages and tobacco	15-16	132	61.9	65.4	1.83	1.59	1.71	0.003	0.019
of which, Meat processing	*151*	*17*	*60.6*	*72.3*	*1.87*	*1.89*	*1.88*	*0.039*	*0.030*
Textiles	17	25	53.8	49.5	2.84	2.35	2.58	0.055	0.069
Wearing apparel	18	39	73.4	40.5	3.59	3.28	3.43	0.030	0.040
Leather products and footwear	19	12	61.7	31.2	2.21	2.12	2.16	0.089	0.123
Wood products	20	13	28.5	51.8	2.11	1.81	1.95	0.083	0.105
Paper products, printing & publishing	21-22	19	16.4	25.7	1.70	1.60	1.65	0.072	0.085
Petroleum and coal products	23	0	0.0	0.0	n/a	n/a	n/a	n/a	n/a
Chemicals and chemical products	24	59	17.5	12.9	1.77	1.88	1.83	0.052	0.061
Rubber and plastic products	25	4	22.9	7.4	2.00	1.75	1.87	0.047	0.151
Non-metallic mineral products	26	23	28.5	22.0	1.50	1.06	1.26	0.052	0.053
Basic metals	27	43	69.6	71.3	1.75	1.56	1.66	0.028	0.027
Fabricated metal products	28	11	3.7	6.5	1.58	1.45	1.51	0.110	0.105
Machinery and equipment	29	39	10.2	9.9	2.03	1.93	1.98	0.075	0.069
Transport equipment	30-33	6	21.9	35.9	2.21	2.16	2.18	0.071	0.054
Office, accounting and computing machinery	30	6	42.9	38.3	1.79	1.58	1.68	0.217	0.131
Electrical and optical equipment	34-35	49	15.3	20.7	2.37	1.70	2.01	0.111	0.123
Furniture and miscellaneous manufacturing	36-37	36	19.0	30.1	1.66	1.47	1.56	0.064	0.062
Total manufacturing		516	27.0	28.5	1.89	1.82	1.86	0.024	0.021

Source: See Table 13.4
Note: Industry and branch PPPs are weighted at gross output

The choice for gross output or value added weights in the aggregation procedure depends on the actual purpose of the comparison. If productivity is ultimately going to be compared on a value added basis, the O–PPP of gross output may be assumed representative of the value added PPP (the 'single deflation procedure'), value added weights are the proper weighting system at industry and branch level.[16] However, single deflation has a number of disadvantages.[17] From the perspective of a comparison of multifactor productivity levels, it is desirable to compute separate O–PPPs of gross output and of intermediate inputs, and to use gross output and intermediate input values as weights respectively.

An important point of criticism on the O–PPP method is that these PPPs are mostly based on unit value ratios. The reliability of the O–PPPs is therefore likely to be greatest in industries with homogeneous products, for which values and quantities are most readily available in the production statistics. For example, in basic goods industries, such as pulp and paper, wood products, metallic and non-metallic mineral products, output coverage is usually quite large as there are relatively few product differences between countries. Product matching is more difficult in manufacturing industries that produce durable consumer goods and investment goods, and the coverage percentages are therefore often lower than for basic goods and the UVRs less representative of all products in an industry.

The 'product matching' problem may be divided into two categories, namely the 'product mix' problem and the 'quality' problem. The 'product mix' problem is caused by the fact that production statistics report quantity

---

[16] Value added weights can only be used for aggregation from industry PPPs up to higher levels as no value added weights are available at the product level.

[17] Firstly, double deflation puts larger requirements on data, as besides output PPPs, input PPPs are also needed. Secondly, double deflation introduces a new possible source of error not present in single deflation measures, that is, errors associated with the measurement of input prices. In many sectors, material input prices are either unavailable or crudely measured. Hill (1971) suggests that the use of double deflation when material input prices are measured with error may be more misleading than using single deflation. This problem is aggravated by the fact that double deflated value added is defined as relative output quantity minus relative intermediate input quantity. This subtraction gives room for errors. A small percentage error in the index of gross output appears as a much larger percentage error in double deflated real value added than in the case of single deflation as value added is smaller than gross output. Double deflation can also lead to measures of output that are unstable and erratic, especially at lower levels of aggregation when value added is a small share of gross output. This explains the ongoing popularity of single deflated value added in international comparisons of productivity levels, despite its theoretical inferiority. Inklaar and Timmer (2008) provide a sensitivity analysis and compare single– and double–deflated measures.

and values for product groups rather than for specified products. This problem is aggravated in international comparisons because of the lack of a harmonized product coding system for industry statistics, so that items need to be combined in order to obtain a correct match between countries.[18] The direction of the bias due to differences in product mix is undetermined. The 'quality' problem relates to differences in characteristics of a similar product. In this case it is not possible to find exactly the same model of a particular product, even if there was value and quantity information on specified products. In practice, detailed product characteristics are difficult or impossible to observe directly from production statistics. Some studies make use of information from secondary, often private, industry sources that may include information on specified product prices. Such sources may prove particularly useful for products from typical high-tech industries, such as information technology equipment (computers and telecommunication equipment), passenger cars and pharmaceutical products. Another fruitful, though data demanding, way forward is to make greater use of hedonic price measurement for international price comparisons. Instead of observing the prices of products themselves, the hedonic method obtains the price of a bundle of characteristics of a product through regression analysis. The international hedonic function hypothesis argues that the coefficients of the product characteristics in the hedonic function should be identical across countries (Triplett, 2004). The increased availability of scanner data makes such an approach possible, but so far it has mainly been experimented with for E–PPPs and hardly for O–PPPs.[19] The estimation of hedonic functions with scanner data can be costly, however, and should therefore typically confined to areas where quality problems are particularly important and where these problems can be addressed by hedonic methods.

---

[18] The recent availability of harmonized product codes in the PRODCOM system for the European Union is a major step forward for international comparisons based on unit value ratios, but comparisons with the United States are still hampered by the use of different product classifications.

[19] For example, the use of a country–product dummy (CPD) method, which relates through a regression analysis the price of a product to its characteristics and to a dummy variable for the country of origin, makes it possible to calculate the quality adjusted PPP from the coefficients of the dummy. Even when hedonic functions are not stable across countries, quality adjustments can be made on the basis of country–specific coefficients to derive PPPs. See Heravi et al. (2003) for an application to television sets in France, Netherlands and the UK.

13.6   EXPENDITURE VERSUS OUTPUT PPPs: AN ASSESSMENT

It may be clear from the discussion in the previous sections that in practical terms neither the expenditure approach nor the industry-of-origin approach is clearly superior to the other in obtaining PPPs for output and productivity comparisons. At the aggregate level, the E–PPP has been mostly applied mainly because it is based on a separate survey of expenditure prices for specified items, and because it avoids the problem of double deflation. However, when using E–PPPs for output and productivity comparisons, one should be cautious about the adjustment for the terms of trade effect. At industry level, the O–PPP is theoretically most preferable. The use of component E–PPPs is theoretically disadvantaged because no price data are available for intermediate product items. The practical disadvantage of E–PPPs is that they require detailed adjustments for margins, taxes and terms of trade effects. O–PPPs are mostly based on unit value ratios as basic prices for specified items at producer level are often not available. But unit value ratios have the disadvantage of introducing 'product matching' problems in international comparisons. The choice on whether to use component E–PPPs or O–PPPs is an empirical one, and will differ by industry. Below we discuss the criteria for choosing between E–PPPs and O–PPPs.

It should be emphasized that the methodology and sources to obtain O–PPPs are fundamentally different from those used to obtain expenditure PPPs in the OECD/Eurostat program. E–PPPs are derived from specified prices that are obtained from a specific survey set up for the purpose. O–PPPs are mostly based on ratios of unit values derived from (national) production censuses and business statistics surveys. The strengths and weaknesses of the two PPP concepts can be classified in the following four broad areas: price concept, representativeness of sampled items, sampling error and weighting systems.[20]

As far as the price concept is concerned, PPPs at industry level should reflect relative prices for domestic production. O–PPPs directly reflect prices at industry level, E–PPPs reflect prices of final expenditure on products, which either have been produced domestically or have been imported. In addition, not all domestically produced goods are destined for final expenditure, as part is being used for intermediate demand or exported. Component E–PPPs therefore only approach the industry level prices in case most of the expenditure is on domestically produced goods and the industry output being produced goes mostly to domestic final expenditure and not to intermediate consumption or exports. This can be assessed using an input-

---

[20] See also the discussion in O'Mahony (1996).

output framework. In this framework total use of goods is given by the summation of final expenditure (consumer, investment and government demand), demand for intermediate consumption and exports. Total supply is given by domestic production (output) plus imports. Both domestically produced goods and imports can be used for final use, intermediate consumption or exports.

Appendix Table A.13.1 shows the shares of expenditure, intermediate and export demand in total use, and the shares of domestic production and imports in total supply for each sector. This is done for a large economy (the US) and a small open economy (the Netherlands). On the basis of these shares a good assessment of the appropriateness of PPPs can be made. For a sector in which the share of final expenditure in total use is low, E–PPPs serve as a bad proxy for the PPP at industry level as the underlying prices do not refer to deliveries to intermediate consumption and export demand. This might not be a problem when the bundle of products and their prices do not differ much between final expenditure and other uses, but in many cases these differences are large.[21] Alternatively, consider a sector with a high share of final expenditure in total use but also a high share of imports in total supply of goods. In that case, E–PPPs also reflect prices of imports, and not only the prices of domestic production. Again, in most cases the prices of imported and domestic production are likely to be quite different (for example clothing). Hence the share of final expenditure in total use and the share of imports in total supply are both good indicators of the usefulness of E–PPPs at industry level. On the basis of Appendix Table A.13.1 it can be seen that E–PPPs are acceptable as measures of price ratios in, for example, sectors such as construction, hotels and catering and real estate. However, the E–PPPs are poor proxies of industry output PPPs in agriculture, mining, many manufacturing industries, public utilities and transport and communication. On the other hand, O–PPPs refer to the conceptually correct price measure in all industries.

Still, when used for comparisons at industry level, component E–PPPs need to reflect basic prices, and therefore have to be adjusted for differences in taxes and subsidies, differences in trade and transportation margins and should be corrected for the inclusion of import prices and exclusion of export prices. The reliability of the adjustments is dependent on the quality of the

---

[21] Consider the case in which prices of products are the same irrespective of their category of demand (final or intermediate). The composition of demand by firms which use these products as intermediates can be rather different from the demand composition of final consumers (for example demand for transportation services being mainly freight services in the first case and passenger transport in the second). This example stresses the importance of using output weights at the lowest level possible when aggregating PPPs.

information on distribution margins and net taxes by sector and especially on the international trade adjustment which requires price and expenditure data which is often not available.

A second issue in the choice for E–PPPs or O–PPPs for comparisons at industry level is representativity of the underlying prices. Representativeness is important in two areas: (1) representativeness of the matched products for the industry output of the countries being compared (also called 'characteristicity'), and (2) the representativeness of the relative prices for sampled products for the relative prices of unsampled products. In the ICP methodology, the E–PPP for a comparison of two countries is constructed from a sub-set of varieties that exist in both countries. In some cases, particularly for comparisons between countries with great differences in income levels or expenditure patterns, this overlapping subset concerns a small number of varieties which may be characteristic of neither country. Characteristicity is less of a problem with O–PPPs, because the measures are not based on specification pricing but on unit value for more aggregate product groups that are being matched. This implies that the output coverage of matched products is substantially larger than the percentage of total expenditure that is covered by E–PPPs. Also, the unit value underlying O–PPPs reflects prices averaged throughout the year, instead of prices at one point of time as in the ICP survey methods. Another important advantage of O–PPPs is that they cover not only final expenditure goods, but also sales of goods for intermediate consumption (see above). Although O–PPPs may be more characteristic of the output in an industry than E–PPPs, there can be a problem of representativity of matched items for non-matched items in the same industry. Due to the 'product matching' problem, O–PPPs are often based on samples of products which are biased towards relatively homogeneous and less sophisticated goods. The underlying unit value ratios may not always be representative of the more upgraded, high-quality varieties in the same industry.

A third issue, linked to the previous one, concerns the sampling error of E–PPPs vis-à-vis O–PPPs. In principle one might expect a bigger sampling error for unit value ratios compared to specified E–PPPs. As more aggregate items are being matched, product mix problems and the quality problem may raise the sampling error of O–PPPs. Lichtenberg and Griliches (1989) showed that in an intertemporal context, producer price indices in the US based on specified product prices are superior to those based on census unit value ratios as price dispersions are much higher for the latter. However, Balk (1999) shows that the sampling error is not only dependent on the extent of price dispersion for a product variety but also on the number of observations. In cases where O–PPPs are based on more observations than the E–PPPs, the final sampling error might well be less than the error introduced by the quality problems.

Finally, consideration needs to be given to the availability of weighting systems for the PPPs that adequately reflect the share of product items in total output. O–PPPs have the advantage of having natural weights attached to the UVRs since they are calculated as the sales value of the products divided by the quantity sold. These weights allow weighting systems to be used at the elementary level of aggregation, rather than only from basic heading onwards as in the case of E–PPPs. They also allow for measures of reliability, such as coverage ratios, to be calculated.

In summary, it is clear that each approach has its advantages and disadvantages. This will differ by industry, and there is no final judgement on the superiority of E–PPPs or O–PPPs in adjusting output for relative price differences at the industry level. In practice, a mixture of O–PPPs and E–PPPs should be used for comparisons at industry level. The importance attached to the advantages and disadvantages of each method differs between industries. In Table 13.6 an assessment is made of the usefulness of expenditure and output PPPs for 19 different sectors in the economy. This is based on an assessment of E–PPPs from OECD for the 1999 ICP–round and O–PPPs for 1997 from the ICOP project at the University of Groningen (Timmer and Ypma 2005). PPPs are ranked from 0 (not useful) to 5 (very useful) on the basis of the following criteria. The usefulness of E–PPPs at industry level depends on the share of final expenditure in total use, the share of import in total supply, and the quality of the E–PPPs. The first two issues can be evaluated on the bases of input-output tables as described above.

The criteria for assessing the appropriateness of using O–PPPs are different from those for E–PPPs. Conceptually O–PPPs refer to the correct prices, namely those of domestically produced products. But as discussed above, the main weaknesses of O–PPPs are the product mix and quality problems. Especially for high-tech goods, or heterogeneous services, O–PPPs can be affected. In addition, for many services there are no data on unit values due to a lack of appropriate value data and the difficulty of defining quantities. O–PPPs are therefore particularly useful for industries for which products are relatively homogeneous and for which differences in product quality problems are small.

Table 13.6 *Assessment of usefulness of adjusted E–PPPs and O–PPPs for industry output comparisons in the OECD*

Industry	ISIC rev. 3 code	Grade		Remark	
		ICP Expenditure PPP	ICOP Production PPP	ICP Expenditure PPP	ICOP Production PPP
Agriculture	01–05	0	5	Small expenditure share	Homogeneous goods, producer prices
Mining and quarrying	10–14	0	4	Small expenditure share	Homogeneous goods
Manufacturing	15–37	2	4		
Food, drink and tobacco	15,16	3	4	High exp.share but also trade intensive	Homogeneous goods
Basic goods	17,20,21,23–28	1	4	Small expenditure share	Homogeneous goods
Non-durable	18,19,22,36,37	2	4	Large import share	Homogeneous goods
Durable	29–35	2	2	Large import share	Quality and coverage problem
Electricity, gas and water supply	40,41	3	4	Homogeneous goods	Homogeneous goods
Construction	45	4	1	High expenditure share	Quality problem
Trade	50–52	0	2	Small expenditure share	Quality problem
Hotels & catering	55	4	0	High expenditure share	Not available
Transport	60–63	1	3	Dif. product mix	Quality problem
Communications	64	3	3	Homogeneous goods	Quality problem
Finance	65–67	0	1	Not available (reference PPP)	Quality and coverage problem
Real estate activities	70	4	1	High expenditure share	Quality and coverage problem
Business services	71–74	1	0	Small expenditure share	Not available
Public administration and defence	75	0	0	Based on input PPPs	Not available
Education and health	80,85	0	0	Mainly based on input PPPs	Not available
Other services	90–95	2	0	Dif. product mix	Not available

Note: Ranking indicates 0 (not useful), 1 (very poor), 2 (poor), 3 (acceptable), 4 (useful) and 5 (very useful).

Source: Assessment based on E–PPPs for OECD from 1999 round and O–PPPs for 1997 from Groningen Growth and Development Centre.

Table 13.6 shows that E–PPPs are not useful as PPPs for output in agriculture and mining. The output of these sectors consists almost entirely of goods destined for intermediate demand (see also Appendix table A.13.1). E–PPPs can also not be directly used for the distribution sector as the output is measured as the margin of sales over purchases. But with an adjustment for the margin to sales ratio for each item, E–PPPs can be used for the retail sector. For the wholesale and finance sectors no E–PPPs are available as financial services are not sampled in ICP. E–PPPs are also not useful for output and productivity comparisons of non-market services (such as education, health and some government services) as those are mainly based on comparisons of input prices or derived from PPPs calculated for private final consumption expenditure.[22] Other sectors for which E–PPPs are inappropriate include transport, business services, basic goods manufacturing and other services. The output of those industries is mainly used for intermediate demand and the differences in product mix between final and intermediate demand are large.[23] For durable and non-durable final goods manufacturing, E–PPPs serve as a poor measure of relative prices due to the high shares of imports in total supply and differences in the product mix of imports and domestic production. E–PPPs appear acceptable for adjusting for relative price differences in food manufacturing, utilities and communications. In food manufacturing, the share of final expenditure is high, and imports are usually much lower than for other manufacturing goods. The share of final expenditure in utilities and communications services is less but one might assume that prices for final expenditure and intermediate demand will not differ too much. Also variations in the output mix of these industries are small as the number of products is limited. This is in sharp contrast to, for example, business services. E–PPPs are also useful for construction, hotels and real estate activities as final expenditure shares are very high for these sectors, and imports are negligible.

O–PPPs are easily applicable to the agricultural sector as the set of goods produced is limited and relatively homogeneous across countries. In addition, O–PPPs for this sector can be based on specified producer prices (not unit values), which alleviates the product mix problem. O–PPPs are also useful for most manufacturing industries and utilities. Much of the output in manufacturing industries such as textiles, pulp and paper, basic metals, non-metallic minerals and chemicals consists of relatively homogenous basic

---

[22] Input price-based PPPs might be the right price concept when output is measured through input indicators. However, for productivity measures, input-based indicators of output are not very illuminating.

[23] In addition, for transport services, subsidies on certain transport categories are very difficult to peel off from the final expenditure price (for example bus, subway and rail transport prices).

goods. The same is true for utilities. For manufacturing industries producing heterogeneous commodities destined for final use, such as electrical and non-electrical machinery and transport equipment, the use of component E–PPPs might be considered. For the wholesale sector, O–PPPs are can also be used although there are quality problems to be considered. O–PPPs are very poor for construction, finance and real estate activity as they suffer from quality comparison problems in these sectors where outputs are highly varied. Finally, O–PPPs are not available for hotels, business services, other services and non-market services such as education, health and government services.

Lastly, the advantages and disadvantages of various types of PPPs also crucially depend on the availability of data. For example, the use of secondary sources on prices, either derived from private data sources or from industry specific surveys, is an important way to reduce the biases in O–PPPs. Another example is that for some industries in small open economies, where industry output is mainly destined for export, export unit values may be used to estimate output prices. When output destined for domestic market and export can be distinguished, one could also combine export unit values with domestic unit values. Alternatively, the use of the exchange rate as a currency converter might be possible in special cases where relative price levels may be expected to be equal, for example, because an industry is entirely under the influence of global competition. However, in most cases these solutions are second-best compared to adjusted E–PPPs or O–PPPs based on domestic production data.

13.7   PPPs FOR INTERMEDIATE INPUT

When double deflated value added measures are used in a productivity comparison, intermediate input PPPs are necessary in addition to the gross output PPPs discussed in the previous sections. The data problems to obtain input PPPs for individual industries are larger than for output. There is often no input price parallel to the industry-of-origin PPPs. Business statistics surveys and productivity censuses provide little or no information on quantities and values of inputs in manufacturing, and for non-manufacturing industries the information is largely absent. Moreover, E–PPPs by definition do not reflect prices of intermediate inputs as they cover only final expenditure categories. However, it is possible to use a combination of O–PPPs and E–PPPs as proxies for relative input prices.

From the producer's point of view, intermediate input PPPs should reflect the relative costs of acquiring intermediate deliveries, hence they need to reflect relative purchaser prices of intermediate inputs. But as for the case of output, the most important issue is to have consistency between the input valuation concept and the input price relatives. So the actual choice for a particular input price concept depends on the input value data used in the productivity comparison. When inputs are measured at basic prices, trade and transportation margins are allocated to the retail and wholesale trade, transport, warehousing and insurance industries. Consequently, intermediate input values in these tables need to be converted using relative basic prices of inputs, rather than purchasers' prices.

E–PPPs for final goods can be used as reasonable proxies for intermediate input PPPs when the same type of final goods are also used as intermediate inputs. One has to assume that the purchasers' prices are the same, irrespective of the industry of use or final consumption destination. The lower the level of aggregation for which this assumption is made, the higher confidence one can have in its validity. For example, the assumption that the E–PPP for a particular telecommunication service, say long-distance calling, is the same for the final consumer as for the intermediate user is less stringent than assuming that the average E–PPP for transport and communication services is the same for final users and intermediate users.

O–PPPs have the advantage that they actually directly cover intermediate deliveries. Hence it is straightforward to use the O–PPPs as a proxy for relative intermediate input prices. For example, the O–PPP for a particular type of paper, say kraft paper, can be used as a proxy for the input PPP for those industries which use kraft paper as an input. Especially for manufactured intermediate inputs, O–PPPs provide a valuable set of proxy intermediate input PPPs. However, a crucial assumption is that import prices do not differ from prices of domestically produced intermediate inputs. This might not hold, especially when imports make up a large share of intermediate consumption. In that case a possible alternative is to deflate domestically produced and imported intermediate inputs separately. Import PPPs based on, for example, trade data may then be used in addition to domestic O–PPPs for the domestically produced intermediate inputs. Exchange rates may be used as a rough proxy for intermediate inputs that are heavily traded in international markets, such as crude oil.

The aggregation method to obtain PPPs of II is not fundamentally different from that for output PPPs, that is, it requires an average PPP for each input category, which is then weighted at the value share of each input category in the total value of intermediate inputs, using either base country or other country weights. Parts of the input-output table which provide the value of products used as intermediate input by industry (so-called use tables) are the key source to obtain the weights of intermediate input categories. These detailed weights are normally not provided in the national accounts nor in production censuses or business statistics surveys. Assume that input prices can be expressed as translog functions of the prices of their components.

Hence the differences between the logarithms of aggregate input prices for the two countries (PPP of II) can be expressed as a weighted average of differences between logarithms of the component intermediate input prices m, each weighted by its share in total input value $\bar{v}_m$ which is averaged over the two countries A and B:

$$\ln PPP \text{ of } II = \sum_{m \,\varepsilon\, II} \bar{v}_m \ln PPP_m^{BA} \qquad (13.6)$$

Inklaar and Timmer (2008) is the first study to provide double-deflated productivity measures for a large set of countries based on this approach. It provides an additional discussion of the problems in the empirical application.

13.8   CONCLUDING REMARKS

This chapter provides an overview of the various issues and problems involved when making international comparisons of productivity using both the industry-of-origin approach and the expenditure approach to purchasing power parity (PPP) adjustment. It has shown that each approach has its advantages and disadvantages. Hence, the two approaches should be seen as complements rather than substitutes. For comparisons of productivity levels by industry it can be recommended to combine information from the expenditure approach (E–PPPs) and the industry-of-origin approach (O–PPPs). O–PPPs are mostly based on unit value ratios, and are best used in those areas where product quality differences across countries are limited, and where output is relatively homogeneous and/or mainly concerns intermediate inputs. These sectors include, for example, agriculture, mining, many manufacturing industries, public utilities and transport and communication. Unit value ratios may be complemented by 'producer price' information from secondary sources. Expenditure PPPs are useful for industries whose products are primarily destined for final use, where the effect of import and export prices is small, and where the expenditure PPPs themselves can be assumed to be of sufficient quality. These industries include manufacturing industries producing, for example, investment goods and durable consumer goods, the construction sector and services such as hotels and restaurants, finance and business services. E–PPPs must be adjusted for differences in trade and transport margins and taxes, and international trade, when applicable.

Recently, this approach has been applied in a study by Timmer et al. (2007). They construct a PPP dataset for gross output for 45 industries (capturing the total economy) for the benchmark year 1997. Based on this set of PPPs, Inklaar and Timmer (2008) provide comparisons of output, inputs and productivity at a detailed industry level for a set of 30 OECD countries. The latter study also discusses the sensitivity of the results to varying approaches such as using single versus double deflation of value added. In addition, they provide alternative sets of results: one based on the use of E–PPPs exclusively and another based on a mix of E–PPPs and O–PPPs, as advocated in this chapter.

In this chapter we have focused exclusively on the construction of purchasing power parities needed when making output and productivity level comparisons. These comparisons are most often based on a two country (bilateral) basis. Comparisons involving more than two countries which need to be internally consistent need multilateral PPPs which have not been discussed here (see for example other contributions in this volume). We also have not dealt with equally important issues of international consistency in nominal output, labour and capital input measures. For a more extensive discussion of these issues, the reader is referred to the recently completed study by Inklaar and Timmer (2008).

REFERENCES

Ark, B. van (1996), 'Issues in Measurement and International Comparison of Productivity: an Overview', in *Industry Productivity. International Comparisons and Measurement Issues*, Paris: OECD, 19–47.

Ark, B. van, and A. Maddison (1994), 'The International Comparison Of Real Product And Productivity', *Research Memorandum*, GD–6, Groningen Growth and Development Centre.

Ark, B. van and R.H. McGuckin (1999), 'International Comparisons Of Labor Productivity and Per Capita Income', *Monthly Labor Review*, July, 33–41.

Ark, B. van and R.H. McGuckin (2004), *Performance 2004*, Conference Board Research Report R–1351–04–RR, May.

Baily, M.N. and R.M. Solow (2001), 'International Productivity Comparisons Built from the Firm Level', *Journal Of Economic Perspectives*, **15** (3), 151–172.

Balk, B. (1999), 'On the Use of Unit Value Indices as Consumer Price Indices', *Proceedings Of The Fourth International Working Group on Price Indices*, Washington, D.C.: BLS.

Bernard, A.B. And C.I. Jones (1996), 'Comparing Apples to Oranges: Productivity Convergence and Measurement across Industries and Countries', *American Economic Review*, **86** (5), 1216–38.

Biesebroeck, J. Van (2004), Cross-country Conversion Factors for Sectoral Productivity Comparisons, NBER Working Paper Series No. 10279.

Cameron, G., J. Proudman and S. Redding (2005), 'Technological Convergence, R&D, Trade and Productivity Growth', *European Economic Review*, **49**, 775–807.

Dollar, D. and E.N. Wolff (1993), *Competitiveness, Convergence, and International Specialization*, Cambridge MA: MIT Press.

Feenstra, R., A. Heston, M.P. Timmer and H. Deng (2009), 'Estimating Real Production and Expenditures Across Nations: a Proposal for Improving the Penn World Tables', *Review of Economics and Statistics*, **91** (1), 201–212.

Freudenberg, M. and D. Ünal–Kesenci (1994), 'French and German Productivity Levels In Manufacturing', In K. Wagner and B. Van Ark (eds), *International Productivity Differences. Measurement and Explanations*, Amsterdam: North-Holland, 53–84.

Gilbert, M. and I.B. Kravis (1954), *An International Comparison of National Products and the Purchasing Power of Currencies*, Paris: OEEC.

Gilbert, M. and Associates (1958), *Comparative National Products and Price Levels*, Paris: OECD.

Griffith, R., S. Redding and J. van Reenen (2004), 'Mapping the Two Faces of R&D: Productivity Growth in a Panel of OECD Industries', *Review of Economics and Statistics*, **86** (4), 883–895.

Heravi, S, A. Heston and M. Silver (2003), 'Using Scanner Data to Estimate Country Price Parities: an Exploratory Study', *Review of Income and Wealth*, **49** (1), 1–22.

Heston, A., R. Summers and B. Aten (2006), *Penn World Table Version 6.2*, Center for International Comparisons of Production, Income and Prices at the University of Pennsylvania, September.

Hill, R.J., (this volume). 'Comparing Per Capita Income Levels Across Countries Using Spanning Trees: Robustness, Prior Restrictions, Hybrids and Hierarchies'.

Hill, T.P. (1971), *The Measurement of Real Product: a Theoretical and Empirical Analysis of the Growth Rates, For Different Industries and Countries*, Paris: OECD.

Hooper, P. (1996), 'Comparing Manufacturing Output Levels among the Major Industrial Countries', In OECD, *Productivity. International Comparison And Measurement Issues*, OECD Proceedings, Paris.

Hooper, P. and E. Vrankovich (1995), 'International Comparisons of the Level of Unit Labor Costs In Manufacturing', In *International Finance Papers*, **527**, Federal Reserve Board, Washington, D.C.

Inklaar, R. and M.P. Timmer (2008), 'GGDC Productivity Level Database: International Comparisons of Output, Inputs and Productivity at the Industry Level', *GGDC Research Memorandum GD–104*, Groningen Growth and Development Center.

Inklaar, R., M.P. Timmer and B. van Ark (2008), 'Market Services Productivity Across Europe and the U.S.', *Economic Policy*, 141–194.

International Labour Office (ILO) (2001), *Key Indicators of The Labour Market 2001–2002*, Geneva.

Jorgenson, D.W., M. Kuroda and M. Nishimizu (1987), 'Japan–U.S. Industry-level Productivity Comparisons, 1960–1979', *Journal of the Japanese and International Economics*, **1**, 1–30.

Kravis, I.B. (1976), 'A Survey of International Comparisons of Productivity', *Economic Journal*, **86**, March, 1–44.

Kravis, I.B., A. Heston and R. Summers (1982), *World Product and Income*, Baltimore, MD: Johns Hopkins University Press.

Kuroda, M and D.W. Jorgenson (2001), 'Economic Growth and Structural Change In Japan', Draft Manuscript, Keio University.

Lee, F.C. and Y. Tang (2001), 'Productivity Levels and International Competitiviness between Canada and the U.S.', in Jorgenson and Lee (eds) *Industry-level Productivity and International Competitiveness Between Canada and the United States*, Ottawa, Industry Canada.

Lichtenberg, F. and Z. Griliches (1989), 'Errors of Measurement in Output Deflators', *Journal of Business and Economic Statistics*, **7** (1).

Maddison, A. (1995), *Monitoring the World Economy, 1820–1992*, Paris: OECD.

Maddison, A. (2001), *The World Economy: a Millennial Perspective*, Paris: OECD.

Maddison, A. and B. Van Ark (2002), 'The International Comparison of Real Product and Productivity,' In A. Maddison, D.S. Prasada Rao And W.F. Shepherd (eds), *The Asian Economies in the Twentieth Century*, Cheltenham, UK and North Hampton, MA, USA: Edward Elgar, 5–26.

Nayman, L. and D. Ünal–Kesenci (2000), 'Comparaison France–Allemagne des Niveaus de Production et de Productivité dans le Secteur Manufacturier', CEPII, Paris, Mimeographed.

OECD (2002), *Purchasing Power Parities and Real Expenditures –1999 Benchmark*, Paris: OECD.

O'Mahony (1992), 'Productivity Levels in British and German Manufacturing Industry', *National Institute Economic Review*, **139**.

O'Mahony, M. (1996), 'Conversion Factors in Relative Productivity Calculations: Theory and Practice', in OECD *Industry Productivity. International Comparisons and Measurement Issues*, Paris: OECD, 245–262.

O'Mahony (1999), *Britain's Productivity Performance 1950–1996: an International Perspective*, London: National Institute of Economic and Social Research.

Paige, D. and G. Bombach (1959), *A Comparison of National Output and Productivity*, Paris: OEEC.

Pilat, D. (1996), *Labour Productivity Levels in OECD Countries: Estimates for Manufacturing and Selected Service Sectors*, OECD Economics Department Working Papers No. 169, Paris: OECD.

Scarpetta, S., A. Bassanini, D. Pilat and P. Schreyer (2000), 'Economic Growth in the OECD Area: Recent Trends at the Aggregate and Sectoral Level', *OECD Economics Department Working Papers No. 248*, Paris: OECD.

Summers, R. and A. Heston (1991), 'The Penn World Table (Mark 5): an Expanded Set of International Comparisons, 1950–1988', *Quarterly Journal Of Economics*, **106**, 327–68.

Taylor, A.M. and M.P. Taylor (2004), 'The Purchasing Power Parity Debate', forthcoming in the *Journal of Economic Perspectives*, **18** (4), 135–158.

Timmer, M.P., G. Ypma (2005), 'Productivity Levels in Distributive Trades: a New ICOP Dataset for OECD Countries', GGDC Research Memorandum, Groningen: Groningen Growth and Development Center.

Timmer, M.P., G. Ypma and B. van Ark (2007), 'PPPs for Industry Output: a New Dataset for International Comparisons', *GGDC Research Memorandum GD–82*, Groningen: Groningen Growth and Development Center.

Triplett, J. (2004), *Handbook on Hedonic Indexes and Quality Adjustments in Price Indexes: Special Application to Information Technology Products*, Washington, D.C.: Brookings Institution.

Vandenbussche, J., P. Aghion and C. Meghir (2006), 'Growth, Distance to the Frontier and Composition of Human Capital', *Journal of Economic Growth*, **11**, 97–127.

World Bank (2000), *World Development Indicators 2000*, World Bank, Washington DC.

World Bank (2002), *Global Purchasing Power Parities and Real Expenditures 2005 International Comparison Program, Methodological Handbook*, World Bank, http://go.worldbank.org/MW520NNFK0 accessed, May, 2008.

APPENDIX

Table A.13.1 Composition of supply and demand in the Netherlands and the United States, 1999

Industry (a)	ISIC rev 3 code	The Netherlands, 1999 as % of total use (b)			as % of total supply (c)		The United States, 1999 (d) as % of total use (b)			as % of total supply (c)	
		Final expenditure	Intermediate use	Exports	Domestic	Imports	Final expenditure	Intermediate use	Exports	Domestic	Imports
1 Agriculture	01-05	13	50	37	69	31	13	81	6	92	8
2 Mining and quarrying	10-14	1	80	19	46	54	1	96	3	71	29
3 Manufacturing	15-37	27	32	41	52	48	41	48	11	82	18
4 Food, drink & tobacco	15,16	34	26	40	76	24	62	33	5	94	6
5 Basic goods	17,20,21,23-28	15	45	40	58	42	19	73	7	87	13
6 Non-durable	18,19,22,36,37	52	27	20	58	42	66	29	5	73	27
7 Durable	29-35	29	22	49	34	66	50	33	17	75	25
8 Electricity, gas and water supply	40,41	34	66	0	98	2	48	52	0	100	0
9 Construction	45	58	40	2	100	0	79	21	0	100	0
10 Trade	50-52	50	50	0	100	0	66	30	4	101	1
11 Hotels & catering	55	72	28	0	100	0	81	19	0	100	0
12 Transport	60-63	21	29	50	91	9	37	53	10	92	8
13 Communications	64	33	59	9	91	9	49	50	1	100	0
14 Finance	65-67	64	33	3	97	3	53	44	3	100	0
15 Real estate activities	70	73	27	0	100	0	63	35	2	100	0
16 Business services	71-74	17	68	15	86	14	26	73	2	100	0
17 Public administration and defence; compulsory social security	75	95	5	0	100	0			not available		
18 Education and health	80,85	94	6		100	0	96	0	0	100	0
19 Other community, social and personal services	90-95	28	52	19	83	17	61	33	5	100	0

Notes: (a) based on use and make tables which list supply and demand of products rather than industries. Products have been used as proxies for industries by allocating them to their primary sector of production; (b) by definition total use is sum of intermediate use, exports and final expenditure; (c) by definition total supply is sum of domestic production and imports; (d) Due to differences in ISIC rev 3 and the classification used in the US Input–output tables, the results for industries 20, 22, 24, 34 and 50 are proxies.

Sources: Statistics Netherlands, Supply and use tables, 1999 and Bureau of Economic Analysis, Input–Output Accounts for 1999.

14. PPPs and the Price Competitiveness of International Tourism Destinations

Larry Dwyer, Peter Forsyth and D.S. Prasada Rao

14.1 INTRODUCTION

Destination competitiveness is inherently linked to the ability of a country or region to deliver goods and services that perform better than other destinations on those aspects of the tourism experience considered to be important by tourists. It is a general concept that encompasses price differentials coupled with exchange rate movements, productivity levels of various components of the tourist industry and qualitative factors affecting the attractiveness or otherwise of a destination. In recent years there has been an increasing amount of attention by tourism researchers to develop a model and indicators of destination competitiveness (Crouch and Ritchie, 1999; Hassan, 2000, Heath, 2003; Kozak, 2003; Enright and Newton, 2004; Blanke and Chiesa, 2008).

Economic theory supports the view that the demand for tourism will be related to its price. There is evidence that international travellers, in particular, are sensitive to price. Following his review of 70 major studies world–wide, Crouch concludes that 'the pivotal role of price (and income) in explaining the demand for international tourism has been thoroughly demonstrated empirically by the large number of studies that have been carried out over the past three decades' (Crouch, 1994, 1995). Of course, the degree of responsiveness depends largely on whether the journey is for leisure or business purposes. Leisure travellers tend to be more sensitive to changes in airfares and relative prices than business travellers. In any case, it is important to pay particular attention to the price competitiveness of a nation's tourism industry, as compared to that of its competitors, if that nation is to prosper as a tourist destination (Papatheodorou, 2002; Ritchie and Crouch, 2003).

Once measures of price competitiveness have been developed, they can be used to analyse a range of issues. It is important to be aware of which factors are determining the price competitiveness of a tourism industry. It is useful for the industry and government to understand where a tourism destination's competitive position is weakest and strongest. It is helpful for both industry and government to know how competitiveness is changing and why these changes are occurring. Patterns of changes in demand need to be assessed in the light of changes in price competitiveness.

The relevance of measures of destination price competitiveness has been recognised. Demand studies now go beyond using the nominal exchange rate as a crude measure of price competitiveness and beyond the use of real exchange rates (nominal rates adjusted for changes in the general level of prices). Thus, studies have attempted to determine exchange rate adjusted changes in the prices of identified 'tourist bundles' of goods and services (Martin and Witt, 1987). However, these studies have not gone beyond trends and do not determine whether a country is more or less competitive than another at a particular point of time. To measure the level, as opposed to simply trends in tourism, prices and cross–sectional studies using the prices paid by tourists in different countries are needed. The Economist Intelligence Unit has undertaken a number of studies (Edwards, 1995) based on prices paid by tourists in selected countries. These studies go into considerable detail. Notwithstanding, they do not incorporate all forms of tourist expenditure and they do not lend themselves to extension of the sample of countries or time periods.

Recognising that, regardless of the quality of attractions on offer, destinations must pay particular attention to the *price* competitiveness of their tourism industry to maintain or increase market share, the authors have sought to construct indices of the price competitiveness of tourism destinations worldwide. These indices can be employed to determine, from the perspective of visitors from different origin markets, destination price competitiveness in absolute and relative terms (Dwyer et al., 2000a, 2000b). They can also be used to assess a destination's tourism price competitiveness from the perspective of visitors having different journey purpose or special interest (Dwyer et al., 1999, 2000b; Dwyer et al., 2001). They can also be decomposed to determine the relative influences of exchange rate changes and domestic inflation rates on destination price competitiveness (Dwyer, et al., 2002a).

These studies by the authors have been based on the very detailed and extensive price comparisons made by the International Comparisons Program (ICP) (World Bank, 1993; OECD, 1987, 1993, 1997). It is appropriate, then, to discuss the role that such data have played in estimating the price competitiveness of tourism destinations and the implications for policy making in different tourism destinations worldwide.

The aims of this chapter are: first, to demonstrate the use of purchasing power parities (PPPs) in constructing tourism price competitiveness indices; second, to identify the types of studies that the authors have undertaken using PPP data in the construction of tourism price competitiveness indices; third, to demonstrate the policy relevance of these measures; and finally, to discuss the implications for the ICP in the provision of data for measuring international destination price competitiveness.

14.2 USE OF PPPs IN CONSTRUCTING TOURISM PRICE COMPETITIVENESS INDICES

Tourism price competitiveness indices compare the prices in different destinations of the goods and services that tourists actually buy. The cost of tourism to the visitor includes the cost of *transport services* to and from the destination as well as the cost of *ground content* (accommodation, tour services, food and beverage, entertainment, and so on). Both types of costs are relevant to the travel decision and can be taken into account in constructing price competitiveness indices. With data on detailed international price comparisons now available from the ICP, it is possible to construct specialised tourism price competitiveness indices.

The construction of price competitiveness indexes for tourism in a selected destination requires several steps to be undertaken:

1. *Choice of origin markets:* Since visitors from different origins will have different purchasing patterns, a set of origin markets must be highlighted. The major current and emerging origin markets for the selected destination can be used to construct the origin set of countries.

2. *Choice of destination markets:* These include the major competitors of the selected destination. A destination's price competitiveness can be fully understood only in comparison to alternative destinations that the visitor can choose.

3. *Expenditure patterns of tourists from different origin markets:* In order to compute price competitiveness indices it is necessary to attach weights to different goods and services consumed by tourists to reflect purchasing patterns. Visitor expenditure, in total and in pattern, varies depending upon the origin market of the visitor, the purpose of travel and the types of goods and services available in the destination. Unfortunately, destinations vary considerably in the comprehensiveness and accuracy of the visitor expenditure data that they collect. The more comprehensive are the visitor expenditure data, the more detailed and accurate will be the price competitiveness indices that can be constructed for that destination.

4. *Compilation of relevant price data:* Price data can be compiled for each of the items purchased by tourists. A major source of data on the prices paid by visitors for goods and services in different destinations is the International Comparison Program (World Bank, 1993). Price data for 255 categories of products and services can be extracted from the ICP for selected years since 1985 and updated to current values using disaggregated consumer price index data for each competitor tourism destination.

5. Prices for the goods and services that tourists buy, are obtained for different destinations and are then combined using weights obtained from their shares in tourist budgets. In order to compute price competitiveness indices it is necessary to attach weights to different products and services consumed by tourists to reflect purchasing patterns. The weights used are the share of expenditure of each of the items in the tourist basket.

    Price data from the ICP are available at a very disaggregated level (255 different goods and services). Since visitor expenditure patterns in different destinations are typically reported for only a small number of broad categories (for example, accommodation, food, shopping, entertainment, organized tours, and so on), it is necessary to establish a correspondence between items in ICP categories and international visitor expenditure categories. This may necessitate fine judgments having to be made as to the specific types of goods and services purchased in different destinations.

6. *Calculation of PPPs for tourism expenditure:* Establishment of a correspondence between tourist purchasing patterns and price data enables derivation of PPPs for each category of tourist expenditure. The PPPs indicate the levels of expenditure required in different destinations to purchase the same basket of tourism goods and services.

7. *Compilation of competitiveness indices:* The PPPs are adjusted by exchange rates to derive price competitiveness indexes. The basic idea behind the index is to measure the level of prices of goods and services in a competitor destination, relative to prices in a selected destination and then adjust for exchange rates.

$$\text{Price Competitive Index} = (\text{PPP/Exchange Rate}) \times 100$$

Interpretation of the price competitiveness index is straightforward. A particular destination is taken as base and its index is 100. For any destination, a price competitiveness index less than 100 indicates that destination to be more price competitive than the selected destination. Similarly, a figure above 100 indicates that the destination is less price competitive than the selected destination.

The values of the indices allow destinations to be ranked according to their price competitiveness. The absolute values of the indexes can also be compared to determine the extent to which different destinations vary in price competitiveness in tourism. Both types of information can thus be used to measure the destination's price competitiveness in tourism in *relative* and *absolute* terms.

14.3   PRICE COMPETITIVENESS OF SELECTED TOURISM DESTINATIONS

Table 14.1 provides an example of the type of expenditure data that provided the basis for a study of the price competitiveness of Australia as a tourism destination. It relates to expenditure patterns of the 'representative' tourist to Australia from different origin markets. It should be noted that the total expenditure relates to the entire trip, not daily expenditure. Thus while visitors from Japan are Australia's biggest spenders per day, these visitors tend to stay a shorter length of time in the destination than others. For the purposes of constructing price competitiveness indices, however, it is the purchasing patterns of these visitors that are most relevant. The Australian tourism expenditure data are very comprehensive and covers other types of tourists also, for example, holiday, business, visiting friends and relatives (VFR), other (Bureau of Tourism Research, 1999). The Singapore Tourism Board publishes the expenditure profiles of eight main purpose of visit categories– Pleasure/Vacation, Business, Business/Pleasure, Stopover, In Transit, Shopping, Visit Friends/Relatives, Honeymoon, Convention and Education (Singapore Tourism Board, 2000). The existence of such data enables the construction of price competitiveness indices for each of the different tourist market segments.

Table 14.1 International Visitor Survey, 1998 – average expenditure by all visitors (in Australian dollars)

	USA	Ger	Jap	NZ	UK	S.Kor	Ind.	Tai	HK	Thai	Mal	China
Food and drink	420	581	289	231	550	280	330	189	394	408	301	435
Accommodation	555	672	277	167	406	506	370	409	335	307	284	481
Shopping	362	414	475	390	387	689	723	656	574	805	597	593
Entertainment	78	82	23	50	105	52	60	43	76	49	48	80
Self-drive cars	70	242	8	43	71	9	22	2	29	10	25	42
Taxis, limousines	43	33	19	26	42	19	47	23	43	46	33	50
Petrol, oil costs	29	126	4	16	43	12	12	9	18	6	17	15
Convention/registration	14	9	1	15	29	6	13	10	17	4	12	8
Organised tours (no accommodation)	73	127	135	23	67	94	33	80	69	29	45	16
Total Expenditure (incl. other items)	1660	2329	1241	970	1749	1677	1616	1423	1559	1668	1367	1722

Source: Bureau of Tourism Research (2003) International Visitors in Australia, 1999-2002 with additional data supplied by Department of Tourism, Canberra

14.3.1   Price Competitiveness of Australian Tourism by Origin Market

Visitors from different origin markets have different purchasing patterns whilst in Australia. Given the visitor expenditure patterns as indicated in Table 14.1, the question may be asked: what would the same bundle of goods and services cost the tourist if purchased in another destination? To answer this question, price data from the ICP were employed. In principle, the cost of that particular bundle of goods and services can be estimated for any destination for which ICP data are available. As noted above, it is necessary to establish a correspondence between items in ICP categories and international visitor expenditure categories. Thus, judgements had to be made, for example, about the composition of the food and beverages consumed by visitors and their match with more disaggregated ICP price data. Ideally, the use of the ICP price data should be based upon detailed surveys of visitor expenditure that distinguish different items purchases in fine detail. Such information is, however, very expensive to collect and subject to argument regarding validity. We may cite the case of Singapore which has very extensive data on tourist shopping purchases but, even here, items such as 'television set', for example, can have wide variations in type and price (Dwyer et al., 2001).

Examples of some destination price competitiveness indices for Australia appear in Table 14.2. Interpretation of the price competitiveness indices is straightforward. For example, from the perspective of a Malaysian tourist, Australia (100) is a more price competitive destination than France (130.9), but a less price competitive destination than South Korea (50.8). This comparison takes the purchasing pattern of the Malaysian tourist as given (according to Table 14.1), and compares the cost of purchasing the same bundle of goods and services in different destinations (for example, France and South Korea), that compete with Australia for visitors. Australia's price competitiveness on the ground component, from the perspective of each origin market, ranges between 7th (for Taiwanese visitors) and 9th (for visitors from Japan, the UK, and Malaysia). Number 1 indicates the top ranking; 18, the lowest. The rankings are also set out in Table 14.2. The rankings disguise some interesting data, however. From the perspective of visitors from New Zealand, Indonesia, and Malaysia, Australia ranks only marginally above Canada and small price increases in Australia could see its overall ranking decrease. On the other hand, New Zealand's price competitiveness from the perspective of visitors from South Korea, Indonesia, Taiwan, Hong Kong, Thailand, Malaysia and China, is very close to that of Australia and small changes in prices in that nation, could, depending on directions, see Australia's ranking increase or decrease.

Table 14.2 Price competitiveness indices for various destination countries – ground component; year 1998; Australia=100

Destination	Origin												All	Rank
	Jap	USA	Ger	NZ	UK	S.Kor	Ind	Tai	HK	Thai	Mal	Chin		
Australia	100.0	100.0	100.0	100.0	100.0	100.0	100.0	100.0	100.0	100.0	100.0	100.0	100	9
New Zealand	97.6	102.7	104.1	–	97.6	98.5	98.7	101.3	102.0	101.6	100.8	98.3	98.8	8
USA	126.4	–	125.6	112.6	123.2	121.5	114.7	120.6	118.1	113.8	115.6	120.8	121.8	13
Canada	110.0	114.1	112.0	100.4	108.9	106.9	101.2	105.5	103.6	99.7	100.6	105.7	106.5	11
France	154.1	159.5	158.2	139.3	151.5	148.8	134.2	148.1	141.4	136.2	130.9	143.1	148.4	18
Italy	119.0	123.0	124.8	113.3	121.7	114.7	109.9	113.5	114.5	110.0	92.4	114.7	117.2	12
UK	148.6	159.8	162.6	139.3	–	147.3	133.7	145.3	141.2	134.4	138.5	143.7	147.3	17
Germany	140.8	140.6	–	129.9	137.7	134.8	126.7	135.0	132.3	128.7	127.6	130.9	135.7	15
Spain	106.2	108.6	110.7	104.1	108.5	103.2	102.5	102.6	104.1	101.0	90.5	103.9	105.6	10
Turkey	68.9	74.2	77.4	69.4	69.6	71.8	71.1	70.2	68.6	68.2	51.2	73.0	70.7	6
Switzerland	149.7	149.3	147.1	141.8	150.4	140.4	137.2	141.2	144.5	141.6	141.2	141.4	145.6	16

Continued

Table 14.2 Price competitiveness indices for various destination countries – ground component; year 1998; Australia=100 – Continued

Destination	Origin													
	Jap	USA	Ger	NZ	UK	S.Kor	Ind	Tai	HK	Thai	Mal	Chin	All	Rank
South Korea	36.1	64.4	67.2	58.4	62.6	–	61.8	57.2	59.6	57.9	50.8	64.4	59.9	5
China	35.0	36.5	36.6	26.6	30.3	33.5	33.3	31.1	29.5	28.4	29.1	–	31.6	2
Hong Kong	115.5	133.2	146.0	125.1	132.5	124.1	119.9	120.5	–	120.8	119.0	129.2	124.7	14
Taiwan	77.2	81.3	77.2	68.5	74.6	75.5	73.9	–	72.5	69.8	66.1	76.0	74.9	7
Indonesia	18.9	20.0	19.6	17.2	18.6	20.0	–	18.7	18.8	18.0	15.4	21.2	19.2	1
Thailand	30.8	35.8	38.8	36.0	35.9	35.5	39.0	33.3	35.4	–	34.3	39.0	34.9	3
Japan	–	157.0	159.0	147.3	160.8	149.0	140.8	146.0	150.2	145.0	128.9	149.0	151.0	19
Malaysia	40.2	44.0	41.5	37.3	40.0	42.0	43.4	40.4	40.0	38.6	–	43.0	41.0	4
Australia Ranking	9	8	8	8	9	8	8	7	8	8	9	8	9	

Source: Authors' estimates

375

14.3.2   Aggregate Measure of Tourism Price Competitiveness

The data allow the construction of aggregate price competitiveness indexes for all destinations in the competitor set. The aggregate index is the price competitiveness index computed for a 'typical' or average tourist. This index appears as the second last column of Table 14.2 and the rankings appear in the last column.

Table 14.2 shows that the top ranked destination in the competitor set is Indonesia and the lowest ranked destination is Japan. Australia is ranked in the middle at 9th.

In respect of the level of price competitiveness, indicated in the final column of Table 14.2, there is a clear gap between 9th ranked Australia (100) and the 7th ranked destination, Taiwan (74.9). It seems clear that Australia and lower ranked destinations will be unable to match the price competitiveness of most Asian destinations in the foreseeable future.

The estimates indicate that there are wide variations in destination price competitiveness. That is, tourism prices differ widely from country to country. The indices provide a quantitative indication of these prices. Any empirical demand study, which uses data from a cross section of countries, would be seriously in error if it simply used nominal exchange rates – tantamount to assuming a price competitiveness index of 100 for all countries.

These observations are consistent with the more general observation that purchasing power parity does not hold across countries – even approximately. There are systematic differences in price levels, even between countries, which trade intensively. Higher income countries tend to have higher prices, and lower income countries lower prices; however, there are important exceptions to this such as Australia and the USA.

14.3.3   Price Competitiveness by Journey Purpose

Since tourist expenditure patterns are associated with purpose of journey, the price competitiveness of a tourist destination will vary according to purpose of visit.

Australia has data on expenditure patterns of tourists classified according to their purpose of visit. Four major purpose of visit categories are: total tourism, holiday tourism, business tourism, visiting friends and relatives (VFR). The different expenditure data are presented in a format similar to Table 14.1. Price competitiveness indices, presented in the same format as Table 14.2, can be constructed for each type of visitor.

The price competitiveness indices that have been published elsewhere by the authors reveal that a destination may be price competitive from the perspective of some tourists, but not for others, depending on purpose of visit. Australia, for example, is relatively more price–competitive from the perspective of business travellers than holiday travellers, given its relatively lower priced accommodation in high standard hotels of the type patronised by business persons (Dwyer et al., 1999).

The analytical framework can, data permitting, also be applied to determine destination price competitiveness for special interest tourism markets such as ecotourism, backpacking, cruise tourism, and so on. The authors have estimated price competitiveness indices for conventions tourism, comparing Australia with other major convention destinations. These price competitiveness indices, constructed using expenditure data of conventions visitors to Australia, indicate that it ranks relatively low in price competitiveness as a convention/conference destination from the perspective of visitors from its major origin markets (Dwyer et al., 2001).

The construction of price competitiveness indices in special interest markets can play an important role in informing the decisions of both private and public sector stakeholders in key tourism market segments.

14.3.4   Price Competitiveness by Tourism Sector

In addition to overall price competitiveness, it is useful to determine the price competitiveness of tourism characteristic industries (Dwyer et al., 2007). The authors have focused on 11 tourism related sectors, including accommodation, food and beverages, organised tours, shopping, and entertainment. Price competitiveness indices can be disaggregated so as to provide information on destination price competitiveness in respect of these key tourism products and services.

Such data can provide a firmer basis for policies to enhance efficiency and productivity in different sectors of the tourism industry. Price competitiveness indices for each of 11 major categories of goods and services that comprise tourist expenditure, were constructed for each destination in Australia's destination competitor set, for 1998 (Dwyer et al., 2000a). Appearing in Table 14.3, these products and services are: food; drink; accommodation; shopping; entertainment; self–drive cars; train and coach fares; taxis; organised tours; petrol; conventions.

Table 14.3 *Price competitiveness indices by tourist products in selected countries, 1998*

Expenditure category	Aust	USA	Canada	NZ	Ger	Italy	Fran	Spain	Switz	Turk	UK	Japan	S.Kor	Ind	Taiwan	HK
Food	100.0	122.5	95.7	100.9	142.8	145.5	152.3	120.9	203.2	67.0	147.1	227.1	82.4	172	69.0	160.0
Drink	100.0	125.5	127.3	96.9	115.3	104.1	107.3	94.2	133.7	57.8	137.0	173.6	82.6	19.5	77.9	198.8
Accommodation	100.0	184.6	152.8	118.4	153.9	131.7	217.7	107.3	130.8	106.6	237.6	177.8	111.	49.3	126.5	197.3
Shopping	100.0	88.2	79.0	93.7	116.7	92.1	114.6	90.2	127.6	61.4	106.1	117.8	39.8	10.5	50.8	97.4
Entertainment	100.0	88.7	106.9	98.5	126.8	159.0	138.1	145.9	139.1	63.2	121.1	130.6	39.5	10.4	50.3	66.1
Self-drive cars	100.0	100.4	91.1	135.5	111.4	109.9	126.0	120.6	108.1	157.4	153.8	98.3	76.2	13.0	62.9	2243
Train, coach fares	100.0	117.5	148.5	24.9	220.8	124.0	227.4	106.3	172.1	30.7	243.7	238.2	28.4	14.4	70.1	56.4
Taxis	100.0	115.5	104.0	72.5	121.3	71.5	130.6	83.6	168.2	30.8	138.7	154.2	29.2	14.9	72.1	58.0
Organised tours	100.0	128.8	148.5	49.6	204.2	150.7	222.4	126.3	123.0	49.7	200.9	195.4	31.1	15.8	76.9	61.9
Petrol	100.0	74.9	95.1	115.2	156.2	225.8	200.4	169.9	197.7	94.5	207.7	200.8	91.2	9.6	46.4	365.3
Conventions	100.0	81.4	70.0	78.3	130.1	128.0	159.5	133.5	139.1	38.6	206.7	155.0	46.9	9.3	45.2	161.1

Source: Authors' estimates

The price competitiveness indices for the particular goods and services, as set out in Table 14.3, are interpreted in the same way as for those relating to destination price competitiveness. Thus, comparing Australia with the USA, the latter is a more expensive destination for the tourist in respect of food, drink, accommodation, self–drive cars, train, coach, taxis, and organised tours, but less expensive for shopping, entertainment, petrol and conventions.

Sectoral price competitiveness indices can also be updated regularly to monitor destination price competitiveness in key products and services over time (Dwyer et al., 2000b). This requires detailed expenditure patterns of tourists according to their country of origin or according to their motive for visit, coupled with accurate price data. Unfortunately, very few countries maintain accurate data on tourist expenditure patterns, and international price data enabling the types of comparisons required are published irregularly.

14.3.5   Sources of and Trends in Tourism Price Competitiveness

Price competitiveness indices can be used to explore questions of how the competitiveness of destinations change over time and what causes these changes.

The authors have sought to extend their earlier studies of tourism price competitiveness by identifying changes in its underlying determinants. The price competitiveness indices were constructed for the period 1985–97, and 1997–98 (following the Asian currency crisis which impacted substantially on both regional outbound and inbound travel, results not shown herein). The year 1985 was selected as the benchmark year as it was the earliest year for which ICP PPPs became available on global basis (World Bank, 1993).

The changes in the price competitiveness of tourism destinations between the designated years are the outcomes of changes in a range of factors.

1.   Nominal exchange rates have changed. These partly reflect differences in inflation, as measured by changes in CPIs, in different countries – though not entirely, since real exchange rates may have altered.
2.   There have been shifts in the structure of prices within countries. Prices in the tourism sector can rise and fall relative to prices in general.

For expositional purposes the information in Table 14.4 may be set out as in Table 14.5. A plus sign indicates movement towards increased tourism price competitiveness while a minus sign indicates the reverse.

Table 14.4   Source of changes in tourism price competitiveness and their sources, 1985–97

Country	P.C. Index 1985	P.C. Index 1997	Ratio 97/85	Exch. Rate Ratio	Relative CPI Change	Tourism/ CPI Change
Australia	100.0	100.0	1.00	1.00	1.00	1.00
USA	116.2	117.6	0.98	0.93	1.06	0.99
Canada	108.7	106.4	1.02	1.00	1.08	0.95
NZ	92.6	105.3	0.88	0.78	0.89	1.28
Germany	98.0	133.3	0.74	0.57	1.23	1.05
Italy	90.9	113.6	0.79	0.86	0.89	1.03
France	100	144.9	0.69	0.86	1.18	0.95
Spain	73.5	101	0.73	0.83	0.85	1.03
Switz	112.4	147.1	0.76	0.55	1.17	1.18
Turkey	50.7	58.8	0.97	93.26	0.04	0.66
UK	108.7	142.9	0.76	0.71	0.94	1.13
Japan	149.2	153.8	0.97	0.51	1.34	1.36
S Korea	82.6	47.2	1.75	1.76	0.81	1.23
Ind	38.5	18.9	2.03	4.69	0.60	0.72
Taiwan	62.3	70.4	0.87	0.77	1.05	1.09
HK	96.2	121.9	0.79	0.93	0.76	1.12
Thailand	58.5	29.7	1.97	1.61	0.89	1.37
Malaysia	53.7	38.5	1.40	1.46	1.08	0.87
China	24.3	31.0	0.80	2.62	0.48	0.63

Source: World Bank *World Development Report 1997*; Accommodation Survey Data (PKF 1996, 1997)

Sometimes exchange rate changes and price changes reinforce each other in their impacts on tourism price competitiveness (for example, the UK), and sometimes they act in opposite directions (for example, Japan).

In table 14. 4, no attempt was made to determine or discuss annual variations in the price competitiveness indices. Comparisons between two data points (for example, 1985 and 1997) may conceal fluctuations in tourism price competitiveness in the years in between. Ideally, estimates of the indices should be produced annually at least. Nevertheless, what emerges from this discussion is that both exchange rate changes and price changes are impacting on tourism price competitiveness, with exchange rate changes appearing to be more important in Asian countries and price changes more important in some European countries.

Table 14.5   Source of changes in price competitiveness of tourism 1985–97

Destination	Overall change in price comp.	Exchange rate changes	Price changes	Tourism/ CPI changes
USA	−	−	+	−
Canada	+	+	+	−
NZ	−	−	−	0
Germany	−	−	+	−
Italy	−	−	−	−
France	−	−	+	−
Spain	−	−	+	−
Switzerland	−	−	+	−
Turkey	−	+	−	−
UK	−	−	−	−
Japan	−	−	+	−
Sth Korea	+	+	−	−
Indonesia	+	+	−	−
Taiwan	−	−	+	−
Hong Kong	−	−	−	−
Thailand	+	+	−	−
Malaysia	+	+	+	−
China	−	+	−	−

Source: Table 14.4.

Note: a plus sign indicates that the relevant change impacted positively on overall tourism price competitiveness (for example, exchange rate depreciation, relatively low inflation rate); a minus sign indicates a negative impact (for example, exchange rate appreciation, relatively high inflation rate). Zero denotes no change.

14.4   POLICY RELEVANCE OF PRICE COMPETITIVENESS INDICES

Price competitiveness indices provide more information on the relative price competitiveness of different destinations than any of the alternatives, since they compare tourist expenditure on the same bundle of goods and services in different destinations.

For the most part, a destination's price competitiveness in total tourism or in some market segments, will be the outcome of its industry structure, the conduct and performance of firms, industrial productivity, and government microeconomic and macroeconomic policies, past and present (Dwyer et al., 2000b; Crouch and Ritchie, 1999).

It is helpful for both industry and government to know how price competitiveness is changing and why these changes are occurring. Patterns of changes in demand need to be assessed in the light of changes in price competitiveness.

The method of constructing tourism price competitiveness indices has general applicability. The price competitiveness indices developed in this study enable comparisons of the prices of the goods and services that comprise the tourism product to be compared across countries and across different sectors of the tourism industry.

The results have implications for the direction of macroeconomic policy, industry policy and destination marketing. Industry stakeholders can employ these results to help assess the impacts of alternative government policies on their international price competitiveness (for example, tourist taxes). The price competitiveness indexes can be used to explore the impact on overall competitiveness of particular policy measures. The price competitiveness indices enable the changing sources of tourism price competitiveness to be identified and analysed. They can provide the basis for tourist industry policy to enhance destination price competitiveness through studies of the productivity and efficiency of different tourism industry sectors.

The price competitiveness indices also have particular relevance for destination marketing. They indicate that a destination may be price competitive from the perspective of some tourists, but not for others, depending on purpose of visit. In an increasingly competitive global tourism environment, the price competitiveness of special interest markets may be expected to assume greater attention by policy makers.

It is acknowledged, of course, that the indices are no better than the data on which they are based. The collection of comparable sets of prices, in detail, across a wide range of centres, is a relatively new process, and there are still problems being sorted out.[1] In particular, some of the individual price categories pose considerable problems. For example, the comparison of airfares across countries is notoriously difficult, since there are a vast array of fares in most countries and it is difficult to compare like with like. Although the authors have developed price competitiveness indices for the travel component of tourism, their results are heavily qualified (Dwyer et al., 2000a)

---

[1] For a discussion on measurement problems associated with different basic headings, the reader may refer to the ICP Handbook for the 2005 International comparison program conducted by the World Bank (URL: http://web.worldbank.org/WBSITE /EXTERNAL/DATASTATISTICS/ICPEXT/0,contentMDK:20962711~menuPK:2 666036~pagePK:60002244~piPK:62002388~theSitePK:270065,00.html).

The same is true with accommodation prices. In the studies undertaken by the authors two different sources of accommodation prices (the ICP study prices and Hotel rate surveys) have been used. Both have their limitations. The main problem with the ICP accommodation price data is that tourists tend to use different types of accommodation than do residents of a country. The main problem with Hotel rate surveys is that they are based on small samples of establishments, and usually undertaken only for selected cities rather than nationally.

In the price competitiveness indices constructed by the authors in their various studies, patterns of tourist expenditure in Australia have been used as the weights. A primary reason for this is the comprehensiveness of the Australian data compared to elsewhere. To the extent that tourists display different purchasing behaviour in different destinations, the price competitiveness indices will vary from those estimated in the various studies. While the consistency of patterns across different origins, with different expenditure shares, suggests that results may not be very sensitive to this difference, useful research can be undertaken on constructing sectoral price competitiveness indices using other destinations as base cases.

Another limitation of the studies is that data used are economy wide data, and there may well be significant variations in tourism prices across regions within a country. For example, the prices charged to tourists in Bali may differ considerably from those charged elsewhere in Indonesia. But all aggregate, economy-wide statistics have this problem. The methodology for constructing price competitiveness indices allows such indices to be completed for different regions within a tourist destination.

14.5   IMPLICATIONS FOR THE ICP

It is possible to identify a number of areas where provision of ICP results could be further improved. Such improvements have the potential to enhance the quality of the competitiveness indices and provide for a wider use and applications of ICP PPPs.

14.5.1   Coverage of Countries

While results are available for the OECD and EU countries on a fairly regular basis, coverage of the Asian countries has been unbalanced and lack of results on a global comparison basis made the application quite difficult.[2]

---

[2] This situation has been remedied to a large extent through the more recently completed 2005 ICP Asia-Pacific project undertaken under the auspices of the

Some of the major destination countries in Asia, such as China and India, are unavailable from the mainstream international comparison publications. The data for China in the authors' studies was based on the work of Ren Ruoen (1996) who constructed reliable PPPs for price comparisons between China and the United States for the benchmark year 1987. The authors' studies used this benchmark year and extrapolated from the study.

The situation with respect to the coverage of the countries has been remedied through the recently completed International Comparison Program (ICP) project with 2005 as the benchmark year. A total of 146 countries have participated in the 2005 international comparisons. The final results are now available from World Bank (2008) at a fairly aggregated level.[3] As these results have become available only recently, no applications based on these results are currently available.

14.5.2   Quality and Detail of PPPs at the Basic Heading Level

During the course of the construction of destination price competitiveness indices, the authors found that results at the more disaggregated level attracted considerable interest from tourism stakeholders. For example, relative costs of purchased transport in different countries (including bus, rail and taxis) appear to be of considerable interest when dealing with destination price competitiveness. One reason for this may be the interest that industry stakeholders have in maintaining or enhancing the price competitiveness of the particular sector in which they operate. It is at the sectoral level that the indices may be expected to have the greatest policy significance. Unfortunately, while such items are listed among the detailed basic headings in the ICP work, often no PPPs are available or, in some cases, available for only a small number of countries.

In cases where PPPs are available it would be useful if there is some indicator of the *quality* of PPP estimates. In ICP related publications there is seldom any indication about the reliability of the PPPs published. Often decisions to use PPPs at this level appear to be made on the apparent 'plausibility' of the published PPP.

It would indeed be a very useful indicator that provides guidance to the practitioner if PPPs at a basic heading level can be used and reported on their

Asian Development Bank. PPPs and real aggregates are published in the final report available on the ADB website (URL: www.adb.org/ Documents/Reports/ICP-Purchasing-Power-Expenditures/default.asp).

[3] The ICP results are released for only major aggregates of the expenditure side of the national accounts. However, results for 155 basic headings are available from the Global Office of the ICP at the World Bank upon request.

own. Based on the authors' experience of Australia's destination price competitiveness, PPPs computed at the level of disaggregation that matches the International Visitor Survey data appear to be quite plausible, and various industry experts are in agreement with the tourism destination competitiveness indices derived using published PPPs for Australia.

14.5.3   Benchmark Comparisons and PPP Updates

Availability of benchmark PPPs at more frequent intervals along with annual updates using national deflators has the potential to increase the applicability of PPPs from ICP.

A related issue concerns the dissemination of PPP results. Usually summary PPP results are made available on the websites of various international organisations. However, detailed basic heading level PPPs are difficult to find.[4] Regular publication of detailed results, similar to World Bank (1993), using electronic or print media would increase the use of PPPs by researchers for various purposes.

14.5.4   Price Data within the ICP Program

The suitability of PPPs in certain applications, such as the computation of indices for tourism, largely depends upon the actual goods and services that are priced within the ICP.

In the construction of tourism price indices, the authors replaced ICP PPPs on hotel accommodation with more detailed price data collected by more specialist bodies that deal with tourist accommodation. As noted earlier, although ICP data do include hotel accommodation prices these are for accommodation across countries such that domestic tourists might use. International tourists are not always likely to use the accommodation, which is typical for a country – for example, international tourists to Thailand tend to use higher than average quality hotel accommodation. An alternative source of hotel prices lies in surveys of accommodation prices and revenues that are periodically carried out by accounting firms.

Currently such decisions are based on industry experience and intuition on the part of the researchers. In order to eliminate any arbitrariness involved in making such decisions, it would be extremely beneficial if a data bank were to be created where price data collected with item specifications were made available on the websites of relevant international organisations or provided

---

[4] It can be seen from the final report of the 2005 ICP, World Bank (2008), that detailed data are available only upon request and published results cover only major aggregates.

to prospective users covering costs of dissemination. Public availability of price data can result in a more reliable database, and may also generate a more enthusiastic participation by the countries involved.

14.6   CONCLUSIONS

Overall destination competitiveness is determined by non-price (attractiveness) factors as well as price factors. Given the evidence on the price sensitivity of the demand for travel, however, tourism destinations need to monitor their price competitiveness relative to alternate locations.

This chapter has sought to demonstrate the importance of price in travel decisions and to highlight the use of PPPs in constructing tourism price competitiveness indices. The method of constructing these indices was seen to rely heavily on price data from the ICP in estimating the relevant PPPs. The existing data were seen to have some limitations of scope and detail however.

The discussion revealed that the construction of price competitiveness indices for tourism is of policy interest to stakeholders in both the private and public sectors. While some underlying causes of destination competitiveness may only be addressed at a macroeconomic level (for example, the level of the real exchange rate), other causes may be addressed at the sectoral or industry level (for example, the affects of a bed tax on the price competitiveness of the accommodation sector). In the context of growing interest in the topic of tourism destination competitiveness, and the development of strategies to maintain or enhance a country's performance on the available indicators, the implications for the ICP in the provision of data for measuring international tourism price competitiveness receive added weight.

REFERENCES

Blanke, J. and T. Chiesa (2008), The Travel and Tourism Competitiveness Index 2008: Measuring Key Elements Driving the Sector's Development, *World Economic Forum: the Travel and Tourism Competitiveness Report 2008*, Geneva, 3–24

Bureau of Tourism Research (1999), *International Visitor Survey 1998*, Canberra: BTR, Canberra

Bureau of Tourism Research (2003), International Visitors in Australia, 1999–2002, BTR, Canberra.

Crouch G. (1994), 'The Study of International Tourism Demand: a Review of Findings', *Journal of Travel Research*, **33** (1), 12–23.

Crouch, G. (1995), 'A Meta–analysis of Tourism Demand', *Annals of Tourism Research*, **22** (1), 103–118.

Crouch, G. and J.R. Brent Ritchie (1999) 'Competitive Tourism Destinations: Combining Theories of Comparative Advantage', Ninth Australian Tourism and Hospitality Research Conference, February, Adelaide.

Dwyer, L., P. Forsyth and D.S. Prasada Rao (1999), 'Tourism Price Competitiveness and Journey Purpose', *Tourism*, **47** (4), 283–299.

Dwyer, L., P. Forsyth and D.S. Prasada Rao (2000a), 'The Price Competitiveness of Travel and Tourism: a Comparison of 19 Destinations', *Tourism Management*, **21** (1), 9–22.

Dwyer, L., P. Forsyth and D.S. Prasada Rao (2000b) 'Sectoral Analysis of Destination Price Competitiveness: an International Comparison', *Tourism Analysis,* **5**, 1–12.

Dwyer, L., P. Forsyth and D.S. Prasada Rao (2001) *The Price Competitiveness of Singapore as a Tourism Destination* for Singapore Tourism Board.

Dwyer, L., P. Forsyth and D.S. Prasada Rao (2002a) 'Destination Price Competitiveness: Exchange Rate Changes vs Domestic Inflation', *Journal of Travel Research*, **40**, 340–348.

Dwyer L., N. Mistilis, P. Forsyth and D.S. Prasada Rao (2002b) 'The International Price Competitiveness of Australia's MICE Tourism Industry', *International Journal of Tourism Research*, **3** (2), 2001, 123–140.

Dwyer L., P. Forsyth and R. Spurr (2007) 'Contrasting the Uses of TSAs and CGE Models: Measuring Tourism Yield and Productivity' *Tourism Economics*, **13** (4), 537–551

Edwards, A. (1995), *Asia–Pacific Travel Forecasts to 2005*, Research Report, London: Economist Intelligence Unit.

Enright M. and J. Newton (2004) 'Tourism Destination Competitiveness: a Quantitative Approach' *Tourism Management*, **25**, 777–788.

Hassan S. (2000), 'Determinants of Market Competitiveness in an Environmentally Sustainable Tourism Industry' *Journal of Travel Research*, **38** (3), 239–245.

Heath, E. (2003), 'Towards a Model to Enhance Destination Competitiveness: a Southern African Perspective', in proceedings of the CAUTHE 2003 Conference, Coffs Harbour, Australia, February 5–8, 2003.

Kozak, M. (2003), 'Measuring Competitive Destination Performance: a Study of Spain and Turkey', *Journal of Travel and Tourism Marketing*, **13** (3), 83–110.

Martin, C.A. and S.F. Witt (1987), 'Tourism Demand Forecasting Models: Choice of Appropriate Variable to Represent Tourists Cost of Living', *Tourism Management*, 223–245.

OECD (1987, 1993, 1997) *Purchasing Power Parities and Real Expenditures*, Paris: Statistics Directorate, OECD.

Papatheodorou, A. (2002), 'Exploring Competitiveness in Mediterranean Resorts', *Tourism Economics*, **8** (2), 133–150.

PKF (1996a), *Trends in Hotel Industry (Asia Pacific Region)*, Report by Parnell-Kerr-Forster, London.

PKF (1996b), *Eurocity Survey Reports*, Report by Parnell-Kerr-Forster, London.

Ritchie, J. R. Brent and Geoffrey I. Crouch (2003). *The Competitive Destination: a Sustainable Tourism Perspective*, Wallingford, Oxon: CABI Publishers.

Ruoen, R. (1996) *China's Economic Performance in an International Context*, OECD, Paris

Singapore Tourism Board (2000) *Tourism Focus 2000*, Republic of Singapore: Singapore Tourism Board, Singapore.

Tourism Research Australia, *International Visitor Survey 1999*, Canberra.

World Bank (1993), *Purchasing Power of Currencies: Comparing National Incomes Using ICP Data*, Washington, D.C.: International Economics Department, World Bank.

World Bank (1997) *Development Report*, Washington, D.C.: World Bank.

World Bank (2008) *Global Purchasing Power Parities and Real Expenditures, 2005 International Comparison Program*, Washington, D.C.: World Bank.

Index